Responding to God

RESPONDING TO GOD

The Life of Stewardship

BY
TURNER N. CLINARD

THE WESTMINSTER PRESS
Philadelphia

BOOK DESIGN BY DOROTHY ALDEN SMITH

First edition

Published by The Westminster Press ®
Philadelphia, Pennsylvania

PRINTED IN THE UNITED STATES OF AMERICA

9 8 7 6 5 4 3 2 1

Library of Congress Cataloging in Publication Data

Clinard, Turner Norman.
Responding to God.

Includes bibliographical references.
1. Stewardship, Christian. I. Title.
BV772.C56 248'.4 79-24762
ISBN 0-664-24292-8

Contents

Continued

Part Three
How a Christian Steward Gives

Preface

In *Grace Abounding,* John Bunyan wrote of how certain passages of Scripture confronted him, accused him, imprisoned, bruised, and tore him. These texts were so real they seemed to him like supporting or tormenting persons, angels, or demons. I do not have Bunyan's visual imagination, but I share his experience of having a verse ring in my consciousness almost daily since boyhood. The verse is Ps. 116:12 (KJV), "What shall I render unto the LORD for all his benefits toward me?" Like the psalmist, I have received great gifts and blessings from the Lord and I keep seeking ways to repay him or at least to show my gratitude.

Since childhood the notion of stewardship has excited me. It filled me with wonder that God would give dominion over his creation into human hands. The blessings he has given through parents, teachers, friends, the church, and especially in Christ have moved me to thankfulness. The stewardship idea gripped me in youth when emphasis was upon "the three T's"—time, talent, and treasure. It stirred me more profoundly as a young minister when the theme of writing and preaching turned to "the stewardship of life." Finally, a congregation that I served for thirteen years courteously heard almost two hundred stewardship sermons without raising an outcry. These people also honored me by joining, and usually leading, me as we grew together in Christian stewardship.

It was inevitable that I would someday attempt this book as a kind of "thank-you note," a response of personal stewardship. But it had to wait until I was captured by the idea that is its theme, that Christian stewardship means our whole and continuing response to the grace, goodness, and guidance of God. If God is the creator and owner of all things and the giver of life, and if God has elected us in Christ and set us in the several houses of our existence and trusteeship, what can Christian stewardship possibly be but the response of our lives in all their aspects and all their contexts to God?

So I have tried to define Christian stewardship as response, to explore some of the personal and social dimensions in which Christians respond, and, finally, to show how giving and tithing are the response of Christians in one particular area of life.

This book attempts to utilize the best in Christian theology as it relates to stewardship today, especially as it may be seen under the rubrics of response, responsiveness, and responsibility. It is simply written so that any Christian of any age who reads it can understand what it has to say. And it is grounded solidly on the Bible. Most of the quotations are from the Revised Standard Version, but when other translations are quoted they are acknowledged in the text.

If you haven't already done so, do join me in the adventure of responding to God with a life of Christian stewardship. I promise you days filled with satisfaction and good cheer, and joyful rest when evening comes.

Turner N. Clinard

Emory & Henry College

Part One
UNDERSTANDING STEWARDSHIP

1
We Are All Stewards

Read Genesis 1, especially vs. 26–31;
Psalm 8:4–8; Psalm 49; Luke 12:13–21

One of the best ways to understand what it means to be a Christian is to study the image patterns of the Christian's relationship to God and man. For example, God is our Father and we are his children; if this metaphor be accepted as spiritual reality, then we also see our relationship to other human beings under the image of brotherhood. Again, God is our Savior and we are sinners in need of salvation; he saves us and brings us into the mutuality and community of sinners saved by his grace. Or, again, Christ is the Good Shepherd and we are his sheep: some are inside and some outside the fold, and the Good Shepherd is concerned about the welfare of both flocks.

These are but three of the several metaphors, analogies, or categories by which our relationship to God and other humans is pictured. Each one throws real light upon the meaning of Christian life. Yet none is perfectly applicable.

One pattern of relationship which has always appealed to me is that of the steward. It seems superior to most others. The Father-son relationship seems largely mystical and is perhaps only figuratively true. The Savior-sinner relationship is certainly real and true enough to our Christian experience, but it operates in a theological realm that is unknown and incomprehensible to nonbelievers without spiritual discernment. The Shepherd-sheep relationship is beautiful and poetic, but a human is not a sheep, so the analogy breaks down when we study it for interpersonal relations. Stewardship is less mystical, less abstract, and more concretely applicable than most image patterns, perhaps simply more literally true.

Stewardship is so concrete a concept that even some who are not Christians and who have no desire to be Christians may yet be impressed by its claim upon their intelligence and their lives. Nonbelievers may see themselves related to God and other people under this image. Almost no one is too insensitive to recognize that some creative mind or force brought our universe into existence; and hardly any normal, noncriminal mind is too self-centered to recognize some kind of relationship and obligation to others.

Genuinely Christian stewardship moves in broader dimensions and at a higher spiritual level, of course. Indeed it may be maintained that genuine stewardship begins only when we respond to God. Only when we perceive God's gifts of love, only when we acquire spiritual discernment to see God's hand in all our good, and only when we see how Christ relates our lives to God and to other persons do we enter happily and satisfyingly into the steward role. That's what this book is all about.

We Are Stewards

At the beginning of our study, however, perhaps all we need to see is what stewardship is. What is a steward? Why are we seen as stewards? Are all people stewards?

I am a steward. Each of the members of your church is a steward. All the people in the pews on Sundays are stewards. But so also are those at home in bed, reading their newspapers, looking at television, playing on the golf course, or vacationing in the mountains or at the seashore.

We are all stewards. We may not have chosen to be. We may have thought that only officers in a Methodist church are stewards, or perhaps that officers in charge of a ship's property are stewards. Or we may have thought that stewards, religiously speaking, are only those who profess the Christian faith, those who have chosen to be stewards, or those who have progressed to that particular point or level in their religious experience.

But we are all stewards. It is not optional. It is not voted to us by others. It is universal. It comes not from the "new birth" but from breathing the first breath of human life.

A steward is and has always been a person who has charge or care of what belongs to someone else. In Old Testament Israel and in pagan Greece a steward was one who administered the affairs of a household. So Joseph in Egypt was steward of the wealth of Pharaoh. The New Testament concept was the same, though the class of stewards might range from slaves to a city treasurer. In early medieval days the *stigweard* (Old English from which our word "steward" derives) was overseer of his lord's livestock. But before long the term broadened, and he became overseer of all his master's goods and, yet later, an officer of the royal household. But never in history did the steward own the things with which he worked or which he invested; he was always responsible to his master for his care of them.

So a steward is a trustee of something that belongs to someone else. Trustees operate many institutions, such as colleges, foundations, children's homes. It is a legal fiction that they own these things; they have a legal title so that they can sue and be sued corporately, but of course they do not own the institution of which they are trustees at all. A steward may be an investment agent for another's capital such as a mutual fund, or even your bank. A steward is an administrator in charge of property owned by someone else.

Moreover, all these examples are precisely of the same nature as our relationship to God in his world. He created it and he created us and he has placed the world in our care and keeping (Genesis 1).

Some, indeed many, will not acknowledge this relationship. But the relationship is nonetheless real and valid, despite its being unacknowledged. Because God created the world and us who live in it, and because all that we have is the gift of his hand, and because even we ourselves are his creatures, it follows plainly that *all is his* and *nothing is ours.* The convenient legal fiction of ownership, invaluable as it may be to an ordered economy, is only a fiction as regards the world and ourselves.

Who Owns the Moon?

In 1959 Russia's Nikita Khrushchev very neatly timed a visit to the United States to coincide with Russia's reaching the moon with a guided missile. It was inevitable that someone would ask the question: Does the fact that a Russian rocket has reached the moon mean that Russia will lay claim to the moon as her own?

This question did come up in Khrushchev's first American-style press conference. When a reporter asked this question, Khrushchev had been expecting it, and he was well primed for his answer.

The question, he immediately pointed out, is a capitalistic question. Only a capitalist, he said, would ask such a question in the first place. Certainly Russia was not claiming title to the moon for herself, for the moon is the property of all people. His was the perfect communist answer to the question. It must be admitted that he scored a propaganda point against us. Moreover, we as Christians must acknowledge that his answer was nearer to the Christian ideology than the answer he implied that a capitalist would give.

Finding, claiming, inventing, and holding have historically meant ownership to us. Possession, we say, is nine points of the law. But communism says that owning property is theft, for what belongs to all should not be monopolized by a few. Yet neither is the Christian answer. Can you plainly say what it is?

Who owns the land on which you live, the soil you till, the cattle you raise, the house you call home, the car you drive —who owns them? Our American economic system permits us to say that we own the things we possess. But do we really?

Jesus told a parable that answers the problem of who owns what. Hear some of the words from his story:

> The land of a rich man brought forth plentifully; and he thought to himself,
> "What shall I do,
> for I have nowhere to store my crops?"
> And he said,
> "I will do this:
> I will pull down my barns, and build larger ones;
> And there I will store all my grain and my goods.
> And I will say to my soul,
> Soul, you have ample goods laid up for many years; take your ease." . . .
> But God said to him,
> "Fool! This night your soul is required of you;
> and the things you have prepared,
> *whose will they be?*" (Luke 12:16ff., italics added)

This story makes quite clear the convenient lie on which our economy operates. Someone else possesses all these things *before* we come on the scene, and someone else will possess them *after* we are gone. So, as a matter of fact, we own nothing.

Job assessed the same situation: "Naked I came from my mother's womb, and naked shall I return; the LORD gave, and the LORD has taken away" (Job 1:21). The writer of Psalm 49 counsels people not to be troubled by the rich, for "when he dies he will carry nothing away" (Ps. 49:17). Building more emphatically on this truth, the First Letter to Timothy declares: "We brought absolutely nothing with us when we entered this world and we can be sure we shall take absolutely nothing with us when we leave it" (I Tim. 6:7, Phillips, 1958).

Once again, since we can take nothing from this world

with us, it is clear that we don't really own anything. Nothing is ours: if it wasn't directly created by God, it is at least fabricated, created, invented, or grown from materials that were created by God. We neither add to nor take away from God's creation. But often because of our basic misapprehension about ownership, we fritter our lives away, striving to accumulate those very ephemeral and evanescent things we cannot remove with us.

The "rich fool" refused to acknowledge that he owned nothing, that all was held in trust from God. There are many like him. There is as much ignorance and human pride in us; we say, "Look what I have made." "I am self-made." "Look at my car, my house, my land, my stocks and bonds." So we become rich fools ourselves, disregarding the fact that we own absolutely nothing.

God has been pleased to give my family food, clothing, and shelter. We even have a legal title to two old cars and some equity in the house we live in. But I have no expectation of riding to heaven in my "Super Beetle," nor do I aspire or expect to see my house beside a golden street, situated as one of the mansions "in my Father's house."

We Hold All in Trust

Yet, though we own nothing, we enjoy, we hold, we use, we manage *everything in the world.* This is the story told in Genesis 1 and again in Psalm 8: "Thou hast given him dominion over the works of thy hands; thou hast put all things under his feet" (Ps. 8:6).

Therefore it is most obvious that we are stewards of God's belongings. All the difference in the world exists between those who recognize and willingly accept their stewardship, realizing the gracious and bountiful and loving gifts of God, and those who set out with the attitude of putting a fence around as much of the universe as possible and saying, "This is mine." It isn't. And nothing we can do can make it so.

Harris Franklin Rall wrote: "For paganism property means simply power and privilege; for Jesus it means trust and responsibility."[1]

We who love God and seek to do his will are happy that he has entrusted us with so much: the world, its beauties, its riches, our health, our minds, our abilities—in short, every good of life. We enjoy all these things as a trust from his hand. Paul said to the Corinthians, "What have you that you did not receive? If then you received it, why do you boast as if it were not a gift?" (I Cor. 4:7).

So we are stewards. We are here looking after this garden Earth as Adam and Eve looked after Eden. Our stewardship is as broad as life itself. It concerns *life,* to be lived for God's glory and the good of people; *time,* a bounty from his hand, to be wisely spent; our *abilities,* the capacities with which he has endowed us, to be used in accord with his purposes and dreams for us—for us all.

"In the beginning God created the heaven and the earth" (Gen. 1:1, KJV). "All things were made by him; and without him was not any thing made that was made" (John 1:3, KJV). "The earth is the LORD's, and the fulness thereof; the world, and they that dwell therein. For he hath founded it upon the seas, and established it upon the floods" (Ps. 24:1–2, KJV). "What is man, that thou art mindful of him? and the son of man, that thou visitest him? For thou hast made him a little lower than the angels, and hast crowned him with glory and honor. Thou madest him to have dominion over the works of thy hands" (Ps. 8:4–6, KJV). "God that made the world and all things therein, seeing that he is Lord of heaven and earth, . . . giveth to all life, and breath, and all things. . . . For in him we live, and move, and have our being" (Acts 17:24–25, 28, KJV).

Such is the story told on almost every page of the Bible: "This is my Father's world." As long as we delight to sing that, we can be trusted to go about and enjoy all that we behold. But when we begin to sound off about "my property" and "what I have made"—beware! We're trying to sneak off with God's good things, dispossess others of them, and lock them up in a private vault somewhere.

God entrusts us with so much. I own those clouds overhead because God has given them to me (and you) to enjoy. I own the wonderful fresh air I shall breathe today, for God has given it to me (and you) to enjoy. But happily I have no way to get a title deed to the clouds or the air, for God intends us all to enjoy them. Jesus said, "He makes his sun rise on the evil and on the good, and sends rain on the just and on the unjust" (Matt. 5:45).

So when next we go to church and offer our gifts, let us rise to sing lustily, "Praise God from whom all blessings flow," or

> We give thee but thine own,
> Whate'er the gift may be;
> All that we have is thine alone,
> A trust, O Lord, from thee.

2
Stewards Live Responsively

Read II Corinthians 5:6–15

If God owns all things by virtue of creation and if, therefore, we own nothing, it follows that all we "possess" we really hold in trusteeship, as stewards. This, however, is by no means equivalent to saying that all people are Christian stewards. What, then, are Christian stewards? How do they get that way? Where does Christian stewardship begin, and how does it differ from the universal stewardship of created human beings?

The answers to these questions may be found in some of the declarations of the apostle Paul to the Corinthians: "For all things are yours . . . and you are Christ's; and Christ is God's" (I Cor. 3:21, 23). "And he died for all, that those who live might live no longer for themselves but for him who for their sake died and was raised" (II Cor. 5:15). These brief biblical texts summarize Christian stewardship, but doubtless some elaboration is needed to clarify the distinctiveness of Christian stewards.

Why Wasn't the Rich Fool a Christian Steward?

If we return to the "rich fool" (Luke 12:16–21), who was a steward without knowing it, we may begin to see the difference. How did he fall short of the descriptive elements in the texts above?

1. He did not recognize the source of his wealth. He thought he had created it and had full title to it. He did not at all see God as his source of supply. Hence there was no sort of responsive turning to God. He had no recognition or appreciation of the real origin of his substance, so he never felt any need to say "thank you."

Of course, mere recognition of the source of his well-being would not have made him a Christian steward. He might still have been a Jew or Moslem or other theist. Nevertheless, recognition is an important step in the right direction. It is at least the beginning of the responding life, the life of thankful appreciation. The psalmist gave a beautiful expression of this aspect of genuine stewardship:

> What shall I render to the LORD
> for all his bounty to me? (Ps. 116:12)

Doubtless all conscious stewardship begins here. God has been good. He has supplied us with life and with all that sustains life; he has given us a beautiful world to live in and enriched us with human companionship. We find it hard to believe that anyone could be so insensitive as to be unaware of God's beneficence in all his good. Nevertheless, the rich man of Jesus' parable showed not an ounce of awareness, not an iota of recognition, not a smidgeon of appreciation; therefore he said not a "mumblin' word" of thanks.

2. To use the biblical texts above to describe him, he "lived unto himself." He did not turn to God in appreciation, and he never thought of turning to other people to share his bounty. Looking at the personal pronouns and possessives that multiply in the parable even more than his crops in his fields, we become aware of a distinctly egoistic and introverted personality. It would be nice to think he was unique, but actually the world is filled with people like him, living for themselves alone.

Perhaps we think: "That really isn't so bad. Why should

I go around singing God's praises when I have worked hard for everything I have? Nothing was ever handed to me on a silver platter."

I am reminded of an old story my father used to tell about how little Johnny was visiting with his friend Bill. Mealtime came, and Bill's father said grace at the table, thanking God for the food. Later Johnny said to Bill, "It sure is funny how your father thanks God for the food; my dad works for ours." There are many adults who think like Johnny, too.

Then there are those who believe that "every man should stand on his own two feet." They believe that every person should look out for himself. They aren't looking to anyone else for help and don't expect to give away what they have earned to others. "If he needs something, let him work for it, as I do."

Actually we rather admire this courageous independence and self-sufficiency, don't we? It doesn't sound so bad to us. We certainly don't like our rugged individualism to be classified as sin. So it may come as a considerable shock to us to read the words of Paul: "He died for all, that those who live might live no longer for themselves" (II Cor. 5:15).

Christ Made the Difference

Had it ever occurred to you that this is why Christ came to earth and taught and died—to keep us from living inturned, selfish, egoistic lives? We know he came to give us "abundant life," but perhaps we hadn't realized that the only abundant life relates us to God and man. We know he came "to seek and to save that which was lost," but perhaps we had failed to realize that to be lost means to be cut apart from relationship, to be isolated from other human beings. We know that he came to effect the will of God ("My meat is to do the will of him who sent me"), and he prayed accordingly ("Thy kingdom come; thy will be done, on earth as it is in heaven"), but perhaps we forgot that God's will is a will for human loving, brotherhood, and interrelatedness. Nothing is clearer in the Bible than that "we neither live nor die as self-contained units" (Rom. 14:7, Phillips). Jesus' mission was to relate us to God and to man in love. And his first and only commandment was, "You shall love the Lord your God with all your heart, and with all your soul, and with all your mind" (Matt. 22:37). But he added that there is a second commandment just like it: "You shall love your neighbor as yourself" (Matt. 22:39).

We speak of atonement (at-one-ment) as though Jesus' only desire was to restore us to right relations with God, to bring the prodigal back from the far country. But the one commandment (with its duplicate) makes it clear that Jesus is as much interested in restoring us to loving relations with others as with God. The parable of the good Samaritan is a paradigm of neighborliness or brotherhood such as Jesus expects to see in those for whom he lived and died.

Possession in the Christian Economy

Perhaps just a word needs to be addressed to the *telescopic nature* of ownership as conceived in Christian relationships. While those nonbelievers who strive hard to fence in as much of this world's goods as they can really own nothing at all, Paul says to Christians, "All things are yours." Admittedly this seems at first to contradict what has already been said, but it is only a paradox. Let us read the whole passage, remembering that it is addressed to the faithful in the Corinthian church:

> For all things are yours, whether Paul or Apollos or Cephas or the world or life or death or the present or the future, all are yours; and you are Christ's; and Christ is God's. (I Cor. 3:21b–23)

Possession is telescopic: I own all because I am telescoped "in Christ" who owns all and is fully identified with God, who owns all. When Paul says all he means all: there is absolutely nothing that does not belong to the faithful "in

Christ." Let me repeat with him to all who stand within the dimension of faith, "All things are yours."

Let me explain what I mean by possession's being telescopic: you know how telescopes work, sliding inward or outward in overlapping cylindrical sections. I remember a collapsible cup I used to carry in my school lunch basket as a boy. Telescoped outward it held a drink of water, but telescoped inward it flattened to the size of a biscuit. I see this image as analogous to possession. Hence, outside Christ, the all-enclosing circle, I own nothing and don't even belong. But hidden in him I belong, and all is mine for all is his.

Ironically we tend to live as though we merely eked out an existence "in the sweat of our brows." Sometimes even some people in the household of believers, the church, live like fearful paupers. This is dramatically illustrated in the latter part of Jesus' story of the prodigal son (Luke 15: 11–32). When the prodigal returns to the open arms and lavish gifts of his father, the older son hears the sound of music and celebration and is bitterly angry. He lashes out at his father, who comes to the field for him: "Lo, these many years I have served you, and I never disobeyed your command; yet you never gave me a kid, that I might make merry with my friends. But when this son of yours came, who has devoured your living with harlots, you killed for him the fatted calf!" No doubt many of us have sympathized with his indignation. Yet if we read more carefully, our eyes are opened: the older son's words, "this son of yours," show no acknowledgment of brotherhood. Then the father replies, "Son, you are always with me, and *all that is mine is yours*" (italics added).

How tragic that one can live such an impoverished life in the very center of generosity and abundance! It is our fault if we fail to enjoy this world which is all ours because it is all God's. All things are ours because we are Christ's and Christ is God's. God is author of all; Christ is co-creator, without whom "nothing was made that was made"; and we are "in Christ"—belonging to Christ, who belongs to God.

Did you enjoy that drink of cool water this morning? Did you enjoy watching the plants and flowers soaking up the rainfall after the last dry spell? Do you enjoy the response of growing corn to the warm sun? What about the bite of that crisp apple, or the flavor of the wild blackberries? You made none of them; you have no deed to any—yet all are yours in God.

Paul is ours and Martin Luther; St. Francis is ours and John Calvin. The rich treasury of devotion in the hymnal from many lands and churches—the Bach chorales, the carols, the devotional poems of Whittier, the treasury of prayer from the Book of Common Prayer, the Apostles' Creed, the Nicene Creed, the wonderful affirmation of the United Church of Christ, the silent seeking of the Quaker for the inner light—all are ours.

Deep snows, buds on plants, June flowers in profusion, streams of water over pebbly beds, the handclasp of friends, the love of family, the happiness of living, breathing, eating, sleeping, reading, writing, talking—all are yours. No one can take them away from you. You need no deed but they are yours. You are rich, rich, rich!—and all through the grace of God.

The American author and naturalist Henry David Thoreau recognized this. He talked with every farmer around Concord about buying his property, but he never bought any. After one such nontransaction, having looked over his neighbor's farm, he wrote: "But I retained the landscape, and I have since annually carried off what it yields without a wheelbarrow." Many New Englanders, Thoreau observed, had become the slaves of their property; but he blithely went about "enjoying the most valuable part of their property," stealing the enjoyment of their hills and fields, stone walls and old apple trees, with only ten cents in his pocket.[2]

In God all is ours: forgiveness; a new start after failure; restoration to a loving family; the sense of direction; a clear conscience; the dimension of spirit; the meaning of life—all is ours. Christian faith is the new dimension that expands our perception of the meaning and richness of life. To come to know the grace of God is to be fully and forever enriched, for so we become "servants of Christ and stewards of the mysteries of God" (I Cor. 4:1), "good stewards of God's varied grace" (I Peter 4:10).

When does all the world become truly yours? When you can know it as a gift of God's love and enjoy it and share it unselfishly with others—not trying to hoard or treasure it for yourself. "And my God will supply every need of yours according to his riches in glory in Christ Jesus" (Phil. 4:19).

Responsive Living: Living Life as Unto Christ

Response to Christ brings us into the realm of Christian stewardship. Christian stewardship begins when we respond to the call of God and the love of Christ, willingly giving ourselves to him. He loved us, he served us, he brought us to God; he saved us from selfishness; he brought us into heaven.

So, as in the parable of the pearl of great price, we sell all lesser things for the greatest value. We forgo all lesser allegiances to become Christ's. We now "belong to that power whom we choose to obey." We are Christ's and "Christ is Lord." That was the first creed of the church and it is the creed of the Christian steward.

To be a Christian is to live a life of grateful response to the outpoured love and grace of God. When we live for Christ who died for us and not for ourselves alone, then Christ is the Lord of our lives.

Paul makes the point that the Christian does all that he does to honor his Lord: "He who observes the day, observes it in honor of the Lord. He also who eats, eats in honor of the Lord, since he gives thanks to God; while he who abstains, abstains in honor of the Lord and gives thanks to God. None of us lives to himself. . . . If we live, we live to the Lord" (Rom. 14:6–8).

Christ "died for us that we should no longer live for ourselves." He shows us how to live for him, to identify with his purposes for our lives and the world—how to reach our own fulfillment by seeking his will for us. So, as Paul wrote the Galatians: "The life I now live in the flesh I live by faith in the Son of God, who loved me and gave himself for me" (Gal. 2:20).

We are further reminded in the Ephesian letter that if we are Christian, our labor and our service, whatever they may be, are not to others but to God. When Christ becomes Lord we become "servants of Christ, doing the will of God from the heart, rendering service with a good will as to the Lord and not to men" (Eph. 6:6–7).

The life lived "as unto God" is the Christian life; it is the responsive life of the Christian steward. And to this life God calls us every one.

3
What Motivates a Steward?

Read I John 4:13–21

Stewardship means holding in trust, using and investing that which belongs to someone else. *Christian stewardship* includes that basic understanding of stewardship, but it is essentially a life of response to God for his goodness and to Jesus Christ for his love.

If response to Christ is that which distinguishes Christian stewardship from the universal stewardship of mankind, then it is worthwhile to ask: "What makes Johnny run?" Why does a person so regard life as to desire to live it "as unto the Lord"? Why does a person seek to do everything to the honor of Jesus Christ?

Not long ago I heard someone speak on the subject "What Motivates Christian Stewardship?" But he gave almost all his time to talking about false motivations: doing things for public recognition, doing them for reward, doing them out of a sense of fear, trying to buy a ticket to heaven, etc., and he kept only a concluding minute or so to say what ought to motivate Christian stewardship. I certainly want to reverse that process.

I am convinced that there are improper motives which cause some people to take a particular position, do a particular deed, or make a particular contribution. That is, there are ulterior motives which cause one to be a hypocrite—for one who is only pretending Christian stewardship is, by definition, a hypocrite.

But there can be no ulterior motive for a life of Christian stewardship. Christian stewardship is, by definition, Christ-motivated. Whatever is done from improper motivation is not, therefore, Christian stewardship. It may be make-believe or "play-like," but it isn't "the real thing." For Christian stewardship *is* properly motivated.

Christian stewardship is a willingly accepted yoke, an embraced obligation, a trusteeship performed in the name of and as before the eyes of Jesus Christ. It is this relationship to Christ which defines stewardship as Christian. We are all stewards, but we are Christian stewards because and when we want to be.

Now, what makes persons regard their lives as God's, see their abilities as a divine trust, think of their time as a gracious endowment, envision all their earthly goods as gifts from the hands of a loving and generous Father, to be enjoyed and shared with others? Why does one claim Christ as Lord? Why commit every phase of life to God? Why seek God's will instead of one's own? Why desire above all else to do what is well-pleasing in God's sight? These, I think, are fair descriptions of that Christian responsiveness which we call Christian stewardship. What, then, makes one do these things?

Duty

No doubt the least common denominator of all the motivations that would so incline a person is the sense of duty. Some people regard this as an inferior motivation, putting it down near the idea of "seeking reward" or "buying favor." I am not among them.

I have never heard anyone running down the worth of duty except someone who was trying to weasel out of doing it. But Christian stewardship as duty comes from the recognition that all one has is given by other hands and that one is accountable for the handling of it all.

Duty is a matter of common decency. All persons of integrity and intelligence recognize some obligation for their sustenance, and only the egomaniac fails to recognize some sort of obligation to other people in this world. Further, persons of common decency want to contribute as much to the future as they have received from the past. They do not want to deplete the treasury of good on earth by taking away more than they return.

Admittedly, duty may not stand as the highest and brightest of motives for Christian stewardship, but it is not selfish or tawdry. I like people who pay their debts, if only out of a sense of duty; who mow their lawns, if only out of regard for their neighbors. What is wrong with that? If one does not live from the sense of duty, what is one's motivation? Is it self-pleasing? Emotional stimulation? Whatever makes one "feel good"?

Gratitude

A second motive that is doubtless related to duty is yet a cut or two higher. I am speaking of gratitude. To receive without the desire to give is unchristian. To be full of thanks for goodnesses and favors received is certainly to want in some measure to reciprocate or repay the goodness received. If we see God as the source of all good, and recognize that all we have is given, how can we be less than thankful?

That which raises us above animality is gratitude, is appreciation. We are never closer to Christian stewardship than in those sober yet joyous moments that we take to count our blessings.

Divine Motivation

Looking at and through these two concepts, duty and gratitude, and looking hard to what lies behind them, one comes to the realization that genuinely religious stewardship of life is divinely motivated or inspired, that real Christian stewardship is not only *to Christ* but also somehow *from Christ,* as well.

John 3:16–17 is necessarily our text at this point: "For God loved the world so much that he gave his only Son, so that everyone who believes in him may not die but have eternal life. For God did not send his Son into the world to be its Judge, but to be its Savior" (TEV).

The same God who creates and sustains us, who sends his sun and rain and who is the source of our every physical good, has taken similar steps for our spiritual lives and eternal welfare. So our stewardship starts in God's love, mercy, and grace. He sought always to bless and save his created children, but they continued in darkness and wilful sin until he took the most dramatic step in all the history of the universe. He sent his Son to light our darkness, to show us the truth, and to guide us in the way. No wonder that Paul exclaims, "Thanks be to God for his inexpressible gift!" (II Cor. 9:15).

It all starts in the heart of God. His grace is prevenient; it goes out to us before anything is expected of us. It was ministered to us through the law and prophets. But above all we recognize the revelation of God in Jesus Christ. Jesus by his life reveals the Father's love and mercy, patience and longsuffering for his wayward and foolish children.

So Jesus finally becomes the ground, the base, the *raison d'être* of our stewardship, when it is real. Christian stewardship starts with Christ. His life reveals God and what God wants of human life. He goes before us; he calls us; he moves us to follow him.

Christ's Love Constrains

This brings us to consider II Cor. 5:14 (KJV): "The love of Christ constraineth us."

Jesus is the ground and motive of Christian stewardship;

and he is even its model and pattern. For before we hear him call us into that relationship, we see him in his own stewardship role toward the Father. Jesus was a true steward: careful to reveal the truth that was his; careful to save and keep all those who have been committed to him; careful to do, not his own will, but the will of the Father. The kingdom of God, which means the rule of God in human life, was always first for him. He was a steward, being always "about his Father's business."

Jesus was dutiful. Jesus was thankful. How often is this made clear in his actions and in his prayers. "I thank thee, Father" was a constant refrain from his lips. He identified his life purposes with the Father's will for him, attributing all power for what he did to the Father.

And Jesus was loving to people. He said: "The Spirit of the Lord is upon me, because he has anointed me to preach good news to the poor. He has sent me to proclaim release to the captives and recovering of sight to the blind, to set at liberty those who are oppressed, to proclaim the acceptable year of the Lord" (Luke 4:18–19).

He loved people: poor, sick, rich, foolish, sinful, good—he loved them all without discrimination. Jesus was the revealer of God; so people could watch him at work and know certainly that God loved them, too.

And so "we love [him], because he first loved us" (I John 4:19). We accept his mission because we see it as the expression of God's love for mankind. His life and teachings inspire us. His vicarious and atoning death magnetizes us. Here in him were perfect love, grace, mercy. Christ loved us and gave himself for us.

This, then, is the inescapable motivation to a life of Christian stewardship. We want our lives to match his; our hearts burn within us, for we want to love as he loved. His motive becomes ours, his mission ours; we follow or try to follow the perfect stewardship of his life: "the love of Christ constrains us."

Christ's Love Controls

Yet the Revised Standard Version of the same verse gives us still more insight into the motivation of Christian stewardship: "The love of Christ controls us" (II Cor. 5:14, RSV). Not only does the love of Christ constrain us to become Christian stewards, but also the love of Christ controls us in living lives of Christian stewardship. Do you follow the distinction?

Jesus said, "And I, when I am lifted up from the earth, will draw all men to myself" (John 12:32). This speaks of the love of Christ, which magnetizes us and causes us willingly to embrace him as Christ and Lord. But Christian stewardship is not one response, but many. It is not a flash in the pan, but a lifelong commitment. We not only respond to the call of Christ; we are then sent on his mission. We do not merely receive the sign of the cross of Christian stewardship—a fitting symbol of our belonging to him—but we are given his commission. He commits to us the word of reconciliation. He says, "As the Father has sent me, even so I send you" (John 20:21).

The love that first drew us to Jesus now becomes the love that motivates our service to humanity in his name. Christ's motive now becomes our motive. Moreover, it is no longer just our love for him which moves us—not just our love *for* Christ but his love *in* us. To identify with Christ's love of the Father and his will, with his prayers and his desire to see the kingdom come, and with his mission to all mankind, is to identify with Christ himself. This is what Paul means when he says, "It is no longer I who live, but Christ who lives in me" (Gal. 2:20).

Don't be embarrassed about this; don't be frightened away because it sounds mystical. Christ identified his own will and his love with the Father's. Christ also identified himself with humanity: "As you did it to one of the least of these my brethren, you did it to me" (Matt. 25:40). If Christ is not ashamed to identify with us, weak, sinful, shortsighted, and foolish as we are, then surely we ought to identify with him, with great love and devotion.

I have often been asked, "But how can you love people you don't like?" It sounds difficult, I grant. Yet the answer is simple. Let Christ in you love them. As a faithful disciple you are "in Christ" and he lives in you. His love can fill you, change you, re-create you. Certainly his love can love even the most unlovely through you.

The Spirit Moves

When Jesus was telling of his own stewardship, his own mission, he said, "The Spirit of the Lord is upon me"—to explain how he held true to his responsibility.

It is a plain teaching of the New Testament that God and Christ are available to us and are indeed with the faithful. Jesus said to his disciples, "I am with you always." The first letter of John affirms: "By this we know that we abide in him and he in us, because he has given us of his own Spirit" and also "God is love, and he who abides in love abides in God, and God abides in him" (I John 4:13, 16.). Paul added: "The fruit of the Spirit is love, joy, peace" (Gal. 5:22).

The love of God was once incarnate in Jesus. He now lives in his faithful followers in the person of the Holy Spirit. So Christians have "the Spirit of Christ." They set the Lord always before them: his mission, his dedication, his love of people, his teachings about stewardship. All these are with us, not only as ideals to inspire but also in the indwelling presence of Christ. Therefore our pattern of life and our daily actions can be Christian indeed, for they can be and they are motivated by that very selfsame Christ whom we first met in the Scriptures and who now lives within us.

4
What Is Required of Stewards?

Read Matthew 25:14–30;
I Corinthians 3:5–9; 4:1–5

It is no secret that many people are "turned off" and "tuned out" by the very mention of Christian stewardship. This is true because they have heard the word used almost entirely with reference to financial campaigns and requests for money. Holmes Rolston is right when he says that for many people stewardship means only a "thinly veiled attempt to separate them from their money."[3]

This is unfortunate, doubly unfortunate. (1) It is unfortunate because, being turned off, they never can enter richly into the understanding of their relationship to God, his world, Jesus Christ, and mankind that can come through the pattern of Christian stewardship. Certainly the sharing or giving of one's possessions *is* an aspect of stewardship as it is taught throughout the Bible. But it is only one aspect of the whole pattern. I have just completed three chapters exploring the basic meaning of Christian stewardship without making any mention of money or giving whatever. (2) It is also unfortunate because those who have closed their minds to the exploration of Christian stewardship can never learn the real significance of giving within their role as Christian stewards and servants of Christ; that is, they may never have the experience of giving because they want to, but only in response to an emotional appeal or under some sort of pressure to "do their duty."

Even this subject, "What Is Required of Stewards?" may cause the turned off and tuned out some pain because of their past experiences, but let me hasten to assure you that we are not going to discuss tithes, budgets, shares, quotas, commitments, or financial pledges. Does that relieve the tension?

What then is required of stewards? One thing only: faithfulness. Faithfulness is all. Christian stewards need no laws, no rules, no regulations. "It is required in stewards that a man be found faithful," wrote Paul in I Cor. 4:2, KJV ("trustworthy," RSV). Jesus said, in concluding one of his parables: "Who then is the faithful and wise servant, whom his master has set over his household, to give them their food at the proper time? Blessed is that servant whom his master when he comes will find so doing. Truly, I say to you, he will set him over all his possessions" (Matt. 24:45–47).

Jesus concluded another parable on stewardship with these words: "He who is faithful in a very little is faithful also in much; and he who is dishonest in a very little is dishonest also in much. If then you have not been faithful in the unrighteous mammon, who will entrust to you the true riches? And if you have not been faithful in that which is another's, who will give you that which is your own?" (Luke 16:10–12).

It is clear that Jesus had one overriding concern about his followers in the stewardship relation: their faithfulness. This quality is first seen in God the Father, who keeps his word and who may be depended upon ("God is faithful," I Cor. 1:9). It was also manifested in Jesus, who was faithful in doing his Father's will and faithful in his mission. Christ set a pattern in faithfulness; he was "a merciful and faithful high priest in the service of God" (Heb. 2:17); "he was faithful to him who appointed him" (Heb. 3:2). And Revelation speaks several times of Christ as "the faithful witness."

Paul spoke of his Christian fellow workers as faithful. "I

sent to you Timothy, my beloved and faithful child in the Lord" (I Cor. 4:17). "Tychicus . . . is a beloved brother and faithful minister and fellow servant in the Lord" (Col. 4:7). With him is "Onesimus, the faithful and beloved brother" (Col. 4:9). And in that deservedly famous passage in Gal. 5:22, Paul tells us that faithfulness is one of the fruits of the Spirit.

"Faith" is the word with the golden aura. We praise people for having faith; we wish we had more faith. But it is faithfulness which carries on the work, does the building, plows the field, and scatters the seed. Jesus prizes faithfulness in his disciples.

Faithfulness in Receiving

Faithfulness in Christian stewardship begins with faithfulness in receiving. To receive faithfully means to recognize all our good as coming from God: "Every good endowment and every perfect gift is from above, coming down from the Father of lights" (Jas. 1:17). To be *full of faith* (faithful) that "my God shall supply every need of yours" (Phil. 4:19), that he is indeed doing so at this very moment —this is faithful receiving.

It is true that we have worked for what we have. It is equally true, however, that our work is our only way to cooperate with God so as to receive his treasures. God gave us life to start with, the universe to live in, the earth to bring forth food—with the cooperation of sun and rain. It is in working with these initial gifts that we "earn our living by the sweat of our brow." Take away the sun, we freeze; the earth, we are hurled into the abyss; the rain, we starve. Yet God has not been content to provide us with physical sustenance alone. He gives us families and friends to sweeten life, beauty to enrich it, and his Son to save us from our folly, selfishness, and rebelliousness. So what do you have that was not given you? The answer is: nothing.

The one thing that is greatest which God gives and which

God only can give is the chief point of contention. God gives us forgiveness, salvation, and eternal life. We don't earn it. We can't earn it; we can only accept it in faith. There is no other way.

Now this is a terrible blow to our conceit. Most of all we like to think: "I can look out for Number One. I can correct my own mistakes. I can find the right way of life and live it. I can do what is right and earn my own salvation." But no. This we cannot do. The rebelliousness and willfulness of Adam and Eve against God, who made them his stewards in Eden on certain contract terms, is an allegory of our condition. The "prodigal son" demanding what is his and going into a far country is a picture of you and me.

None of us can ascend to heaven by some tower of Babel that we construct. We cannot earn, buy, or pay our way into the kingdom of God. As Paul says in Rom. 3:27–28 (Phillips): "What happens now to human pride of achievement? There is no more room for it. Why, because failure to keep the Law has killed it? Not at all, but because the whole matter is now on a different plane—believing instead of achieving." He adds again in Rom. 4:16 (Phillips): "The whole thing, then, is a matter of faith on man's part and generosity on God's."

We are all sinners, falling short of God's plans and dream for us: "All we like sheep have gone astray; we have turned every one to his own way; and the LORD has laid on him the iniquity of us all" (Isa. 53:6). Not only have we all followed our father Adam in rejecting God's will, but we can't find our way back to God's presence without Christ, "the way, the truth, and the life." So faithfulness must begin with receiving.

Faithfulness in Holding and Investing

The main area for faithfulness in stewardship, however, is holding and investing. Life, already seen as a gift of God, can be more perfectly lived as unto God. Breath seen as a gift of God can be more profitably expended so as to give glory to God. Strength of mind, body, and spirit, seen as God's gift, can be more easily employed in his service.

Faithfulness at the level of holding, using, and investing for God means primarily *honesty* and *dependability.* Some of us are not honest. When we take things that are gifts of God and act as though they were not, using them to our pleasure or aggrandizement, we are being dishonest. Christian stewards will not do that, because they have received faithfully; hence they will use honestly, being motivated by the love of God and desiring only to please him.

Many who would like to be considered Christian stewards are not faithful, for they are not dependable. When you took the vows of church membership you promised faithfulness in several areas of life. Unless you are dependably keeping those vows, you are not meeting Christ's requirement of stewards, faithfulness. When you accepted a place as a teacher, youth counselor, or officer in the church and were duly installed in that position, you were publicly accepting a stewardship, not just an honor or title. If you have done less than your best, if you have used less than your full ability, if you have been irregular in your attendance or have not tried earnestly to discharge your responsibilities, you have not been faithful. You have not met Christ's requirement.

The great thing about being Christian stewards is that we become fellow workers with Christ and partners with God. Since Jesus takes the concept of stewardship from the realm of economics to describe our mutual interrelationships, it is only right that we should say that as Christian stewards "we are in business with God." Those who faithfully accept their Christian stewardship soon discover that they are not only servants of their Lord, they are also partners with God. Jesus said, "My Father is working still, and I am working" (John 5:17). By this he was explaining to us that he and God the Father have always been working together to effect God's purpose in the world. Then one day when Jesus was talking with his disciples, he said, "No longer do I call you servants, for the servant does not know what his master is doing; but I have called you friends, for all that I have heard from my Father I have made known to you" (John 15:15).

Historically the steward was never an ordinary servant. He always stood next to the master of the household. He was on intimate terms with his master, was taken into his master's confidence, planned with his master in the administration of the estate. And all this has real implications for Christian stewardship.

Once you have willingly accepted such a position in the household of God, you will begin to be seized with this wonderful truth: God and I are working together for the good of men, for the enrichment of life, for the coming of the kingdom. If you are a farmer, you are working with God in bringing forth his good from the earth to sustain the lives of his children. If you are a carpenter, you are building under the direction of the Master Carpenter; if you are teaching, you are in league and covenant with the Great Teacher; if you are in business, you are in business with God.

All of us as Christians are members of the greatest company in the world. God started this business and he remains head of the firm.

1. He decides what product we shall produce: mature persons in Christ.

2. He makes clear the company's goals: "the rule of God in human lives" or, as H. Richard Niebuhr put it, "the increase among men of the love of God and neighbor."

3. He sends out the corporation's representatives: "Go into all the world."

4. He commits to our trust the word of his grace, the Christian gospel, "entrusting to us the message of reconciliation" (II Cor. 5:19). So our business is God's business.

If this analogy sounds shockingly modern and irreligious, let me remind you that it simply follows the custom of Jesus in his parables. Many of them turn on making God the householder and men and women the servants in charge of his estate. The superintendent or steward was responsible to the master or householder and must at any time be ready to give an account of the management of the Lord's affairs.

One suggested reading for this chapter is familiarly called "the parable of the talents." A talent was a sum of money, equal perhaps to $1,000 or more. When the lord left his country for a long visit abroad, he left his money in the care of his servants for investment. They became stewards and business partners by virtue of their trust. He recognized that they did not all have equal ability, so he left to each servant an amount for investment that he felt he could handle, and took his journey. The man with $5,000 invested his trust and earned $5,000 more; and the man with $2,000 earned $2,000. But the man with $1,000 hid his money in a hole in the ground.

After what was probably several years, the master returned and called each of his servants in to give account. The first two reported on their success, and each in turn received this judgment: "Well done, good and faithful servant! . . . You have been faithful in managing small amounts, so I will put you in charge of large amounts. Come on in and share my happiness!" (Matt. 25:21, TEV).

But the servant who had received $1,000 excused himself: "Sir, I know you are a hard man, . . . so I went off and hid your money in the ground. Look! Here is what belongs to you" (Matt. 25:24–25, TEV).

The greeting he received from the master was quite different from that of the other two. He was called "wicked and slothful" or "bad and lazy," for having failed to use his trust. He was told that he might at least have earned interest on it and returned that to the owner. Then his trust was taken from him and he was shut outside the door.

Nobody needs to be told that Jesus' purpose in telling this story was to dramatize our accountability as stewards to God. But perhaps not everyone has noticed that the first two stewards were applauded not for the amount they had earned but *for faithfulness.* The third servant was rejected and condemned for proving unfaithful, not because he didn't turn a 100 percent profit, but because he had shown himself undependable. Jesus is careful to make the point that the master would have been pleased even if the third servant had only earned interest on his money.

The essential teaching of this parable is that faithfulness is everything in one's stewardship role. The third servant had kept his lord's money, but he had not invested it. So he was both unfaithful and unprofitable. The implication is clear: *God requires faithfulness* and he expects a profit on what he invests in us. God expects our lives to be fruitful, for he knows that if we are faithful in investing them for him they will be. Jesus said, "It is your Father's will that you bring forth much fruit."

God is bountiful in his gifts to us, but he is not an indulgent grandfather, expecting nothing. He expects the investment of our lives. If we really enter into stewardship, we work in active participation with God. God expects a profit from our labors, for Jesus said, "A good tree brings forth good fruit." As surely as God has poured all his bounty so lavishly into our hands, just that surely does he expect faithfulness in our handling of it.

As Christ was faithful in his stewardship, so are we expected to be faithful. The Father's word to him was, "This is my beloved Son, with whom I am well pleased." We too may share his purpose, his will, and his work. We know what he is about; and we may work in double harness with him. As we labor with him we may know his joy and hear his "Well done, good and faithful servant!"

Part Two
AREAS FOR RESPONDING TO CHRIST

5
Responding with One's Life

Read Romans 12:1–2; I Corinthians 6:9–20

As we have seen in Part One, we are all stewards because God created and owns all things; hence whatever we have we hold in trust. But we rise to Christian stewardship as we respond in gratitude to the love and mercy of God, living no longer to ourselves but to him. So it is the love of God and of Christ Jesus which constrains and controls us. Christian stewardship is, by definition, Christ-motivated; his motives become our motives. And what is expected of stewards? One thing only: faithfulness. We should be full of faith in receiving and honest and dependable in holding and investing all God has entrusted to our care.

Having explored the concept of stewardship, we become interested next in the fullness and extent of our trust. If I am a steward, what am I a steward of? What is specifically in my control? For what am I personally responsible? What are the limits and boundaries of my trusteeship? What has God put into my hands in expectation of faithful keeping, and of what does he expect from me an honest and trustworthy accounting?

The most obvious answer to this question is, "Everything that I have," for all comes from God. Another answer is equally obvious and even better: all of my life, for all of life is a trust. But the trouble with summary answers is that they don't clarify themselves. What do we mean by "everything" or "all of life"? The answers themselves need analysis and explication.

Responding with Life and Breath

If Christian stewards are responsible for their entire life and all they possess, how does that break down into components? First of all, it means *life itself,* for life itself is God's initial gift. We are God's creatures. He made us. "The LORD God formed man of dust from the ground, and breathed into his nostrils the breath of life; and man became a living being" (Gen. 2:7). Surely responsive living must start here—for without this first trust we are nothing and we have nothing. Hence the principal stewardship is stewardship of the very life we live. Since God gives it, it is to be used, administered, lived in accord with the ends and purposes of God.

Once, while Paul was waiting in Athens for his traveling companions to arrive, he noticed that the city was full of altars to the gods of the Greeks, one even inscribed "to an unknown God." When the Athenians demanded that he preach to them, Paul took the "unknown God" for his subject. He told them that this is the God "who made the world and everything in it"; that he "does not live in shrines made by man"; but that "he himself gives to all men life and breath and everything" (Acts 17:24–25).

It is interesting that Paul, like the Genesis writer, calls attention to the breath. Both seem to emphasize the breath of life. Life certainly depends on breath. It came to our first father by the breath of the Creator; and it comes to every newborn baby as the first requisite. We can live only when and while we breathe. When the breath stops, life stops. This has a further interest for us, also, because the Hebrew word *ruach* and the Greek word *pneuma,* which we translate "breath," also mean "spirit." Without laboring the point further, life exists and continues only by the breath, or spirit, of God. So we are stewards of the air we breathe and of every moment that we breathe. Life is not a matter merely of the body's existence. No wonder the psalmist cries out, "Let everything that breathes praise the LORD!" (Ps. 150:6).

Yet life no more consists in breath or spirit alone than it consists in body alone. Nor is our purpose to debate which is the prior gift: body, breath, heartbeat, spirit, or soul—for all come from God, and all come in the same package.

So if it is the Spirit of God which lights the dull candle of man's body into incandescence, let the flame of his candle glow brightly to honor the source of his light. If it is the breath of God which gives man breath, let man's breath be expended for God's praise and human good; or if it is the magic of the loving heart of God which wakens an earthly body to warm and breathing life, then let that life exult, let it live, let it honor and serve its creator—our love answering his deep love for us.

Life is all these gifts of God, not just one. The old Roman poet Lucretius made much of this in *De Rerum Natura,* "On the Nature of Things." We do not encounter spirits existing without bodies, he said; nor can bodies continue to live when the spirit, soul, or breath has gone out of them. Life is one—a unity—of all these things together.

Therefore when a complete response to God is called for in the Old Testament, it comes in words like these: "Hear, O Israel: The Lord our God is one Lord; and you shall love the LORD your God with all your heart, and with all your soul, and with all your might" (Deut. 6:4–5). These words were kept and treasured and became the opening of the confession of faith known as the Shema, an ever-recurring liturgical element of synagogue worship. Judaism recognized the emotional, spiritual, and physical aspects of human life and with these words called for total response to God. The repetition of these words in worship became a constant reminder to the devout that God calls for the devotion not of a part of a person's life but of the whole of it.

The Greeks, however, split the person asunder for a time, and their influence brought about a heresy with which the early church had to contend. Indeed, we still have to contend with it today. The Greeks believed that body and soul were separable, separate entities; and the body, being material, was evil. Hence arose an early Gnostic heresy among the Greek Christians, that religion is only spiritual: God is spirit, human beings are spirit; they relate to God in the spirit. Hence the body, being naturally evil, is free to cater to its lusts, that having nothing to do with a person's religion.

Judging from the behavior of some people, that heresy still exists. But it is not so in Christ or Christian stewardship. Personal Christian stewardship is the stewardship of everything that makes me me and you you. Thus it is a package deal: we received it all together, and we return it all together. We give the heart to love and compassion, the mind to contemplation of God's beauty and truth, and the body to doing his will with our arms and hands and legs and feet. God has given all that makes human life; we as Christian stewards respond to him with all that life contains.

Christ and Christianity have never sought a split personality but always a unified one. The command of the Shema became the first commandment of our Lord: "You shall love the Lord your God with all your heart, and with all your soul, and with all your mind." So reads Matt. 22:37, with Jesus changing "might" of Deut. 6:5 to "mind." But in Mark the saying is recorded as "with all your heart, and with all your soul, and with all your mind, and with all your strength" (Mark 12:30).

Jesus is careful in the Markan version to improve the first commandment as restated in the Shema just a bit in order to emphasize that every part of the human personality, every aspect of life, is included. Jesus does not want fractured persons who give him some part of their being in response to his own self-giving; he wants whole persons.

Stewardship of the Body

Let us now look at another part of the wholeness of life. The body is the package in which the whole of a person's nature lives. So Christian stewardship should begin with the body. Paul at Corinth ran into Greek Christians who were continuing to live immorally according to the Hebrew-Christian ethos. So there were constant moral problems arising in the congregation. Paul had attempted to teach them the Christian's freedom from the law, the freedom of a person who is directed by the Spirit of Christ. But they with their Greek background had interpreted what he said as meaning that the body is free from the control of the spirit—the Gnostic heresy.

I Cor. 6:12–20, which makes the situation quite dramatic for us, is a kind of mock dialogue between Paul and those taking the Greek libertine position. The libertine says, "all things are lawful for me," and Paul rejoins, "but not all things are helpful." The Greek says, "Food is for the stomach and the stomach for food." Yes, answers Paul, but one day God will put an end to both. The context makes it pretty clear what the next libertine argument is to be: the body is made for sex and sex for the body. But before it can be said, Paul answers, "The body is not meant for immorality, but for the Lord." Food may fill the needs of the stomach, but only Christ can fill the needs of a human person: "The body is meant for the Lord and the Lord for the body," he declares. Christ dwells in the body of a Christian. "He who is united to the Lord becomes one spirit with him," he says. Therefore to sin sexually with the body is to join Christ to a prostitute. Perhaps Paul's line of thinking was not yet altogether clear to the Corinthians, but the concluding statements are plain and emphatic: "Do you not know that your body is a temple of the Holy Spirit within you, which you have from God? You are not your own; you were bought with a price. So glorify God in your body."

Christians no longer belong to themselves. Once created

and belonging to God by creation, they have been purchased a second time by the sacrificed body and blood of their Lord. Hence they belong to God twice over. And their lives are properly directed by the indwelling Holy Spirit.

Therefore unlimited freedom to gratify the body by food and drink, by sexual indulgence, or anything of that sort, is not properly regarded as freedom at all but as enslavement of the person to the lower, animal nature. Paul avers, "I will not be enslaved by anything." In Christ we have been made free from the law of sin and death. We have been given "the glorious liberty of the sons of God." But this is liberty *from sin;* sin no longer reigns over us. We belong to that power which we have chosen to obey. When Christ is Lord, Christian stewards will glorify God in their bodies.

Offering the Living Body

There is another Scripture passage, however, which clarifies the personal stewardship response with a kind of dazzling clarity. Paul is again writing about the whole response that the Christian steward will make to God. He says, "I appeal to you therefore, brethren, by the mercies of God, to present your bodies as a living sacrifice, holy and acceptable to God, which is your spiritual worship." This is Rom. 12:1 according to the Revised Standard Version. The King James Version is quite similar but it translates the last clause "which is your reasonable service" rather than "which is your spiritual worship."

Making sacrifices had long been the Old Testament way of serving and worshiping God. One sacrificed to God to acknowledge his sovereignty, to thank him for his goodness, and to symbolize the giving of life back to God. But the sacrificing of animals—calves, lambs, doves—ended with Christ. For Christ had performed the one effectual and eternal sacrifice for all, so no more sacrifice of that nature would ever be needed.

Yet there was an efficacy and symbolic value in animal

sacrifice which Paul implicitly acknowledges as he turns to the New Testament usage in worship as response to God. Paul calls for the New Covenant sacrifice: "Present your bodies"—not to be burned, not to have their blood spilt upon the altar, not to be quartered and cooked for food. "I appeal to you . . . by the mercies of God," he says, "to present your bodies as a living sacrifice."

God wants our bodies, not dead, but living. He wants us to give him a body that is active and alive to do his bidding, to serve his beloved people, to seek and save the lost, and to go on errands of mercy. Such a sacrifice is "holy and acceptable to God."

Therefore the apostle calls for the offering of our bodies. God can't get much worship, praise, honor, or service from our personal stewardship if it comes disembodied. Faith is nice; the words used in the liturgy may be beautiful; and an excellent sermon may fill us with wonder. Yet it is only with their bodies (containers of the whole person) that Christians can truly worship and serve God.

Sometimes a sluggish, lazy church member will inspect his farm or factory, or even play golf or fish on Sunday morning. Such a person must be gently rebuked for not sharing in the work of Christ in the church. Often his rejoinder will be: "But look at my pledge. I am giving as much as anybody to the church." It won't do. Christ wants not yours but you. He accepts no substitutes.

Christ desires the gift of the human body in living sacrifice, not because he is more concerned with bodies than souls or spirits, but because it is only in the body that he can get the full response that constitutes Christian stewardship. The apostle Paul told the Athenians that God gives us "life and breath and everything." Jesus said that we must love with "heart, mind, soul, and strength." If Christ is to have the personal response he so richly deserves, he must have the offered body. This is doubtless what Paul had in mind when he said to the Corinthians, "So glorify God in your body."

Paul's word makes me think of Bill Wade, Vanderbilt's All-American football player of about 1950, who went on to play professional football for many years. It is a great thrill to see a powerful, highly developed human body doing its tasks so excellently on the football field. But Bill Wade glorifies God in his body on and off the field. He is a Christian churchman, has been a dedicated worker in his local congregation in Nashville, has worked faithfully with the Fellowship of Christian Athletes, speaking in preaching missions and visiting colleges, schools, and athletic groups to share his faith. He has given his time, talent, money, and strength as a sacrificial offering on the altar of Christ's church. Carroll Dale of Bristol is another who has done very much the same things. Not only has he given his time; but over and above his own tithe, he has also given to the church all the dollars he has made in speaking engagements.

Then think of Christ's own beautiful acts in his body. Remember the hands breaking bread for the hungry, extended in mercy, blessing little children and the old, giving the touch of healing—and the final sacrifice of his body on the cross.

What, then, is the first response of a genuine Christian steward? It is giving one's whole being back to God for a life of worship and service, offering one's body together with all the gifts and strengths that God has given—giving it all back for the honor and glory of God.

We can do it, too; and so we shall be transformed by the renewing of our minds, so that we also will prove "what is that good, and acceptable, and perfect will of God."

6
Work, Vocation, and Ministry

Read I Corinthians 3:5–9;
Ephesians 6:5–9

The apostle Paul taught that work is subject to the divine will and purposes: "Let every one lead the life to which the Lord has assigned him, and in which God has called him" (I Cor. 7:17). Yet work is perhaps the area of life most frequently divorced from God. We are apt to be least responsive to God in our daily labor. It is the area which we tend most to secularize. We may exercise stewardship at church, on Sunday, maybe even in our homes, but we are apt to think of our work as a completely separate, secular compartment of life where we earn our living "by the sweat of our brow." We think our work is surely our own business. So God is not involved in much of our labor, and altogether too frequently we tend to shut him into some compartment of life labeled "religious" and put up the "no visitors" sign at our place of work.

But consider that about one third of every day is spent in work and among people with and for whom we work. Every one of those days is given us by God. It should therefore be quite obvious that the Christ who wants heart, soul, mind, and strength devoted to God must necessarily be much concerned with our labor. Someone has suggested that God may be more interested in our work than our worship. As Holmes Rolston said: "Men reveal their character more by the way in which they work than by the way in which they pray."[4]

God has always been concerned about our work. Even in Eden, God assigned the first people their labor to do. Very early the Hebrews accepted as divine the principle, "Six days shalt thou labor," for this provided for livelihood, productivity, rest, and worship. Still another ancient biblical teaching was, "In the sweat of your face you shall eat bread." The Jew recognized that God had created a world filled with plenty for human needs, but he knew that people needed to work to receive it. Still later in history the principle was announced: "If any one will not work, let him not eat" (II Thess. 3:10). Paul applied this principle at Thessalonica, and Captain John Smith followed it in the Virginia colony. Today, however, there are some who believe the government owes them a living, whether they are willing to work or not. No idea is more destructive of human dignity and character. On the contrary, the New Testament enunciates the principle that "the laborer deserves his wages" (Luke 10:7; I Tim. 5:18).

God ordained work from the beginning. He himself worked and, as Jesus pointed out, is still working. He is still creating the world. Christ worked. He labored for more than a decade as a carpenter before entering into his individual ministry of teaching, healing, and preaching. Paul earned his living, at least in part, as a tentmaker. When we work, then, we are in excellent company. And, despite the Yahwist's view in Genesis 3 that labor was a curse upon Adam for disobedience, the long view of human history shows work to have been one of our greatest blessings.

1. God established work as our way of cooperating with him in bringing forth the world's good. Work was, in his eyes, and should be in ours, an altogether good thing. God knows human need. He intends to supply our need, as Jesus pointed out in the Sermon on the Mount, as naturally as he supplies the birds of the air and the lilies of the field. But if you think birds and plants don't work, you don't know

much about birds and plants. A robin will eat sixty feet of earthworms in a day, and a swallow will catch and eat an almost innumerable quantity of insects. Also, it is not unusual to see a bit of grass, a weed, or other plant work its way through four inches of asphalt or concrete. These living things work, and they are fed and clothed. Even so God plans on feeding, clothing, and sheltering all of us, but he expects labor as our way of cooperating in getting what we need.

2. This, however, is only the first reason for work. Work is good also because it is good for us. When we work we exercise, we develop, we grow—physically and otherwise. To work is to put one's hand or mind to something positive and constructive. So work has therapeutic value. One successful farmer said: "When you feel like working, work. When you don't feel like working, work. When you feel happy, work. When things are going wrong, work. When nothing seems to work, work." Perhaps work is no such universal panacea as his statement suggests. But if you have mental or emotional sickness and are institutionalized for a period of time, as soon as possible you will be given work therapy to help you recover. Work gives us fulfillment; it gives us a sense of usefulness; it helps us express our creative desires.

3. Work, then, is a way of achieving purposiveness in life, fulfilling our creativity, and actually co-creating with God. Every Jew was taught a trade, just as Jesus and Paul were. For every Jew was expected to make a useful contribution in the world. People are probably closest to God when they are working for good and useful purposes in the world.

4. For the Christian, then, work is clearly an area of stewardship. By work we serve the needs of others. We not only get God's good for ourselves but we channel it to others as well. Christ's teaching is that when we serve others we are serving God: "As you did it to one of the least of these my brethren, you did it to me." By work we share our good with others.

5. Obviously whatever work we do that becomes a "service," providing physical, mental, or spiritual necessities to others, must be work that is intrinsically good. It must be in accord with God's purposes. It must help others' lives to be richer and fuller. If it disseminates the truth, comforts the sorrowing, heals the sick and the hurt; if it heals divisions and brings peace—then it is work which can be applauded with the words, "Well done, good and faithful servant."

Without presenting other necessities for work or benefits of work, let us summarize the concept of work as stewardship: Life, health, strength, and time (which is what life is made up of) are all God's gifts to us. Hence life, health, strength, and time should be accepted, treasured, and used as aspects of "the manifold grace of God." If this is true of life, health, strength, and time, it is also true of what is commonly called "talent"—the particular gift of God which makes it possible for us to be individuals, unique in our personal labor and responsiveness.

What is the nature of your genius? You can't say "none," no matter how normal, average, or dull you may consider yourself. Every one of us is as individual as the leaves on a tree or the snowflakes that fall from the sky. The essential difference lies in something we generally call a "gift." A "gifted musician" is one whom we recognize as having received a special aptitude, bent, and ear for music. Gifts can be developed, of course, but however much they are improved, they are still gifts, first of all. One has a "green thumb," another has the gift of putting others at ease, another has charismatic leadership ability, and another mathematical genius. But each person, however humble, has a gift. So Peter advises: "As each has received a gift, employ it for one another, as good stewards of God's varied grace" (I Peter 4:10).

Now, having looked briefly into the meaning and significance of work up to the point of seeing it as service to God through service to people, let us turn to consider the meaning of "vocation."

Response to Vocation

Vocation is a word with two widely different outcroppings of meaning. The common meaning, the secular twentieth-century meaning, is: one's selected work by means of which one earns a livelihood. To enable all persons to select the proper vocation in which they will realize their desires and be happy, we have filled the schools with a plethora of materials, instruments, tests, and vocational counselors. Aptitude and preference tests multiply. Vocational counselors and placement officers abound from junior high through graduate schools. A recent U.S. Commissioner of Education maintained that our schools from the first grade on should be busily engaged in vocational training. Also, the Federal Government subsidizes retraining programs for those who don't fit into and find happiness in their first vocations. This is the most common and generally accepted meaning of the word "vocation."

But the etymology of the word reveals an older and once dominant meaning that was quite different. Vocation derives from the Latin *vocare,* meaning "to call"; hence one's vocation is the task to which he or she is called. Moreover, the old and accepted understanding of vocation until recent times was that such vocation meant "divine calling."

The idea of divine calling to different kinds of tasks may be found throughout both the Old and New Testaments. Abraham, a nomadic shepherd, was called by God to leave his country and kindred and take his immediate family and flocks to a new land (Genesis 12). Moses, a politician exiled from Egypt, was called by God to go back to Egypt to assume leadership of the Israelites and shape them into a nation (Exodus 3). Samuel was called to the political leadership of the Jews in Israel, and Gideon to be their military leader. Jesus was called to his ministry; and he in turn called twelve men to be his disciples. Paul received a vocation on the Damascus road. Any sober reading of the

Bible brings the clear judgment that biblical history is the history of people whom God has called to several varied positions, and they have attempted to "walk worthy" of their vocations.

This concept of vocation would be a foreign language to the average vocational counselor or placement agency of our time. If the word happens to be used in conversation, e.g., "What is his vocation?" it means only "What kind of work does he do?"

Within the confines of the church itself we still speak of the "call" to preach, or of being "called" to a missionary field. But I believe it would be safe to say that 95 percent of church members are not aware that they are themselves called by God, that they have a divine vocation.

There are several vocations, or callings. Allow me to illustrate from my personal experience:

1. The call to faith came to me early in life, through the ministry of the church I attended and the devout lives of my parents.

2. Then in a few years I experienced what William Law spoke of as "the call to a devout and holy life." My heart burned for righteousness before God and my being ached to know him.

3. Next there came a deep desire to follow Christ in such a way as to make my life a blessing. I wanted to feel that I was not sponging on life but was making a contribution to pay my rent for the space I was occupying in God's world.

4. With this there followed strong inclinations toward teaching and toward the pastoral ministry.

5. Finally, more than once, as God's man I have felt what I believed to be his leadership in moving me to particular places of work. So, as you see, even a single individual may know several calls. God calls us to discipleship, then to Christian maturity. He calls us to exercise the means of grace; and he calls us to serve humanity for his sake.

The Universal Calling to Christian Ministry

Among these several calls there is, however, one that is universal to Christians, and that is the calling or vocation to Christian ministry. There is no teaching in the New Testament that is clearer than the teaching that every Christian is called to ministry, to service to others for Jesus' sake.

To Roman Catholicism, with its cleavages between clergy and laity, this perception was lost in the Middle Ages, but it came back with the Protestant Reformation. Every Christian receives a loud and clear call to the service of God. Paul put it: "For we are his workmanship, created in Christ Jesus for good works, which God prepared beforehand, that we should walk in them" (Eph. 2:10). This means, not that you must leave your present job or position to be God's servant, but that in your present work you must seek opportunity to serve God, that you must turn your work to service, that your motivation in your work must far transcend the question, "What can I get out of this work?" and become "How can I make my labor most serviceable to God and my brothers?"

Whatever you do, you can honor God and serve humanity. A teacher, a coach, a businessman, a farmer, or a garbage collector can consecrate his work—the product of his life, health, strength and peculiar gift—to God and his kingdom.

There are, moreover, some clear inferences which can be drawn from the statements above, and they should be emphasized:

1. If the work I do is to be my divine vocation and ministry, it will call for the dedication of my "gift" to bless others, whatever my gift may be. If I do not employ my gift in my job, I must either learn how to do so, leave my job and seek another, or do double duty by more fully employing my gift for God at other times.

2. As already indicated, whatever I spend my strength

and gift upon must necessarily accord with and further God's purposes in the world. If my work strengthens others, that is good; if it weakens them, it is no Christian vocation. I am then fulfilling no ministry and am being faithless in stewardship. If it is morally questionable or if it in any way deprives others or draws them away from God, I must abandon it.

3. But, as already indicated, when I work in partnership with God, when I have the consciousness of doing God's will and walking with Christ, when I am "increasing among men the love of God and neighbor," then my work is transformed to worship. Work can and does become, for the life responsively lived, sacred and sacramental.

There is an old symbol of the Moravian Church that defines the Christian stewardship of work. An ox is pictured standing between an altar and a plow, and underneath are the words "ready for either." Truly Christian stewards are ready to give themselves to God either in work or worship; and they so fully dedicate their strength to God in work that it becomes worship.

Even so do Christians attain to their highest fellowship, the fellowship of which Paul spoke to the Corinthians: "We are laborers together with God" (I Cor. 3:9, KJV).

7
The Family and the Church

Read Deuteronomy 6:1–9, 20–25;
Acts 16:14–15, 25–34;
I Corinthians 12:4–31; Ephesians 4:1–16

We cannot understand either the full meaning or the complete dimensions of our responsiveness and responsibility unless we see our stewardship in relation to its "houses." From its earliest beginning the Greek word *oikonomos,* which we translate "steward," was always defined by its relationship to a house or household. *Oikonomos* ("steward") combines *oikos* ("house") with *nemein* ("to distribute," "to manage"). The steward was a person deemed trustworthy to whom the head or proprietor of a house entrusted the management of all the affairs of the household, including not only receipts and expenditures but also the actual care of the servants and children of the household.

Up to this point we have dealt with the steward primarily in terms of individual response to God as trustee of all he or she has received. This is valid, but it is not complete. The steward responds to God and is characterized by sensitive responsiveness. But when Christ saves us he sets us within a company of the saved. Hence a Christian steward also and invariably responds within the context of a household. For a steward is by definition the trustee or overseer of a household.

Such information may cause our minds to jump immediately to the pastor, elder, bishop, priest, or deacon who has designated responsibility for the care of God's household, the church. This instant intuition is by no means amiss. But, as we shall presently see, (1) the first house of our responsibility is our own household, and (2) the care of God's family is by no means left entirely in the hands of ordained ecclesiastics.

The First House of Christian Stewardship

It was no accident that the first Christian churches met in private houses. There were several first-century historical factors that caused it: the poverty of the Christians, the hostility of the authorities, the need for a place for common worship and catechetical instruction, and the lack of public meeting places after it became clear that the Christians were not merely a Jewish sect. But there were also traditional and cultural factors that brought it about. Though there was a Temple and there were synagogues, it is clear that the really basic unit of the family of God in Old Testament days had been the individual household. Here worship had been conducted, the laws were taught and kept, the truth was inculcated, and every member had responsibility to the whole household. The father was the priest and head of the family, but the larger and richer households frequently had stewards, slave or free, to whom much of the administration of the affairs of the household was committed.

So it is by no means surprising that the first Christian groups met in homes and were identified by the houses where they met. Worship, instruction, celebration of the sacraments, missionary planning, and care for the unfortunate were concerns of these tiny congregations. But as the individual congregations grew and spread, they could no longer be contained within single domiciles. Moreover, the management of the affairs of the religious unit (as at Philippi, Colossae, Ephesus) had to be more fully organized, and more specific tasks had to be committed to deacons, bishops, presbyters, and the like.

But before we move from the individual household of faith to the congregational family, let us briefly consider the first house. Its stewards (mother, father, or whoever) had the care of every aspect of family life. Food had to be placed on the table and the family had to be housed and clothed. The values of the family had to be inculcated by precept and example—and values were taught perhaps even more indelibly by example when precept was slighted or ignored, as today. Lines had to be drawn, traditions observed or established, decisions made, judgments rendered for each household. The household, even though each individual was given due place and respected, acted as a unit. Hence in the New Testament we frequently read how a certain man "and his house" believed and were baptized.

The stewardship of the family is at once one of God's greatest gifts to us and one of our heaviest responsibilities to him. Remembrance tells me that God's best gift to my childhood and youth was the family that surrounded me with love and care. I learned that a good conscience is better than any material things. I learned what it meant to trust God when my father gave up a prosperous business to begin preparing himself for the pastoral ministry. My parents never gave their children much, materially speaking, for they didn't have it to give. But they gave us a deep conviction of life's being under God's care and judgment and inculcated in us a strong sense of personal responsibility.

They were good stewards in their house. And each of us receives the responsibility for such stewardship in his own family. A care is laid upon us, a responsibility for sharing. Did anyone learn the truth that "it is more blessed to give than to receive" before he experienced doing without something he wanted in order that another member of the family might have something he wanted? Did anyone really begin to know the privilege of laboring with God in stewardship before becoming responsible for a family? How blessed it is to rear children "in the nurture and admonition of the Lord"! How happy an occasion it is to give back to God in Christian baptism the child he has given us. The loving, suffering, rejoicing, enduring together, and sharing of the family are treasures of inestimable worth. In the Christian family every person learns and is taught to sacrifice some personal pleasure for the greater good of the whole. There every life is treasured, and all things are done for mutual edification and happiness.

The family unit remains the building block of God's kingdom in the twentieth century. Fathers and mothers are the chief priests and stewards. They have the principal care of the family. They must keep alive the sense of God's presence with grace at meals, family devotions, prayers, and the natural discussion of what the real values are. They must be "examples to the flock." This doesn't let others off the hook, however. There are important tasks that may be committed to the other older members of the household; and there are appropriate responsibilities that may be delegated to every member. There is a stewardship of something deemed important that is placed in the hands of every member of the family, from grandmother down to the smallest child. Faith was a family affair in biblical times and it remains so today.

The Second House of Stewardship

Stewardship in the church, the household of God, the family of faith, is not more important than stewardship in the single family, the individual *oikos.* But it is more visible, more public. It is also more palpably that stewardship to which Jesus and Paul and Peter so frequently referred, as seen in the New Testament.

1. Doubtless we who belong to the church need to think first about stewardship *of* the church. The church is another supreme manifestation of the manifold grace of God. God creates us, Christ redeems us, and the Holy Spirit continues

with us to guide and empower us. These are the greatest gifts, but the church into which we are set is a great gift too. God may be said to have called it into being in the election of the Jews, and Christ may be said to have redeemed and reshaped it by his life and death, but it was the Holy Spirit who first revealed it with clarity and beauty to Christ's disciples. After Pentecost the disciples worshiped together, ate together, witnessed to their faith, and shared their possessions for the good of all. Instruction, preaching, the sacraments, and the care of the poor became intimate concerns of the whole body of believers.

Other than God's giving himself in Christ and the Holy Spirit, no other universal gift ranks with that of the church. For in that one gift are many gifts: the Bible, Christian fellowship *(koinōnia)*, opportunities for worship, service, and Christian growth—all the means of grace. So, in a time when the church has been derided and is under criticism, it especially behooves the people of God to reflect on the many gifts they have received in the Christian church.

To our limited understanding the church is absolutely essential to the completion of God's purpose to build his kingdom on earth and to Christ's mission to bind all humankind in loving fellowship under God's rule. But God is resourceful beyond all our thoughts: when the descendants of Abraham fell short of their missionary responsibility as God's elect, he chose the one perfect steward to continue his redemption of mankind. If one can conceive of the failure of the Christian church as God's instrument for the redemption of mankind in our age, God will doubtless have some other "faithful remnant" with which to start afresh. But while we have the church among us and may experience therein the continuing action of God through the Holy Spirit, let us be good stewards *of the church.*

2. Practically, of course, it is responsiveness and responsibility to God *in and through the church* which is the essence of being Christ's faithful and true stewards. Paul Schilling has written, "We have been called into Christian

community not for mutual self-congratulation but for service in God's name, and not for unique privilege but for special responsibility."[5]

What, then, are our stewardship responsibilities in the church? They vary, doubtless, with changing times; and individual responsibilities differ according to our several gifts. We have already named some of the things Christians began to do as stewards in the first flush of realization of the church, as recorded in the first chapters of Acts. The whole of the book continues this story. For example, in Acts 3 and 4 we read how Peter and John had no gold but gave "what they had" to heal the lame man; how they then witnessed to the healing and saving power of Christ before the people and before the Sanhedrin; and how, being forbidden to say more, they declared, "We cannot but speak of what we have seen and heard" (Acts 4:20).

Perhaps the best clarification of stewardship responsibility in the church is seen in those New Testament letters where the church is pictured as the body of Christ (Romans 12; I Cor. 4:1–7; 12:4–31; and Ephesians 4). Though these passages differ somewhat, each is like a piece of one whole stewardship mosaic. They make it clear that Christian stewardship in the body of Christ is churchmanship. In summary, this is what they say: Each Christian is a member of the body, having a different gift and being responsible for the performance of his distinctive function. Some serve, some prophesy, some teach. But all should love and honor one another, living in harmony. They should collectively contribute to the needs of the saints and practice hospitality. They have the truth to share as "stewards of the mysteries of God," and they must seek to help one another live "according to Scripture."

The stewardship of these several members in the body is directed by the Holy Spirit "for the common good." Some have faith, gifts of healing, or the utterance of wisdom. Each member must respect and appreciate the gifts of the others, for all are needed; and each should rejoice or suffer with the others. So, whether one is a prophet, teacher, pastor, evangelist, or other worker, one has a responsibility to employ his gift "for the equipment of the saints, for the work of the ministry, for building up the body of Christ" (Eph. 4:12, RSV 1946). The writer of this book is in full agreement with John Mackay's declaration that the comma after "saints" is heretical.[6] For all stewards are responsible "for the equipment of the saints for the work of ministry" ("to equip the saints for the work of ministry": RSV 1972)—a translation that accords with the teaching of the universal vocation to ministry.

Since the church has spread worldwide and taken on many and various new operations, the categories of Christian service in the church have multiplied. There are special ministries now to the young—and the old. There are multiple committees in every church, organized to plan and fulfill the church's full ministry more completely. There are athletic directors, choir directors, directors of education. There are leaders of study groups, prayer groups, church visitation groups, and so on almost ad infinitum. The categorical designations change, but the stewardship responsibility remains unchanged; and whatever the graph or chart of services performed, each Christian still "is given the manifestation of the Spirit for the common good" (I Cor. 12:7).

The Priesthood of the Believer

The apostle Paul saw himself as a steward "of the mysteries of God" (I Cor. 4:1). Protestants generally see him as a special spokesman of God's truth and make him at least the equal of Peter in authority. Because the church in early centuries had to designate certain persons as rulers and administrators, tradition across nineteen centuries has divided Christians into clergy and laity. But this division and distinction was not established in New Testament times. During the Reformation, efforts were made to return to

New Testament understandings and practice by stressing (1) the universal vocation to the ministry and (2) the priesthood of the believer.

Yet even today most of us regard pastors and priests as *the important stewards* of God's household. We reason that they have pastoral care, they order the services of worship, and they make priestly intercession for the people; they administer the sacraments, perform weddings, bury the dead, and have general oversight of the entire program and business administration of the church. Assuredly, there is some truth in our human reasoning. Moreover, churches do not grow and develop and serve their communities where the clergy are not zealous stewards. Hardly ever will churches be distinguished by active, responsible members if the clergy do not set the example in stewardship.

But when all this is said, and when we have rationalized ourselves into subordinate roles in the administration and work of the church, we must be reminded once again—and with emphasis—that each of us is a called minister, each of us has a gift to employ for the good of all, and every believer is a priest of God. Therefore answering roll call and pledging financial support, however good and necessary, do not by any means fulfill our responsibility as stewards in God's house.

We have already called attention to passages picturing the church as the body of Christ. These passages also show that the health and growth of the body is dependent upon the functioning of every member. Ephesians 4:15–16 describes the body of Christ as growing and upbuilding itself in love "when each part is working properly." Other New Testament Scriptures that picture the church as a growing temple also make the individual member responsible for growth. Ephesians 2:19–22 pictures the church growing into a holy temple of the Lord, with each person as a growing stone. I Peter 2:4–8 also pictures the church as a spiritual house with Christ as the cornerstone and the members as "living stones." Therefore, "let all things be done for edification" (I Cor. 14:26).

It is interesting that Peter moves directly from his picture of the church as a spiritual edifice to his emphatic declaration of the priesthood of believers:

> But you are a chosen race, a royal priesthood, a holy nation, God's own people, that you may declare the wonderful deeds of him who called you out of darkness into his marvelous light. Once you were no people but now you are God's people; once you had not received mercy but now you have received mercy. (I Peter 2:9–10)

The words of Peter here intentionally remind us of the failure of God's first chosen people to perform a sharing and priestly ministry to all humanity, and so they doubly strengthen the charge laid upon God's new people, Christians (who once were "no people"), to perform their priestly role with responsibility—to share God's mysteries, to declare his mercies, to serve as God's intermediaries in continuing Christ's redemptive ministry in the world. Christian stewardship is a continuation of the priesthood and ministry of Christ. Every believer becomes a priest to others, seeking to restore right relations between them and God.

Yet even the believer's priesthood is but one of the aspects of the total responsibility that is his or hers as *oikonomos,* a steward of God's household.

8
The *Oikoumenē* and the Cosmos

Read Psalms 8:5–8; 24:1–2;
Isaiah 61:1–3;
Matthew 25:31–46; 28:16–20

Perhaps the most obvious truth that has been trying to break through in the previous chapter is that our stewardship under God does not confine itself to the home and the church nor, indeed, to religion. For God is not the God only of believers in family groups or worshiping congregations. If we tend to confine our stewardship to a "happy little family group," and if we are concerned only with the working of the well-oiled machinery of the church, we, like Israel of old, have not yet understood the meaning of our election.

God did not select the Jews because of any superlative worth they had, as he plainly told them (Deut. 7:6–8; 9:4–6). They were elected to share their understanding and their good with mankind, to be "a light to the nations" (Isa. 49:6). Much as God is concerned to build his church, even the church is a means to an end, not an end in itself. God is concerned for all people in all places. He intends to rule in the lives of "all people that on earth do dwell." And the church is the instrument chosen to complete his purpose.

Moreover, God is not concerned only with the religious aspects of human lives, but with every aspect. The church sometimes serves the needs of people *in order* to bring them into the church. But Christ is concerned with feeding hungry people for their stomachs' sakes and healing sick people for their bodies' sakes. He said, "I will build my church," but he didn't announce this as his ultimate goal.

But wait: before further discussion of responsible stewardship of Christians that lies outside the church, let me name and identify the larger circles of Christian responsibility. *They are two* and they seem almost to coexist; that is, they overlap and are largely coextensive. Yet they are two. They are two bigger, broader, wider houses of responsibility into which God sets us as trustees when we respond to his loving grace and mercy. These two houses of our stewardship are (1) the *oikoumenē*, or inhabited world, and (2) the cosmos, or natural world.

The *Oikoumenē*

You will recognize the Greek *oikoumenē* because it is the compound word from which our English word "ecumenical" is drawn. The word *oikos,* as we have seen, means house, residence, or household, referring almost always to an inhabited house. And the verb *menō* means "reside" or "remain"; so the compound is a rather confusing tautology, something like "the residence of residency" or "the house of dwelling." It presents no problem to translators of the New Testament, however, who nearly always translate it simply as "the world." So as we shall be using the term here, it means "the inhabited world."

This house of our Christian stewardship extends to the borders of the inhabited earth. God created all earth's people, as the reading of Genesis 1–2 makes clear, for he created man and woman, our progenitors. This was the final and climactic action in the series of words by which he spoke all things into being. So God is "father of all mankind" on every continent, in every land and clime.

As a good father, God loves all his children—"red and yellow, black and white," rich or poor, educated or ignorant, weak or powerful. No one escapes his concern. God's plan for redemption embraces all people of every station in society, of every race and nationality.

It follows that when the church is what it should be, it is not concerned primarily for its own existence or continuance, but it is concerned about its service in the world. It exists for the sake of the world, not itself; and it is concerned for the coming of God's rule in the world. Following the Christ who gave up all things in discharging his stewardship, the church gives itself in service to people, offering itself as a living sacrifice to God. The church, when it becomes fully aware of itself as God's servant and steward, operates on the principle that "he who loses his life for my sake will find it" (Matt. 10:39). God builds the church when it becomes the willing instrument of his purposes in the *oikoumenē*.

I shall make no effort to discuss or even to list all our responsibilities in the inhabited earth. But it is appropriate to suggest some of them.

Clearly the first stewardship obligation of a Christian toward others inside or outside the church is to love them. This, you will remember, is the second commandment of Jesus. But this love is no sentimental affair. It is, in fact, the same sort of love God in Christ has shown toward us. It is neither *erōs*, the love of attraction, nor *philia*, brotherly love; but it is *agapē*, an outgoing love which, though not motivated by the beauty of its object yet seeks only his highest welfare. Since Christ exercised this kind of love toward us, our stewardship responsibility manifests it toward others "as unto Christ."

This love is "the fruit of the Spirit" (Gal. 5:22); that is, the Spirit dwelling in us loves others through us. As a Christian steward you must love your neighbor as yourself. But who is your neighbor? According to the parable of the Good Samaritan, he is the person in need, violated and bruised by someone and ignored by others. It is the task of Christian stewardship to find this needy person, to bind up his wounds, and to get for him the care and necessities his condition requires. As Warren A. Quanbeck writes, "Love of neighbor . . . is discipline in behaving toward the neighbor as God acts toward man."[7]

Since Christ is the model of stewardship for us, it is well to be reminded of how he pictured his own ministry to those "outside the gates." When he read from the prophet Isaiah in the Nazareth synagogue, he chose the following passage as descriptive of his own ministry:

> The Spirit of the Lord is upon me,
> because he has anointed me to preach good news
> to the poor.
> He has sent me to proclaim release to the captives
> and recovering of sight to the blind,
> to set at liberty those who are oppressed,
> to proclaim the acceptable year of the Lord.
> (Luke 4:18–19)

Most of the responsibilities which become ours as Christians fall under the umbrella of this description from Isaiah 61.

Robert E. Cushman says that Christian stewardship "may be seen also as an extension of Christ's ministry in and for the world."[8] In such terms it can be equated with the mission of the Christian church. And that, I believe, is true *if* we read the church's mission in broad enough terms. "All the world" into which Christ sends us is, indeed, the *oikoumenē;* but God's kingdom means his rule in every aspect of life on earth—in government, economics, labor-management relations, owner-renter relations, race relations. Integration of the public schools was a step in the right direction, but God wills equal rights for each human being, equal opportunity, equal respect among all races, and mutual human concern among us all. Christian stewards see many shortcomings yet to be overcome in race relations and human rights.

The Christian steward has an obligation to society which he can discharge only through good citizenship. God may be as interested in our politics as he is in religion, for it is through government that education is controlled, research is done in medicine, people are given or not given justice and their human rights. Because of scandals and corruption, which sometimes become highly visible in government, church members tend to throw up their hands, pronounce anathema on all politics, and refuse to take an active part in it, even to the extent of failing to vote. Precisely the opposite is called for in Christian stewards, however. For we cannot actually have nothing to do with government, since it will continue to regulate almost every part of our lives. As a pastor I used to preach the responsibility of Christians to become active in politics, and I was pleased when several members of my church began to stand for election to city, county, and state offices.

Our God is a god of justice and judgment. He comforts and delivers those who suffer under the heel of tyranny and the violence of oppressors. Christian stewards cannot believe that he plays favorites in the world. The prophets denounced ancient Israel when the people became unconcerned about human welfare. God would not accept their worship, demanding that "justice roll down like waters, and righteousness like an ever-flowing stream" (Amos 5:24). Christ reminded certain tithers that God is more concerned about "the weightier matters of the law, justice and mercy and faith" (Matt. 23:23). God does not countenance the domination of the people of one class, nationality, or color by another—in South Africa, in India, or in America.

God is concerned with the economic imbalances and maladjustments in our nation and world. It cannot accord with his will that less than 10 percent of the people should live in great luxury, consuming 90 percent of the world's resources, while the great mass of the population must try hopelessly to exist on what is left. God will not hold his people guiltless who live in luxury, spend lavishly, and satisfy every desire for material things while millions of people on every continent never know a day without hunger, are ill clothed and ill housed, and die like flies from starvation and hunger-caused diseases.

The will of God is peace, and the dream of his people is

peace. It is inconceivable that his rule in the world would fail to include peace among all nations. So there is no way that Christian stewards can support that which makes for war in wrongheaded international relations—in seizing and monopolizing the world's goods or arming sufficiently to kill everything alive in the world many times over, all in the name of defense. God is a god of love and mercy. So his steward must operate in love and mercy in social and international affairs. Christian stewards will seek the well-being of the people of all nations. They follow the Christian principle that the strong ought to help the weak. They are concerned about international hunger, poverty, and militaristic nationalism, or any imbalances that awaken strife and destroy peace. The God of peace seeks not only a cessation of hostility but amity and mutual understanding and helpfulness among peoples, which will make for lasting concord.

It is obvious that government, national or international, is not going to abdicate and turn its prerogatives over to the church. If so, what church? But the church through Christian stewards can influence government. At the 1976 Democratic convention the better speakers asked for integrity, moral leadership, and human compassion in our government. They nominated for President a declared Christian who said in his acceptance speech, "Love must be aggressively translated into simple justice." He was elected. But great problems have arisen and deferred his initial hopes. This does not mean, however, that we need abandon Christian ideals. It simply means that "the good fight" must be kept up. It is up to Christians to see that love *is* translated into justice.

We have hardly begun to enumerate the many Christian concerns in this big house outside the church. Add what we call "welfare"—the care of those who are old, sick, handicapped, or disabled. Add the need for jobs for the unemployed, so they may earn a living for their families in dignity. Add a governmental reform and regulation of our economy that will no longer allow the greedy with power to enjoy all material goods while others must do without common necessities. Add a program that will make health care available to all people, rich or poor. These may sound like political goals, but they are also clearly things that Christian stewards must help to bring about. Christ in the parable of the Last Judgment (Matt. 25:31–46) identifies with the needy, the deprived, and the unjustly treated. He praises those who serve him in serving them. Because of this there can be no human concern in the world that is not within the purview of Christian stewardship responsibility.

Stewardship of the Cosmos

While there is general coincidence between Christian stewardship of the *oikoumenē* and the cosmos, there is also discernible difference. Stewardship of the *oikoumenē* limits itself to the populated earth and the welfare of those persons who populate it; but stewardship of the *kosmos* involves that portion of the earth which is not populated, the depths of the earth beneath the crust on which we live, the skies and seas around it, and all other portions of the universe over which the human race has any measure of effect or control. Since July 20, 1976, our cosmos extends not only to the moon but to Mars as well. Cosmic stewardship also takes into account human "scientific" tinkering with the heavens for purposes of altering the weather. Though still having human welfare as its first end, cosmic stewardship is coming to realize the claims of *all life.* The problem has finally become clear: if we continue to destroy other life forms in the natural world, can its balances be so preserved as to make human life possible?

Cosmic stewardship is also a stewardship of the future. How long can mankind exist if we continue to waste, destroy and pollute all that makes life possible and good? A Methodist conference on stewardship in Dallas in 1968 approved a "Foundation Statement for Christian Stewardship." I should like to include three paragraphs here from the section on stewardship of our natural resources:

> The conservation of God-given resources must become a major concern of those who care for the future of the human race. Minerals, forests, water, air, soil and wild life are of prime importance. Each resource needs to be studied and plans formulated by which its best use and preservation may be achieved. The preservation of natural resources and their restoration and enrichment are major objectives for the Christian steward. . . .
>
> The problem of conservation must become everyone's concern since everyone is dependent upon natural resources. The indispensability of these resources should stir a concern to preserve them in order that coming generations may have the necessities of life. Exploitation must be replaced by careful planning to conserve where the supply of resources is limited, and to replenish where this is possible.
>
> Conservation becomes a matter of stewardship inasmuch as natural resources are gifts from God to all people and because they are necessary to the preservation of human life. Stewardship calls for use without abuse, with all possible preservation of the existing supply.[9]

Stewardship of the cosmos, ecological stewardship, is stewardship of the largest house of all—the universe God created and is creating, the house within which all human activity of the past, present, and future takes place. The boundaries are enlarged and the stewardship role becomes more complex as we consider the whole creation and attempt to understand our place in the ecology ("the word about our house"—*oikos* plus *logos*). But simple and clear biblical and theological foundations for this area of stewardship have already been laid, especially in Chapter 1.

It is noteworthy that human beings began centuries ago to perceive their relationship to the natural world as trusteeship, not ownership. In ancient and simpler days no one would have been so egotistic or so naïve as to claim ownership of the earth. Stories of the beginning clarify this. Adam and Eve are put in a garden to enjoy it and care for it for the owner.

"The earth is the LORD's and the fulness thereof" sings the psalmist, "for he has founded it upon the seas, and established it upon the rivers" (Ps. 24:1–2). All other biblical references to creation are but reaffirmation or commentary on that statement. "In the beginning God created the heavens and the earth" (Gen. 1:1); "The earth is the LORD's" (Ex. 9:29); "Behold, to the LORD your God belong heaven and the heaven of heavens, the earth with all that is in it" (Deut. 10:14); "Thou hast made heaven, the heaven of heavens, with all their host, the earth and all that is on it, the seas and all that is in them" (Neh. 9:6). "Of old thou didst lay the foundation of the earth, and the heavens are the work of thy hands" (Ps. 102:25). Dozens of additional references from Old and New Testaments could be quoted to underline the same ideas.

Yet only in the past two decades have people in general become much concerned about ecology, and Christians have even more recently begun to recognize the created world or natural environment as properly within the purview of Christian stewardship. In my school days I occasionally heard speakers talk about conservation, but then they were primarily concerned with protecting land from misuse and preventing soil erosion.

However, within the lifetime of any young adult today other and mounting concerns have been added: the pollution of the atmosphere and the water supply, the population explosion, increasing world hunger coupled with a reduction of tillable land and depletion of water to grow food, the serious depletion of minerals from the earth that can be transformed into energy.

To these broad and basic concerns more have been added. It is now known that the use of tobacco can cause cancer and heart disease, that certain chemical sprays for insects can pollute both earth and water and set up chain reactions in nature that lead to human disease and death, that aerosol sprays may be destroying the ozone layer that makes life on earth possible. Certain foodstuffs, dyes, and food additives are now known to cause cancer. Chemical wastes and human sediment dumped into our rivers and seas have made use of the water unsafe and poisoned the supply of fish for eating. The list could be lengthened to fill more pages than this whole book contains.

As a consequence, fear—fear of suffocation, disease, cold in the winter in unheated houses and dark at night in unlighted ones, fear of hunger, fear of human violence springing from overpopulation and the inability of people to feed themselves—fear has doubtless caused the mounting concern for the environment, the rise of organic gardening, the eating of health foods, "the return to nature," and at least some slight improvement in conservation practices.

Genesis records that when God completed creation he called it good. Then he placed all created things under the dominion of mankind. The human race was not given a title deed to land, water, fish, or fowl, but it was given control. Now that many of the things we once thought limitless are dwindling away, we are beginning to be aware of what poor stewards we have been. We have cut our forests, denuding the earth and sending its topsoil into the rivers; we have polluted the air we breathe and filled our rivers and seas with wastes; and we have made our garden of Eden look more and more like a garbage dump—and most of this has been done in the name of progress! It was man who fell, but we begin now to see how the created world itself was cursed in that fall (Rom. 8:20–22). Human selfishness and thoughtlessness of others have been the real causes behind dwindling resources and the earth's becoming less and less habitable. Now that more and ever more people have less and less land to till, water to drink, and air to breathe, human extinction may be nearer than we think. Today changing weather patterns in the world (possibly brought on by nuclear explosions, space travel, our manipulations of the weather, and the squirting of 600,000 tons of fluorocarbons into the air each year) mean not only further diminution of arable soil but also (many scientists insist) that we are nearing another ice age.

In general, fear is a terrible thing. But in this instance it may have helped to some degree to bring us to our senses.

But why is all this related to Christian stewardship? Because God loves his human creatures and has chosen some of us to share his love with all the others; because the intent of Christ is "abundant life" for all, but the ravaging of nature has shown that abundance can be so depleted by some that all will suffer lack; because "life" is biblically defined as the highest good, but the present cosmic ecology threatens life itself; because I am my brother's keeper; because life must be preserved in order that God's plan for the redemption of humankind may be effected—and we could keep on adding reasons. The highest possibility and greatest responsibility of human beings is to love. If we love, we shall try to do all necessary things to make earth a better place to live for all God's creation. Paul Schilling writes:

> Christian stewardship likewise involves concern about the ways in which society uses the natural resources which God has given us so abundantly, but which are nevertheless limited. . . . We are blasphemously denying our trusteeship and assuming rights that are not ours: when we pollute the air of our cities and the water of our rivers with poisonous exhaust fumes and waste products, when we denude forests through strip-mining in Pennsylvania or chemical defoliation in Vietnam, when we scorch God's good earth with fire and bomb, and when we expend, in futile and inhuman destruction of life and property, billions of dollars of our national wealth and thousands of our most promising young men.[10]

There are many more environmental and human concerns for Christian stewards that we have not room here to discuss. But some must be mentioned. Was it in the interest of human welfare to spend billions of dollars on the space program, to reach the moon, to photograph Mars? Is it enough to say that human curiosity must be satisfied or that our need for adventure necessitated these expenses? Weigh them against what this money could have done to feed the hungry and care for the sick. Nuclear weapons systems, poisonous gases, and plans for germ warfare—are these ever defensible on human, not to mention Christian, grounds? Will we continue to permit strip mining to poison waterways and make no real effort at land reclamation (there is still no satisfactory regulatory law)? Shall our oldest wild river, the New River, with its beautiful natural wilderness surroundings, be destroyed for the benefit of a small increase in electric power? It has at least been given a temporary reprieve. Will we continue to allow our best lands to be used for housing developments, roadways, electric power dams, new industries? Is it progress that destroys more and more of God's good earth on which we and future generations must depend for food? And must we always give in to industrial polluters when they say that they cannot afford needed control equipment, and if government regulations are enforced, many people will be thrown out of employment—the cry of wolf heard at every effort to save the environment for human habitation? These are Christian concerns, for they concern the welfare and life of God's creation and the survival of the human race.

But what can I as a single individual do? Let's begin at the simplest level: Don't be wasteful. Don't prepare more food or take more on your plate than you need. Eat what you need but don't waste food. Use the water you need for drinking, bathing, and keeping growing things alive, but don't waste it. Why waste the energy and the water for a hot steam shower for thirty minutes when a warm shower for five minutes will get you just as clean?

Use the energy you need, but don't waste it. Why take off at traffic lights as though on your way to the emergency room of the hospital when you're only driving home from work? Is it really essential for you to drive seventy-five miles an hour, passing all other cars and running the chance of arrest, and using almost twice as much gas as would be required to cruise along at fifty? Why run the television set when nobody is watching? Why burn lights in six rooms when only one is occupied?

"Give a hoot; don't pollute." In recent years college students have been gung ho for preserving the environment, even marching and demonstrating for this cause. But some of those same students leave cigarette packs and soft drink cans about the campus or toss them out along the highway. In celebration or protest, they decorate all the trees on campus with toilet tissue, desecrating their beauty and ignorantly destroying other trees—those used to make the paper. The waste costs little, but the cleaning up may run into hundreds of dollars.

We are responsible as Christian stewards for the health, productivity, and beauty of this great house, our natural world. We can act more responsibly. We do not have to waste, destroy, pollute, or do anything to hurt our fellow humans. We must not "hog" but share our good. We must be concerned, not just for ourselves but for all God's children.

As citizens we can exercise our influence in regulating or terminating those concerns which put the making of money above human welfare. We can put more pressure on industries that pollute our water supply. We can tell our representatives in Congress that pollution controls on automobiles must be both speeded up and tightened. We can resist through every possible means the destruction of natural wilderness by housing, commercial recreational areas, or industries that destroy them. We can call for laws to protect endangered species of birds, animals, fish—even humans. When wanton determination to increase productivity and profits violates human welfare, we must bring to bear all the organizational and governmental power available. There are organizations to which we can contribute and through which we can work. Common Cause, the Nature Conservancy, the Audubon Society, the National Wildlife Federation, the Sierra Club, and many other worthwhile agencies now exist through which we can channel our influence and help preserve the cosmic environment in which all people live.

The environment affects us, but we can affect the environment too. "This is my Father's world," created for the life, livelihood, and enjoyment of all people. Christian stewards must see that it continues to effect its Creator's purposes.

9
The Stewardship of the Gospel

Read Matthew 16:13–19a; 28:16–20;
II Corinthians 5:14–20;
I Peter 2:9–10

Christians who fully respond to the love and grace of Almighty God become, as Peter said, "good stewards of God's varied grace" (I Peter 4:10), or, as Paul wrote, they are "servants of Christ and stewards of the mysteries of God" (I Cor. 4:1).

The "varied" or "manifold" (KJV) grace of God is so broad that we cannot fully describe it, but by looking at certain of the most significant aspects of it we should have a better conception of the whole. Life, breath, and the body are the initial gift of God, to which one responds by offering to God life, breath, and the body in worship and in service. Work, labor, and vocation are another area of the given, for God guides and calls us to our labor; hence this aspect of life is dedicated to God by the responding Christian. Family, church, *oikoumenē,* and cosmos are graces and gifts of God on the one hand, but the faithful steward also recognizes them as the ever-widening circles of his responsibility on the other hand. But when we think of the whole realm of the grace of God, the one superlative gift of his grace, the one Sinai of his grace, towering over the plain of all other gifts, is Jesus Christ and the good news he means for all people.

The gospel is the greatest gift ever received by any living

person. Therefore it becomes the Christian's greatest stewardship responsibility. Ephesians 3:3 speaks of "the grace of God that was *given to me for you"* (italics added). In a similar vein Paul writes to the Colossians, "I became a minister according to the divine office which was *given to me for you,* to make the word of God fully known" (Col. 1:25, italics added). If any gift we ever received was plainly marked "to you, and for others," it was this gift. We are all recipients, we all become trustees, and we must all become sharers of Christ.

The Meaning of the Gospel

It is strange that one of the central words in the Christian vocabulary should need any explanation, but the word "gospel" is still ambiguous to many because they have so frequently heard it misused. For example, when they have heard some "hellfire and damnation" preacher denouncing the sins of everyone except himself, they may also have heard someone evaluate, "Man, he's really preaching the gospel." That is a misuse of the word "gospel," even an abuse of it.

Jesus came preaching "the gospel of the kingdom of God"; Ephesians speaks of "the gospel of your salvation"; and Paul tells the elders of the church at Ephesus that his purpose is "to testify to the gospel of the grace of God" (Acts 20:24). Always the gospel is spoken of with great joy. The gospel is "good news." It comes from Greek *euangelion,* meaning "good tidings." In Anglo-Saxon it became *godspell,* literally "the good story." I should like to define it first historically and then somewhat circumferentially, that is, including all the legitimate meanings it has since developed.

In its narrowest and first meaning the gospel appears to have been the good news of Jesus' resurrection from the dead. That was great good news to the first-century faithful, for it meant the verification of what they had been taught and the vindication of their belief that Christ was the one sent from God. But as early Christians reflected about it, they came to realize that the crucifixion was as much a part of the good news as was the resurrection. When they had thought about it for a century or so, they realized that Jesus' coming into the world was as much a part of the good news as the crucifixion and resurrection. So within about two centuries the gospel came to stand, not just for one event in the life of Jesus but for the coming, the life, ministry, teaching, death, resurrection, ascension, and return—indeed for all that Christ had come to mean to his faithful followers. So to share the gospel means to share the good news of Christ.

About the beginning of the second century John recorded as the words of Jesus what we have come to call the "Golden Text" of the Bible, and it is a summary of what the gospel had come to mean: that God loved the world so much that he sent his Son so that everyone who believes on him might not perish but have everlasting life (John 3:16). Soon early Christians began to refer also to the writings about Jesus' life and ministry as the Gospels according to Matthew, Mark, Luke, and John.

As the years have passed, the gospel has come to be even broader than the good news about Jesus himself. It has come to include the salvation of countless millions and the changes in society and morality caused by the influence of Christ as well as the countless institutions for human service built in his name. So it may be said in truth that the term now includes not only the mighty acts of God in Old Testament times and the acts of Jesus Christ but also the works of his faithful disciples and stewards across the years.

But summarily the gospel includes the good news of God's love for us; the news that Christ came, lived, and died for us; the news that Christ saves us and that he lives in us, enabling us to live joyous and victorious lives. It also includes the good news that God plans to unite all things in Christ and to make "the kingdoms of this world" into "the kingdom of our Lord."

The Importance of the Good News

When we reflect on the full meaning of the gospel, it hardly seems necessary to talk about its importance. Yet the greatest Christian theologian spoke of it with these words: "I am eager to preach the gospel to you also who are in Rome. For I am not ashamed of the gospel: it is the power of God for salvation to every one who has faith, to the Jew first and also to the Greek" (Rom. 1:15–16).

Experience has also confirmed the value and importance of the Christian gospel. Paul wrote to the Colossian Christians: "Wherever that gospel goes, it produces Christian character, and develops it, as it has done in your own case from the time you first heard and realised the truth of God's grace" (Col. 1:6, Phillips). Each of us will readily affirm the truth of that assertion.

History, too, testifies to the importance of the gospel. Where the gospel went, slaves began to be treated as human beings, there developed a new concern for women, and children came to be valued. In time the gospel began to make people reform unjust laws and become concerned about equal rights and privileges for all persons as children of God. The Christian gospel of human worth in God's eyes has caused reformation in many areas of life, built hospitals and schools, and sent missionaries, doctors, and teachers to the ends of the earth.

But Why Must We Become Stewards of the Gospel?

Thinking back upon the whole concept of life as response to the love, grace, mercy, and gifts of God, we recognize that every good gift of God to us is to be received with thanksgiving, treasured, invested, or shared with others, and finally given account of by the recipient. The thankful heart responds with thanksgiving, and the faithful heart responds in faithful stewardship of every gift.

In Romans 1, where the apostle Paul is expressing his

eagerness to come to Rome and share the gospel with the people there, he writes that he feels himself under a sort of universal obligation: "I owe something to all men" (Rom. 1:14, Phillips). We can easily understand Paul's feeling indebted to Christ for his salvation, but why did he feel an indebtedness to Jews and Gentiles, Greeks and Romans, rich and poor, cultured and ignorant—to all people? Most of us can easily think of several people to whom we feel we don't owe anything! But that is because we haven't realized our stewardship obligations as fully as Paul. He knew that in sharing the gospel with others he was actually ministering to Christ, since Christ identified with all people. Moreover, later in the same letter Paul advises, "Owe no one anything, except to love one another" (Rom. 13:8)—which is at least an implication of a universal obligation to love. Actually the necessity of Paul's universal indebtedness arises from his own acceptance of God's love. He knew that God loves all and has plans for all, that Christ came for all and died for all. So his obligation arose from the "allness" of God's love. Paul had accepted what was purposed for all and his conviction of the need to share it was so great that he declared: "Necessity is laid upon me. Woe to me if I do not preach the gospel!" (I Cor. 9:16).

The gospel is precisely the one gift more than any other which is for you and me *because* it is for every person under heaven. It is the gift that must not be hoarded or kept. For the "allness" of God's love offers the truth to all, extends help to all, and grants forgiveness, reconciliation, restoration, and eternal life to all. "All this is from God, who through Christ reconciled us to himself and gave us the ministry of reconciliation" (II Cor. 5:18).

You and I are among the relatively few, that small percentage of the human race who already fully enjoy all these blessings. To have received these blessings with Christian understanding is not a reason to congratulate ourselves or to point to them as an evidence that we are more favored than others; it is not even a reason just to praise God for them. As Paul Schilling writes; "We have been called into the Christian community not for mutual self-congratulation but for service in God's name, and not for unique privilege but for special responsibility. We have been entrusted with the good news of God's forgiving, transforming love in Jesus Christ partly in order that through our witness in word and life others may be brought to him. Hence stewardship involves evangelism. The steward is inevitably a missionary. If he really has been given victory over the ways of thought and life which alienate men from God, he is impelled to share the gift with others."[11] All the gifts of the gospel have been placed in our hands *for us and also for others* with whom we must share them. The grace of the gospel must not come to a dead end in us.

So, since we love Christ, "the love of Christ constrains us" to share our knowledge, understanding, and newness of life with others. First-century Christians, thinking on all that was happening in their lives, made this emphatic: "We cannot but speak of what we have seen and heard" (Acts 4:20). Really good news is too good to keep. We are called to Christian ministry and given a holy priesthood in order that we may declare the wonderful deeds of him who called us "out of darkness into his marvelous light" (I Peter 2:9). As Christ's love for us demanded his giving his life for us, so the love of God demands our sharing the good news with others for whom Christ died.

Moreover, Jesus both implicitly and explicitly placed us under the obligation of stewardship of the gospel. When we read the story of Simon Peter's confession in Matthew 16, we tend to concentrate on his words, "You are the Christ, the Son of the living God," or Jesus' response, "You are Peter, and on this rock I will build my church." But we as Protestant Christians have largely avoided the important words of Jesus: "I will give you the keys of the kingdom of heaven."

What were the keys Christ gave on that occasion? What are the keys of the kingdom then, now, and always? Whatever this gift was, it was first given to Simon Peter as a rather typical Christian, much like all of us, loving Christ but weak, fallible, fearful, and sometimes betraying him. What then was the thing that Christ dared to place in Peter's hands as a representative disciple?

The key Simon received was the key every believer has received from then until now. *It was the Christian gospel.* Christ's words announced the one thing by which believers can unlock the mysteries, graces, and goodnesses of the kingdom of heaven for others. It is the gospel which brings persons to the knowledge of God; it is the gospel which makes us know Christ's loving thoughts to us; it is the gospel which turns the lock and makes available all the riches God has in store for all his children. Peter was given this key—and Paul (how often he spoke of the gospel committed to him)—and every sincere believer has possessed it ever since.

Yet Christ did not rest content with an implication that the treasure of the gospel had been placed in our hands for sharing with all humankind. More than once he made the obligation for Christians quite explicit. When he was bidding good-by to his followers on that last night in the upper room, he said plainly and unmistakably, "As the Father has sent me, even so I send you" (John 20:21).

Christ came, the gospel incarnate, to "draw all men," to seek and save the lost, to give believers abundant life, to restore them to the Father. Quite explicitly he left in the hands of his followers the task of witnessing to his ministry, carrying out his mission, and sharing his gospel. The Great Commission makes it most emphatic: "Go . . . and make disciples of all nations . . . teaching them to observe all that I have commanded you" (Matt. 28:19–20). So we are not only to share the good news, but in the very sharing we are to make it plain that those who receive it from our hands are also to pass it on. There can be no question that each of us is under the obligation of love and command to share the gospel.

So, as Harvey H. Potthoff comments: *"Evangelism* is transformed in the light of stewardship. Too often so-called evangelism is little more than institutional promotion or public relations, a technique for increasing church membership. . . . To see the Christian life in terms of stewardship is to move into a deepened view of evangelism. Evangelism is a reaching out to share what has been received as a precious gift of new life. It is to witness and to invite. It is to go forth to identify with persons where they are. . . . It is to invite persons into a new life and into the fellowship of the new life."[12]

How Can I Discharge My Responsibility for the Gospel?

How is the question that troubles us. It is a question of great importance. Right away we are apt to say, "But I'm no apostle, no preacher; I've had no training to spread the gospel." But that rationalization excuses no Christian steward.

Perhaps our first obligation is to enter more fully into the meaning of the good news for ourselves. Many can't share it because they haven't much to share. But we can all "follow on to know the truth" and we must if we are "disciples indeed." The Christian religion is not a matter of shaking hands with Jesus but of entering vitally into an ever-deepening relationship with him.

In a practical way, we can prepare ourselves to share the gospel through full participation in the life of the church. The preaching, worship, instruction, and opportunities to serve afforded through the church enable every one of us to turn the key fully for ourselves and enter into God's riches. The church also becomes an instrument for sharing: Paul wrote to Thessalonica, "Therefore encourage one another and build one another up, just as you are doing" (I Thess. 5:11). As administrators in God's household we are responsible to see that all members receive "their portion of food at the proper time" (Luke 12:42)—

milk for babes and strong meat for the mature.

But more than this, the church becomes a vehicle for the gospel. Your support of its ministry is support for the gospel; your sharing in its program of ministry, education, and social service are ways of spreading the gospel. Paul saw the generous gifts of the Philippian church as "fellowship in furtherance of the gospel" (Phil. 1:5, ASV).

Yet, even when you have done all these things you have not completely fulfilled your stewardship of the gospel. You are still personally obligated to share your good news, to witness to what God has done for you. The man who had called himself "Legion" was told by Jesus, "Go home to your friends, and tell them how much the Lord has done for you, and how he has had mercy on you" (Mark 5:19). The good news that is the gospel is not merely theological doctrine to be stated in general homiletic terms. It boils down finally to "the good news according to you and me." Christianity is experiential, not theoretical, and the gospel we can share is our experience with Christ.

For the woman at the well it went like this: "Come, see a man who told me all that I ever did. Can this be the Christ?" (John 4:29) For Andrew, Simon's brother, it was: "We have found the Messiah" (John 1:41); and he brought his brother to Christ. For the blind man to whom Jesus restored sight, when the Jews called upon him to proclaim Jesus a sinner, his gospel was, "Whether he is a sinner, I do not know; one thing I know, that though I was blind, now I see" (John 9:25). Notice the great variety of their testimonies. Yet it is all one good news, the good news about Jesus Christ.

You and I are not responsible for being theologians like Paul or preachers like Stephen. But I am put in trust with the gospel according to me, and you are entrusted with the gospel according to you.

So what is your story? Has God lifted your feet out of the miry clay? Has he kept your feet from falling? Has he made peace in your heart when it was a ground of conflicting loyalties? Has he filled your life with new love, wonder, and understanding?

We are all stewards of our own experience with Christ: his outreaching love, his redemption, his grace. It is not just the same for us all because we are different and our needs were different. Yet, like Paul, each of us can tell one simple and true story: "By the grace of God I am what I am" (I Cor. 15:10).

Peter and John met a crippled beggar at one of the gates of the Temple. He pleaded for help. Peter responded: "I have no silver and gold, but I give you what I have; in the name of Jesus Christ of Nazareth, walk" (Acts 3:6). They shared their gospel, and it was enough.

How will you share the gospel? In the way God opens up for you: through living the life of faith in your home before those who know you best; at your work, through the simple witness of a good life and right words in season. I cannot tell you specifically. I try to witness to the gospel as a teacher and Christian writer. You and I can witness, each in our own place.

For "we are ambassadors for Christ, God making his appeal through us" (II Cor. 5:20). Let us both pray and determine by God's strength and the guidance of his Holy Spirit to share the good news.

Part Three
HOW A CHRISTIAN STEWARD GIVES

10
Christian Giving

Read Micah 6:6–8; Mark 12:41–44; 14:3–9;
II Corinthians 8–9

"Now concerning the collection," writes Paul in I Corinthians 16:1 (KJV). Paul was much concerned about a large offering from the new, principally Greek Christian churches he had established, to go for the relief of the poor in the Jewish Christian church at Jerusalem. Perhaps he was the first Christian fund raiser, and the offering was the first "One Great Hour of Sharing." Paul really threw himself into this effort, which would relieve the needy as well as give the Greek Christians an opportunity to know the joy of sharing. For most of all he hoped the offering would be a means of binding together the Jewish and Gentile Christians. So the apostle was also the first "ecumenicist."

But Paul's "pitch" for the offering from the Corinthian church is especially interesting for its context. In previous chapters of the letter the apostle has answered some practical questions about church administration that the Corinthians had written him about. He has discoursed upon "spiritual gifts" and their place in the church; he has sung the beautiful hymn on the "more excellent way" of love; he has directed that all gifts are to be used for edification, and he has written with great fervor of the resurrection and its importance to Christian faith. Then, having reached a kind of spiritual eminence in the declaration of his faith, he brings up the matter of the offering. That is, his request for the offering has been set against important items of Christian faith in the theology of the church. And this is where it belongs.

Similarly, in our own discussion of stewardship *we are now ready for the first time to speak of giving*—of giving as an aspect of Christian stewardship. It is amazing that stewardship theology has survived, achieved clarification, and become as rich as it has, for the modern stewardship movement came into existence only after the churches were disestablished and had to be supported by voluntary giving. The first emphasis was (and had to be) on giving to support the church. But before long the emphasis broadened to include stewardship of time, talent, and treasure. Even as late as 1946, however, the United Stewardship Council came forward with this limited definition:

> Christian stewardship is the practice of systematic and proportionate giving of time, abilities, and material possessions, based upon the conviction that these are trusts from God to be used in his service for the benefit of all mankind in grateful acknowledgment of Christ's redeeming love.[13]

Note that, even so recently, stewardship was still being defined principally as a doctrine of giving. But Christian stewardship as we have discussed it is the total response of persons to God, receiving all of life as a trust, and living all of life "as unto God." Giving is neither the beginning nor the essence of stewardship, but giving is an expression that finds its significance only within the total response of a person to God.

The purpose of this book is not in any way to deemphasize giving but only to put it in its place. For giving is but a part of stewardship. The prophet Micah saw that giving is not enough:

> With what shall I come before the LORD,
> and bow myself before God on high?

> Shall I come before him with burnt offerings,
> with calves a year old?
> Will the LORD be pleased with thousands of rams,
> with ten thousands of rivers of oil?
> Shall I give my first-born for my transgression,
> the fruit of my body for the sin of my soul?
> He has showed you, O man, what is good;
> and what does the LORD require of you
> but to do justice and to love kindness,
> and to walk humbly with your God? (Micah 6:6–8)

Micah's point is that the right response to God is more than sacrifice, more than giving in any amount. For it is the whole life response which God seeks. Christian stewardship does not call for money but for the whole person, and it is impossible to enter into it fully apart from the total surrender of one's life to Christ.

The Response God Seeks

Interestingly, the best story to illustrate Christian giving as an aspect of total response to Christ is also a story about Paul's collection for the saints in Jerusalem. The story is told in II Cor. 8:1–6. Paul is writing the Corinthians and trying to stimulate their giving when he tells it:

> We want you to know, brethren, about the grace of God which has been shown in the churches of Macedonia, for in a severe test of affliction, their abundance of joy and their extreme poverty have overflowed in a wealth of liberality on their part. For they gave according to their means, as I can testify, and beyond their means, of their own free will, begging us earnestly for the favor of taking part in the relief of the saints—and this, not as we expected, but first they gave themselves to the Lord and to us by the will of God.

Even before the apostle had presented the matter of the relief fund to the Macedonians, they asked to be allowed to help. Their response was so generous as to astonish him: they were poor, yet they gave, gave liberally, out of their poverty. Somehow (such is the grace of God) they added their abundant joy to their extreme poverty and came up with "a wealth of liberality." It is not, after all, the amount of the gift that counts, as Jesus explains in the story of the poor widow who gave *more than the rich,* though she had only two small coins (Mark 12:41–44). Einstein could not have evolved the Pauline equation, and ordinary mathematics cannot explain Jesus' saying. Yet Paul explains how this "arithmetic of grace" works: "First they gave themselves to the Lord and to us by the will of God." We or our churches may be poor in the secular economic sense, but if we first give ourselves to the Lord, God is able to do "far more than we ask or think" for others through us.

Martha Berry once visited Henry Ford to ask for money for her school for the poor children of northwest Georgia. The result was a gift of ten cents. Miss Berry planted the ten cents in peanuts and bought a piano with the proceeds. Then she reported her stewardship to Mr. Ford. Today the multi-million-dollar Ford Quadrangle, comprising several magnificent Gothic buildings, stands on the Berry School campus as mute testimony to what can be done with stewardship of a little.

The gift God wants, the supreme gift of stewardship, is ourselves. No matter how much of money, talent—or whatever—we give, we have not entered into full Christian response until we give our lives to him. But after this first and basic gift is made, the rest becomes easy.

Giving God Loves

All of II Corinthians 8 and 9 concerns the Palestinian relief fund. Paul wants a strikingly generous gift from the Corinthians, but he also stresses that they are not under any compulsion or command to give. The important thing is that their giving shall be a proof of their love to the recipients. Paul writes:

The point is this: he who sows sparingly will also reap sparingly, and he who sows bountifully will also reap bountifully. Each one must do as he has made up his mind, not reluctantly or under compulsion, for God loves a cheerful giver. (II Cor. 9:6–7)

Some years ago the young pastor of a congregation that had just completed a beautiful new church building set a special Sunday for an offering of $25,000 to apply against the indebtedness. He wrote excitedly in his church paper, telling of gifts already received by mail. Then he said something that might seem to negate all he was trying to do: "Please do not give unless you really want to give out of a sense of gratitude."

Did this make sense? Yes. It makes complete sense in Christian stewardship, though it may sound foolish to a non-Christian. When we have given ourselves to God, there is no struggle or problem about giving of our means. I remember several years ago that my family set a goal and had a burning desire to give $1,000 a year to the church. That amount was far more than a tithe of our income at that time, and it was a year or two before we could reach it, but we never doubted that we would be able to, because we wanted to do it.

I hesitate to include this negative note, but it is true and important and should be mentioned. Paul said, "He who sows sparingly will reap also sparingly" (II Cor. 9:6). We recognize the truth of this principle in farming, and we need to be aware that it works in stewardship too. I have seen churches wither because they did not want to give to Christian outreach, evangelism, or missions but to keep their money for local uses—new buildings, organs, facilities. Also I remember Bill Jones (not his real name), an officer of the church. He wanted so much to have a new home. When he got it he had to have new furniture. Then he totaled his monthly payments and found he could no longer give to the church. He was ashamed not to give, so he dropped out of the services and soon became cross with the church and asked for his letter. His is but one of thousands of similar stories.

Why is willingness in giving so extremely important? Perhaps it begins where John Milton put it long ago in his sonnet "On His Blindness": "God doth not need / Either man's work or his own gifts." This is the same truth the apostle Paul spoke to the idol-worshiping Athenians:

> The God who made the world and everything in it, being Lord of heaven and earth, does not live in shrines made by man, nor is he served by human hands, as though he needed anything, since he himself gives to all men life and breath and everything. (Acts 17:24–25)

God neither expects nor desires our gifts out of a sense of need. He is the Giver and we have nothing to give but his gifts to us. So the Christian responds to God with gratitude, with love, and with cheer. But there is no joy and no happiness in giving our leftovers to God. Cheap and inadequate giving makes us ashamed. God's gracious giving must have a gracious response.

Paul often reminds us that Christ "though he was rich" became poor, giving up all heavenly prerogatives for our sake. And when we read Christ's life, we see that the nearer he came to the cross, the more he spoke of his peace and joy. He told his disciples to "be of good cheer" for he had "overcome the world," and he left the legacy of his peace and joy with them. How could this be? Apparently the most joyous act of Jesus' life was his embracing the cross for you and me. Contemplating his self-giving and his joy, we know there is no satisfaction to be found in returning the small change of our lives to him who gave all, even life itself, for us.

Returning to the giving of the Macedonians, we can see why it was a source of joy to them. For they gave:

> according to their means . . . and beyond their means,
> of their own free will,

> begging us earnestly for the favor of taking part in
> the relief of the saints—
> and this, not as we expected, but
> first they gave themselves to the Lord.

Small wonder that giving of this kind should be full of joy.

Our Need to Give

Knowing that he would not be allowed to come to them again, Paul delivered his valedictory to the Ephesians at Miletus. He admonished the elders about the care of the church and reminded them of "the words of the Lord Jesus, how he said, 'It is more blessed to give than to receive' " (Acts 20:35). Most of us quote this saying when we want a pious-sounding platitude about giving. It sounds like dreamy-eyed idealism. We don't openly question it—that doesn't seem religious, and it puts us in a bad light to deny a teaching of Jesus.

But Jesus never talked idealistic nonsense. He characteristically spoke "the plain, unvarnished truth." Therefore what we need to do is to recognize this statement as an eternally true law of being and to investigate what Jesus meant. Let's do that.

When I was a pastor, the congregation I served was spending about a quarter of a million dollars on the renovation and expansion of our church building. We decided to call in a professional fund raiser. Despite the fact that we were trying to get a great deal of money pledged to the building fund, our director continued to tell us we must not stress the need for money but "the need of the giver to give." The entire campaign was based on this theme. We raised our needed money, but, far more importantly, the congregation trebled its regular giving and the entire church was revitalized. The campaign director was anchored firmly to Jesus' principle: "It is more blessed to give than to receive."

Jesus did not say it is nicer to give, or better to give, or more fun to give; he said it is *more blessed* to give. Neither did he deny that it is good and fun and pleasant to receive. And Jesus wasn't fooled. When hardheaded advocates of common sense chuckle at the nonsense of Jesus' saying, it is they who are deluded. Christ's word is as solid as granite.

The word Jesus used is the same as that translated "blessed" in the Beatitudes. It is the Greek word *makarios,* which means more than good, nice, pleasant, or even happy. The blessedness of which Jesus speaks is life's highest good and God's greatest gift. Jesus meant: to give, rather than to receive, is life's superlative good, its supreme benediction.

Obviously receiving is a good. For we have needs. Jesus pointed out that the heavenly Father knows about our human needs. But receiving adds nothing to the quality or character of one's life. Receiving makes us no better or nobler. The millionaire is no better than the pauper.

What shows that we are more than blind mouths is that we long to give, to share, and to help others—which shows that we have some affinity with God our maker. God loves and gives; and we begin to show our likeness to him in loving and giving. It is giving which reveals us. The measure of our lives is in what we have given and the attitude with which we have given. Old Dr. Finis Ewing Perkins of Birmingham, who gave away everything he ever made, used to say joyfully, "You know, all I have now is what I have given away." It is a valid question whether any of us has anything but what he has given away. So it is in fact more blessed to give than to receive. And all the great persons whom we fondly remember and venerate were great in their giving.

Giving acknowledges our spiritual awareness of God's providential care. It expresses our gratitude, a lovely human attribute. It demonstrates our response to God. And by giving we enter into partnership with Christ, we share the purpose of God and the mission of the church.

Jesus by the Treasury

That giving is a proof or manifestation of our gratitude and love to God brings to mind once again the fact that God as universal owner is interested in our giving because it is an evidence of our response to him, a symbol and sign of our love. We must not forget here or elsewhere that as stewards we are responsible and accountable. This is a principal teaching in several of the stewardship parables of our Lord. Christians recognize both the gifts of creation and the gifts of redemption and see the obligation that falls upon them from receiving both.

A story that calls visual attention to our accountability is the story of how Jesus sat down by the Temple treasury and watched the people making their gifts (Mark 12:41–44). It includes the heart-warming story of the widow's gift as well as a cautionary implication about the rich people who put in large sums. We rightly emphasize the generosity of the widow's gift, but we frequently pass over the significance of Jesus' watching by the treasury. What does it indicate that Jesus watched? It shows his concern, his oversight, and his judgment. And it fully accords with what we already know of Jesus' teaching. He talked as much about people's handling of money as about any other subject. He commented on how hard it is for a rich person to enter the kingdom. He said that his disciples must seek the kingdom of God first, rather than things. And the one idol of mankind that he spoke against was mammon, a personification of money.

This does not mean that Jesus saw the handling of money or the giving of money as the most important part of stewardship. But he did say, "Where your treasure is, there will your heart be also" (Matt. 6:21). Our handling of money and giving of money are good indicators of our inner stewardship response to God. Jesus weighs the integrity of our stewardship, and he finds clues in our giving. He evaluates our gifts, whether they represent real gifts of love and sacrifice or are merely the pocket change of our wealth. So he can say justly of a widow who gives only two tiny coins. She has given more than all the others.

It was Jesus who said, "By their fruits ye shall know them." Scripture also reveals that "man looks on the outward appearance, but the LORD looks on the heart" (I Sam. 16:7). So Jesus watches the treasury of the church in order to see if our giving reveals the prior giving of our lives or whether we are merely tossing off an unneeded bit of our surplus.

When we spend more for cigarettes or alcohol than we give to the accomplishment of God's purposes on earth, when we spend more for pleasure and entertainment than we give for God's work, we not only have lost the joy of giving but also the approbation of our Lord.

"Think not, because no man sees, / Such things will remain unseen," wrote Henry Wadsworth Longfellow in "The Builders." And James Russell Lowell even more poignantly pictures Christ as saying to the old knight returning from his search in "The Vision of Sir Launfal":

> Not what we give, but what we share,
> For the gift without the giver is bare;
> Who gives himself with his alms feeds three,
> Himself, his hungering neighbor, and Me.

These lines are based upon Jesus' parable and his saying, "As you did it to one of the least of these my brethren, you did it to me" (Matt. 25:40).

Giving as Worship

Nothing is more obvious than that a single chapter does not say all there is to say about Christian giving. I have written little or nothing about giving for evangelism, giving as a stewardship of the future, giving as cooperation with God in bringing the kingdom, or giving as an escape from human selfishness. I have not referred to one tenth of what the Bible says about it. Many readers will miss favorite passages. But I have tried to set giving in its place within the overall picture of Christian stewardship, not to exhaust the subject.

Yet one other thing must be said. Christian giving is an act of worship. Sacrifices, first fruits, and the tithe in Old Testament times were not prescribed to answer the question, "How much must I give?" but to make giving an act of worship. Worshipers did not come before God without an offering (Ex. 23:15; 34:20). Rather they brought their first and their best in appreciation and thanksgiving to God and as a declaration of their trust in God's providential care. So they fulfilled the word of the proverb, "Honor the LORD with thy substance, and with the first fruits of all thine increase" (Prov. 3:9, KJV). Parenthetically, the Bill Joneses who come to worship without an offering will soon cease to come.

Christians reach highest when they bow in worship. Their "spiritual worship" is the giving of their bodies (Rom. 12:1). They do this both symbolically and literally in bringing their offerings to the Lord's house. Their gifts, part of their salaries or earnings from labor, are a symbol of the giving of their bodies. Money is labor converted into cash; hence a generous offering signifies self-giving. Giving is physical expression of spiritual reality, the reality of thanksgiving and honor to God.

Two days before the Passover, Jesus was with his disciples in the house of Simon the leper, in Bethany. As he was sitting at the table, a woman came with an alabaster jar of expensive ointment and anointed him with it. Some of the disciples indignantly called her action waste. But Jesus said, "She has done a beautiful thing to me" and "Wherever the gospel is preached in the whole world, what she has done will be told in memory of her" (Mark 14:3–9). Hers was the extravagance of true love and worship. Acts of sincere worship are always beautiful and memorable.

11
Tithing: At the Frontier of Grace

Read Proverbs 11:24–25; Malachi 3:1–12;
Matthew 6:2–4, 19–21, 24, 25–34

It is appropriate to begin here where we left off in the previous chapter, for tithing is a norm of giving long practiced as a way of worshiping God. And, like the broken alabaster jar of ointment, it has had its share of criticism, even by disciples. But the first and most important thing to remember is that tithing came into existence as an act of worship, not in response to law.

Tithing originated before it was practiced by the Jews, and the Jews themselves practiced it long before it became law. That it did finally become law is evidence that it was found to be a good and healthy practice. But tithing was not law and not legalistic in its origin. It had its origin in grace, and it lives at the frontier of grace today. We might go further and say that tithing can be vital, healthy, and joyful *only* in the realm of grace. The true rewards of tithing are quashed by formalism and legalism. Christians do not get these rewards if they are tithing for any of the following reasons: (1) they think it is law and binding upon them; or (2) they expect it to bring them material dividends; or (3) their church demands it of them. None of these things that destroy the beauty and happiness of tithing was present in the beginning.

Tithing started because primitive people in the East, living as shepherds or farmers, were aware that the source of their good was not in the earth or natural world itself but in whoever created it. When we read across several Old Testament books, especially the Pentateuch, we find such a primitive people, thankful for their substance and, as their God-consciousness and understanding expand, thankful also for God's mighty acts for their redemption. Filled with gratitude for the grace they have received, they are eager to worship the God of their sustenance and salvation.

God, they reflected, should have the first fruits because he had given them everything. He should have their best; less would be selfish and grudging. God, who succoured Abraham, received a tithe in grateful acknowledgment of his help. And God, who had brought the Children of Israel out of Egypt, was certainly entitled to the firstlings of their flocks.

Even so, out of grace and through gratitude flowed the gifts of God's people in early Judaism. Their giving was clearly and only an act of worship, a remembrance of God's generous dealing with them, and a celebration of their provider and sustainer.

In time, it is true, Hebrew worship became regularized and ritualized. Jewish leaders decided the tithe should be brought to the Temple. The Levites and the priests began to be supported from the tithes. Also, there were the poor to care for, and a special tithe was collected every third year to care for them. So, by the time of Jesus, tithing had become legalistic and formalized in the extreme. But even then Jesus did not advocate its abolition. He upbraided the scribes and Pharisees, not for paying the tithe but for leaving undone weightier matters of the law, justice and mercy and faith (Matt. 23:23). Doubtless the legalism of tithing at that time caused Jesus, Paul, and the New Testament writers generally to place their emphasis instead upon free will, generosity, and regularity in giving; but it is significant that the practice of tithing was neither condemned nor abolished.

Tithing had originated from free will; it had been "an outward and visible sign of an inward and spiritual grace" in its inception. Thus it has been many times in human history and certainly can be today.

It would be idle to speculate or investigate why so many peoples in ancient times practiced tithing or how, as if by a preestablished agreement, they decided on the same giving pattern. Maybe "God told them" in their hearts. It would be harder to explain by mere coincidence.

Let it further be stressed that the Jews were *not giving a tenth of their property to God.* They were worshiping with the first-fruits, the tithe, and other offerings in token of the fact that all was God's. God was creator and still owner; they were but his tenants. God had chosen them for his people as an act of divine grace. As Moses told them, "It is because the LORD loves you" (Deut. 7:8). They liked to remember God's gracious dealing with them, the covenants, the deliverance from Egypt, his blessings in the wilderness, his faithfulness and steadfast love. Also, they knew themselves to be a nomadic people, sojourning in a land not their own. And they had been slaves in Egypt. So they ordered their giving, in time, not only to praise God but also to help the enslaved and the poor.

Those who continue today to argue against the tithe on the ground that it is legalistic, who affirm that we are under grace, not law, and hence not required to tithe, are not really objecting to legalism. Objections to the practice of the tithe under grace usually come from those who want to give less than a tithe. But a truly grateful and graceful response to what God has done for us in Christ treats the tithe as a traditional norm, a basic minimum that may serve as a springboard from which to vault into higher levels of giving. Nothing in Christian teaching ever indicates that less is expected of the Christian than law required of the Jew. Jesus updates some old laws in the Sermon on the Mount (Matt. 5:17–48), internalizing them and making them more demanding. At the same time he also tells his disciples that their righteousness must exceed the righteousness of the scribes and Pharisees, who were experts in keeping the law.

But being a Christian is not a matter of keeping certain laws. It is living with the attitude and spirit of Christ. All our stewardship—whether of time, talent, or treasure; whether at home, in church, or outside the church; whether of holding, investing, or sharing—*all begins with the grace of God,* in creation, in election, and in redemption. We are stewards because of God's love. His gracious giving provokes our grateful response. His lavishness makes us cry, "What shall I render to the LORD for all his bounty to me?" (Ps. 116:12) That which, above all other things, makes us respond is Jesus Christ, the gift that includes all gifts. He not only practiced a ministry of love, healing, teaching, encouraging, and helping in his life. He also gave his life for us and comes back to us in the Holy Spirit to dwell in our lives and to keep on loving others through us. He guides, inspires, comforts, and empowers us to live such lives as God would have us live, and he helps others through us. The Spirit helps us to pray and strengthens our witness in order to make our words effective in winning others. Even so, the whole stewardship response of our lives is occasioned by and rises from the artesian well of God's grace, which waters the deepest thirst of our being. Graceful response is by no means automatic, but our stewardship begins in the heart of God.

Getting Things in Perspective: Learning to Trust God

One important aspect of our stewardship is "overcoming the world," getting *things* in proper perspective. It is difficult for us to see past things to the Creator who provides them. Things, essentially good in themselves, serve to blind us and keep us from seeing God. Perhaps the greatest battle in the human soul is the battle to overcome the "thingification" of life. Jesus was deeply troubled for people who "gain the whole world and lose their own souls."

To live well and happily one must overcome the tyranny of things. I remember an elderly lady who waved her hand about over her accumulation of priceless antiques in a great mansion: "Look at all these things we have," she said, "but they haven't brought a moment's happiness." I also remember a remarkable man, a chance acquaintance. He told me how as a poor boy he used to pull his little wagon past one of the town's finest houses and dream that one day he might get to go inside. "Now," he said, "I live in that house and drive the Cadillac you see out there. But you know, none of it is mine. It all belongs to God." I never got to know him; we simply spent a night in the same motel. But the joy and radiance of his life were inescapable. Both these persons were wealthy in things, but only one had achieved dominion over them.

How tragically true it often is, as Emerson said, that "things are in the saddle, and ride mankind." Money and things are good servants but they are horrible masters. Jesus wanted to help his disciples overcome this lust that destroys life. Even more strongly he wanted his followers to place their full trust in God. So he said, "Seek first his kingdom and his righteousness, and all these things shall be yours as well" (Matt. 6:33). To encourage their trust he pointed out how God in his economy takes care of birds and wild flowers. Without worrying or being anxious, the birds of the air and the flowers of the field fill their place in God's plan. The birds work diligently catching insects, scratching for worms, seeking seeds; and God provides. The flowers reach down for water and food and up for sunlight, and God clothes them in great beauty. Surely, said Jesus, you are of more value in God's eyes! God knows that you need food, clothing, and shelter, so you don't have to be anxious about these things, though unbelievers frequently are. But if you fill your place (seek first his kingdom) in God's plan as birds and flowers do, then "all these things shall be yours as well."

Jesus encourages his disciples to have an attitude toward

life that is untroubled, calm, and trustful. He knows that the only way to arrive at that trust which enables one to live on the frontier of grace is by the full commitment of life to God. For only one thing can hold first place in our lives. "You cannot serve God and mammon" was Jesus' way of putting it. So long as we are fretful, worried, and anxious about things, we show that we have not committed our lives totally to God's loving care. It goes without saying that worriers don't tithe.

Not only is there no joy in things; there is also no security in them. It is ironic but true that the more stress we place on accumulation and the more we seek our security in things, the more insecure we feel and the more we worry. So long as we seek our security in things we shall be insecure. George Buttrick once said, "God has made us insecure in all things that we might put our trust in him." So Jesus counseled, "Do not lay up for yourselves treasures on earth . . . but . . . treasures in heaven." It is sheer folly to depend for safety and security upon things. Banks fail, the stock market takes a tumble, businesses go broke, mines and oil wells give out, crops are blighted, and farms are washed away. Only God may be depended upon. He has been "our dwelling place in all generations" (Ps. 90:1); he is "our refuge and strength, a very present help in trouble. Therefore we will not fear" (Ps. 46:1–2). God alone is fully faithful, reliable, trustworthy. He is the eternal sustainer. Years ago I learned a bit of unpretentious verse that I want to quote because it reinforces Jesus' teaching here:

> Said the Robin to the Sparrow:
> "I should really like to know
> Why these anxious human beings
> Rush about and worry so."
>
> Said the Sparrow to the Robin:
> "Friend, I think that it must be
> That they have no heavenly Father
> Such as cares for you and me."
>
> Elizabeth Cheney

Moreover, halfway commitments or seeming commitments will not help. Ananias and Sapphira, living a lie before God in pretending to sell all and share it with the church (Acts 5:1–11), found not security but death. Finally every dependence of faith upon things brings death, for the rains descend and the winds blow and beat upon every house. Poor Malachi has been denounced for legalism in our century because he asserted that God's people had been stealing by robbing him in tithes and offerings. But one should read his statement in its full context (Malachi 3). The real problem that Malachi pinpoints is that God's people have proven sinful and disloyal. Their withholding of tithes is only symptomatic of their far more serious disease: they have been withholding themselves from God. God's call is, "Return to me and I will return to you" (Mal. 3:7). For Malachi their payment of full tithes would symbolize their returning to God. In God's household there is no lack. Here Malachi is quite in agreement with Jesus.

"Prove Me": Working Within Natural Law

Malachi has been sharply criticized for saying that God asks us to "prove" him by tithing. But this criticism is hard to understand. Paul says, "Prove all things; hold fast that which is good" (I Thess. 5:21, KJV). John admonishes us to "test the spirits" (I John 4:1). Paul's call to full commitment to Christ in Romans 12:1-2 (KJV) has the stated purpose: "that ye may prove what is that good, and acceptable, and perfect will of God." Jesus clearly promises rewards to right discipleship; and when he calls disciples to seek the kingdom first, he adds that "all these things" shall be added. Moreover, the psalmist had long ago declared that the righteous person "is like a tree planted by streams of water, that yields its fruit in its season. . . . In all that he does, he prospers" (Ps. 1:3). Why then do we object to the idea that humans prosper and are blessed by living in accord with God's will rather than at cross-purposes with God?

We recognize "natural law" working in the physical universe. Nobody cries or curses because of the law of gravity. It does not seem to outrage us that water freezes at 32 degrees Fahrenheit, that the sun rises every morning, or that the winter and summer solstices recur regularly. Jesus enunciated similar laws or principles that operate in the human dimension: "Whoever would save his life will lose it, and whoever loses his life for my sake will find it" (Matt. 16:25). "Give, and it will be given to you; good measure, pressed down, shaken together, running over. . . . For the measure you give will be the measure you get back" (Luke 6:38). "It is more blessed to give than to receive" (Acts 20:35). Surely we cannot condemn his statements as legalism. Rather, they are pronouncements of the truth containing an implicit challenge to spiritual adventure. "Try giving yourself away" is the challenge contained in these principles. Do we really believe that we will impoverish ourselves by sharing our good, by giving in worship, or by giving to relieve human need?

What do we have, that is worth having, that did not come to us by sharing or giving? Everything we have which came through the acquisitive drive is really temporal, passing, and of no eternal value. It can bless our lives and others' *only by our sharing and giving it away.* Shall we deny that this principle is true?

> One man gives freely, yet grows all the richer;
>   another withholds what he should give,
>   and only suffers want.
> A liberal man will be enriched,
>   and one who waters will himself be watered.
>
> (Prov. 11:24–25)

Sharing and giving operate on the principle of the vacuum. We must exhale to inhale. We must give to receive. We are always insisting that one can't share what one doesn't have (e.g., faith). But it is equally true that we can't have what we are unwilling to share. Can we keep and hoard God's goodness, love, and mercy? No. But the more we share them, the more we have. Even the gospel is "too good to keep."

Tithing is a symbolic way of confessing our dependence on God and our faith in a universe over which God has real and ultimate control. It exists at the frontier where faith meets grace. We express confidence in God, and our confidence multiplies. Our gifts go to God's purposes and human good; and so as tithers we gain the realization that we have entered into partnership with God. We adventure upon our faith in trust, and by God's grace our trust in God becomes deeper and deeper.

There are many thousands of tithers who will testify to the blessings that come to them through tithing. Most will not speak of material rewards, for stewards who tithe from love and in order to serve Christ's cause are fearful of encouraging tithing from wrong motives. The gifts of God are not for sale, as Simon the sorcerer learned (Acts 8:9–24). But tithers will more readily speak of the joy and newness of life into which tithing has brought them. As L. E. Meyer writes, "The chief reward is increased spirituality, manifesting itself in the blessings of heart, soul, mind, and strength that come through conscious unity with God."[14]

Tithing Is Biblical and Practical for Christians

I will not take the time to review what the Bible, especially the New Testament, has to say about right giving. But you will remember four principles taught there, namely, that giving should be (1) entirely voluntary; (2) proportionate; (3) regular and systematic; (4) an act of worship. We have already touched upon these biblical principles.

Now tithing, motivated by the love of Christ and given in love and gratitude, meets every standard of giving taught in the New Testament and fits all the practical lessons implicit in the Scriptures.

Practically speaking, by tithing in faith and trust in God we do overcome anxiety. It opens up channels of communication, allowing God's grace and love to flow into and fill our lives. Tithing is a way of sharing our good with others for Jesus' sake. Tithing lets us enter into partnership with God in evangelism, missions, and human service, accomplishing God's purpose in the world.

Another practical consideration must be mentioned. Tithing enables the church to fulfill its mission. Practically speaking, tithers make it financially possible for the church to do Christ's work. Most churches spend most of their money on themselves, maintaining the property and program, for they don't really give enough money to serve the community, help the poor, evangelize the lost, send out missionaries, establish schools and hospitals. It can't be done on the approximately 2 percent of members' incomes that churches receive. But there is almost no limit to what a tithing church can do. The Mormons and the Seventh-day Adventists should convince us of this. Nevertheless the main advantage of the church's tithing is that the conversion of our pocketbooks also inspires the conversion of our attitudes and lives. Tithing is commitment; it is love in action—and when we see it working we tend to stop our holding back, our self-centeredness, and our cautionary restraint and "launch out into the deep," giving ourselves fully and wholeheartedly to Christ. Tithing is an adventure of faith that gets the spirit right.

And So, Across the Frontier

There is magic in tithing. The real magic is in *what begins to happen to us.* How many persons can you name who tithed for several years and then quit? It is possible, but highly improbable. For one who responds to the grace of God with the tithe, who responds in love and worship, begins to undergo a radical transformation.

Costen Harrell writes, "The tithe began as a custom, was later written in a law, and at long last in the radiance of the New Testament becomes a means of grace and a way by which the humblest may labor with God in the redemption of his world."[15] The employment of the means of grace is a way to Christian growth and maturity. Regular worship, Bible reading, private devotions, meditation and prayer, working in the church, serving people—all these keep the spirit healthy and growing; all these develop the strength of body, mind, and spirit; all serve or assist that power by which we become true children of God. Generous and sacrificial giving is by no means least among the means of grace. Many who began to tithe from a sense of duty soon became excited about how the practice became a channel of blessing. Tithing begun in duty is usually continued in joy.

As already indicated, one of the first great changes that comes to tithers is their victory over fear and anxiety. They no longer worry about sustenance. When they see that they are living as well on nine tenths as they did before on ten tenths, their worries are sloughed off. The budget and bills don't disappear; they just become less central in their lives, less formidable and threatening. Tithers begin to believe that *the God who has sustained them will sustain them.* Though they may not hear the command to go and sell all they have and give it to the poor, they no longer clutch their possessions to themselves or depend upon them. They are no longer tempted to make a god of things. Rather, they begin to sing with the psalmist, "The Lord is my shepherd, I shall not want," and to believe with the apostle that "my God is able to supply all your need." Earl Barfoot writes:

> Anxiety is relieved only when we learn to trust the source of supply. . . . Life opens up when we trust God. . . . To trust him is to claim him, and in the claiming, there is implicit the sense of knowing where the source and support of life are. . . . If we do believe that the scriptures are full of the promises of God, we must know also that those promises are not offered out of a bare cupboard.[16]

If God is the real master of our lives, we are in his hands.

This trusting is the first great step that carries us out of the realm of self-centeredness and through the door into the realm of grace. Once anxiety is overcome, the Christian steward quickly discovers the joys of the shared life. G. Ernest Thomas writes: "The return from tithing is in the form of spiritual blessings and reflects itself in changed inner lives. . . . Tithing contributes to the happiness of the individuals who tithe. . . . Shared money becomes a source of abiding joy."[17]

The life of the founder of Alcoholics Anonymous was transformed by such sharing. Awaking for the fiftieth time in a hospital for drunkards, he was told by his doctor that liquor would soon kill him. He asked the physician for another drink "to straighten me out." The doctor promised to give him his drink if he would first show himself as a horrible example to a young man in the next room who was there for the first time. He agreed. Then, talking to the young man, he was deeply moved with the desire to save him from his own fate, and in helping him he found his own help. He never went back for the promised drink. Instead he founded A.A. and became a blessing to hundreds of thousands of other alcoholics. Even so, in tithing we begin to see how we can bear another's burden and so fulfill the law of Christ. When we really begin (in grace) to share, we come to realize deeply that the God of grace, who gives all, gives for all, and the Christ who sacrificed everything did it for everyone. So we enter into the joy of sacrifice. We come to realize the folly of the old saying "Give till it hurts," because the more we give, the greater becomes our joy in sharing.

Also at about this point the tither, having responded to grace with grace, ceases to ask the old question asked by so many impoverished Christians, "How much *must* I give?" and begins to ask instead, "How much *can* I give?" As Robert Paul Roth puts it, the tither ceases to regard the tithe as a ceiling and begins to think of it as a floor.[18] It is certainly true, as Julius Earl Crawford writes, that "the true steward finds genuine joy in the constant enlargement of his offerings to the cause of Christ."[19]

Material giving has become only a way of expressing our desire to give ourselves wholeheartedly and fully to Christ. As L. E. Meyer writes:

> Our responsibility in partnership with God is to give our hearts in love. . . . Our wealth but returns to the Giver His own, but our love is the gift of our own free will returning to do the will of God. It is not so much the giving of the tithe as the attitude in which it is given that blesses both the giver and the receiver.[20]

When the attitude has so changed, one's whole stewardship life has begun to be lived in the realm of grace. Tithing is like priming the pump: a bit of water (grace) is poured in and much more comes out.

Amos John Traver writes:

> The Christian who responds without reservations to the grace of God will be a graceful person in all his ways. Grace will inevitably express itself in beautiful lives. These lives will not be formal, for they will grow from within. This beauty is more than skin deep. Applied to giving, it goes beyond rules of "tithing mint, anise and cummin."[21]

In the same vein G. Ernest Thomas writes: "I have discovered that many followers of Christ who possess an inner radiance are those who have the habit of tithing."[22] God's grace makes the Christian steward graceful (grace-full). The awareness that God has fully accepted us in his household works a change of personality and makes us responsible and graceful stewards in his house.

So, finally, as the old gospel song puts it:

> I'm living on the mountain, underneath a cloudless sky,
> I'm drinking at the fountain that never shall run dry,
> O yes! I'm feasting on the manna from a bountiful supply,
> For I am dwelling in Beulah Land.
>
> C. Austin Miles[23]

Beulah Land sounds like the realm of grace in which the responsive and responsible Christian truly resides.

Christian stewards care for all God's children as God does.

Christian giving is giving in the spirit with which God gave his Son. Christian living is living in the same spirit as our Lord, Jesus Christ. So for us collectively, as T. A. Kantonen says, "Stewardship is the re-enactment of Christ's life in Christ's people."[24]

Notes

1. Harris Franklin Rall, *The Teachings of Jesus* (Abingdon-Cokesbury Press, 1930), p. 139.

2. Henry David Thoreau, *Walden*, in *The American Tradition in Literature*, ed. by Sculley Bradley et al., 4th ed. (Grosset & Dunlap, 1974), Vol. I, p. 1274.

3. Holmes Rolston, *Stewardship in the New Testament Church*, 4th ed. (John Knox Press, 1953), p. 51.

4. Ibid., p. 47.

5. S. Paul Schilling, "A Theological Interpretation" in *Theological Perspectives of Stewardship*, ed. by Edwin A. Briggs (General Board of the Laity, United Methodist Church, 1969), p. 10.

6. John A. Mackay, *God's Order* (Macmillan Co., 1953), pp. 149–150.

7. Warren A. Quanbeck, "Stewardship in the Teachings of Jesus," in *Stewardship in Contemporary Theology*, ed. by T. K. Thompson (Association Press, 1960), p. 50.

8. Robert E. Cushman, "Twentieth Century Development in Stewardship," in Briggs (ed.), *Theological Perspectives of Stewardship*, p. 103.

9. "Foundation Statement for Christian Stewardship," in Briggs (ed.), *Theological Perspectives of Stewardship*, p. 163.

10. Schilling, "A Theological Interpretation," p. 12.

11. Ibid., p. 10.

12. Harvey H. Potthoff, "The Mission of the Church," in Briggs (ed.), *Theological Perspectives of Stewardship,* p. 123.

13. Definition quoted in Helge Brattgard, *God's Stewards,* tr. by Gene J. Lund (Augsburg Publishing House, 1963), p. 5.

14. L. E. Meyer, *As You Tithe So You Prosper* (Unity School of Christianity, 1953), p. 13.

15. Costen J. Harrell, *Stewardship and the Tithe* (Abingdon Press, 1953), p. 61.

16. Earl Barfoot, "The New-Every-Day Lifestyle," in *Shalom: A Vision of a New World,* ed. by George Morris (Tidings, 1974), pp. 59, 65, 62, 58.

17. G. Ernest Thomas, *Spiritual Life Through Tithing* (Tidings, 1955), pp. 57, 61, 62.

18. Robert Paul Roth, "A Twentieth Century Conception of Christian Tithing," in Thompson (ed.), *Stewardship in Contemporary Theology,* p. 149.

19. Julius Earl Crawford, *The Stewardship Life,* rev. ed. (Abingdon Press, 1947), p. 141.

20. Meyer, *As You Tithe So You Prosper,* p. 29.

21. Amos John Traver, *Graceful Giving* (Muhlenberg Press, 1946), p. 7.

22. Thomas, *Spiritual Life Through Tithing,* p. 56.

23. From "Dwelling in Beulah Land," by C. Austin Miles. Copyright 1911, Hall-Mack Co. © renewed 1939, The Rodeheaver Co. Used by permission.

24. T. A. Kantonen, "Stewardship and Christian Doctrine," in Thompson (ed.), *Stewardship in Contemporary Theology,* p. 181.

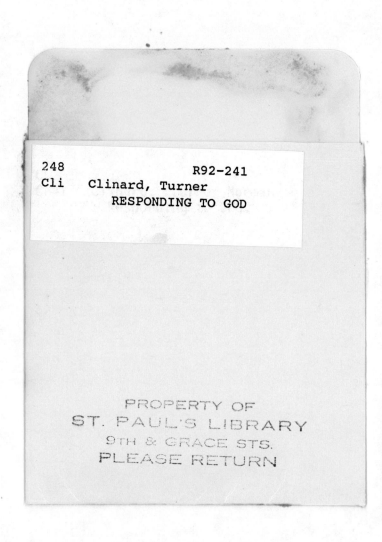

BLANCHE CLEANS UP

Books by Barbara Neely

Blanche on the Lam

Blanche Among the Talented Tenth

Blanche Cleans Up

Blanche Passes Go

BLANCHE CLEANS UP

A BLANCHE WHITE MYSTER

BARBARA NEELY

The characters and events portrayed in this book are fictitious. Any similarity to real persons, living or dead, is coincidental and not intended by the author.

ISBN: 1941298435
ISBN 13: 9781941298435

library of congress cataloging-in-publication data
Neely, Barbara.
Blanche cleans up / BarbaraNeely.
p. cm.
ISBN 0-670-87626-7
1. Afro-American women—Massachusetts—Boston—Fiction. 2. Women detectives—Massachusetts—Boston—Fiction. 3. Women domestics—Massachusetts—Boston—Fiction. I. Title.
PS3564.E244B56 1998 97-39834
813'.54—dc21

Published by Brash Books, LLC
12120 State Line #253,
Leawood, Kansas 66209

www.brash-books.com

This book is dedicated to the people who literally made it possible: Andrea, my dearest Babs Bigham, Beth Baldini, Denise Barry, Diane Bird, Donna Bivens, Alan Brush, Dick Cluster, Peggy and Peter Dickey, Priscilla and Junie Dickey, Lisa Dodson, the Economics Dept. at U. Mass Boston, Nancy Falk, Roz Feldberg, Deborah George, Charlene Gilbert, Gladys, Hilary Gomolin, Hattie Gossett, Gloria Harris, Chanel Hunt, Miz Janie, Lisa Kirchner, Deborah McGregor, Terri Malloney, Steve Mentzer, Alberta Neely, Miss Ann who took it like a big girl, Bernard Neely, Bryan Neely (the all-time gold medal winner in the brother department), nephew Rasheen Neely, my wonderful sister Vanessa Neely, Claes Nillson, James Page, Barbara Reeves, Liz Roberts, Elaine Thomas, Charles Tolbert, Suki Tye, Pauletta and colleagues, Gwen and Tommie Williams, Emani Wilson, the women and men of lla & b (especially Judy and Jay), Chu-Han Zhu, and finally, foremost, and always, to Jeremiah Cotton who did it all with grace, courage and love.

ACKNOWLEDGMENTS

Many, many thanks to the people who did their best to make this a better book: Babs Bigham, Dick Cluster, Juanita Guidry Copeland, Jeremiah Cotton, Pamela Dorman, Deborah George, Charlene Gilbert, Mimi Hersh, Amy Manson, Ann and Vanessa Neely, Alice Roberts, Terri Small-Turner, Phyllis Wender, and Kate White, with special thanks to my dear friend, Joycelyn Moody.

AUTHOR'S NOTE

This book is a work of fiction. Characters and events are the product of my imagination. Any resemblance to real people, organizations, institutions, or incidents is entirely coincidental. While the novel is set in the Roxbury section of Boston, some of the area's features have been altered for the purpose of telling this story.

ONE

MAY 1998
DAY ONE—THURSDAY

Blanche climbed out of the cab by the mailbox that read 1020. She ignored the sharp little wind that smacked at the backs of her legs—a reminder that spring in Boston could often pass for winter—and walked down the sloping driveway. She stopped halfway to the house. Her hand automatically rose to her hip as she gave the Brindle place a good looking over.

The house reminded Blanche of her mother's friend, Miz Alicemae, who still wore lace-up corsets and knee-length cotton bloomers as though the year were 1902. It was an old-fashioned brick house, with shutters and trim in richest green. It rose up from the ground like a grand diva reaching her full height. Vain like Miz Alicemae, too, Blanche muttered. She adjusted the strap of her slip and continued down the drive.

Understanding houses was part of how she made her living. Just like a good surgeon didn't open up a patient without an examination, she didn't clean or cook in a house until she'd done the same. She couldn't remember when she'd first understood how much houses had to say about themselves, but it was information she'd come to depend upon.

She had an uneasy feeling about this place but wasn't sure if it was due to the house itself, the job she'd promised to do here, the people who lived inside, or all of the above. She wondered if the house had a secret, like those nips of Beefeater gin Miz Alicemae kept hidden all around her house.

This was not the sort of job Blanche liked. Being housekeeper-cook was the kind of position she woke up worrying about in the middle of the night. She wasn't scared of it. There was no type of domestic work that she hadn't aced in the twenty-six years since she'd taken up the profession. It was her ability to cook, sew, clean, launder, wait table, and all the rest that made it possible for her to make her way in the world and feed and clothe her dead sister's two children. Part of the problem with this job was that she never liked supervising folks—too much like being an overseer. She hoped that Carrie, the housemaid she'd met yesterday, and Wanda, the cleaning woman, didn't need somebody looking over their shoulders, because she already had two kids at home.

She had Cousin Charlotte to thank for this job. Charlotte had shown up at Blanche's house first thing last Saturday morning, one of her ever-present hats cocked on the left side of her head. (Did she sleep in those things?) That day she'd had on her what-to-do-with-old-dishes hat: two overlapping, grungy, gray, felt-covered saucers turned face-to-face with a long, nervous, iridescent feather poking out to the side. That feather had danced a jig while Cousin Charlotte explained that she expected Blanche to stand in for Miz Inez, Cousin Charlotte's friend, so Miz Inez and Cousin Charlotte could travel down home to Farleigh, North Carolina.

"Are you sure you can't get somebody else?" Blanche had asked. She'd been smart enough not to add how badly Miz Inez got on her nerves with all that tiresome talk about her wonderful white employers and best-in-the-world son.

"Blanche, I ain't got no time to be foolin' with you!" Cousin Charlotte had told her. "If you ain't got the common decency to help out my oldest and dearest friend, a poor woman who ain't never had a real vacation in her life, as a favor to me, your own mama's first cousin, then I..."

Blanche had tuned Cousin Charlotte out. It was all over but the shouting, and she was the loser—not that she'd gotten a bit of thank-you from Cousin Charlotte. Of course, Cousin Charlotte didn't need to thank her: She'd taken Blanche and the kids in when they'd moved to Boston in a hurry three years ago. And then there was Mama. She'd tongue-lash Blanche up one side and down the other if Blanche refused to help Mama's favorite cousin.

Blanche just hoped her usual day customers got good service from Cousin Charlotte's niece, Larissa. Cousin Charlotte said Larissa used to work for a housecleaning service, but that didn't mean she knew what she was doing. Blanche had called her clients and warned them that she'd had to replace herself for a week. She'd made note of which ones complained so she could replace *them*. Any employer who couldn't understand an emergency would likely be a problem before long. One of the major reasons she chose to do day work was being able to pick up and drop clients as she saw fit. This meant she didn't have to take no mess from nobody, her preferred way of living.

Now she let herself into the Brindle house with the key Miz Inez had given her. She'd gotten here early so she'd have some time to get a feel for the place. She stashed her bag and jacket on a hook in the utility closet. The house felt like sleep was still in charge, but she walked through the downstairs, looking into each room, making sure the Brindles were still upstairs.

It was a good-sized house: five bedrooms with baths, two master suites, and another bathroom occupied the two upper floors. A living room, breakfast room with sunroom, dining room, library, an office, two bathrooms, the kitchen, and the laundry room took up the first floor. Each of the major rooms was nearly the size of a small apartment in Blanche's neighborhood. The house was furnished in what Blanche called undeclared rich: gleaming wood chests and tables with the kind of detail that said handmade, sofas and chairs that looked like they'd grown up in the rooms, Oriental carpets older than her grandmama, and pictures so ugly they had to be expensive originals. Light streamed down from a large window over the stairs to the second floor. The library, with its battered hassocks and mashed throw cushions, looked like the most used room. The office smelled of smoke and men.

Blanche went back to the kitchen to make a cup of tea. While the water boiled, she looked around the room where she'd be spending most of her working hours for the next week. It wasn't the most modern, the largest, or the best-appointed kitchen she'd ever worked in. There was a microwave but no convection oven. There was enough work space on the counter between sink and stove, but Blanche was partial to a butcher-block station in the middle of the floor, especially one with wheels. The appliances were on the older side, too. It had been a while since she'd used an oven she had to bend over to reach, and the dishwasher looked to be in its teens. What did impress her about the kitchen was how well Miz Inez had organized it: the bottles and cans arranged by size, the spices alphabetized, and labels on the shelves so you didn't waste time looking for beans where only canned fruit lived. From the looks of what the shelves contained, not a lot of fancy eating went on here, which was fine with Blanche. Less work.

She carried her tea and the note from Miz Inez to her already favorite spot: the sunroom off the breakfast room. She always liked to use the front of the house if she was going to be working in a place for a week or more—a way of reminding herself of her equality with her employers. She took a deep breath and felt her pores soak up some of the moisture. There were palms and rubber plants nearly touching the curved glass ceiling; Boston ferns on narrow columns drooped to the ground. A spleenwort with leaves wider than her hand took up a whole corner. A huge anthurium with what she could think of only as an erect penis in the middle of its flat red flower shared a five-tiered stand with a spider plant, a piggyback plant, and several others she didn't recognize. Another circular stand held at least twenty plump African violets in every possible color. The white-sailcloth-covered chairs seemed to float among the plants. She leaned back in an armchair and kicked off her shoes. The tile floor felt warm beneath her feet.

She sipped her tea and looked over the four-page note from Miz Inez. It included mealtimes: eight-thirty for breakfast (she checked her watch; she had over an hour to get that together), one o' clock for lunch, drinks in the library at four-thirty, dinner at seven. Next came the list of meals for the week and the name of the grocer to call, if necessary. Inez reminded her that Mr. Ted Sadowski, who worked for Mr. Brindle, usually arrived for breakfast (he had his own key) and would take lunch if he was in the house. Allister Brindle himself took care of the plants in the sunroom. The Brindles' schedules followed, including lots of lunches and dinners out, Blanche was pleased to see. This job was looking up.

As for the staff, Carrie had Sunday off and a half day on Wednesday; Wanda Jackson, the cleaning lady, came on Tuesdays to do the downstairs and Thursdays to do the upstairs, which meant she'd be working upstairs today. Blanche got Inez's regular days off—Saturday afternoon and all day Tuesday. Felicia Brindle's personal trainer was due today, too, and her masseuse tomorrow. Friday was payday for Blanche and Carrie; Wanda's check got mailed to her.

Blanche didn't have much information on the family, except that there were just two of them, a man and wife. She'd met the woman, Felicia Brindle, yesterday when Miz Inez had brought her in to show her around.

"Inez says they're real nice people," Cousin Charlotte had said when Blanche asked her about the Brindles. "They even hired her son, but it didn't last. He didn't used to be so—You'd think he'd spend some time with his Mama, stop by and—But don't get me started on Ray-Ray. What was I sayin'? Oh yeah.

Inez been with these Brindles since Jesus was a child. I know she told you how they just love her."

Exactly. In Blanche's experience, the more a person believed love was a part of what they got from their employer, the more likely it was that the person was being asked to do things that only love could justify. Who knows what all Inez did for these people? Blanche thought about the woman down in Farleigh who routinely told her maid how much she loved her and insisted the maid call her Auntie—things the young maid had bragged about. But the woman also emptied her bowels in a slop pot so the maid could keep a written description of its contents. Blanche doubted Inez went anywhere near that far, and like it or not, this was the job she was stuck with, but only for a week, she reminded herself. She drank the last of her tea and sighed. It was time to get to work.

Blanche was cutting the biscuits when Carrie arrived, breathless and grumbling about the bus being late.

"I'll serve breakfast this morning, Carrie. I haven't seen Allister Brindle yet. I want to check him out. And this Ted who works for him, too."

"Do anything you wanna do. You the boss," Carrie said, but didn't sound like she meant it.

Great! A sister with an attitude, Blanche thought. Thank you, Cousin Charlotte; thank you, Miz Inez. She gave Carrie a sharp look. Carrie was a plain-faced, dark brown-skinned woman—nowhere near as dark as Blanche—with permanent frown lines in her forehead and a chin round as a Ping-Pong ball. Her deep-set black eyes peered suspiciously out at Blanche from behind dinky little metal-framed glasses. Who could tell her age? Anywhere from fifty to eighty, Blanche figured. Straightened, gray-streaked hair was visible through the thin black hair net that covered her hair, the tops of her ears, and her upper forehead. She held her mouth as though she'd just had a vinegar cocktail. Blanche had never seen a grumpier-looking woman. Probably constipated, she thought.

She set the biscuit cutter down. "Am I stepping on your toes by serving breakfast?"

"Ain't got nothin' to do wit me."

Blanche waited, sure this lie wasn't all Carrie had to say on the subject.

"It ain't no job of mine, noway. It's Ricardo's job," Carrie said.

"Who's Ricardo?"

Carrie blinked at her. "He works here."

Okay, it's like that, Blanche thought. If I don't ask, she won't tell. Is she mad because a stranger's come in to tell her what to do? Or does she have a constipated personality, too?

"So where's Ricardo?"

"Mr. B sent him and Elena home to Argentina."

"Because . . ."

"Till after the election. That's why Inez said I could wait table and get the door. It don't make me no never mind."

"Why'd he send them home?"

" 'Cause Mr. Ted said it wasn't right for somebody running for governor to have personal servants like that in these times."

"Who's running for governor?" Blanche wanted to know.

"Mr. Brindle." Carrie's tone said everyone in the world knew this but Blanche.

"So Elena is Felicia's personal maid, and Ricardo is his valet and the butler?"

Carrie barely nodded. "That's right."

"What about Elena's work?"

"I'm s'posed to help Mrs. B with her toilet, but she don't seem to need me much, so I just wait table and . . . I'm just doin' what Inez said for me to do. It ain't no big thing."

"Yeah, right." Blanche folded her arms and stared at Carrie.

Carrie tossed her head. "Well, it do make a change."

That's better, Blanche thought.

"Well, honey, you can keep on waiting table, but not this morning. This morning I wanna check out the household, like I said. After that, you got it."

Carrie gave her a barely visible nod. She didn't look happy but she went off to set the table without further comment.

Sweet Ancestors! If she'd known she was going to have to arm wrestle the housemaid, she'd have gotten more rest. And what a hypocrite this Brindle character was, sending off their personal servants! As if anybody would mistake somebody who lived in this kind of house for just your average Joe.

One of the two men at breakfast looked to Blanche like a high school boy in his dad's best suit. Ted Sadowski, no doubt. His bright blue eyes snapped with energy. Hungry eyes, Blanche thought. He sat on the edge of his chair.

Allister Brindle looked like what Blanche called The Leadership: square face, graying Kennedy hair, and squinty eyes. Was there a men's grooming shop that specialized in making white men look like born politicians or was it a gene thing?

The two men talked and chuckled together. Something about them reminded her of a couple of dogs sniffing each other and romping in the park. Felicia Brindle showed no interest in either of them.

"Morning, ma'am, gentlemen."

Felicia looked over the top of her newspaper. She was a thin, sharp-boned woman who reminded Blanche of ribbon candy—all curves and gloss. Her pearly white skin, red jumpsuit, and red-blond hair only added to the effect. She looked directly into Blanche's eyes.

"Good morning, Blanche. Just juice and coffee, please. I hope you enjoy working for us even though it's only for a short while." She smiled up at Blanche.

Enjoy? If she wanted the help to enjoy it, she'd pay more for fewer hours. Still, Blanche was partial to employers who looked her in the eye.

Neither of the men spoke or even looked in Blanche's direction. She considered giving them a loud, bustling greeting that forced them to acknowledge her, but she knew the advantages of not being seen. Still, there was no excuse for their bad manners. She made a mental note never to greet either of them first again.

Ted Sadowski was going over his boss's schedule for the day. "The lunch should be a snap, sir. Then there's the good government panel followed by an interview with you and Mrs. Brindle for prime-time news and a small reception at the Plaza. The Drake Society dinner tonight. That should be pretty low-key."

Allister Brindle nodded. "Excellent, excellent," he said, rubbing his hands together.

Both men loaded up on the biscuits, ham, curried eggs, and mango slices. But not even Blanche's food stopped the flow of their talk.

"We'll give 'em a bang-up lunch, make them feel included. They all need that, you know, all of them. They're like children!" Allister Brindle spoke like an authority.

"Oh, it'll be fine, sir. You've got them in your pocket. They're behind us a hundred percent."

Brindle reached over and slapped Sadowski on the back. "That's why I hired you, Ted. Even *I* believe you when you mouth that bullshit." Brindle's smile faded. "Let's not be overconfident, Ted. You can never quite trust them. You must never forget that." He gave Sadowski's shoulder a little shake for emphasis. "They've got different values. In the end, they're in the pocket of whoever pays them."

Blanche left for the kitchen. She wondered which *They* Brindle and Sadowski meant—blacks, women, gays, Puerto Ricans, people in wheelchairs? It didn't matter which. What mattered was that Brindle and Sadowski believed in *They*; talked about *They* as though *They* lived on the underside of a public toilet seat. Is this what Inez listened to every day? Poor Inez. Poor Inez, hell! Poor Blanche.

When the front doorbell rang, Blanche waited for Carrie to come running from wherever she was to do her Ricardo job. The bell rang again. Still no Carrie.

"Carrie! Door!" Blanche called toward the laundry room.

"I'm in the bathroom!" Carrie called out.

Blanche went down the hall and looked out the long narrow window in the front door. The man on the other side was the color of old, old gold. He could have been a mulatto or a Latino, but the ease with which he stood at rich white folks'door in his shorts and T-shirt convinced her he was Caucasian. She looked him up and down. Ummm, Soccer Thighs. She didn't know zip about the game, but she watched it on TV occasionally for the stud muffins—particularly for those long, muscular, almost girlish legs and tight butts.

She opened the door. The man picked up his gym bag and turned toward her. He looked at her as though she were the center of the universe and everything else was background. He smiled a closed-mouth smile that warmed his dark blue eyes even more.

"Hi, I'm Saxe Winton. I'm Felicia's trainer." He held out his hand. "And you're?" His voice was deep and warm.

"Blanche." She unintentionally mimicked his tone. She took back her hand and stepped aside. He gave her another of those Mr. Mona Lisa smiles as he passed her. I bet his dick curves up when it's hard, she thought. Every man she'd ever known with an upturned dick had sex seeping out of his pores, just like this boy. No, not boy. Those wrinkles around his eyes and mouth weren't all about laughing. Mid – to late thirties, probably. She closed the door behind him.

"Is that you, Saxe?" Felicia called from the top of the stairs.

Saxe turned to Blanche and gave her a regretful look as though duty were calling him away from where he really wanted to be. Great Googa Mooga! How much of that hot lustiness pouring off him like water over a fall was under his control? Did he want to present himself as lunch to every woman he met, or couldn't he help himself? Maybe both. Pity the poor cow who thought it had anything to do with her. Awright, Blanche, get your mind out of your drawers, she told herself. Still, how long had it been? She got to two years and stopped counting.

Carrie came out of the bathroom off the kitchen. "It was Mr. Saxe, wasn't it?" She sounded like her number had come out and she'd forgotten to play it.

"Yeah, he sure makes answering the door worth the trouble."

"Humph." Carrie stuck her nose up in the air. "He sure ain't why I want to answer the front door. Like I said, that's my job from Ricardo. I just think Mr. Saxe is nice, is all." Carrie didn't look at Blanche.

"Nice? I don't know about nice, but I bet he could make your panties melt before you could get them off."

Carrie looked as shocked as if Blanche had lifted Carrie's dress to check on the state of her panties.

"What you mean?" Carrie smoothed her dress over her hips. "I wouldn't take off my . . . I don't want . . . I got to get the panties, I mean the sheets, folded." Carrie darted into the laundry room quick as a lizard and closed the door behind her.

Blanche shook her head. Poor thing can't even admit that a part of her heartthrob is coming from lower down. Probably won't even let herself feel that sweet drum beating down there. Blanche put on the kettle, then turned from the stove to watch the back door, knowing that it would open. It was an ability so old she no longer asked herself where it came from.

A woman stepped inside. Blanche had no idea who she might be. Wanda Jackson, the cleaning lady, was due about now, but this white woman surely wasn't Wanda Jackson.

"Well, darlin', you must be the replacement," the woman said.

She was about Blanche's weight but a little shorter. They had the same stout-hipped, big-butt, big-busted frame, although this woman had the kind of shapely legs Blanche had cried for in her youth. Her hair was braided, too—not in two thick cornrows on either side of a center part, like Blanche's, but in a circle of plump gray plaits wound around her head. Her face was as rosy white as Blanche's was blue-black. The fine lines in her face reminded Blanche of the cobweb-thin cracks in very old paintings she'd seen in museums and wealthier employers' homes.

"It's Wanda Jackson here." She thrust out her hand. "And what might your name be, darlin'?"

"Blanche. Blanche White."

Wanda gripped Blanche's hand as though she meant to keep it. She cocked her head to the side. "And what a pair of names for one such as yourself, eh?"

Blanche was impressed. A white woman who brought up color without stammering and quaking and going on about how some of her best friends had color as a sign she wasn't a racist! What a nice surprise.

"Speaking of names, you're the first white Wanda I ever met."

Wanda peeled off two sweaters and a woolen scarf. "Well, you're the fifth or sixth colored I've had to tell that Wanda is an old Polish name I inherited from my Polish great-grandmother on me sweet dead mother's side; then I married a Brit from Liverpool, just like me mum, name of Jack Jackson. Who named you, darlin'?"

"Great-Grandmama Ruth. She never said why, and she wasn't the kind of woman who took kindly to being questioned."

Wanda nodded. "Just the kind of woman I'm lookin' to be meself." She sat down at the table and changed her heavy brown tie-up oxfords for the pair of paisley carpet slippers she took from her tote bag.

"Tea?"

"And what a welcome change you are from our Inez, darlin'. Hardly willin' to part with a bit of water, not to speak of a cuppa tea."

Blanche heated the potbellied teapot and fetched a tin of cookies from the pantry.

Wanda hovered over her cup, sugaring her tea and sniffing the fragrant steam, as if preparing to drink tea was as tasty and satisfying as sipping it. She settled into her chair as though she had no plans to clean the upstairs today.

"I hope I didn't offend with what I said about Inez," Wanda said. "I didn't mean no harm, you know. She's a decent soul, even if she spends a tad too much time with her Brindle glasses on."

"Her Brindle glasses?"

"The rose-colored ones, darlin'. You know the ones I mean."

"Ah, those. Well, I got twenty-twenty vision myself, at least on the job."

Wanda winked at her. "Better to see than to be seen, me old gran used to say."

"Wanda, honey, you're somethin'. "

Wanda gave Blanche a long, level look. "And are you that taken with yer own good sense, darlin'?"

"Sometimes," Blanche told her. She thought about the conversation she'd heard in the breakfast room. "But I get your point." Maybe the Ancestors put Wanda in her path to remind her not to fall into a *They* trap of her own.

Wanda blew and sipped, sipped and blew. "A fine house, this, don't you think? Although I can't always say the same for him what owns it."

Blanche knew when she was being led and to somewhere she wanted to go. "Who are these folks, anyway?"

Wanda leaned back in her chair. "Robber barons they were. Ran opium to the poor Chinese with Franklin Roosevelt's grandda, then—"

"You mean the grandfather of President Franklin Delano Roosevelt?"

"The very same, darlin'. Didn't stop there, either. The Brindles was also in cahoots with old man Kennedy runnin' bootleg whiskey in the Prohibition. They say the father to this Brindle was a decent sort. Worked for the poor, tried to get laws passed to help the likes of us. I met him once, in a way of speakin', when he come here to stay for a bit. This was years ago, before I come here to work regular. Back then I was hired in to help out at the shindigs they were throwin'. This particular time it weren't just good works the old gentleman was pursuin'. Panted after my precious, he did, right there in the front hall. Now this one ..."

Blanche held up her hand. "Wait a minute, wait a minute. I'm still back at your *precious* being panted after. I've heard it called many a thing, honey, but I got to tell you, this is *new*."

Wanda shrugged. "As I was saying, our current Mr. Brindle is more than a bit to the right of his dear old da."

"Carrie tells me he's running for governor."

"That he is, darlin', although some say he's just practicin' for a Washington run later on."

Blanche passed Wanda the tin of cookies. "What about the wife?"

"Bit of a cold fish, personalitywise. Still, better'n him, At least she's got a good side."

"How do you know?"

"Saw her name in a paper. Not your regular paper. A newsletter like. Said she gave a considerable lot to one of them shelters for the homeless."

Blanche freshened Wanda's tea. "Rich folks give money for reasons that ain't got nothin' to do with having a good side."

"Not money, darlin', time. It's time she's been puttin' in at that place." Wanda nodded at Blanche's look of surprise. "She's in one of them do-gooder women's groups, too. Not too good," she added. "No intentions to parcel out their booty to the likes of us or anythin'. More in the way of socks for the poor wee kiddies and birth control for their mums." Wanda dumped three teaspoons of sugar into her tea and reached for the cream. "Still, I know for a fact the Missus is still sendin' checks to Lucy, who used to do the cleanin' here. She's the one got me the job when she had to quit. Knocked down by a hit-and-run driver on her way to the supermarket. In a wheelchair since then. That was two years ago."

Blanche wasn't surprised about Allister's politics, given what she'd seen of him, but Felicia's generosity *was* a surprise. "That's a lot of checks. You sure it wasn't Felicia's car that knocked her down?"

"Blanche! That's a mite cynical, my girl!"

"No," Blanche disagreed, "just realistic. You said she's a bit of a cold fish."

"I see your point. But what a dull place the world would be if people only did what was expected, eh?"

"What about Felicia's people?" Blanche asked.

"Well, socialwise, she married up, to be sure, but she's got gobs of money. She don't have relations hangin' about. I think she comes from wig makers or some such, while his mum's side came over on the *Mayflower*, I think. Her parents used to come to dinner from time to time, but they've both passed now. Same as his."

"What about Allister's money?" Blanche asked.

Wanda spread her hands. "Old but not as deep as it once was. His old man lost a good bit, I think. His mum's money was really her family's money. They kept most of it for their own line—accordin' to Lucy."

Wanda looked into her almost empty cup and sighed but refused Blanche's refill. "I've got to get on with upstairs sometime," she said.

Blanche looked over Inez's menu for today's buffet lunch: ham, cold roast beef, potato salad, shrimp salad, pasta salad, green salad, and a platter of high-end cold cuts. All of it ready but the green salad, thanks to Inez. But it wasn't what Blanche called a "bang-up lunch." It was the kind of lunch people like the Brindles served to guests they weren't trying to impress, except with quantity. Good enough for *They*, no doubt.

Carrie hummed "Just a Closer Walk with Thee" in a high nasal whine as she moved between the kitchen and the dining room. On her last trip, she took a detour down the front hall and came back so sparkly-eyed, Blanche knew she'd just shown Saxe out. Felicia Brindle sailed into the kitchen before Blanche could tease Carrie about Saxe.

"Just wanted to make sure everything was coming along," Felicia said, peering over Blanche's shoulder to see what she was doing.

As if she could do anything about it if it wasn't. "Everything's just fine, ma'am," Blanche said, blocking Felicia's view out of sheer cussedness. Blanche always called her employers ma'am and sir to their faces. It put just the right amount of distance between them and her and was good cover when she couldn't remember their names.

Curiosity—disguised as helping Carrie hand around the canapés—carried Blanche into the library where the guests had gathered for drinks before lunch.

Blanche was generally delighted to come across a group of black people, but her stomach dropped when she saw that the *They* Brindle had referred to were what she called The Downtown Leadership—the black men that the big downtown white folks talked to when they needed blacks with positions and titles to support the latest cut in programs for the poor, or to amen some closet racist like Brindle. Do the Brindles of the world really think we're all stupid enough to believe that shit is sunshine because the idiot who says so is black?

She recognized Ralph Gordon, the new head of the Roxbury Outpatient Care Center. His face had been all over the papers a couple of months ago when the *powers that be* hired him after firing the woman who'd directed the health center for years. Her mistake had been complaining about cuts in her budget to the newspapers. Gordon was talking to James McGovern, the head of the Association of Afro Execs. He kept himself in the news by complaining about affirmative action and lying about black women taking jobs away from black men. Jonathan Carstairs, a lawyer who'd run for city councilor from Roxbury, was guzzling something from a highball glass. His campaign platform had included arresting welfare mothers if their kids got into trouble. Naturally, he'd lost the election. Blanche thought of him as a prime example of how racism made black people crazy. A tall, paunchy man Blanche thought was a high muckety-muck at one of the banks and a couple of men she didn't recognize were hovering around Felicia Brindle.

She watched Allister Brindle work the room, shaking hands and slapping backs. Was it phoniness that made him look like he was made of cardboard? His guests melted before him like butter under a hot knife. The talk was partly about sports and partly a sermon from Brindle against those homos, welfare mothers, and drug-dealing teenage gangsters who were ruining the Commonwealth and the country. Blanche kept waiting for one of the guests to take exception. None did.

Blanche wasn't at all surprised that nobody from what she considered the helpful groups in the community was there. It wasn't likely any of them would be hanging out with someone as far right as Allister Brindle. Like Allister had said, this was a paying gig. Every one of these suckers expected something in return for their sellout—a slot on some board of directors, some photos of them with the governor to hang in their offices and homes as a sign that they were somebody, or a reference to them in the newspaper as black leaders, which was important because they were leaders nobody followed.

Except for one of them.

Why was Maurice Samuelson hanging around Brindle? The Reverend Maurice Samuelson, founder of the Temple of the Divine Enlightenment. He certainly wasn't a leader without followers. She'd walked by Samuelson's Temple a couple of times just before services began, and there'd been so many people, mostly women, trying to get in, she'd had to cross the street. He was also probably the only one of these boys who actually lived in Roxbury, where most blacks in Boston lived. There were signs all over Roxbury about the Temple and its programs for elders and young people. He was the best-known outside of Boston, too. There'd been a story about Samuelson in *Jet* magazine. The article said his Temple was a new kind of African-American religion where Christian, Jewish, and Muslim holy books and beliefs were mixed together. She watched him as she offered the tray around the room.

He was a short man who tried to make himself look taller by walking with his shoulders up to his ears and wearing thick-heeled shoes, both of which Blanche thought made him look like an old-time gangster. He slicked his long hair down with pomade heavy enough to turn his kinks into waves that curled at the top of his collar in the back. His dark blue suit fit as though he and Allister Brindle had the same tailor. His blue-and-cream-polka-dot bow tie and cream silk shirt were a perfect match. Of course, it wouldn't matter to her how he looked. She was suspicious of anyone who was pushing not one, not two, but three male-led religions rolled into one.

And was Samuelson the only minister here? In this town, white politicians and black ministers seemed to go together like tears and tissues. At election time, the pols got religion and came looking for the blessings of black ministers as a way to get black votes without providing the kinds of services to black communities that they at least promised to East Boston and Charlestown and the other mostly white Boston neighborhoods.

"I wouldn't raise a dog in Roxbury," she heard someone say, but turned too late to see which man had spoken. She wished a pox on the speaker and all the listeners, too, since not one had disagreed.

Brindle clamped his hand on Maurice Samuelson's shoulder and steered him toward an empty corner. They looked like bad boys up to something nasty. Blanche worked her way close enough to hear what they were talking about.

Brindle set his glass on the mantle over the fireplace. "Now, about the election." He gave Samuelson's shoulder a little shake. "I really need your help in Roxbury, Maurice."

"Not to worry, not to worry," Samuelson assured him. "Aunt Jemima and Uncle Ben know which side their bread is buttered on. And if they don't, it's my job to tell them."

Both men laughed.

Flames engulfed Blanche's brain. She'd never before heard a black person promise to keep the Darkies in line for Massa. A tremble went up her arms as she fought the urge to smash Samuelson over the head with the tray of hors d'oeuvres, an urge so strong she could see bits of smoked salmon in his hair. She told herself to breathe deeply, to stay calm, to simply ease away. But before she could stop herself, she turned abruptly and jabbed a sharp elbow into Samuelson's lower spine, knocking him off balance and splashing whatever he was drinking onto his shirt. Uncle Ben and Aunt Jemima that, you butt-sucking maggot!

Samuelson staggered a step or two before he recovered his balance. He whipped out a handkerchief and dabbed at the stain.

"Oh, so sorry, excuse me." Blanche turned her head so that Samuelson, but not Brindle, could see that her apology was just words. She was pleased by the momentary flicker of uncertainty in Samuelson's eyes. Was he wondering if she'd bumped him on purpose? She certainly hoped so.

Samuelson hardly missed a beat. "No harm done, sister. No harm done." He reached out to pat her arm.

Blanche stepped back. If he touched her, she'd break his face in four places, and she let her eyes tell him so. He pulled his hand back.

"Everything all right?" Felicia Brindle made hostess sounds at Samuelson, but her eyes were on Blanche, who felt a sudden chill.

Two other men gushed up to Brindle, and he began telling them a joke about a Jew, a gay man, and an old black woman stuck in an elevator together as he led them toward the dining room. Blanche hurried off. Her blood was already sizzling. One more insult and she was likely to really go off in here.

She threw herself onto a kitchen chair, as startled by what she'd just done as Samuelson had been. What had possessed her? She'd been riled before. Worse than this. Once in a while she'd been messed with so badly, she'd had to let her finger slip into somebody's drink, put too much salt or hot pepper in the eggs rancheros, or add a couple tablespoons of cat food to the beef bourguignon. But never anything like this.

Of course, she wasn't about to deny the wave of pleasure she'd felt when her elbow found Samuelson's spine. He'd deserved it, no doubt about it.

Still, what she'd done was unprofessional behavior of the worst kind—the kind that made you lose your job—and this job wasn't even hers to lose. So why had she acted like it was? Had she passed her sell-by date? Had she lost the looseness needed to roll with the kind of blows that came with this work? Or maybe she was just sick to death of nigger-minded dickbrains like Samuelson making pacts with the devil in the name of black folks.

"Spiritual leader, my foot!" She fiddled and fumed, moving pots from the sink to the dishwasher, emptying the kettle, wiping the counter, anything to help her fidget away the last of her outrage. At the same time, she was depressed by the knowledge that there was really nothing surprising about what Samuelson had done. She knew that all these years of being hated for no reason beyond color had convinced some black people that the racists must be right. Did Samuelson hate himself as much as he did the people he called Aunt Jemima and Uncle Ben? Or did being a man of the cloth make him an honorary white in his own eyes?

She didn't go into the dining room, but she listened at the door to Brindle announcing his run for governor. He also thanked his guests, men he knew would help him "convince your people that old-style liberalism must give way to new-style pragmatism," which Blanche understood to mean that the few crumbs being passed down to poor black people would be taken back if Brindle were elected—for their own good, of course. Brindle spoke in a kind of imitation Martin Luther King singsong she'd once heard Ted Kennedy on TV while giving a speech to some black group. She liked to think some black consultant with a wicked sense of humor had suggested this black-speak strategy. When Brindle was done, his guests all clapped. Blanche went back to the kitchen, wondering what their mothers and children would think of them.

Voices in the hall told her when the guests were leaving. Felicia lurched into the kitchen like someone struggling to remember how her legs worked. She stood in the middle of the room staring in Blanche's direction but looking at something only Felicia could see.

"Can I help you, ma'am?" asked.

Felicia pulled herself back from wherever she'd gone. "We'll be back for drinks and out for dinner," she said.

Blanche could have driven a car through the spaces between Felicia's words, as if she had to search for each one and figure out how to say it before she spoke. Blanche wondered what had happened to dull those sharp edges she'd sensed earlier. Something surely had. Felicia had the slack-faced look of someone who'd just had a serious shock. Blanche's curiosity pushed her to ask Felicia what was wrong, but her mother wit wouldn't have it. As far as she knew, she wasn't being paid extra for hand-holding.

She helped Carrie put the library back in order and load the dishwasher.

"So, no more nice Saxe what's-his-name until Saturday," Blanche teased Carrie.

Carrie sniffed and tossed her head. "Don't mean nothin' to me who comes and goes in this here house, not even that one who does the massage. She'll be stompin' in here tomorrow right on time. She don't miss a day. She—"

"Why you call her 'that one who does the massage,' like she ain't got a name?"

" 'Cause God don't mean for women to do what she do."

"A lesbian, hunh?"

Had Carrie been a few shades lighter, Blanche was sure she'd have seen blood rush to the woman's face.

"It's against God. It says so in the Bible."

"But what's it got to do with you?"

"Ain't none of my business. But my pastor say it ain't natural. It's ungodly!" Carrie hissed.

"I don't get it," Blanche said. "You Christians say God made everything and everybody, which has gotta include lesbians. But then you say lesbians are ungodly. Seems to me that you, your pastor, or your God is very confused, honey."

Carrie looked at her as though Blanche had just grown horns. "I'm gonna put you in my prayers." She hurried away to the laundry room and closed the door firmly behind her. Blanche could hear her shrieking some hymn about being delivered from the heathen. It was so tuneless and off-key, Blanche suspected Carrie had made it up for her benefit.

Wanda came down the back stairs lugging the tools of her trade. She hauled the vacuum, bucket, mop, sprays, and sponges into the maintenance closet and took out her tote bag and sweaters.

"Well, darlin', it's been more than a pleasure. I'm lookin' that forward to our next meetin', I am." And she was off.

Blanche sat down at the kitchen table, thinking about her best friend, Ardell, down in North Carolina, and what she'd say about the Samuelson thing. She also thought about going to the Y for a sit in the sauna, about calling home to check on the kids, but right now she didn't have the energy to move. Her eyelids lowered; her neck and shoulder muscles relaxed; her hands folded over her belly. She was a breath away from sleep.

Then she was wide awake. Why? She straightened up and looked around. Carrie was still in the laundry room, Wanda and the Brindles had gone, and there was no one else in the house. She walked through to the front hall. But there *was* someone else in the house. Someone who'd just been in the front hall, judging by the whiff of soap or deodorant she caught. She didn't even think about going upstairs. If there was somebody up there stealing the Brindles' shit, she wasn't about to put her life in the way. But she didn't need to go up. The person upstairs was just coming down.

"What are you doing here?" Blanche and Ray-Ray asked each other at the same time.

From this angle, Miz Inez's overgrown son looked even more like a chocolate-covered tank than usual. Blanche didn't care for overmuscled men; she always suspected those extra muscle bulges were substitutes for a pea brain or a pencil-stub penis and not enough sexual imagination, along with a bad case of low self-esteem to make up for it. Ray-Ray was an exception. When they'd first met, Blanche had found it hard to believe that anyone could be so in love with himself, so sure that whatever was good in life was his by right. Then she'd thought about it. Who needed more self-love and confidence than a black man in America? He was smart, too, and usually found a way to make her laugh or otherwise get on her good side. But there were limits.

"I'm where I'm supposed to be," she told him. "You ain't. What you doing in these people's upstairs?"

"Oh, that's right. This is the week Mama's away. I was upstairs stealing from your white folks, of course," he teased.

"You must mean your mama's white folks."

"Touché, Miz Blanche, touché." Ray-Ray bounced down the last of the stairs and gave her a peck on the cheek. As usual, he managed to move in ways that showed off his muscles.

"What *were* you doin' up there, Ray-Ray?"

"Getting my shirt." He held it out to her. "I left it here when I fixed the window on the third floor. See? My initials." Ray-Ray headed for the front door.

Blanche stepped in front of him. "How'd you get in here?"

"Through the front door, like everybody else." He gave her an amused look. "You're not pissed because I came in through the front door, are you? I always do. I used to play in this house. And no one is ever going to make me use the back door. Not ever."

Blanche wished him luck with that. But given the many shapes and forms the back door could take, she was pretty sure he'd already been through a couple of them, whether he knew it or not. Was it even possible to grow up a poor black man in America and avoid the back door?

"Honey, I don't care what door you use; I just wanna know how you got in here."

Ray-Ray held up a key. "From the usual place under the mat," he said. "I'll put it back on my way out."

"Well, I'll tell the Brindles you came to call."

Ray-Ray spun around. "You don't have to. They might not like the idea of you letting me in their upstairs when they're not home. Let's just pretend you never saw me." He gave her a full-faced grin.

"Ray-Ray, I don't want no mess from these people about the missing gold cuff links or—"

"Don't worry, Blanche," Ray-Ray told her. "You'll be glad I came, trust me." He opened the door and slipped out.

Oh shit. "Ray-Ray!"

He was gone.

Blanche hurried upstairs. She could feel he'd been in Allister's rooms, but didn't know if anything had been moved. She checked Felicia's rooms. She couldn't tell if Ray-Ray had been in there because the rooms reeked of that moist, bleachy smell of clean-body sweat, vaginal juices, and sperm. Saxe might tease the help with his sex appeal, but he was obviously delivering more than just promises to his client. She wondered if Allister knew, and why Felicia had sounded so down after having just had one of the world's greatest mood lighteners.

She went back to the kitchen and brought out the food she'd held back from the buffet for her and Carrie's lunch, and tapped on the laundry room door.

"Ungodliness can seep through wood, honey, so you might as well come on out here and help me eat this food."

Blanche didn't want to tell Carrie about Ray-Ray's unexpected visit, but she couldn't shut him out of her mind.

"Do you know Ray-Ray, Inez's son?" she asked Carrie when they'd settled at the table.

Carrie filled her plate. "Um-hum. Useta do odd jobs around here."

"How come he left?"

Carrie shook her head and forked some potato salad into her mouth.

"What happened?" Blanche asked her.

Carrie kept chewing. Her eyes strayed to the platter in the middle of the table.

"Try some of this ham. It's good." Blanche eased a large slice onto Carrie's plate.

"He useta be around here all the time, working and not working."

"You want that last piece of roast beef?" Blanche pushed the platter closer to Carrie. "What was he doing here if he wasn't working?" she asked as Carrie speared the meat.

"Come to visit Mr. Marc. Mr. Brindle useta take them both to ball games, stuff like that when they was boys."

The kind white folks thing, Blanche thought. Proving your decency through the help. But she was surprised Allister went in for it. Wanda said he came from old money. They didn't usually go in for touchy-feely with the help. It didn't fit with their deep belief that they deserved what they had and the poor deserved to be poor.

"It's a shame to waste the rest of this food," Blanche said. "I couldn't convince you to take it along home, could I?"

The first big smile Blanche had seen lit up Carrie's face as she bobbed her head up and down.

Blanche got some plastic bags and aluminum foil to wrap the food. "So, why did Ray-Ray stop working here?" she asked.

Carrie cut her roast beef into bite-sized pieces. "Seems like him and Mr. B had some kinda fallin' out."

Oh shit! Ray-Ray coulda been upstairs cutting up all of Allister's clothes. Blanche leaned forward. "What kind of falling out?"

Carrie shrugged. "Don't know. Happened on my day off. Inez just said they had a fallin' out and Ray-Ray wasn't working here no more."

"When was this?"

Carrie wiped her mouth. "Year or so, I guess." She folded her napkin and laid it beside her plate. "Well, better git back to work."

She left Blanche sitting at the kitchen table, glad it was the Brindles' and not her own food she'd used to pay for that paltry bit of information.

"I'll get it!" Carrie shouted almost before the front doorbell stopped ringing.

She was wearing her sparkly eyes when she came back a few minutes later.

"It was Mr. Saxe."

Men running in and out of here like it's a cathouse, Blanche thought. "What'd he want?"

"He was looking for his pictures."

"What pictures?"

"Ones I put on Miss Felicia's dresser, I guess," Carrie said.

"What kind of pictures?"

Carrie shrugged. "One of them envelopes you git pictures in from the drugstore."

"Where'd you get it?"

"Found it on the floor in the hall. Outside Miss Felicia's room."

"So you figured they were hers?"

Carrie nodded. "Put 'em on her dresser."

"Did Saxe get them?"

"He went up to get them, but he said they weren't there no more. Miss Felicia musta moved 'em."

Or somebody else moved them, Blanche thought. Somebody who claimed to have been getting his shirt. But why?

"Pictures of what?"

"Don't know."

"You mean you didn't look at them?"

Carrie adjusted her hair net. "Weren't none of mine. I didn't have no business to look at . . ."

Blanche tried to imagine herself a person who could find an envelope full of pictures and not look at them. She thought Carrie would be better off if she was lying about looking in the envelope, but given what she'd seen of Carrie, Blanche was surprised she'd even picked it up from the floor. She shook her head in wonder and went to the library to set up for drinks.

Inez's note said Allister liked a Bourbon and branch in the afternoon and Felicia took an olive and an onion in her martini.

Allister looked tired but upbeat when he and Felicia got home. "It all went very well, don't you think?" he asked.

Felicia shrugged as if she couldn't care less.

Blanche gave her a closer look. Felicia's hair and clothes were clean and in order, but there was something smudged about her, as though she'd been flattened against a windowpane and smeared like a bug. Felicia ran her hands over her hair. It didn't help. It's them eyes she needs to do something about, Blanche thought.

"Where'd you disappear to?" Allister asked Felicia.

"What?"

"At the reception. I looked around and you were nowhere to be seen."

"You're running for office, Allister, not me. I don't have to be ever-present." Felicia's hand shook when she took her drink from the tray Blanche held. She looked up at Blanche and quickly away.

"A candidate's wife can be more important than his platform. You know that. You promised you would . . ."

Felicia rose with the martini glass still in her hand.

"Blanche, please send the shaker upstairs," she said, and walked out of the room and up the stairs as though Allister didn't exist.

Allister closed his eyes, laid his head against the back of his armchair, and sighed a sigh that was almost a moan. Then he, too, rose and left the room.

Blanche was expecting Felicia to send for her and ask what had happened to Saxe's pictures. She was relieved when it didn't happen. Maybe she was wrong about those pictures. Maybe Ray-Ray had taken something of Allister's, as she'd first thought.

Allister was in the breakfast room when Blanche passed by on her way to the kitchen. She waited half a minute before she strolled past the breakfast room again. Allister was now in the sunroom leaning over the stand of African violets. She couldn't see his face, but she watched his hands. He slowly, gently removed browning leaves, moved pots from one spot to another, and brushed his fingers lightly against the blossoms. His body looked softer, more rounded, as if he'd been stiffening his spine and sucking in his gut until this moment when he thought he was alone. Like everybody else, Allister had more than one side, but she didn't think it mattered. Was a rattlesnake sunning itself all that much less dangerous than one on the hunt?

When Allister finally went upstairs to dress for dinner, Blanche waited again for shouts of "I've been robbed!" but all was quiet. Either Ray-Ray had pinched something of Allister's that wasn't obvious, or she'd been right the first time and it was Saxe's pictures he'd taken and Felicia just hadn't missed them yet.

The wind had died down by the time Blanche left work. The air was still on the cold side, but she could feel spring just waiting to burst out. She climbed the driveway and walked up Cottage Street—really a one-lane, one-way road.

This was the greenest part of the city she'd seen outside of Boston Common and the gardens downtown. It looked like country around here. Just like the Brindles' place, the few other houses along the road were all down in a kind of valley tucked away out of sight behind stone or wooden fences. Following Inez's directions, Blanche turned left at the top of the hill and followed a two-lane road until it turned into Perkins Street, where she saw the lake she'd noticed on the way in. The sign she passed said BROOKLINE, and she realized the Brindle house was about three blocks outside the city of Boston.

But she'd crossed the line and was back in Boston now. Another sign announced that her lake was called Jamaica Pond, which told her she must be in the Jamaica Plain section of Boston.

Her regular jobs took her into the South End, Back Bay, and Beacon Hill, but she'd never been here before or to other neighborhoods like East Boston, Charlestown, South Boston, or the North End. Somebody had told her that some of these places had once been separate towns, but that was a long time ago. But it was now 1996, and from what she heard and read, the major use of these neighborhood names seemed to be to keep people apart and suspicious of one another. And she knew there were Boston communities unfriendly to folks from outside, particularly black, brown, and yellow folks.

From where she now stood, she couldn't see the other side of the pond. Canada geese and ducks skimmed along its surface. People strolled, jogged, and pushed strollers on the path beside the pond. Blanche stretched out her arms to the greening trees and blue water. She missed all of this over in the part of Roxbury where she lived. There were some trees on its streets, but if there were any bodies of water in the neighborhood, besides public pools and mud puddles, she'd never heard about them.

She'd been in Boston nearly three years, but having to build up her clientele and take care of the kids and the house, along with winters that demanded she stay indoors as much as possible, had reduced her learn-about-Boston time down to about six months. Still, she hadn't even done six months worth of exploring. Maybe it was because she hadn't had much choice about moving here. It was not so much her idea as her only alternative: She'd needed to get out of Farleigh in a hurry, and Cousin Charlotte had been able and willing to help her out. Blanche would have left Boston by now if it weren't for Taifa and Malik. They'd been in three different school systems in as many years. It didn't feel right to ask them to move again.

She waited for the light to change at Jamaica Way and Perkins Street, where the traffic was moving at expressway speed. She looked down Jamaica Way with its huge houses on one side and the pond on the other. Nice. When the light changed, she hurried across and walked on toward Centre Street, where she'd get the bus. It was a longish walk. Miz Inez had offered her banged-up car, but Blanche had seen enough of Boston driving to know she didn't want to be on the road unless she had to. Anyway, her fast-approaching-fifty-year-old body could use the exercise.

She walked up Perkins Street, past big old houses that were now apartments, and over to Centre Street, where the store signs and street language were in Spanish, past the Bromely Heath

Projects to the Jackson Square bus depot next door. She was on the tip of Roxbury now. She got the number 44 bus and let her mind slip back to the other events of her first day on Miz Inez's job.

Lord! Had she really poked that man? She had a feeling she'd be hearing about *that.* Shit! And didn't Ray-Ray have a nerve, which was probably one of the reasons she liked him in spite of herself. A poor black person without nerve was a dead person. But that didn't mean she approved of his sneaking onto his mother's job to steal something, which was the only reason she could think of for him sneaking around upstairs. From what Carrie said, he was definitely no stranger to the house, but if he hadn't worked for the Brindles for at least a year, why hadn't Carrie or Wanda found his shirt and given it to Miz Inez to take home, and what did Ray-Ray mean when he said she'd be glad he came? She still didn't know what he'd been doing in the Brindle house, but she knew his shirt didn't have doodly-squat to do with it. Maybe Saxe's pictures did, although it was hard to figure out how Ray-Ray would know Saxe had left them there. But she definitely intended to ask Ray-Ray about those pictures the next time she saw him. And that Carrie! Her and her pastor and her thing for "Mr. Saxe"! Lord! did she have stories to tell Ardell. Blanche got off the bus on Humboldt and walked up the street to Rudigere Homes, eager to be on her own turf.

TWO

DAY ONE—THURSDAY

Even after all these months of living in the housing development, Blanche was still put off by the large, square, concrete court that doubled as parking lot and playground ringed by a narrow sidewalk. She was bothered by the circled-wagons feel of the place, the way the houses all turned in on the square as though snubbing the rest of the community. She knew it only looked that way. Rudigere Homes Tenants' Association met and held community events, like the kids' carnival and the barbecue in the park, with Warren Gardens and other cooperative housing tenants' associations in the area. There was really nothing wrong with the place; she just missed living on a street where people strolled by or slowed their cars to look at the flowers in somebody's bit of garden or window box, or to holler at a friend. What she liked most was that Rudigere Homes was a cooperative. She enjoyed the sense of semi-ownership that meant she wasn't going to be asked to move because the landlord's cousin's girlfriend needed a place to stay, or the building was being condo'd.

She also liked the development's redbrick houses with their alert, lean faces and high narrow stoops. Each house had a postage-stamp square of grass and a baby tree flanking the front door. They were houses with few frills, but their no-nonsense attitude made her feel safe. They looked like houses that wouldn't take no mess.

She was still only on nodding terms with the four or five folks in the complex who belonged to what she called The Passing-Through Club—people who clearly saw Rudigere Homes as a stepping-stone to a house in Milton or Dedham or some other suburb, so they didn't have time for folks who planned to stay. She got along fine with the rest of the residents, including plump, slow-moving Joanie, who lived next door. Like Blanche, Joanie had raised her dead sister's two children, only Joanie's two were now in college on full scholarships. Jack and Evelyn Morton—a young couple with two little kids—lived directly across the square. More than once Blanche had heard shouting coming from their house and went to the window in time to see Jack storm out and slam the door behind him. The three Saint Pointer Sisters lived side by side. They weren't really sisters, and from the way they screamed at their kids, she doubted they were saints. The three women and a couple of their older children sang in a gospel group that traveled around giving concerts. But when they practiced at home, they always sang "Shaky Flat Blues" and "Love in Them There Hills." The other families on the square included the Porters, an elderly sister and brother, and Miz Murphy and her grown son, Tongues. Miz Murphy spent a lot of time yelling at the children for playing in front of her house and did a lot of her shopping at Warren Liquors. Mr. and Mrs. Addison lived in the last house. Joanie said they were in their late eighties. Every evening, rain or shine, they ambled five times around the court, holding hands and laughing together like any other lovers. Then there was Karen.

Blanche hurried by the house three doors from her own, almost tiptoeing in the hope of getting by without having to pay what she'd started calling The Karen Subsidy. But Karen was either watching at the window or had a sixth sense that told her when a possible contributor was within borrowing distance. She came lumbering out of her front door in a housedress so dingy, its pattern was almost a memory. She scuffled toward Blanche in her beat-up bedroom shoes. Blanche set her mouth to give Karen a faceful of "No!" Blanche was always ready to help out a neighbor with a cup of this or that, especially if the neighbor was worse off than she was. But Karen's husband and oldest, living-at-home daughter both had jobs, plus Karen was collecting disability. Yet the items she borrowed and never replaced were growing, from a bit of cornmeal to slices of bacon, from salt to tampons.

"Hiya doin', Blanche? I was just heading for your house. One of my kids got a sore throat. You got any honey?"

Blanche stared at her. Damn! How was she supposed to say no to a sick child? She rolled her eyes at Karen but motioned for her to come along. She showed her pique by making Karen wait outside on the stoop while she fetched the honey instead of inviting her inside. A person had to fight back any way she could.

It wasn't yet dinnertime, so she decided to cook instead of letting the children have the soup and sandwiches they'd have had if she hadn't gotten home early. She gathered her favorite mixing bowl, an iron skillet, and a large loaf pan. Being home early also meant she'd be here when Shaquita came over.

The only painless part of standing in for Miz Inez was Shaquita, Cousin Charlotte's live-in granddaughter. Cousin Charlotte wasn't about to leave a sixteen-year-old home alone for a week, no matter how much Shaquita argued that she was old enough to take care of herself. So Shaquita was staying with Blanche, who was pleased to have the girl around to show Malik and Taifa how a responsible teen behaved.

Shaquita's presence also ensured that someone would be at home with Malik and Taifa before and after school. Blanche decided to give the girl some extra cash in addition to the money she was already paying her to help Taifa with her Spanish and Malik with his English.

Blanche peeled and quartered eight potatoes and put them in a pot with some salt water. She checked the clock. She had about twenty minutes of conversation time before the kids got home—time enough for a quick chat. She'd dialed the 919 area code and half of Ardell's phone number before she remembered her old friend was off playing nanny on some yacht. It didn't feel natural to be out of touch with Ardell. They'd always been on the phone to each other, even when Blanche was hiding from the police and when Ardell was hiding from her crazy-assed and now ex-husband. Blanche sulked for a few minutes, until she heard Ardell tell her to get over it.

Blanche had just diced an onion and a couple cloves of garlic and was about to sauté them when she realized she was no longer alone in the house. She wouldn't have known Malik had come home and gone right up to his room if she'd had to depend on her ears alone. It was her ability to sense when people she cared about were nearby that sent her upstairs. Although his door was open, he looked at her as though she'd caught him doing something he shouldn't have been. Lately, she was shocked every time she saw him. Just last year he was a chubby, stocky little boy who loved being hugged and tickled and never went to bed without a goodnight kiss. Now he was tall and lanky, with a voice she barely recognized. And she wasn't ready to think about who he might be kissing.

"Yo, Mom."

Or at least she thought that's what he said. "You hungry?" she asked, going somewhere she felt on solid ground. He shook his head and continued emptying his backpack onto his bed. She watched him from the doorway for a few moments, his bowed head and bent neck so unprotected, so young. She saw him curled up next to her hanging on to every word of the story she was reading to him; she saw him learning the alphabet and so proudly reading a story on his own for the very first time. Now his room was full of books she'd never heard of. He'd be thirteen soon. Was she giving him what he needed to take his next step, to run the obstacle course of teenhood into adulthood? There was so much he didn't know about growing up and girls and ego and pain. She hoped she'd be able to find the words when she needed them. She could hear music leaking from under his door almost the moment he shut it. She went back to the kitchen. At least I know where he is, she thought as the beat made the walls throb. She sautéed the onion and garlic and dumped them into her big crockery mixing bowl. She added a pound and a half each of ground turkey and ground beef.

"I'm home!" Taifa announced loud enough for the neighbors to hear her even with the front door closed, which it wasn't. Blanche waited for it to slam. It took so long, she began to suspect Taifa of having some of her all-look-and-dress-alike girlfriends trailing in the house behind her—all sporting the same stiff-as-straw hairdo and enough earrings to stock a store. Blanche strode into the living room. Taifa knew homework came before company. But instead of friends, she found Taifa lugging a carton of candy bars—her school's latest scheme to save the arts and athletics programs. Taifa dropped the box, kissed Blanche on the cheek, then dragged the box into the coat closet. Blanche figured there must be a hundred bars of candy in the box, but she didn't complain. Taifa could sell fleas to a dog and make him come back for more at a higher price. Blanche had once seen her convince their stingiest neighbor to buy candy he swore he didn't even like. But that was last year, before Taifa's new boom-box voice and cracking gum.

Blanche went back to the kitchen and added a couple tablespoons of tomato paste and a splash of milk to the mixing bowl. Taifa switched on the radio in the living room and began ooh-baby-babying in a high, screechy voice.

"Moms!" Taifa shouted during the commercial.

Blanche waited for whatever was to follow and wished the changes in Taifa didn't bother her so much. She also wished Taifa and Malik would go back to calling her "Mama Blanche" instead of "Mom" or "Moms." She knew who they were talking to when they used her name. As they got older, "Mom" and "Moms" felt like jobs that could be filled by anyone willing to do the work without either of the children taking much notice of the change.

The song on the radio segued into a commercial for blemish cream.

The phone rang. "It's for me!" Taifa shouted.

Blanche sight-measured some cumin and chili powder into the bowl and marveled at how quickly the girl's voice went from a bullhorn to a phone whisper so low Blanche couldn't hear a word.

Taifa danced into the kitchen and opened the refrigerator. "Moms! Can you get me some new rollers when you go to the store?" She stared into the fridge as though it were a TV. "I seen these new bendy kinda curlers they be better than the…"

Blanche sighed over the "they be better" but let it pass. She knew Taifa was bilingual. She also knew Taifa was trying to out-'hood girls who'd spent their entire lives in this community. It was Taifa's way of making up for having been a private-school girl her first year in Boston. The school counselor had told Blanche it was just a phase the child would outgrow once she settled in and made some friends. But Taifa was now on the volleyball team and the school newspaper and had more friends than Blanche and Malik combined. As far as Blanche could see, there still hadn't been any change in her wannabeness.

"… really dope curlers, Moms. My hair will look so fine!"

Taifa reached into the fridge. Blanche sent her to the sink to wash her hands.

She took milk and peanut butter from the fridge. "Moms! Did you hear me?"

As if she could avoid it. Didn't people in Ohio hear her? "I heard you, Taifa. Like I've told you a hundred times, if you want new rollers, you gotta buy them with your own money. I won't have anything to do with you frying your hair up like a batch of pork chops. Now, if you want to get your hair cornrowed, dread it, or just wear it natural, I'll be glad to…"

"Moms! You are so out of it. I mean truly, really, totally out of it!" Taifa slapped a sandwich together and flopped down at the kitchen table. "You said I could do what I wanted with my hair, but you won't let me do nothing I want to with it."

Blanche dumped some bread crumbs into the meat loaf mixture. Taifa gave her a look as sour as month-old milk.

"What I said was that you could be in charge of your hair on three conditions: no dye, no extensions, and you pay for all your hair stuff with your own money."

Taifa poked out her mouth. "You just want me to look like a geek. You don't care if my friends laugh at me and talk about me and stuff." She bit into her sandwich.

Blanche washed her hands, then squished meat loaf ingredients together and tried not to pretend it was Taifa's tender throat between her hands. She took a deep breath.

"I ain't even sure what a geek is, and I don't want nobody to make fun of you, baby, including yourself, which is what you'll be doing if you grow up to be a black woman who thinks your hair's gotta be processed or have extensions made out of Dacron or some poor Indian woman's sacrificial hair to be beautiful." Blanche mentally patted herself on the back for sounding so reasonable and even-tempered. She turned the meat loaf into the pan, covered the potatoes with a bit more water, and went on.

"Look, if I had my way, every black person in the world would wear their hair in some kind of natural style instead of making themselves look foolish imitating white folks' hair."

"Oh, Moms! That race stuff is *so* old! I keep tellin' you, it ain't even about white people. I—"

Blanche held up her hand. "Yeah, yeah. So you say. I think it is about white folks. I think it's about being ashamed of having nappy hair."

"Yeah, but my girlfriends' mothers don't..."

Blanche felt her left nerve beginning to fray. She couldn't seem to stop herself from reacting to this holdover from years of having Mama tell her she needed to be more like Miz Mary's or Miz Caroline's daughters, who'd be happy to lick the kitchen floor clean, let alone mop it, if their dear old mother even looked like she wanted the floor cleaned.

"... and Rasheeda's mother said she'd never let Rasheeda go out with naps all over her head like some kinda ..."

That did it! Blanche spun around and leaned across the table so that her face was close to Taifa's. "Now, I've let you get your hair straightened. Even let you get a permanent. If that ain't good enough for you, put a paper bag over your head and stop bugging me about it!"

Taifa looked at her as though Blanche had just invented child abuse.

Damn! She'd been doing that calm-parent thing so well there for a minute. Most of the time she remembered the cost of childhood to the child and tried to act accordingly, but it didn't always work. Taifa twisted around in her chair so that Blanche couldn't see her face. Blanche slammed the meat loaf into the oven and set the timer.

"I'm going to see Miz Barker," she told Taifa. "When the timer rings, please take the meat loaf out of the oven and put on the potatoes."

Taifa sucked her teeth hard enough to loosen a couple. "Why I got to do everything? Why can't Malik take out the meat loaf? Why I always ..."

Blah, blah, blah, Blanche mouthed behind the girl's back. She put on her sweater and took her handbag down from its hook. She was out the door before Taifa finished complaining.

Four little girls were jumping rope across the way:

"Miss Mary Mack, Mack, Mack,
All dressed in black, black, black ..."

Their voices were as light and high as birdsong. Blanche's toes twitched with double-Dutch memory. If she wasn't headed somewhere, she'd go ask them for a turn. She waved to Evelyn, pushing the baby's stroller around the square. The security guard waved to them as he U-turned in the parking lot. He was another reason she felt lucky to be in Rudigere Homes. The development had hired a security company that kept a guard on the premises, or near the premises—whichever guard was on duty seemed to spend 90 percent of his time down the hill and around the corner at McDonald's. But at least the tenants had his cell phone number if something happened.

As usual, traffic on M. L. King Boulevard was like a practice track for the Indy 500. Music loud enough to make your ears bleed was pumping out of every fourth car, usually driven by somebody who looked like he needed to be at home doing homework. A long, slow funeral procession nearly brought traffic to a walk. Cars going in the opposite direction reduced their speed as well.

"It's the Franklin boy," a passing man said to his companion. "It's a damned shame, too. I don't know what's gotten into these kids."

Sunlight glinted off the hood and bumper of the hearse, turning it into a silver shield that hid some poor mother's grief. Another child killed by a child. There'd been four killings in eight weeks, as though the four boys arrested for the murders had declared open season on themselves. She knew it wasn't permanent. Teen killings had gone way down over the last couple years. The police liked to take credit for it, but the cops couldn't stop it alone. The children had clearly decided there was no benefit in seeing so many of their friends die. But every once in a while, there was an outbreak that reminded her there were still some teenagers using bullets to solve their differences. Of course, it was easier for them to get guns and sell drugs than it was for them to get decent educations or jobs. Now folks in D.C. were acting all surprised about the possibility that the CIA was involved in shipping drugs into black communities—like black folks hadn't known that for years. These kids sure as hell weren't flying the stuff into the country.

No matter who started it or who kept it going, kids killing one another frightened her like nothing else she could think of. Taifa and Malik had given her a bucketful of grief when she'd tightened their curfew and demanded that they phone her if their plans changed the slightest bit. But she'd also recognized a light of relief in their eyes. It seemed it was true about teens wanting limits, although she didn't recall wanting any at their age. She crossed the street once the procession passed, resisting the urge to turn around and hurry home to see what her kids were up to.

She walked up the block to Miz Barker's store. As usual, she marveled that the building was still standing. Its single gray story leaned against the house next door for support. The two steps down into the little space sagged as if they held the weight of the world. Inside, the store was dark and cool and smelled of dust, stale candy, and old paper. Miz Barker sat on her high-backed stool behind the cash register. Nothing moved but her eyes.

"Hey, Miz Barker. How you doin' today?"

Leathery eyelids blinked slow as a sunning lizard's.

"I can't complain, daughter. I can't complain." She shifted on her stool. "Glad you doin' what you doin'. I know you don't care for Inez Brown."

Blanche wasn't surprised Miz Barker knew about her standing in for Miz Inez. Miz Barker knew everybody's business, almost before they knew it themselves. But Ardell was the only person to whom Blanche recalled telling her feelings for Miz Inez. It was useless to ask Miz Barker how she knew what she knew. She would only stare at you as though you were a talking cockroach.

"It's true Miz Inez ain't exactly a favorite of mine, but…"

"Oh I know, I know," Miz Barker said. "Family's family And Charlotte' s a whole lotta woman to say no to."

How in hell could Miz B know about her conversation with Cousin Charlotte? Blanche just shook her head and smiled.

"I ain't ever been able to warm up to Inez much myself, but I always liked that boy of hern, no matter what they say about him."

Blanche wasn't quite up to singing praise songs to Ray-Ray today, so she applied the lesson her kids were teaching her about not having to have an answer to every comment and said nothing. She looked around the store.

"All the mess is gone," she said.

"Got the last of it cleared out last night. I hope them little thugs is through with me now."

So did Blanche. Miz Barker's store had been broken into and trashed three times since she'd barred a bunch of boys from her store after she'd caught one of them stealing.

"You best watch out. Them thugs'll be hangin' round your place now."

"Why would they do that, Miz B?"

Miz Barker gave Blanche a pitying look. "You don't know much, do you? Well you'll be finding out. Ain't my place to—"

"Miz Barker, if there' s something I need to know about Taifa and Malik..."

"Ain't nothing goin' on with them two of yourn. I'd tell you if there was."

"Then what?"

"Got that girl stayin' with you, don't you? What you expect? Boy still like girl, last I heard."

"Shaquita? I doubt whether she's fast enough for that bunch."

"Useta give them little hoodlums candy when they was babies. Now..." Miz Barker looked so frail and disappointed, Blanche wanted to hug her—a very different urge from the one the old woman had first aroused in her.

Before Blanche bought into the cooperative, they'd lived in an apartment around the corner from Miz Barker's store. Blanche and Miz Barker had had words after Taifa came home from the store and told Blanche what Miz Barker said about hincty negroes sending their children to private school so they'd grow up thinking they were better than other black people. Blanche had gone to the store and called Miz B on her signifying, telling her that where Malik and Taifa went to school was none of her business, unless she was planning to pay for their education.

That conversation seemed to have convinced Miz Barker that it was better for them to be friends. She'd taken Blanche and the children into her inner circle of special care, which meant she was deep in Blanche's business and full of advice on everything from what kind of underwear Blanche should buy Taifa to the best deodorant for Malik.

Now Blanche asked for a box of toothpicks and a can of Ajax, neither of which she needed. Like many people in the neighborhood, she frequented Miz Barker's store more to keep the store alive than out of necessity. Miz Barker was a cantankerous old woman with mostly useless stock and prices higher than the supermarkets. But her store had survived for nearly sixty years. Joanie, Blanche's neighbor, said she and her childhood friends had made their first candy transaction here and that Miz Barker had been the adult of last resort for many a troubled child who now credited her with keeping them out of jail or worse.

While Miz Barker shuffled around collecting and bagging Blanche's purchases, Blanche wondered what was in those dust-encrusted boxes on the very top shelves of the store. They'd been up there so long, dirt and age had combined to turn them all a uniform shade of greasy brown.

"That granddaughter of mine is come to stay, you know. Weren't my idea."

Blanche looked sympathetic but she wasn't really. Somebody around the house and store was just what Miz Barker needed right now. The boys who'd been hanging in front of the store were gone for the moment, but they'd be back. Where else could they go? The recreation centers were overflowing, the basketball courts were packed, and she doubted they were involved in extracurricular stuff at school.

"She all upset 'bout these break-ins. Wants me to have a keeper, I guess. Like I ain't got sense enough to come in out the rain. Like I'm a child."

Blanche had met Miz Barker's granddaughter, Pam, for the first time last year and liked her right away.

"She must love you a lot to change her life around and come stay with you for a while. Putting family first. You must be real proud of her."

"Humph. Oughtta be findin' a man and having babies 'stead of tryin' to make one outta me."

Blanche inched toward the door without replying. She'd said what she had to say. Life was too short to try to soften this tough old bird.

"Wait! I'm closin' up right now. I'll walk out with you."

Now Blanche was doubly glad Pam had come to look after Miz Barker. There were neighborhood stories about Miz Barker's independence, about how she'd refuse a ride, even when it was raining; about her turning down offers to walk her home, even in the winter when it was icy and dark by store-closing time. The break-ins had clearly frightened the old woman in a way Blanche had thought nothing could. Blanche walked her around the corner and up the block to her house.

Shaquita's suitcase was standing at the bottom of the stairs when Blanche got home. Shaquita came in from the kitchen.

"Hey, sugar, how you doin'?"

Shaquita put her arms around Blanche. "Hi, Aunt Blanche. I'm good. How're you?"

"Glad to see your sweet self."

They walked arm in arm into the kitchen.

"Hey, you two."

"Hi, Mom." Taifa was setting the table.

Malik slipped the meat loaf out of the pan onto a platter. "Yo, Moms."

She looked at the table, at the mashed potatoes Shaquita was working on, the warmed-up greens waiting to be dished up. Shaquita had even made the gravy. "Shaquita, honey, I can see it's going to be a real pleasure having you around."

Shaquita smiled in the way that always made Blanche want to squeeze her. She had a full-cheeked, pug-nosed face with something delicate about the set of her mouth that probably fooled some people into thinking she was timid.

"I don't want you waitin' on these two, Quita." Blanche sliced the meat loaf. "The list of their chores is on the refrigerator. Don't let them give you no excuses, and don't let them leave this house till they've finished their chores. Same goes for homework. And just let me know if anybody gives you a hard time." She gave Taifa and Malik a warning look.

"I'm going to pay you extra to manage these two."

"Supervising us!" Malik and Taifa shouted in unison, temporarily united in their indignation. The similarity in their expressions highlighted how much they looked alike—red-brown, hazel-eyed images of their dead daddy with their mother's high cheekbones.

Taifa put her hand on her hip. "I surely don't need nobody to manage me! I can manage or—"

"You can hardly manage to get to school!" Malik hooted.

"An archaeologist. That's what I want to be." Shaquita said. "Too bad I have to go to college to do it. I wish I could just—"

"Phew! Digging in the dirt and touching old dead people and stuff! You must be crazy," Taifa told her. "I'd rather be a talk-show host or a model."

Malik hooted. "A model? With that face? Not unless they're looking for the most funny looking—"

"You ain't the finest thing in the world either, you know." Taifa rolled her eyes at him.

"But just think," Shaquita went on, "I might find the tomb of some African queen that nobody'd been in since she died."

"Yeah," Malik said. "It could be full of her jewels and things and the walls all covered with paintings and—"

"Yeah, but it'd still be dirty. And hot. Not for me! I want a job with air conditioning," Taifa said.

Blanche doubted Taifa would grow up to be a talk-show host, because she liked to do all the talking, or a model, unless there was going to be a call for models with hips. But she was pretty sure that whatever the girl did, there would be air conditioning.

When Blanche left the kitchen, Malik and Taifa were arguing over whose turn it was to wash dishes. Shaquita went upstairs to unpack. Malik and Taifa knew that if the dishes weren't done by nine, both of them would be grounded for three days—without music or phone calls, in or out. The kids had told her this was cruel and unusual punishment. Blanche thought of it as a way to get the dishes done without having her left nerve frayed to a frazzle.

When the bell rang, Blanche went to the front door prepared to say this wasn't a good time for Malik or Taifa to have company, or, no, Taifa or Malik couldn't come to the door right now.

"Ray-Ray! Just the person I wanted to talk to. Come on in." She stepped back from the door.

Ray-Ray looked excited and even more lively than usual. He moved around on the stoop like he was eager to start jogging or doing jumping jacks.

"No thanks, Blanche." Ray-Ray shifted from foot to foot, flexing arm muscles that looked too big for his skin, as if a pin-prick would burst his biceps like overdone sausages. "I need you to do me a favor," he said.

"Yeah, well, I need to talk to you about this afternoon first. I really don't appreciate you showing up on my job, your mama's job, like some kinda cat burglar. What if somebody caught you? Miz Inez mighta got fired behind that shit!"

"Aw, c'mon, Blanche."

"Don't c'mon, Blanche, me ! You was wrong and you know it." She paused to give weight to her words, then added, "Now tell me what you took."

"No, Blanche, I don't think that's a good idea. You—"

"Did you take Saxe's pictures? Or was it something else? Tell me the truth, Ray-Ray."

He stepped back a step. "Pictures? What pictures?" He took a square, cream-colored envelope out of his jacket pocket. "Give this to Allister," he said.

The envelope had Allister's name printed on the front.

Blanche didn't know why, but she didn't want to touch it. She looked from the envelope to Ray-Ray. "Is this about what you took from the house? What's going on, Ray-Ray? Why can't you give him the note yourself? Or put it in the mailbox?"

He stopped jiggling and looked directly at her. "It's just better this way. Quicker. And I don't want to go back up there again right now. Just tell him you found it in front of the mail slot." He held the envelope out to her. "Please."

"Ray-Ray, what are you up to?"

He gave her a devilish smile. "You are going to love it, Blanche. Trust me. It'll be good for everybody in Massachusetts—maybe even the country."

Ray-Ray looked directly into her eyes and spoke as though he believed what he was saying. Maybe that was what made her believe him. Maybe she just wanted to. He thrust the envelope at her again. This time she took it.

"But what's in it?" she asked him.

"You can't tell what you don't know," he said. He waved before jumping off the stoop.

Blanche slowly closed the door, still looking at the envelope. Something told her she was going to be sorry about this. She slipped the envelope in the zipper compartment of her handbag.

Later, she thought about calling Miz Barker before it got too late, still uncomfortable about Miz Barker's request for an escort home. But then she remembered that Miz Barker wasn't alone; Pam was there. A checkup phone call *and* a caretaker granddaughter would likely send the old girl into a major hissy fit.

THREE

DAY TWO—FRIDAY

Place oughtta be called Prozac House, Blanche mumbled to herself. The Brindle house was practically bouncing with Upness.

Carrie came down the back stairs and slid Felicia's picked-over breakfast tray onto the kitchen counter. "Miz Felicia wants you, Blanche. She said bring up some fresh coffee, too."

Here it comes, Blanche thought. On the way to work she'd wondered what Felicia was going to do about the Samuelson thing. She was sure Felicia had seen her. She'd thought about how to handle this on the bus, so she was ready; she just wished she didn't have to be. She took a deep breath and tapped on Felicia's door.

Felicia was sitting at her desk looking through some papers. Something about the angle of her head and the extra concentration she was giving to what she was doing made Blanche think she was pretending to be busy.

"Good morning, ma'am. You wanted to see me?" She set the coffee tray on the far end of Felicia's desk.

Felicia continued to flip pages for a few more seconds, then hitched her chair around. She looked up at Blanche and quickly away.

"Good morning, Blanche."

Felicia looked as though she'd spent the night with five horny young men who'd made her jump hurdles between bouts of being jumped herself. Even her hair looked beat.

"Tonight's the big night, you know. The big man makes his bid for the big job. It's all so big, isn't it?" She poured her own coffee and took a sip.

Blanche took a mental step backward. This wasn't the conversation she'd expected. Maybe Felicia *hadn't* seen her poke Samuelson.

Felicia picked up a sheet of paper from her desk and turned the subject to changes in the household schedule. She told Blanche that Allister would be campaigning in Springfield on Saturday and Sunday and would be gone until early Monday morning. They'd both be out for lunch and dinner on Monday. While Allister Brindle's run for governor surely wasn't in any poor person's best interest, having him out glad-handing was going to make Blanche's work life a little easier. She relaxed her guard against being put on the hot seat and half listened to what Felicia was saying until she realized it centered on her.

"Inez's note says you need to leave early today, Blanche." Felicia's smile quivered like it was nervous. "But that's not why I sent for you."

Shoulda known, Blanche thought. Miss Mistress just likes to play with people. Shoulda known. Needing somebody to yo-yo was pretty common among women she'd worked for whose powerful husbands treated them like toys. She gave Felicia an inquiring look.

"Yes, ma'am?"

Felicia avoided Blanche's eyes. "I saw the quote accident unquote you had with Reverend Samuelson. What do you have to say for yourself?"

Blanche had to concentrate on not laughing. Was this fool joking? What did she have to say for herself? Did Felicia think this was grade school and she was the schoolmarm? Oughtta tell her "kiss my butt" is what I got to say for myself! Instead, she stared at Felicia as though she had half an avocado stuck to her forehead.

"Well?" Felicia crossed her arms over her chest.

"Well, what, ma'am?" Blanche's right hand rose, unbidden, to her hip.

"Please don't take that attitude with me, Blanche. I could have fired you the moment you touched him. I still might."

"Well, ma'am, you got a right to have whoever you want working for you, but you can't fire me because this isn't my job. It's Inez Brown's job. I believe she's been working for y'all for some years. Of course, you can get somebody in from an agency until Inez gets back, which is fine with me. I just hope you aren't planning to fire Inez for something you seem to think I did, although I'm not quite sure what it is I'm supposed to have done... ma'am." Blanche watched Felicia figure out how much trouble would be involved in finding a new housekeeper-cook just to finish out the week.

Felicia nodded her head a couple of times. "You know how to protect yourself, I'll give you that." She let her hands fall into her lap. "You're not going to tell me the truth, are you? I wouldn't if I were you. But let me say that I saw what you did to Reverend Samuelson. I don't know what he said or did to you, but men being men, I can imagine. Nevertheless, I cannot allow such behavior in my house. Do you understand?"

She was going fine till that last question, Blanche thought. Now it's back to grade school. But Felicia wasn't through.

"You don't think I understand at all, do you?" She looked into Blanche's eyes for just a second. "You think because I'm... You think I don't know how it feels to have someone disrespect you so badly you just have to..."

She ain't trying to convince me she knows something about life, is she? Blanche asked herself. Probably thinks being disrespected means having somebody come late to her dinner party. Blanche had no thought of confessing, but if she had, Felicia's doing the I-feel-your-pain thing wouldn't have changed her mind. Confessing was something she did with people she trusted, people who cared about her. People in her world. Her world and Felicia's were on different planets. Only one of them ever took the spaceship called the city bus to the other's planet. Felicia's attempt to get her to stab herself in the back was evidence that only one of them lived in the real world.

Blanche watched Felicia closely, waiting for her to finish her sentence. When they'd first met, Blanche had noticed that Felicia was one of those employers who actually looked you in the eye and spoke directly to you instead of acting like you were a machine they spoke into to get their meals cooked and their drawers washed. But Felicia wasn't making much eye contact today. For while Felicia acted like what they were talking about was important, in the pauses between what Felicia had to say, Blanche could feel the woman slipping away to think about something more pressing—something that was making Felicia look like a vampire's leftovers.

"Well, as you say, it's only temporary," Felicia said at last.

She handed Blanche two small white envelopes—one with Blanche's name, and one with Carrie's name written on the front of it. Blanche put the pay envelopes in her pocket. She hadn't expected to get paid today since she'd only been on the job for two days, but she liked the fact that Felicia paid her on the regular day anyway.

"Will there be anything else, ma'am?"

"No, Blanche, there's been more than enough already."

Blanche was glad Carrie wasn't around when she got back to the kitchen. She needed a few minutes alone to take herself to task in a way Felicia couldn't. She plopped into a chair and leaned her elbows on the kitchen table. How could she have been so sloppy? Had she even looked around to see if anyone was watching? Samuelson had just pissed her off so badly! Still, she should have been more careful.

She rose in anticipation of a tap on the back door.

"Hi. I'm Mick Harper, Mrs. Brindle's masseuse."

She had the same red-brown coloring that Taifa and Malik had inherited from their Creole daddy.

Blanche stepped back so Mick could enter. "Blanche White," she said, "Pleased to meet you. I'm holding down Inez's job while she's on vacation."

If Mick Harper's mannish haircut, bone-crushing handshake, and butch walk didn't deliver her message, her purple T-shirt did. I CAN'T EVEN THINK STRAIGHT was plastered across her chest in hot-pink letters. She was one of those midsize women who managed to make themselves seem taller and bigger by the way they moved their bodies. Blanche was tickled. She knew instinctively that Felicia's having a very out lesbian masseuse was meant to be a slap at that righteous-assed Allister.

"Love that shirt," she said.

Mick grinned and pushed her granny glasses further up her freckled nose. She lowered her eyes when she smiled in a way that gave Blanche a glimpse of someone who was not quite as brash as Mick's big bad woman front.

"She ready for me?" Mick gestured with her head toward the second floor, exactly as Wanda and Blanche and, Blanche suspected, hundreds of thousands of other women did every day when referring to their employers.

"If acting shifty-eyed and nervous is what you mean by ready, I guess she is."

"She have breakfast?"

"If that's what you want to call it."

"They fight?" Mick asked. "They usually do when she has to play the politico's wife. Didn't he have some kind of campaign lunch yesterday? She wanted me to come early yesterday morning, but I was booked. Well, let me get to it." Mick stomped up the back stairs.

When Mick came back down, the kitchen table was set with cups and plates for three. A plump carrot cake adorned the middle of the table flanked by a plate each of sliced-turkey-and-Havarti sandwiches and one of smoked salmon and Boursin.

Mick didn't hide her surprise. "Wow! Food! I don't think Miz Inez would approve, not unless you're planning to charge me. You'd swear she was paying for the groceries around here."

"Well, I won't tell her if you don't." Blanche waved Mick to a chair. "Carrie should be through in a little bit. I don't think she'll mind if we start without her."

Mick gave Blanche a skeptical look. "You don't really think Carrie's gonna sit down and have lunch with me, do you?"

"Bet you a nickel food will win out over foolishness," Blanche said.

"You're on." Mick straddled a chair and helped herself to a couple of sandwiches. Blanche allowed her a few bites before she began asking questions. This wasn't exactly a free lunch. She'd never met a black masseuse before. She was all but drooling with curiosity.

"You been doin' this kinda work long?"

Mick screwed her snubbed nose and thinnish lips into an *I'm thinking* arrangement and pushed up her glasses again.

" 'Bout eight years." She took a huge bite of her sandwich.

"Started with a Swedish girlfriend," she said, talking around half a mouthful. She gave Blanche a challenging look and hesitated a beat.

Blanche figured the look must be about the Swedish girlfriend's color, since they'd already jumped over the sexual preference hurdle. She waited for Mick to go on.

"Ingrid was into massage, got me interested. I went to the Massage Institute in Waltham, got my certification, and quit my job at the phone company." Mick reached for another sandwich.

"So, you do good business?"

"I do okay. Being my own boss, in charge of my own time, makes up for what I lose in cash."

"I know just what you mean." Blanche filled Mick's coffee cup. "Course, your clients probably recommend you to people, same as mine. I know that helps."

"Oh sure. I work on all Felicia's friends now."

"She seems decent enough."

"Felicia? She's okay, I guess," Mick said.

Blanche waited for her to go on, but Mick finished her sandwich in silence.

"So, Felicia's a good employer?" Blanche prompted.

Mick shrugged. Crumbs dotted the corner of her mouth. "She's okay, I guess."

"You already told me that. But that don't tell me much." Blanche failed in her plan to keep irritation out of her voice. What did these Brindles do to hush up the help? First Carrie and now Mick.

Mick fiddled with her coffee cup but didn't speak.

If politeness didn't open her up, maybe a little jab would help. "Of course, not everyone knows how to get information about the people they work for."

"Oh, I know how to get it, all right," Mick huffed. "I'm just not sure I oughtta be talking about my client's business."

"Well, I don't know how it is in *your* business," Blanche told her, "but in my business, information is just like a pot or a broom, just another something I use to do my job in a way that works for all concerned, just like you need to know if your client's got a bad back or a tricky kidney so you can give them the best service. And anyway, I'm working for Felicia, too. So, this is just a little talk between two professionals about our mutual client."

Mick laughed.

"Now, tell me everything." Curiosity made Blanche nearly squirm in her chair.

"Everything like what?"

"Well, how'd these two wind up together, for a start. Or don't you know?" Blanche put plenty of challenge in her voice.

Mick leaned back in her chair. "I know, all right, Blanche. It ain't about not knowing."

"Well?"

"Well, Felicia met Allister at an anti–Vietnam War rally in college. It sounds weird, now that Allister's become Mr. Right-Wing Republican. But it's true. Felicia was big in Women Against the War, or something like that, and Allister burned his draft card."

Blanche snorted. "Figures. I bet Allister was more interested in keeping his butt outta the line of fire than he was in ending the war!"

"Tell me about it," Mick said. "But Felicia sure thought he was the real deal. She said he was magnificent back then. That's the exact word she used."

"Then what the hell happened? She acts like she can hardly stand him now."

Mick shrugged. "Allister changed after they settled down and had a kid. At first she thought his right-wing thing was Allister's way of sucking up to his grandfather, making sure he got all of whatever the old man had to leave. Or at least that's what one of Felicia's girlfriends told me. But Allister was just showing his true colors. He didn't switch back to being a liberal when the old man died. That's what I don't understand: Why a good-looking, intelligent woman with goo-gobs of money, who claims to be against war and poverty, and a feminist and all, stays with a man who now says he hates everything he used to believe in, everything she still believes in."

"Well, there's believing and believing," Blanche said. "Maybe she believes in being Mrs. Overclass just a little bit more than she believes in peace and feminism."

Mick looked disgusted. "You're probably right. She sure don't have no problem letting you know—in a very nice way, of course—that she's a big deal in this town. Allister's related to people who own this state. Or should I say, people who killed the

Indians and stole their land? Being his wife means something whether he's a Republican or walks around in a monkey suit. Being his ex-wife don't mean jack, and being a liberal don't mean nothing nowhere, these days."

Blanche thought about the difference between this picture of Felicia and the one Wanda had painted. She had no doubt that both versions were true. Like everyone else, Felicia was put together with pieces from different jigsaw puzzles so you got a little bit of a tree, half of a horse's leg, and a bit of lake that taken together meant something different from anything the individual pieces showed.

"Honey, I was wrong about you! You are *deep* in these folks' business!" Blanche said. Nothing like a little flattery to keep a person's tongue loose.

"Oh, Felicia's not my only source," Mick told her. "It's really kinda funny. While I'm working on them, Felicia and all her friends tell me rosy stories about their own lives and all the sad and juicy stuff about their friends. Told in the most sympathetic way, of course, at least on the surface. But you have to ask yourself... Anyway, I don't get a lot of information directly from the source, but I sure get plenty from the girlfriends. If I hear the same story from three of them, I figure it's probably mostly true. And, man, do they have stories to tell! I'm thinking about writing a book one of these days."

"I hope you're planning to hire a good lawyer."

Mick laughed. "And a couple of bodyguards, too. These real upper-crust girls hate it when their shit gets in the street."

Blanche wasn't ready to move on to Mick's alternative career; she Blanche cut Mick a healthy slice of cake. "What about their son?"

"Marc. Him and Allister fight a lot. Marc lives right over in Arlington, not a half hour away. Close enough to visit, but never does."

"I wonder what they fight about."

Mick ducked her head and picked at the crumbs on her plate. "Usual father-son bullshit, probably."

She knows something, Blanche thought, and wondered what Mick didn't want to tell.

"Felicia meets Marc for lunch a couple times a month," Mick went on. "I used to think she did it just to piss Allister off. But she talks about Marc like my mom talks about my brother—like there was something real special between 'em."

Carrie came down the back stairs and stared first at the sandwiches and cake and then at Blanche and Mick.

"Just in time. Have a seat." Blanche held her breath.

Carrie took a step forward and one back. She put her hands in her apron pockets and took them out. She looked at the sandwiches again. Blanche could almost feel Mick adding another layer of protection around her most sensitive self.

"I think you'll like these salmon sandwiches," Blanche said to Carrie. "Would you rather have juice than coffee?" she asked as if there was no doubt Carrie was going to join them.

Carrie eased onto the chair in front of her place setting. Under the table, Blanche poked Mick on the thigh and held out her hand for her nickel. Mick dug into her pocket and slipped the coin to Blanche. Blanche grinned and offered Carrie the sandwiches. Breaking bread with a lesbian. A step in the right direction, even though Carrie couldn't make eye contact with Mick. Blanche wondered if Mick would change the conversation now that Carrie had joined them, and was pleased when she didn't.

"I thought Allister Brindle was going to have a heart attack the first time he saw me!" Mick laughed. "Yeah, I'll always remember that day."

"You think that's why she hired you?"

Mick didn't pretend not to know what Blanche was talking about.

"I used to, when I first found out what a right-wing asshole Allister is. In the beginning, every time I came here, she made sure he saw me. I felt like I was being used to jag him. That was before I realized how good I am at what I do. Now I charge her extra because I'm working in a hostile environment." She put out her palm. Blanche slapped it and laughed.

"I pray for him every night," Carrie said. She kept her eyes on her sandwich. "I pray that God won't make him suffer too much."

"Better to pray that bastard gets just what he deserves." Mick stood up and thanked Blanche for the lunch. "See ya Monday!"

Blanche gave Carrie her pay before Carrie went off to set the table. Blanche was ready to slip the Brindles' lunch into the microwave—something she rarely did, but she didn't feel like working over a hot stove for Allister Brindle. Anyway, she'd discovered very few people could tell the difference between the cooked and the zapped.

By the time the lunch dishes were in the dishwasher, both Brindles and Sadowski had left the house. They'd been gone about an hour when one of the three phone lines rang. Allister and Felicia each had their own lines with voice mail. Miz Inez had said the house line was the only one Blanche was responsible for answering. She checked to see if it was the one ringing. It was.

"Brindle residence."

"Inez?"

"No. Who's calling?"

"This is Marc, Marc Brindle."

"Oh. I'm Blanche White. Inez isn't here. I'm working for her this week. Your parents are both out. Do you want to leave a message?"

Silence, except for breathing.

"Hello?"

"You... you wouldn't happen to know where I can reach Inez's son, Ray-Ray, would you? He left a message on my machine, but he didn't say... I called Inez's house but there was no answer, so..."

Blanche opened her mouth to say she'd just seen Ray-Ray yesterday, but changed her mind.

"Sorry, I don't have a number for him."

Another silence.

"Your parents are both out. Would you like to leave a message for—"

"Uh, no, never mind. Thanks."

The line went dead.

"And good-bye to you, too," she said to the dial tone. Mick said Marc and Felicia were on good terms, but what kind of relationship did you have with a son who called your housekeeper and didn't even leave you a "hi"?

Greedy-eyed Sadowski wasn't with the Brindles when they came home. Felicia and Allister both had that stretched skin and squinty-eyed, dazed look Blanche had seen on other employers who'd had to glad-hand with the public for long hours. They drank their drinks in total silence—not the kind of silence that comes after a fight, or the kind of comfortable silence that happens between people close enough not to need to talk much, but the kind of screaming silence where there's so much that hasn't been said for so long, neither party would know where to begin if they dared.

Blanche thought it best not to mention Marc's call to Felicia. He hadn't left a message for Felicia—so why call herself to the woman's attention, given their morning run-in? But, as often happened, Blanche's curiosity got the better of her.

"Your son called, ma'am."

"When? What did he say?"

"He was looking for Inez."

"What did he want with Inez?"

"He said he was looking for Ray-Ray. He didn't leave a message."

Allister had been ignoring them until he heard Ray-Ray's name.

"Ray-Ray? Marc dared to call here looking for that—"

"Please, Allister, haven't you caused enough grief already?"

Felicia took her drink and went quickly up the stairs. To the phone, Blanche guessed.

The bus ride home was like being on a mental merry-go-round—one thought leaping up as another one dipped to the bottom of her brain. How were things going to work out between her and Felicia after this morning? She liked Mick. She reminded Blanche of an iceberg or an underwater mountain with only the tip of herself showing. And Carrie wasn't nearly as tough a nut as Blanche had thought—softened by sandwiches, she chuckled to herself. Shit! She'd forgotten about the note Ray-Ray gave her for Allister. She'd have to do something about that tomorrow.

She got home just in time to listen to Taifa and Malik squabbling over which of them had knocked over her Swedish ivy and broken the pot. All thoughts of the Brindle household quickly disappeared.

"Moms, Miss Downing said we gotta have the money in tomorrow for the museum trip." Taifa smacked gum in Blanche's face on the way to kissing her.

"Waste of time paying for that ignorant child to go to a museum." Malik remarked in his new voice.

"Child? Child? Who you callin' a child? I'm older than your baby butt! Your big sister, that's who I am and always will be, whether you like it or not."

"Maybe I'll always be your brother, that's up to you. But you may not always be my sister," Malik told her. "I could change my name, move to the other side of the planet, and forget I ever knew you." He picked up his book and walked out of the room.

Taifa gave Blanche a startled look. "He couldn't really do that, could he?" Taifa's voice was a whisper.

Blanche knew what Taifa wanted to hear. She also knew that Malik had taken a giant step away from Taifa and from her, just by raising the possibility of disappearing from the family. His words had put a hairline crack in her heart, too. Once again, she was faced with the major contradiction of her parenthood: wanting both to be shed of these kids and to be as much mother as they needed for as long as they needed her—within reason, of course. It was like wanting to be a rock and an eagle at the same time. She gave Taifa a hard hug but didn't answer the girl's question.

Shaquita broiled a decent pork chop, Taifa's sautéed spinach with fresh garlic was delicious, and Malik had baked the sweet potatoes till they were done but still moist. Blanche wasn't really hungry—fallout from handling food all day. Still, she tried to show some gusto as she moved her food around.

Taifa talked nonstop through dinner—about the school play, what girlfriend A said to girlfriend B about boy C, and her latest favorite song. Despite Taifa's chatter, Blanche was more aware of Shaquita, who was altogether different from the perky future archaeologist of last night's dinner. Both her shoulders and her mouth looked like they had invisible weights pulling them down. She was red-eyed, too.

"You okay?" Blanche asked Shaquita when Taifa let her get a word in.

"I bet her and her boy—"

"Butt out, Taifa," Shaquita said in a voice that meant business.

Boyfriend trouble, Blanche thought. If she asked Shaquita about it, she'd not only have to listen to the girl's account of puppy love gone wrong but take it as seriously, at least on the surface, as Shaquita did. Was she ready for that?

Blanche was almost grateful when Malik reminded her of the environmental meeting he wanted to go to that evening. Almost. She'd much rather take a hot bath and go to bed early, but she knew this meeting was important to Malik, and she had no intention of letting him go alone. She wasn't one of those parents silly enough to think their child wasn't the type to get into trouble. There was no type.

Neither one of them would be going to the meeting if it weren't for Miss Wagner, Malik's social studies teacher. When he told her he wanted to write his environmental paper on Roxbury, Miss Wagner insisted the environment wasn't important to black people in inner-city neighborhoods. Malik had come home from school determined to find black people in Roxbury working on some pollution problem. This would make the third environmental meeting she'd taken him to. He'd turned his nose up at both of the other organizations. One of them had been run by white people who did all the talking while the black residents listened; the other meeting had started nearly an hour late, and while the talkers had been black men, they hadn't had much to say. Malik had seen the notice for tonight's meeting in Dudley Square. Neither of them had heard of the organization before. Blanche had meant to ask Miz Barker about it, but it had slipped her mind.

They took the number 28 bus over to Blue Hill Avenue, past the Nation of Islam mosque and Ma Dixon's restaurant. They got off the bus at Columbia Road, then began looking for the address on the flyer. Malik did what Blanche had come to call the not-with-you walk where he strolled either three steps behind or three steps ahead of her. He and Taifa had adopted this method of walking with and without her over the last year. Blanche had resented it until she remembered ducking out the side door of her junior high school to avoid Mama, who was waiting out front to walk home with her.

They almost missed the place. They'd been looking for an office-type building or a storefront, but the office of the Community Reawakening Project was up a narrow stairway to a third-floor apartment across the street from the check-cashing place. A hand-lettered sign invited them to walk right in.

There were fourteen people already there. Six of them were white—the largest group of whites Blanche ever had seen in Roxbury, except cops. They were all sitting together with tight little smiles on their faces, their hands folded in their laps like schoolchildren under a mean teacher. If they were so uncomfortable, why had they come? She took the flyer from Malik and read the answer down at the bottom in very small letters: "Also sponsored by the Multicultural Environmental Coalition."

Blanche and Malik sat in the last row of metal folding chairs set up in what was probably once a living room. Malik took out his notebook. The seats were filling up, except for a ring of empties surrounding the island of whites. Blanche wondered if they had the minority jitters: Did they think everyone was looking at them? Did they think they felt an unwelcoming vibe from some people in the audience? Were they worried about getting home safely? Were they getting a hint of the stress of being black in a mostly white and often evil-acting country?

She watched a young dread sister gather her hair in one hand and dig in her shoulder bag with the other. She pulled out a pair of chopsticks and used them to pin her hair on top of her head. When a couple of stray dreads fell in her face, she flipped them back with a toss of her head that made Blanche smile.

She used to think the Hair Ballet that white girls did was all theirs until she'd noticed dread sisters flipping their hair over their shoulders, lifting it from their necks to catch a breeze, flinging it back from their faces in ways that women with false or processed hair rarely seemed to do. And wasn't it funny that after all these years of horsehair, other people's hair, Dacron weaves, wigs, and extensions, it was our own naturally nappy hair that was making black women's blow-hair dream come true? Like Lady Day sang, God bless the child that's got her own.

Blanche closed her eyes and took a deep breath—cocoa butter, perfume, a razor-sharp cologne, chewing gum, greens. She tuned in on the talk.

"Yeah, but he's fifteen years younger than her. She must be outta her mind!"

"Maybe she's just looking for staying power," came the laughing response.

"... and my foot swole up big as a cantaloupe ..." came from another quarter.

She listened to the jazz and gospel, rhythm and blues, and rap in the voices around her. Something loosened deep down in her belly. She relaxed into the melody of voices like a child curled up in her mother's lap.

"Hi, Blanche."

Joanie, Blanche's next-door neighbor, angled her hips into the seat on the other side of Malik.

"Hey, Malik, whatsup?" She asked the question like the answer was important to her, which was one of the reasons Blanche liked her. She took young people seriously.

"I gotta do this paper. On the environment. I want it to be about the Bury, too," he said, and told her about his difference of opinion with his teacher.

"Good for you!" Joanie told him. "Everybody in this city got something bad to say about Roxbury and most of 'em don't even know how to get here from downtown. I'm glad you stickin' up for us."

A woman took the chair in front of Malik and turned to speak to Joanie.

"These are my next-door neighbors, Blanche and Malik." Joanie told her.

The woman turned her narrow, sharp-featured face first to Blanche. "Hi," she said, reaching an arm over the back of her seat. "I'm Lacey Monroe, sex worker."

"Blanche White, temporary celibate."

Malik's eyes widened, but he minded his manners enough to say hello to Lacey when she spoke to him.

Lacey turned toward the front of the room.

A pecan-brown woman with a short, angular natural was looking the crowd over. Maurice Samuelson was with her, and so were two white men and one of the black men Blanche had seen at Brindle's lunch but couldn't identify.

The woman stepped toward the audience and clapped her hands. "Our panel members are all here, so we'll get started." She looked around the room as she spoke. She didn't smile. Shadows played around her deep-set eyes and under her full bottom lip.

"I'm Aminata Dawson of the Community Reawakening Project. Tonight is one in our series of events to make sure the community knows how our lives, and our children's lives, are being affected by pollution, toxic waste, and other environmental hazards, especially lead poisoning.

"I started this organization almost a year ago, when my only son was sent to Walpole for shooting his best friend. My boy, who I raised to respect life, to love life, this boy who was so gentle and sweet when he was little that he could have been an angel. Ask anybody who knew him. But he changed after he was poisoned by the lead in our apartment. Even his teachers noticed the difference. Asking me if everything was all right at home, like it was my fault the boy got into fights and wouldn't listen. Didn't nobody care whether the medicine they gave him was going to fix what that lead had done to his mind. Nobody cared then and nobody cares now. Doctors try to tell me lead poisoning don't make our kids kill each other. But I know different. I know that medicine wasn't enough to stop my boy from turning into somebody who could kill his best friend, my boy who was so gentle and sweet when he was little that he could have been an angel. Ask anybody who knew him. I raised him to respect life, to love life. But he changed after he was poisoned by the lead in our place. Even his teachers noticed the difference. Asking me ..."

A hum vibrated through the room as Aminata began retelling her son's story. People shuffled their feet and squirmed in their chairs. From the side of the room, a big black man with SECURITY printed on his orange armband took half a step toward

Aminata. Aminata looked at the man and blinked like she was waking from a trance. Or a nightmare.

Blanche reached for Malik's hand. He let her hold it for half a second—long enough for her to know she wasn't the only one moved by Aminata's story.

Aminata began again: "A lot of our kids are still getting sick from lead poisoning. How do we know all these kids out here killing each other ain't just like my boy? My boy who was so gentle and . . ."

The man with the security armband coughed.

Aminata continued: "We got to do something, y'all. This is genocide. This racist system has found perfect ways to get rid of us: give guns and drugs to our children who don't go to school; give legal drugs, like Ritalin, to our kids who do go to school just so they'll sit still for teachers who don't care if they learn as long as they keep quiet; and poison our babies with lead in their own homes. Roxbury is the most lead-polluted community in Boston. We got to do something, and we got to do it now. I'm asking every one of you to have your kids tested for lead. One of our speakers will tell you how easy it is to get your children tested. And it's free. But you got to do it now. By the time the poison gives your child stomachaches, or makes your child be tired or mean and irritable all the time, it'll be too late to stop what happened to my son." Aminata paused.

Blanche looked around the room. There was no hum and shuffle now.

"Take your time, sister," someone said.

Aminata went on: "Tonight we're going to hear from people who can tell us what we need to do to protect our families from lead poisoning."

The first speaker was a white man in a shirt and pants as rumpled as used pajamas. He was from the also-sponsored-by group mentioned on the flyer. Pajamas looked puzzled by people's laughter when he told them they had to fill out an application and apply to be in an organization with someone who didn't even respect them enough to press his clothes. But there was no laughter as he talked about the amount of lead in old paint and water pipes, and the harm that just breathing in lead dust could do to a young child, even one still in the womb.

The black man Blanche didn't know turned out to be second in command at the Roxbury Outpatient Care Center, where kids could be tested for lead free of charge.

The second white man stared at the audience with eyes so pale they looked blank. He was from the state agency that was responsible for lead removal, and talked about the laws and regulations to make landlords and realtors responsible for lead cleanup. But by the time he had used the phrase "what you people need to do" three times, the room was alive with people talking to one another as if he weren't even present.

Then it was Samuelson's turn.

"Now you know," he said. "Can't none of y'all say, 'I didn't know.' You been told and you know what's got to be done. We got to do what we always got to do here in devil land: take control, take control, take control!

"The Temple of Divine Enlightenment is in the forefront, the forefront of the attack on these racist dogs who would defile our community with their evil..."

It was a good performance, if you went in for what Blanche called minister speak. She always felt like the person using it was trying to put something over on her, so she hardly listened. She was more concerned with the damage Samuelson was doing to the ozone level with all that hot air he was blowing. When she tuned back in, Samuelson was ticking off the ways in which the Temple was working on environmental problems.

"...keep the mayor's and the governor's feet to the fire and remind those white folks in the legislature that we are here, we are powerful, we are great! That's why you got to not only get your children tested for lead but register yourself to vote and join the Temple's Community Cleanup Campaign!"

Blanche waited for him to tell Aunt Jemima and Uncle Ben they should vote for Brindle, but he didn't. People clapped when he sat down. Blanche didn't.

The man who'd helped Aminata get off her gentle-son speech came up to speak. He moved with that kind of big-man grace that always reminded Blanche of her ex-lover, Leo.

"My name's Othello Flood. Most of y'all know me. I grew up around here. Probably stole something from half the people in this room."

The audience laughed with him.

"But I looked up one day and understood I'd been doing wrong and what I needed to do to make things right. So me and a couple other brothers started Ex-Cons for Community Safety. Our group tries to get brothers coming home from prison to take responsibility for making our neighborhoods safe and to help turn our young brothers around so they don't go the prison route. As far as lead poisoning and the environment is concerned, we have an environmental patrol that deals with illegal dumping and trashing. We make sure abandoned buildings are secured and not being used by junkies or drug dealers. We also provide security for meetings like this and escorts for our elders and other people who need it. We're working with some of the youth to start a breakfast program for the little ones next year. Thank you."

A chorus of "Amen" and "Good for you, brother" went up from the audience. You could secure me anytime, you fine thing, Blanche thought. She crossed her legs and tried to pay attention to what the man was saying instead of the size of his hands and the way the light played on his cheekbones. He responded to the applause with a big grin that made him look very, very sweet. Blanche licked her lips.

After the meeting, some people lined up to sign the volunteer sheet and pick up the brochures on lead poisoning. Maybe she and the kids should get involved. After all, if the environment went, nothing else mattered. It would also give her a way to be with Malik and Taifa where she wasn't giving orders and correcting them all the time. And it would be good for them to have something to do with all that energy that would benefit somebody besides themselves. On the other hand, she didn't think this was the right organization. Too much pain.

The front of the room was quickly transformed into a buffet with huge jimmiejohns of orange soda and cola and mountains of sandwiches separated by mounds of fresh fruit. Malik excused himself and headed for Aminata. Blanche was tempted to go see what they were talking about but knew better.

She walked deliberately to the back of the room and stood near Lacey and Joanie, who were talking about where to find the freshest fish in the 'hood. Blanche gave Lacey a sly looking-over and felt curiosity gnawing at her belly like hunger: Lacey was a good-looking woman, not pretty, but with the kind of regular, narrow features that got attention. She was smaller than Blanche expected—one of those short women with a tall presence. There was an elegant drape to her wool knit pants, and her blouse had a made-to-fit look. Blanche figured the pants alone probably cost her five or six hundred bucks. Her rings, bracelet, and earrings weren't gold plate, either. Blanche wondered just what kind of sex work she did.

Blanche turned, her blue-black searching for Malik. He was still talking to Aminata, who was watching him closely, nodding her head every once in a while. Even from here there was something forlorn about her. Blanche thought about Miz Pearl, her mother's old hairdresser. When Miz Pearl's husband of thirty years died, Miz Pearl expected to die of grief. When she didn't, she turned her life into a monument to her husband. She sent his clothes to the cleaners twice a year to keep them fresh, joined the women's auxiliary of the lodge he'd belonged to, and held poker parties for his cronies. The walking wounded, Blanche thought.

Lacey's eyes followed Blanche's. "It's a real shame. She was—I guess I should say *is*—one of the best mothers I ever saw. Patient, loving, involved. For all the good it did her."

"I was just thinking how life can carve us out a path we had no plans to take," Blanche said.

"The three of us went to high school together," Joanie said. "Losing her son really messed her up."

"Remember all that volunteer stuff she used to do?" Lacey said. "Working on public housing tenants' rights, helping homeless girls—and didn't she start a food pantry at some church around here? She gave all that up when her boy went to jail."

"Not exactly," Joanie said. "You know she'd been hassling with a couple of them groups for years."

"About what?" Blanche wanted to know.

"The same old thing," Joanie told her. "Women doin' the work, men getting the glory. But writing that letter to the feds about the housing development boys ripping off the funds ended her thing with most organizations around here."

Now Blanche understood why none of the well-known community groups she read about in the black newspaper had been represented at the meeting. Being down on crooked male leadership was one thing, but writing letters to try to stop it was something else. Honesty might be the best policy, but it didn't necessarily lead to popularity.

"You know, she used to live in this apartment," Joanie said. "Moved out and got a room so she can use this place for the organization."

Blanche was momentarily distracted by the sight of Othello Flood in the front of the room. He definitely reminded her of Leo. He didn't look like Leo, except that they were both big and dark-skinned. It was his air that really called Leo to mind—that same gentle, slow way that, to Blanche, meant a man sure enough of himself not to have to prove anything to anybody. She wondered if, like Leo's, his skin felt tight as a drum and extra warm, like there was a banked fire waiting inside to set her parts ablaze. Now, what could she go talk to him about? Suddenly, it dawned on her that Othello was watching Aminata as though she were the last bit of sandwich in a soon-to-be-foodless world. Damn! Blanche turned to Lacey.

"So what line of sex work are you in, exactly?"

"The rent-my-body-for-pleasure line." Lacey took a leather case from her handbag and handed Blanche her card. "We're a cooperative. We work the big hotels and private parties for men with lots of money."

Blanche looked down at the card:

Family Values, Inc.
555-767-7979

She covered her mouth with her hand, but not quite soon enough to stifle the whoop of laughter that turned the heads of people standing nearby.

"Girl! Are you serious?"

"As any other incorporated entity out here." Lacey didn't even smile when she said it.

"Yeah, I nearly split my sides the first time I saw that card," Joanie said. "They even got an investment club."

"You should hear some of the phone calls we get," Lacey told them. "People thinking we're part of the religious right. I give them some righteous religion, all right." Lacey tipped her head toward Maurice Samuelson, who was in the middle of a group of smiling women. "Of course, for some religious folks, our brand of family values is just what they're looking for."

"No shit! You never told me Samuelson was one of your customers!" Joanie sounded seriously cheated.

"He's not one of ours. I hear he likes them white, young, and not too expensive—which keeps him away from us."

Blanche looked at Samuelson and wondered what he would say if he knew Lacey was back here putting his business in the street.

Samuelson looked up and caught Blanche's eye. He began working his way toward her.

"Uh-oh. I'm outta here." Joanie turned toward the door.

"Next time we'll talk about *your* sex life, or should I say, the lack of it?" Lacey winked at Blanche and hurried out the door behind Joanie.

Blanche made a wide circle around the room and joined Aminata and Malik.

"You're lucky," Aminata said after Malik introduced her to Blanche. "He's a fine young man. Concerned about his community."

Malik ducked his head. Blanche grinned her pleasure.

"He's been telling me about this paper he's gotta do. I'm honored he's decided to focus on the Community Reawakening Project. It's important to get our message out to young people *before* they start having kids."

Blanche put her arm through Malik's.

Malik turned to Aminata. "I'm gonna read these pamphlets and papers you gave me and write my outline; then I'll call you, okay?"

"You can call me anytime, Malik," Aminata told him.

Blanche and Malik had nearly made it to the door when Blanche realized Samuelson was there and waiting for her.

"Well, hello! You're the sister who almost knocked me over yesterday."

Blanche just looked at him.

"Reverend Maurice Samuelson at your service, my sister." He bowed to her, then turned to the two men behind him. "Y'all wait by the car." Facing Blanche again, he pressed his hand to his heart. "I'm just sorry our first encounter had to be while I was trying to get the man to do right by our people."

"Oh, is that what you were doing?"

Samuelson gave a little laugh that made Blanche think of having her pockets picked. She waited for him to ask what she meant, but he didn't.

She understood what he wanted from her, but she'd be damned if she'd help him convince himself it was all right to dis blacks to Brindle.

"We all got to do the distasteful sometimes," he said. "I'm sure you run into this problem in your line of work."

"I try to do my job in a way that don't make me ashamed to look black people in the eye," she told him.

Samuelson refused to bite. "May I know your name, sister?"

Blanche told him and introduced him to Malik.

"I'm at your service, Sister Blanche. May I call you that?" Samuelson's voice was as greasy as his hair.

"Certainly, Brother Maurice."

His face went sour for half a second, but he recovered quickly enough. "Have you considered joining us at the Temple? Many have found peace there, Sister Blanche. Many. Some have come from Islam; some have come from the Baptist, Catholic, Pentecostal, or other faiths. All have found a home in the Temple. Join us." The last was said in a whisper she thought was meant to be spiritual but reminded her of an obscene phone call.

His invitation to the Temple of Divine Enlightenment made her wonder if he thought she'd be more respectful on his turf.

"What a creep," Malik said.

"He is that," Blanche agreed. "Kind of preacher that gives *God* a bad name."

"So why'd you decide on this group for your paper, Malik?" Blanche asked while they waited for the bus.

Malik turned bright eyes toward her. "She da bomb, Moms! Don't you like her?"

"But you're supposed to do a paper on an organization, not a person."

"Yeah?"

Blanche always marveled over how much defensiveness the boy could load into one word.

"Well, I just wondered, why this one? I know you weren't crazy about the other groups, but . . ."

"You don't like her."

"Malik, it's not about Aminata. It's the Community Reawakening Project I wonder about. I mean, is *she* the whole organization? I didn't see nobody else there who claimed to be a member, did you?"

Malik thought for a second. "Well, just because people didn't say they were members don't mean they weren't. She gave me a whole lot of pamphlets and stuff. And she didn't treat me like a dumb kid when I tried to talk to her, like those guys at the other places we went to."

"Well, I just wondered if you didn't want a more . . ." A more what? An organization that wasn't run by a woman drowning in grief, who talked like she just might be across the street from sane? An organization that didn't meet in the founder's ex–living room? That didn't invite Samuelson to speak?

"This is the only group that talked about teenagers and violence and lead poisoning," Malik said.

Exactly, Blanche thought. She'd never seen or heard any news reports that said lead poisoning could cause violence. She was sure the lead poisoning–violence connection was something Aminata had cooked up to ease the pain of a murdering son. But if she said as much to Malik, he'd likely take it as another sign that she didn't like Aminata. She just hoped he wouldn't be too crushed when he found out Aminata didn't know what she was talking about.

"But nobody else who spoke said anything about lead and violence. Just Aminata."

"Yeah?"

Here we go again. Tension seized Blanche's back and lifted her shoulders nearly to her ears.

"Don't you think it's strange that nobody else mentioned it?"

"Maybe the others don't care as much about teens. Maybe they just care about little kids. Miz Aminata said sometimes it's hard to make people see what's right in front of their noses."

Blanche twitched. "Miz Aminata said" was a phrase she had a feeling she could get sick of hearing. "Well, you don't have to decide tonight, you—"

"Mom, I already decided." Malik looked at her from stern eyes nearly level with her own. "Miz Aminata's gonna see if she can get some interviews with the parents of the four guys in jail for killing people to see if they had lead poisoning when they were little."

"I don't know about that, Malik. Maybe you need to think about this. If Miss Wagner already believes nobody cares about the environment in Roxbury, does a paper on an organization with one member prove her wrong? At least you need to find out if there really are other members of the organization, or if the whole thing is Aminata."

"So what if it's just her? You gotta start somewhere. Probably a lot of groups had just a couple of people in the beginning. You're always saying if you want something done, get up and do it. That's what Miz Aminata's doing."

Blanche wanted to shout "No fair!" She wasn't raising him to use her own arguments against her! But he was right. Whatever problems Aminata might be having, she was living what she believed. Malik could probably do a lot worse.

"Okay, Malik. It's your choice, but I want to think about this interviewing parents thing." What she really meant was that she wasn't sure she wanted him off doing interviews with Aminata about something that could cause her to get lost in her gentle-son story and scare somebody half to death. What happened when Othello wasn't there to call her back?

Blanche settled into her bus seat and wished it were her bed.

Malik poked her in the side. "Moms! What exactly is a sex worker?"

Shit! Didn't she ever get a break? She pulled herself up and cleared her throat. "A sex worker is somebody who sells sex for a living, or maybe a counselor or somebody who works with people who sell sex."

"You mean like ho—prostitutes?"

"Um-hum."

"Is that what she is, that lady we met? Lacey?"

"Yes."

"She don't look like a ho—prostitute."

"And what do prostitutes look like?"

"You know, Moms, they wear a lot of makeup and their . . . all their stuff is hanging out." Malik hesitated a moment. "And they don't go to meetings about the environment, either."

She thought about the times in her life when her money was so low, her prospects so dim that if the right stranger had asked her to have sex for the right price, she didn't know how she would have answered. She thought about the more than a handful of women she knew and worked for who talked about sex with their husbands and lovers as though it were a price they had to pay for help with the cost of food or school clothes for their children.

"Looks like you're wrong on all counts," Blanche told him. "Looks like prostitutes are the same as computer programmers and lawyers."

"What do you mean?" Malik gave her a suspicious look.

"I mean you can't tell what they do by looking at them—*or* whether they're interested in the environment." Was this where she should launch into her thing about the need to legalize prostitution or jail more johns? She knew parents were supposed to know shit like how much to tell a child and when, but she sure as hell didn't. The books generally said something about when the child is ready and nothing about how to recognize ready when it asked you a question.

Malik poked her again. "Moms, what did you mean about being a temporary celib—"

"Here's our stop," Blanche was delighted to announce. She jumped out of her seat. "Hurry up, I gotta pee!"

As she scurried to the bathroom, she saw Shaquita curled up on the extra cot in Taifa's room looking like butter wouldn't melt in her mouth. Maybe it's just boyfriend trouble. Maybe it was something else.

When she came out of the bathroom, Blanche stuck her head in Taifa's room and asked Shaquita to come with her. Blanche waved Shaquita into her own room and closed the door. She took off her shoes and knee-highs.

"Tell me what's wrong, honey." Blanche looked straight at her.

"Nothing's wrong, Aunt Blanche. Nothing's wrong, honest."

Blanche gave the girl a close, hard look. Was her face even fuller than usual? Her eyes were certainly bright, and her skin almost glowed, even though she didn't look particularly happy. Damn!

"You're pregnant, aren't you?"

The tears that quickly sprang to Shaquita's eyes were all the answer Blanche needed.

"Oh, Shaquita!" Blanche plopped down on the bed and turned her face away so that the girl couldn't see how deeply disappointed she felt.

"Don't tell Grandma, please, Aunt Blanche. I know I have to tell her, but..."

"I don't hardly mind not being the one to break the news to Cousin Charlotte, believe me." Blanche took Shaquita's hand and pulled her down on the bed beside her. "How far along are you?"

"Five weeks. I just found out today." Her voice broke like a dropped glass.

Blanche almost jumped for joy. There was still time. She looked at Shaquita. "Have you thought about what you're going to do?"

Shaquita shrugged and looked like she wanted to cry.

"I mean, you're not very far gone, you could still..."

"Pookie doesn't know yet."

"Pookie?" Was this child telling her she was pregnant by somebody called Pookie? Ancestors save us!

"I tried to tell him this afternoon, but..."

"Well, maybe you should think about whether you want to tell him at all. Depending on what you decide to do, he—"

"He's my baby's father!" Shaquita sounded as though not telling Pookie was a crime that could land her in jail. Worse yet was the way she said "my baby." Blanche thought she heard jail doors clanging shut. Poor Cousin Charlotte. Shaquita wasn't the only one caught between a rock and a hard place.

"I don't want to try to make any plans until I talk to Pookie."

Pookie. Right. The more the child talked, the more depressed Blanche became and the more reluctant to say what she had to say. But she couldn't let that stop her.

"You're a very mature and steady young woman, Quita, but I think you're still too young to have a baby." Blanche congratulated herself on her diplomacy, for not saying *We don't need another child having a child.* But from the way Shaquita's back stiffened, diplomacy hadn't helped.

"I'm as old as my mom was when she had me." Shaquita looked at Blanche, then away.

From the look on Shaquita's face, it wasn't necessary for Blanche to point out that Shaquita's mother was not exactly a role model: She'd begun a serious love affair with heroin soon after Shaquita was born. She'd died when Shaquita was just four years old.

"Then tell Pookie soon. The two of you need to have a real heart-to-heart. A child needs more than love, Shaquita, and I don't think you and Pookie—"

Shaquita stopped her. "You don't even know him. He's not like everybody says, he—"

Blanche raised a hand to stop her. "You're right. I don't know him. Okay. You talk to him. Then we'll talk." She gave Shaquita a hug. Shaquita leaned heavily against her and began to cry. "What will Grandma say? She's gonna be so mad!"

Blanche wiped Shaquita's eyes and kissed her on the cheek.

"The big question is not what will Cousin Charlotte say, but what you're gonna do. Talk to Pookie. Tomorrow." She gave Shaquita another squeeze and told her everything would be all right. She hoped it was true.

Blanche shut her bedroom door and sat on the side of the bed rocking and hugging herself as the memory of her own teenage pregnancy and decision to have an abortion played in her mind. She'd been older than Shaquita, almost nineteen, and determined to do what Mama would not have her do: get out of Farleigh, take her life in her own hands, and try to live it her own way. Had she already decided at nineteen that she didn't ever want to have children? She felt a rush of warmth and protectiveness toward Shaquita, and the girl she herself had been. Is that what this was all about? Wanting to help Shaquita, the way Cousin Murphy had helped her? But an abortion might not be the kind of help Shaquita wanted.

Blanche went to her altar and lit a candle and a stick of incense, then spoke to the Ancestors about what was on her mind. If only I knew how to keep my mouth shut, she told the picture of her mother's mother. Why did I have to even notice that the girl's pregnant? She closed her eyes and listened to their silent answer confirm what she already knew: Whether she liked it or not, she had to talk to Shaquita about her options, just in case Cousin Charlotte turned out to be useless on the subject. But she didn't have to do it tonight.

She switched on her radio, already tuned in to WGBH. *Blues After Hours,* her favorite program, was on. She fell asleep to Sippie Wallace singing "Black Snake Blues."

FOUR

DAY THREE—SATURDAY

Blanche could feel the tension before she turned down the Brindles' driveway. The house looked glum. She hadn't cared much for the house's airs when she'd first seen it, but having met the family, she now felt some sympathy for the place. She silently apologized to the house because she had a feeling she was about to add to its blues.

She put on her apron and took Ray-Ray's note to Allister Brindle from her handbag. Ray-Ray's childish handwriting stared up at her. Did the note mention that he'd been in the house when the Brindles were out? If it did, she'd have some explaining to do.

She heated water in the kettle but didn't let it boil much. Too much steam would make the paper soggy. For a quarter of a second she felt bad about opening someone else's mail, especially since Ray-Ray had told her the less she knew the better. But while she was prepared to play dumb if it suited her, she wasn't interested in *being* dumb. She held the sealed flap of the envelope over the kettle spout, then carefully opened it and read the note inside:

> Man, this is a grate tape. I bet the voters will love watching it, too.
>
> R-R

A videotape! That's what Ray-Ray took the day she'd caught him in the house, damn him. Wait till she saw him! She read the note again. Ray-Ray couldn't spell, but he knew how to threaten without using a threatening word. But what was he after? The note didn't mention money. And what was on the tape, anyway? Damn! What to do now? What if she didn't give the note to Allister at all? Would that fool Ray-Ray show up here again or call Allister to make sure he'd gotten it? She found some glue, resealed the envelope, and put a stamp on it. She studied Ray-Ray's childish handwriting, then imitated it as best she could, adding the street address and city under Allister's name. She bent the ends of the envelope and scooted it across the floor with her foot to give it a mailed look before she put it in her apron pocket.

She peeped into the breakfast room while Carrie was serving breakfast. Brindle and Sadowski looked as though Carrie were offering them arrest and bankruptcy instead of Blanche's buttermilk pancakes and Canadian bacon. Felicia had already called down to say she didn't want anything just now.

"Them two look like their mamas just died," Blanche said when Carrie came to the kitchen.

"Ain't none of my business." Carrie adjusted her hair net so that it just touched her eyebrows.

"I didn't say it was your business, Carrie. I want to know *their* business. What were they talking about?"

"Ain't my job to pay no attention to what they say."

Blanche stepped in front of Carrie and looked directly into her eyes. "Well, you ought to make it your business. If they're all being dragged off to jail, or lost all their money and can't pay us this week, I think we need to know about it, no matter whose business it is."

Carrie frowned up at her from behind her narrow glasses. "Well, if you put it that way, Mr. B. was poutin' about sharing the newspaper with some broken-down athlete. Mr. Ted said it wasn't so bad and they could make up for it, but he didn't sound like he believed it hisself."

"You sure remember a lot for somebody who don't pay attention."

Carrie tilted her head and gave Blanche a sly look. "Didn't say I wasn't payin' attention; I just said it wasn't my job."

Blanche laughed as she dug out her as-yet-unread copy of the *Boston Globe.* BRINDLE ENTERS GUBERNATORIAL PRIMARY was the main headline, complete with a picture of Allister and Felicia dancing at the announcement party the night before. To the left of the Brindle-for-governor story was a picture of Saxe Winton over a caption that said "Champion skier dies."

Blanche read the caption again, struggling to connect its message to the picture of Saxe smiling his sexy smile, to the feel of his fingers wrapped tenderly around her hand just a day or two ago. And now he was dead. Just like that. Life's latest little surprise. She suddenly wanted to get up and dance, to kiss the kids and Mama, to find a way to get to Africa, to learn how to sing alto, to do all the things she loved to do and every and all the things in her dream box that were labeled "someday," "maybe," "if I'm lucky." She gave Saxe's picture a last look and read the article.

> Saxe Winton, six-time Olympic downhill skiing champion, was bludgeoned to death in his Back Bay condo sometime Thursday. Police believe Winton frightened a burglar and was killed in the subsequent struggle. A pillowcase full of small valuables was found on the scene. Winton's Olympic medals and other trophies are reported to be missing.
>
> Winton was a distant relative of Bradley Winton, one of New England's founding fathers. Since retiring from competitive skiing, Winton had become personal trainer to a number of prominent people in the Boston area. He was 37.

Blanche stared at Saxe's smiling face once again. A shadow crossed her mind and made her shiver.

"Carrie, look." She handed Carrie the paper.

"Oh no! Oh sweet Jesus! God rest his soul." Blanche watched tears well in Carrie's eyes as she read. While Blanche felt the sadness of a young life ended, she and Saxe had been nowhere near on crying terms.

"This is a wicked, wicked world," Carrie moaned.

The intercom interrupted her tears: Felicia. Carrie wiped her eyes on her apron and hurried up the back stairs mumbling to herself. Blanche pictured the two of them upstairs boo-hooing over the loss of all that dick power.

She took a fresh pot of coffee and clean cups into the breakfast room. She replaced Brindle's and Sadowski's half-filled cups with fresh ones. Brindle was talking.

"I don't want her questioned, mentioned, or interviewed. My name cannot be attached to this in any way. You understand that?"

"Of course, sir. No problem. We're covered at police headquarters, and the D.A.'s office. I'll call in a favor or two in the newsroom of both papers. But Mrs. Brindle…"

Allister sipped his coffee. "I'll talk to her. She can't go running around.… You know how emotional she can be."

Sadowski was smart enough not to respond to that.

Blanche took a detour to the front hall. The mail was scattered on the floor under the slot in the door. She picked it up and stuck Ray-Ray's note in the middle of the pile. This was her half day. She'd be gone before Allister got to the mail. She shuffled the envelopes into a neat stack and put it on the hall table.

Carrie came back to the kitchen carrying Felicia's scarf to be pressed.

"How's Felicia holding up?" Blanche asked her.

"Look like she been crying. Couldn't hardly make up her mind what to wear."

Not know what to wear! Now ain't that a sign of grief, Blanche said to herself.

"Anybody'd think Mr. Saxe was a relative 'stead of just her trainer, not that I ever did know just what he was training her for."

Blanche gave Carrie a sharp look, not at all sure the woman wasn't putting her on.

Sadowski came to the kitchen to tell Blanche that Allister wanted some ice water. Blanche was drinking from one of the squat crystal glasses the Brindles used for their morning juice.

"I don't think that glass was meant for you." Sadowski looked at her as though he'd caught her stealing the silverware.

Blanche sipped her water slowly until it was all gone, all the while looking at Sadowski. He didn't return her gaze. She set the glass on the drain board. "Thanks for telling me," she told Sadowski. "I'll ask the Brindles which glasses were bought for the help's use and make sure to serve your drinks in them next time you eat here."

Sadowski's blush became a full-face flush. Blanche filled a pitcher with water and ice, plopped it and a glass on a tray, and thrust it at Sadowski.

He tried to stab her with his eyes before he turned and left without speaking.

"Asshole," Blanche muttered, and went back to her work.

She didn't see Felicia until she knocked on her door to say she was leaving for the day.

Felicia was on the phone: "Please call me back, Marc. I need to talk to you. I... I love you, darling." She hung up and turned toward Blanche.

Blanche could see why Carrie thought Felicia had been crying. Her eyes were glassy and underlined with half circles so dark they might have been painted on with eyebrow pencil.

"Morning, ma'am. Sad news about Mr. Winton." Blanche watched for Felicia's response, wondering if it would be bigger and louder than Carrie's had been.

Felicia didn't respond—not what Blanche expected from a woman whose joy boy had just bought the farm.

"Had he been working for you long?" Blanche asked.

Felicia didn't seem to hear her. Maybe Saxe was one of a set, so he wouldn't be missed much.

"I just left a message for my son," Felicia said, as though Blanche hadn't mentioned Saxe's name. "He didn't say where he could be reached? He hasn't called again?"

"No, ma'am, and he only called once, yesterday."

"I've been calling him for days now. I haven't seen him for nearly two months."

Blanche wondered why Felicia had taken so long to notice her son was out of touch. And why the hurry now?

"Oh, you know what kids are like," Blanche said. "Don't think of calling home unless they need something."

"Yes, of course." Felicia said, but she looked as though she thought Blanche was lying through her teeth.

Blanche suddenly saw trouble swirling around Felicia like a swarm of flies.

If Blanche hadn't spent so much time upstairs with Felicia, she'd have been gone by the time Carrie crashed into the kitchen.

"Mr. B wants to talk to you!"

"About what?"

"The mail. I took it in, like usual, then went to do the beds. He come runnin' upstairs while I was making his bed, told me to wait in the hall. He shuts the door, then comes out asking me where did this letter come from, was it in the regular mail? I told him I didn't know 'cause the mail was already on the hall table, so somebody else musta picked it up."

Shoulda left it on the floor, Blanche thought.

"He was cursin' and sweatin', and told me to git you," Carrie said. "I think he's having some kinda fit!"

Blanche went to the front of the house and stopped just outside the library doorway.

"Cocksucking black bastard! How the hell did he get in the safe? Who—"

Sadowski broke in: "But sir, I was just in the safe and there was—"

"Not that safe, you fool."

Sadowski was standing by the sofa looking as though he didn't know whether to sit or shit. "Sir, I still don't understand. This other safe—"

"Just shut up, Ted." Allister suddenly looked almost too tired to stand.

"Sir, is there something I should know, something you'd like me to do?"

"Get Samuelson on the phone," he told Sadowski. "Tell him we have a problem."

Sadowski headed toward the phone, then stopped. "Sir, if it's of a delicate nature, perhaps Reverend Samuelson isn't exactly the right—"

"Let me handle this, Ted. I can trust Samuelson completely. Unless he wants to go to jail."

Allister noticed Blanche standing in the shadows on the other side of the doorway. He took a deep, pull-yourself-together breath, but it didn't help. He shook the note from Ray-Ray at her as she moved into the room.

"You! Er, ah, um…"

"Blanche, sir," Sadowski told Allister.

Allister looked from Blanche to Sadowski and back to Blanche, as if checking the difference between what he saw and what he was being told.

"That's right, Blanche White," she said. "What can I do for you, sir?" She looked him hard in the eye and held him for a few moments before he remembered he was supposed to be in charge.

"It had to be you! Everyone else denies it."

Blanche stared at him without speaking. What could you say to someone who believed a person was guilty just because other people said they weren't—even if it was true?

"Where did this come from?" he demanded.

"Excuse me?" Blanche said in her calmest voice. She could smell Brindle's panic.

"It doesn't have a zip code or a postmark!" He pointed to the corner of the envelope. "Was this in the mail when you picked it up at the front door?"

"I didn't go through it. I just picked it up and put it on the table. Is something wrong?"

"Just answer my question. Did this note come in the mail?"

Blanche shrugged. "Like I said, I didn't go through it, so . . ."

"No one gave it to you? Asked you to put it in with the mail?"

"Why would anyone do that? They could just stick it through the letter slot."

"What if I told you someone saw a black man come in the front door on Friday? What would you say to that?"

Blanche folded her arms across her resentment at being treated as though she had no more brains than a marshmallow. Did he really think she'd believe this trumped-up story? He didn't even have the right day.

"If somebody came in here, I'd say he must have had a key."

"Then someone was here?"

Blanche shrugged. "Maybe."

"What the hell does that mean? Either he was here or he wasn't."

She'd never seen anyone's eyes get bloodshot while she watched. Could she make him froth at the mouth next?

"If somebody with a key came quietly in the front door, I wouldn't know a thing about it." They say if you're gonna lie, stay as close to the truth as you can.

"You know Ray-Ray Brown, don't you?"

"I'm working in his mama's place," she said.

"Was he here?"

"I didn't let him in."

"When did you last see him?"

"I don't quite remember."

Allister stared at her as though she'd just announced that she didn't remember her name.

She could hear Sadowski murmuring on the phone.

"Is something wrong?" she asked again, then looked over her shoulder.

"Seems to be," Felicia said. Blanche had sensed her coming down the stairs. Now she glided into the room wearing enough makeup for the stage. She curled up in one of the big armchairs. "Has somebody finally got the goods on you, Allister?"

"Stay out of this, Felicia; just stay out of it."

"How can I stay out of it when I find you badgering the help? The woman has answered your questions. What more do you want? You may go, Blanche."

Blanche hurried back to the kitchen wondering just what it was that Allister had on Samuelson that was serious enough to give Allister the right to call Samuelson to deal with darky problems. She snatched her handbag and hurried up the driveway, almost giggling with relief that this was her half day so she didn't have to hang around the fire raging in the Brindle house.

At least she hadn't got singed. She laughed at that ass Allister trying to trick her into telling him about Ray-Ray. No wonder so many women thought all men were fools—but a fool could be as dangerous as any other man. She wondered what would have happened if Felicia hadn't shown up. And what was up with her playing champion of the help? Playing was right. Blanche was sure Felicia's attitude was less about looking out for the help and more about going against Allister.

She was glad she'd gotten Ray-Ray's note out of her hands, but she knew she hadn't heard the last of it. She could see now that she'd have been better off flushing it down the toilet. Where was that negro? She had some talk for him! Although she had to admit she enjoyed watching Allister jump up and down like somebody put a hot coal in his drawers. And Ray-Ray really deserved a medal if he was going to use that video to keep Brindle out of the governor's office—even though she had a strong feeling that Ray-Ray had a more personal reason for wanting to bring Brindle down than simply saving the state from Brindle's brand of leadership. But what did Brindle expect Samuelson to do? Ray-Ray didn't impress her as a person likely to be moved by Scripture.

She brewed some tea when she got home and drank it while she made her grocery list: apples, pears, toilet paper—what *did* Malik do with all that toilet paper?—tissues, honey (Karen was never bringing *that* back), baking potatoes, toothpaste. She didn't expect Taifa or Malik to show up for hours. Taifa had talked Malik into helping her sell candy bars in front of the new supermarket on Centre Street in exchange for two days of doing his dishes. Shaquita had gone to the mall with some friends.

Blanche's own legs were eager to be on the move again. All that business with first Felicia and then Allister had made her edgy. The sun was shining, too, something that hadn't happened all that often during this so-called spring. Lord! What she wouldn't do for some real heat. She sorely missed North Carolina's weather. The dogwood would be in full, sweet-smelling bloom down there about now. Buds were just appearing up here. She put her jacket back on, grabbed a couple of reusable shopping bags, and headed toward Dudley Square.

Dudley Square was full of Saturday afternoon bustle: kids running out of the library, police cars taking up too many parking spaces, women jockeying strollers and shopping bags, men checking out the women and one another's cars. She never tired of looking at folks, particularly her own. Of course, she'd never seen a face of any color that could be called average, but she thought this was particularly true of black people, who seemed to have a wider range of feature sizes and shapes than other people. She figured this was because most blacks born in America were the children of a lot of African nations thrown together in slavery and most black families had also picked up European and Native American blood, whether they liked it or not. So, every black face was like a picture of the world: one or more of a zillion shades of brown or black; lips from dime thin to bee-stung plump; eyes that slanted up or down or were round as coins; flat noses, fat ones, long and pointed ones. Black folks had them all.

The smell of Jamaican meat pies from Dudley Pastry wrapped around her like a mother-made cloak. The music snaking out of Nubian Notion across the street put extra rhythm in her walk. For a moment, Dudley Square put her so much in mind of 125th Street, Harlem, USA, that she looked across the street half expecting to see the Apollo Theatre. There was also something about the low, crumbly buildings that reminded her of downtown Farleigh.

Maybe these similarities were signs that there was a place here for her, just as there was a place for her in Harlem and Farleigh. But those two cities were special. Farleigh was her birthplace. Her great-grandparents had lived and died there. The dirt knew her. It was her root place. And she knew she was always welcome in Harlem, it being home to all American blacks; plus, actually having been her home for nearly twenty years, before she moved back to Farleigh. In either place she could plop herself down and be herself.

But she was in Boston now, and the way she was ignored by salesclerks and followed by store security people downtown was just one more sign that this city wasn't putting out the welcome mat for her. Boston didn't seem to allow much room for differences either. If you were white and lived on Beacon Hill, you had to wear a lot of navy blue and worship old money. If you were an Irish Catholic from South Boston, you had to have big hair and a bad racial attitude. As for Roxbury, when she'd first moved in, three women in Rudigere Homes had, without being asked, given her the names of their hairdressers, as if there was something wrong with her unstraightened hair. And practically every mother in the housing development had found time to tell her how wrong she was when she'd said it was just as bad to scream at, curse, and dis your kids as it was to beat them.

Folks in Harlem and Farleigh might have had the same attitudes toward her beliefs and looks, but they had more class than to get in her face. But did she really care whether this place felt like home? Wasn't she already dreaming about packing up and getting out of here as soon as the kids were finished with school? The only problem was that her dreams never lasted long enough for her to see where she was headed.

She took her time with the shopping. She hated getting the groceries home and finding that the label stuck on an apple covered a bruise, or that the broccoli stems were rubbery with age. She checked contents, too. If a product had too many ingredients she couldn't pronounce, she looked for another brand. She finished her shopping, dropped her groceries off at home, and hurried on to Miz Barker's store. She had a couple of questions she needed to ask.

Miz Barker was in her usual spot, peering over the counter like a soldier over the castle wall. She raised her slow-moving eyelids and shifted in her seat when Blanche opened the door.

"Hey, Miz B. How you doin'?"

"I'm fair to middlin'. Ain't no useta complaining noway."

Blanche set her handbag on the glass-fronted counter full of Snickers bars, Reese's peanut butter cups, and jars of loose candy.

"Where's Pam?"

"She went up to the house to start dinner. Child's still sweet as pie and smart, too."

Overnight, all Miz Barker's harrumphing about her granddaughter coming to stay had disappeared.

Blanche got right to one of her reasons for stopping by. "Me and Malik went to a Community Reawakening Project meeting the other night. It was about lead poisoning."

"What kinda meeting?"

"That group Aminata Dawson started."

"What the name of it again?"

Blanche told her.

"Humph. Don't make no sense. Just like some of these names these young girls give they babies. Where they get these names from, I'd like to know. Now, Aminata's name..."

Oh shit! What was it about old folks that made them think they had the right to take your conversation anyplace they liked? Blanche promised herself that when she was eighty-five she'd answer the question she was asked and not go rambling in the middle of her answer.

"...African she told me. That's all right. But some of these made-up names they be coming up with, I just don't..."

Blanche decided to keep her mouth shut on this issue to keep from disagreeing. She thought it was great that black parents were making up their children's names instead of depending on European names. She especially liked the names that were some combination of the parents' names, like Malik's friends Janel, whose parents were Janice and Nelson, and Charmita, named after Charles and Juanita. A name made up for you was really your name, one that had never belonged to anyone else, had never even been said out loud before. A name couldn't get more personal than that. But if she told Miz Barker what she thought, they'd be there all night while Miz Barker lectured her on all the ways she was wrong. Be cool, she told herself. She could get Miz Barker back on the subject if she just hung in.

"She grew up around here, didn't she?" Blanche asked.

"Who?"

Blanche sighed and hoped they weren't going to have to go back to the beginning of this conversation before they could get to the end.

"Aminata."

"Sure did. Married that Dawson boy. Didn't last long. He went off somewhere and never come back. Wonder what become of him?"

"But she stayed."

"Where she gon' go with a child to raise? And look what all that mother loving and looking out got her. Boy sitting in prison for murder. Don't make no sense."

"She acts kinda strange when she talks about him."

"And wouldn't you? Your only child in prison for the rest of his natural life?"

"I mean *real* strange, Miz Barker. It's like she goes into a trance and just repeats..."

"I know how she do. I seen it. Better than crying herself to death or taking to drugs. Aminata ain't crazy. She trying to keep herself from *going* crazy. When she goes off on her son talk, all a person got to do is touch her or speak to her and she straightens right up. Right up."

"Malik wants to do a school project with her. She's supposed to take him to some interviews."

Miz Barker's lizard lids rose to reveal eyes sharp as shale. "Wondered what this was all about. What kinda interviews?"

Blanche told her that Aminata was convinced that lead poisoning had made her son violent enough to kill his friend. "And not just her son. She wants to talk to the parents of those four boys they're holding on murder charges to see if any of them had lead poisoning. Malik wants to do his school paper on Aminata's idea." There was a hard ring in her own voice that Blanche didn't like. Just because Malik believed Aminata and not her was no reason to be a bitch. "I think Aminata made up the whole lead poisoning and violence thing because her son killed—"

"I don't know nothing about no lead poisoning," Miz Barker interrupted. "But that boy of yourn'll be as safe with Aminata as a black man-child is gonna be round these parts."

But her own son hadn't been safe with her, Blanche thought, then cringed at her own unfairness and the probability that Miz Barker had also heard the green-tinged edge in Blanche's voice and knew what it meant. She was grateful Miz Barker didn't speak on it, which didn't mean she never would. Blanche bought some baking soda and a six-pack of kitchen matches—atonement for her meanness.

"You seen Ray-Ray lately?" Blanche held out her hand for her change.

"You sure full of questions today."

Blanche felt herself blushing but decided to bluff. "Who else am I supposed to ask? Mr. Al?"

Mr. Al owned the barbershop around the corner and had been in business as long as Miz Barker had. Like her, he was a source of community history and current goings-on, but he and Miz Barker hadn't spoken for years. Neither one of them would say why, but each bristled at the sound of the other's name.

"I ain't no bear, woman, so don't try to bait me." Miz Barker rose from her wooden stool and rubbed her behind with both hands. "Umm. Butt near 'bout gone to sleep. Old butt can't handle too much hard stool. When I was a girl..."

Here we go again, Blanche thought, so she was surprised by Miz Barker's next words.

"Why you looking for Ray-Ray?"

"I didn't say I was looking for him."

"You was going to." There was no doubt in Miz Barker's voice.

"I got something I want to talk to him about."

Miz Barker gave her a long look.

"Ray-Ray did something I didn't like, and I intend to tell him 'bout hisself," Blanche said.

Miz Barker's eyelids slow-lowered to half-mast. "Well, if I see him, I'll tell him you looking for him." She turned her back to Blanche and fiddled with something on the shelf behind the cash register.

"So now you got an attitude." Blanche's voice was as sure as Miz Barker's had been a bit ago.

The older woman turned to face her. "People been bringing that boy trouble ever since he was a child. I never seen a person try as hard to be good as that boy did when he was young. Went to school. Didn't steal. Always polite. And being beat up right and left by these hoodlums round here 'cause he didn't want to be in no gang or steal cars and such. It didn't stop when he growed up neither. Some people can't stand folks different from them. Make trouble for 'em. Don't make no sense."

And what made Ray-Ray so different from everybody else—the fact that Miz Barker thought he was special? Or the fact that he was male? All her life Blanche had been listening to women make excuses for some man acting like a boy—many of the same women who raised their own sons to believe that taking care of their trifling behinds was women's greatest joy.

"Most black people I know been brought trouble at one time or another," she told Miz Barker. "Sometimes it's 'cause they're different, but sometimes it's 'cause what goes around comes around. This ain't about me wanting to pick on Ray-Ray. It's about him doing me wrong and me having the right to speak on it. Nobody's perfect, not even Ray-Ray." Blanche picked up the greasy little bag Miz Barker had put her purchases in. "I'll be seeing you, Miz Barker."

"Humph!" was the old woman's only reply.

Irritation made Blanche walk even faster than usual. "That woman's too old to be so silly about that boy!" she said to the sidewalk. But she did feel better about Malik going off with Aminata tomorrow.

She was halfway up the hill to Rudigere Homes when she saw Miz Johnson grown son, Tongues, heading down the hill toward her. She couldn't help but smile.

Tongues hopped and bobbed toward her like a man walking on hot coals. His jacket and shirttail flapped around him as though a windstorm had gotten under his clothes. If he owned more than one shirt, they all looked like the plaid flannel one currently hanging over a pair of wrinkled khaki pants.

"I dreamed 'bout you, Blanche." He wheeled around and bounced back up the hill alongside her. "I dreamed 'bout you, just like last time. I told you, remember? I said—"

"Don't even go there, Tongues, okay? Just like I told *you* last time, I don't wanna be your girlfriend."

"I know, I know, I know what you said, I know what you said, but you sure is one fine woman, Blanche. I loves me a big strong woman, yes, I do, Blanche, I do. You make my heart—"

"Tongues, am I gonna have to get mad to shut you up?"

Tongues spun around and did a little leap before acting out how he'd got his nickname. "Sha lal kall ba Somalla damalla na kah hola maka..."

Blanche watched him for a second, laughing to herself and shaking her head. Crazy as he can be! But she loved that speaking-in-tongues thing. She'd heard it started when he'd tried to use the speaking in tongues he'd seen in the Pentecostal church to convince the army he wasn't fit to fight in the Korean War. They drafted him anyway. But whatever he'd seen in combat had changed his game into a way of dealing with any threat, no matter how mild. Otherwise, he was quiet and polite, with a shy smile and a sweet hello for everybody. Except that every couple of months he'd fall in love with some woman and declare his feelings whenever he saw her on the street—until he fell for someone new. He'd never done any harm, and Blanche had to admit there was something spirit-lifting about being adored, even by Tongues.

Taifa, Malik, and Shaquita showed up in time for dinner, all with plans for the evening: Shaquita was meeting Pookie—to tell him about her pregnancy, Blanche hoped. Taifa wanted to go to a party around the corner, and Malik wanted to go to Janel's to play some video game Blanche probably wouldn't let in her house. But that wasn't all he wanted.

"So, whaddaya think about the interviews, Moms? Aminata's gonna do 'em tomorrow." Anyone who didn't know him would have thought from his tone that he didn't care one way or another about going with Aminata.

"You can go, sweetie." Blanche paused to make room for his huge grin. "But you gotta be prepared to interrupt her."

Malik frowned at Blanche as though it were her fault Aminata was slightly off. But he listened closely to what she told him Miz Barker had said about how to stop Aminata's gentle-son speech.

"Have fun and don't get pregnant!" Blanche had whispered to Taifa as she was leaving the house. It was a standing joke with them—something Blanche always said when Taifa was on her way to some hormone-laden activity. With Shaquita in the house, it wasn't really funny, but seemed even more important to say than ever—like lighting a blue candle for protection.

When they'd all gone, Blanche made herself a gin-and-tonic and carried it to her favorite armchair. She sat sipping her drink and listening to the silence. Suddenly loneliness slithered up her legs and wound round her body like a boa constrictor. Lately, it attacked her more and more often. She was still looking forward to being her own woman again, with the kids grown and gone, but the closer she got to that, the more clearly she remembered that life alone wasn't all joy. She'd gotten used to being needed. She didn't always like it, but it was now so much a part of who she was, she couldn't quite see herself without it—like trying to imagine herself with a different face. She fought off thoughts of Leo that flooded her mind as they always did when she was feeling like she wanted to be attached to someone for a while.

How long had he been married? Two years? Three? Sometimes she forgot he now had a wife and thought of him down in Farleigh still waiting for her to come back to him, like he'd always done. It was time to get over being hurt about it. If she'd wanted the man, she could have had him. He had been really clear on that. She was the one who hadn't been clear. She still wasn't. Would she have felt differently if she and Leo hadn't known each other since grade school? If he hadn't been her first boyfriend and the man everyone down home expected her to marry? She hoped she hadn't let a good thing get away from her just to prove she was her own woman. But she'd hated the idea of being matched and labeled, and she'd never been keen on marriage. Yet, for the hundredth time, she wondered exactly when Leo had given up on her—if there'd been a way she could have stopped him, short of becoming Mrs. Leo.

Well, it was too late now. He'd decided to take second best. Blanche moved her shoulders as if to throw off an itchy sweater. She didn't need all this will-I-be-a-lonely-old-lady bullshit.

Yes, she was likely to be alone and, if she was lucky, old, but she didn't see herself talking to strangers just to hear her own voice, or buying younger men just to have a warm body in the bed. Leo or no Leo. Wasn't everybody alone inside their own mind? Anyway, she and Ardell had talked about getting a place together once the kids were grown. They'd be fine together, just fine.

She leaned over and picked up her copy of *Working Writer* from the floor beside her chair. It had become one of her favorite books. Joanie, who worked as a dietician at Boston Medical Center, had given it to her. The poems and stories by hospital laundry workers who'd recently gotten their GED and improved their English skills through the Worker Education Project were about people like her—people who worked with their hands at jobs that could murder your back and didn't provide a livable pension. They wrote about things she understood too well—like hardly ever having enough but deciding to love life anyway. Reading the book, she wondered what would happen if she and everybody like her decided to take the same week off and let their employers scrub the floors and empty the garbage while the workers got massages and sailed around the harbor on the old yacht.

She was still reading when Malik came in at nine, as instructed. At ten-twenty, she walked over to Dale Street to meet Taifa, who knew to leave the party at ten-thirty.

"Why I always got to be home so early? Other girls my age can stay until midnight, and I'm the only one whose mother..."

Blanche yawned. If she had a nickel for every time this child complained about what she wasn't allowed to do, she'd be richer than a Republican congressman.

On the way to the bathroom at two in the morning, something moved Blanche to look into Taifa's room. When she opened the door, Shaquita ducked her head under the covers. Taifa was sound asleep.

"Shaquita, are you sick, honey? You feel all right?" Blanche whispered, thinking miscarriage and ectopic pregnancy.

"I'm okay," Shaquita said tearfully. The blankets shuddered from her sobs. Right, Blanche thought.

"I'll be back." Blanche went to pee, then pried Shaquita out of bed and tugged her down the hall.

"What's wrong, Quita?" Blanche demanded, back in her own room.

"It's Pookie," Shaquita said, snuffling and sniffling. "He was supposed to meet me in Dudley Square so we could talk about... about things. But he never showed." Welling tears turned her large, dark eyes to liquid. "I called his house when I got home, and some girl answered and hung up when I asked for him." She was crying again in earnest now.

"Maybe his family had company or something; maybe the person didn't understand—"

"When I called back," Shaquita interrupted, "whoever answered the phone laughed in my ear, then laid the receiver down and left it off the hook. I could hear Pookie talking and laughing."

The little shit! Blanche put her arms around Shaquita and rocked her. "Shaquita, this is all the more reason for you to think seriously about whether having a baby right now is a good idea. If you can't get Pookie's attention before you tell him you're pregnant, what do you think it's going to be like when your belly is poked out and you're puking all over the place?"

Shaquita pulled away from Blanche. "You just don't understand!" She stomped out of the room.

Blanche lay back on her bed. Maybe Shaquita was right. Maybe she didn't understand. But Shaquita didn't understand either. Blanche saw her a year from now: one more too-young mother, like a half-finished building trying to provide shelter and safety when she was still only the shell of the woman she might become. Blanche fell off to sleep, hoping to be around when Shaquita was old enough to recognize Pookie-itis as a childhood disease.

FIVE

DAY FOUR—SUNDAY

It was one of those sunny mornings that almost made Blanche believe Boston was going to have something she'd recognize as a spring day. Almost. It wasn't one of those down home days when the varieties of new green and the smell of honeysuckle made spring air a thing you could almost hold in your hand. Most of what made such a day did show up in Boston, but in trickles—one week buds, then weeks of cold followed by some flowers, after which the scents of coming summer might meander in on the back of a chill breeze. The full effect was lost—it was like eating the strawberries, then the cream, and then the cake.

She got off the bus and fast-walked as far as Jamaica Pond. The trees had that gauzy look, as though their new buds were bashful—hiding behind a fine veil until they were ready to be seen. Blanche slowed down and watched the sun glinting on water like poured silver. She never stopped being amazed at how beautiful the natural world could be, even when it was surrounded by whizzing cars and gray concrete.

The Brindle house was quiet this morning. Today was Carrie's day off and Allister was away. Blanche was finishing up her tea when Felicia called down to say she'd have her juice and coffee in her room. Blanche collected the newspapers from the stoop and took them upstairs along with the tray.

"Morning, ma'am."

"I'm expecting someone," Felicia said. She looked like she was running for Miss Rainbow: blue eyelids, burnt-orange cheeks, and beige powder that didn't hide the purple half circles under her red eyes. She was pacing around and up and down the room like a power walker on a very small track. She made a pit stop at her writing table to pick up a business card and look at it. "A Mr. Cleason, Charles Cleason," she said. "Please show him into the library when he gets here."

"And a good morning to you, too, ma'am," Blanche said as she turned to leave.

"I'm sorry, Blanche. I didn't mean to be rude."

Blanche paused in the doorway. "Still worrying about your son, ma'am?" Blanche was immediately sorry she'd asked. Felicia's face crumbled like dried clay.

"I'm sure he's fine," Blanche said, eager to leave for fear that Felicia might reach out for support Blanche wasn't prepared to provide.

She put Felicia's misery out of her mind and made herself a lovely vegetable omelet and cheddar biscuits for breakfast.

Damn! The doorbell *would* ring in the middle of her meal. She tore off a small chunk of biscuit, popped it in her mouth, and quickly chewed it. She wiped her fingers on her apron and adjusted her panties on the way to the door.

"Morning." The man tipped his hat.

Blanche nearly jumped, his voice was so much bigger than the short, slight, olive-skinned white man the voice belonged to. He followed her down the hall so silently, she looked over her shoulder to make sure he hadn't slipped away.

Felicia was down the stairs before Blanche could fetch her. Blanche held the library door open.

"Thank you, Blanche."

Blanche smiled and practiced her knack for closing a door in a way that made it seem tightly shut but left just enough room between door and jamb for a sensitive ear to hear what was going on inside.

"I've called all of his friends; no one's seen him or talked to him in days," she heard Felicia tell Cleason. "I'd rather not involve the police."

Private detective, Blanche figured.

"You said something about the death of someone close to him?" Cleason asked.

"I don't even know if he knows about Sa—his friend." Felicia's voice went up and up like a singer's reaching for a high note. "Of course, it's been all over the news and . . ."

"Is there anything else you can tell me?" Cleason asked.

Felicia cleared her throat. "Well, he was my personal trainer."

"Your son?" Cleason sounded surprised.

"Oh no. Of course not. I meant his . . . his friend who . . ." Felicia paused again. "Forgive me, Mr. Cleason, I'm a bit upset, as you might imagine. I . . . Here's the picture you requested."

"No need to apologize, Mrs. Brindle. I understand completely."

I'm glad *you* do, Blanche said to herself. This was the first she'd heard about Marc and Saxe being friends. What was that funny catch in Felicia's voice when she'd mentioned the friendship? Did Marc know about his mother and his friend? Was that it? Blanche tiptoed away as Cleason assured Felicia that he would get right on it. He promised she'd hear from him in a few days.

Blanche scraped the cold remains of her breakfast into the garbage disposal and washed the few dishes by hand while her mind went elsewhere: It was like one of those Bill-loves-Mary-but-she-loves-Bob-who-loves-Susie kind of things. Felicia wanted to talk to Marc, who wanted to talk to Ray-Ray, who left word for Allister, who told his boy, Sadowski, to get Samuelson. But Felicia hadn't shown any interest in locating her son *before* Saxe died. And why was Ray-Ray looking for Marc? Did he want to show Marc the tape? From what Ray-Ray had said about doing something good for everybody in the state, she had a feeling he wanted to put that tape on national TV, if he could. Why? Ray-Ray admitted he'd been tight with the family; then he'd had a big fight with Allister. Did Ray-Ray want to ruin Allister because of that fight? But how serious could their fight have been? After all, Inez was still working for Allister.

While Felicia was still in the library, Blanche went upstairs for Felicia's tray. She made the bed and looked around. She appreciated the room: a queen-size spindle canopy bed without a canopy, a slipper chair and matching footstool, a writing alcove with bookshelves and a desk. She checked the bathroom for towels. There was a Jacuzzi and a shower lined with jets and showerheads. It even had a built-in seat. The shower was totally enclosed, so it was probably a steam cabinet, too. But it was the big cedar box with a door in it that stood next to the shower stall that made Blanche want to strip immediately: a sauna. Imagine! Your own sauna in your own bathroom! As much as she enjoyed the community sauna at the Y, she would have loved the privilege of a private sauna when the blues made her feel like crying over something she either couldn't or didn't want to name.

An hour later, Felicia came to the kitchen to say she was leaving for lunch and would be out for dinner as well. She had on a dark skirt, a beige sweater, no jewelry, and flat shoes, which made Blanche wonder if she was off to the shelter where she volunteered. Felicia told Blanche she could leave early if she liked but to double-check to make sure the answering machine was turned on.

No wonder Inez was so fond of this job. So far, there'd been very little of anything like hard work.

The phone rang before Felicia left the house. Blanche picked it up at the same moment Felicia did, even though it was the house line. It was Malik.

"Oh, sorry. I thought it might..." Felicia hung up the phone.

Malik ignored Felicia. "Mom, we finished the interviews and guess what? Three of the four guys in jail for killing people had lead poisoning when they were little. But listen to this, Moms, listen to this! One of them had a little sister who maybe died from lead poisoning when she was a baby. The building where they lived is still there, but it's boarded up. Aminata says we should check to see who owns the building and . . ."

So, who cares what Aminata said? Blanche mouthed at the receiver. Just because three of those kids had been poisoned by lead didn't mean lead poisoning had anything to do with their growing up to kill people. As for the child who'd died . . . All right, Blanche, get a grip, she told herself. She knew her attitude had nothing to do with lead poisoning and teen violence and everything to do with "Aminata says." Malik said it the way members of the Nation of Islam used to say, "The Honorable Elijah Muhammad says."

". . . check at City Hall. Can I go with her? Moms? Are you listening?"

"Sorry, honey. Where does *Miz* Aminata want to take you?"

"She said to just call her Aminata." Malik had that religious-experience tone in his voice again. "She's going to City Hall to find out who owns the boarded-up building. Aminata says we should make an example of the owner if the building still has lead in it."

Blanche didn't miss the "*we*."

"The buildings where the other kids lived have been de-leaded." Malik had barely paused for breath.

Environmental Man. My junior expert, Miz, excuse me, Aminata's boy sidekick. She managed to tell Malik she was glad the interviews had gone well, and even sounded like she meant it. "Let's talk about City Hall when I get home," she told him. She sighed and leaned her head against the wall after they hung up.

How was she going to act when the boy got a girlfriend? But that would be different. His girlfriend would be his age, not some woman old enough to be his mother. Malik looked up to Aminata in a way he could never look up to her. He didn't see Aminata when she woke up evil. Aminata would never be the one who told him he couldn't see that movie or hang out on the corner with his buddies. She watched herself trying to work with her feelings, understanding for the first time what jealousy was. It tasted of sour milk. She vowed to be extra nice to Aminata. If Malik was going to have a hero, at least Aminata was better than some woman-dissing rapper.

Blanche stopped by Miz Barker's on her way home. She wanted to put their Ray-Ray tiff to rest. Like Mama always said, it didn't make any more sense to let a man come between you and your women friends than it made to trade meat for a bone.

Pam came out from behind the counter and gave Blanche a hug. Miz Barker wasn't there.

"Don't tell me your grandmother actually left you in the store on your own without her supervision!"

Pam's face was solemn when she pulled away from Blanche.

"She was so upset about Ray-Ray, she had to go home."

"What about Ray-Ray?"

"You haven't heard? Mr. Porter who works at the morgue told us. Ray-Ray drowned last night in the public pool around the corner on M. L. K. Boulevard."

Blanche could feel her mouth gaping open but couldn't give her brain instructions to close it. Ray-Ray's larger-than-life grin flashed across her mind. The last time she'd seen him, life had spilled out of him like wine from a too-full glass. Her knees felt funny. She leaned against the counter, glad she hadn't had an opportunity to lay Ray-Ray out for stealing Allister's tape while she was around, glad that Ray-Ray had had the last word. Allister can relax now, she thought. Her stomach lurched.

"You okay, Blanche?"

"Hunh? Oh, yeah. Just shocked, I guess. I'm working his mother's job while she's away, and I just saw him..." Oh shit.

Would she have to break the news to poor Miz Inez? At the very least, she had to call Cousin Charlotte.

"Gran is taking it real hard. Ray-Ray was a favorite of hers. Ever since he was a little kid. She just broke down when she heard."

"You say he drowned? At the city pool?"

"People around here have been sneaking into that pool after it's closed since I was a kid. I guess Ray-Ray was one of them. The fence has been broken forever. Ray-Ray's not the only person to drown there either. It seems like every other summer some child sneaks in and ... Mr. Porter said he heard there was blood on the edge of the diving board, like Ray-Ray tried to do some kind of fancy dive, hit his head, and knocked himself out, then fell in the pool and drowned."

"Maybe I'll stop by the house and see Miz Barker."

"Please do, Blanche. I'm really kinda worried about her. I wanted to close the store and stay with her, but she shooed me out. Told me she needed privacy. 'Like my own boy,' she kept mumbling to herself. Nearly broke my heart."

Both women looked at each other through a shimmer of tears.

Miz Barker peered out through the space between the door and the safety chain.

"I'm so sorry about Ray-Ray, Miz Barker. I know he was special to you."

Miz Barker unchained the door and opened it. She looked up and down the street, then stepped back. "Come on in, daughter."

Her house was gleaming clean, but it had the same dry-paper-and-ancient-candy smell as the store. Miz Barker's shoulders seemed more bent than ever as she shuffled into the living room to a high-backed rocker. Blanche sat on the sofa. The room was so narrow, their knees nearly touched. The walls were covered with photographs of adults holding babies like they were the first prize in a contest, couples in their wedding gear, teens in caps and gowns, and old folks looking stiff and brittle as month-old bread. Blanche recognized Pam in some of them. Miz Barker rocked slowly and shook her head.

"No more than a child, really. Just a boy." Her eyes glittered with tears. "I 'preciate your stopping by, Blanche. I know you had a bone to pick with him."

"I'm glad I didn't get a chance to do it. I feel so sorry he lost his life."

"He was a good boy. Many a time he'd come here and mop my kitchen floor, wash the windows, things I wanted done but just didn't seem to have the... People always did take against him, even though..." Miz Barker raised her head. "It wasn't no accident, Blanche. I know that sure as I know my name. Feel it in every bone I got." She turned her head and frowned out the window as though she expected to be challenged from outside, then looked defiantly at Blanche.

Blanche could feel Miz Barker ordering her to ask what she had to ask but wasn't sure she wanted to. Did she really want to know the meaning of the lurch in her gut every time she thought about how much safer Allister Brindle was now that Ray-Ray was dead?

"Tell me," she said, almost against her will.

Miz Barker sat forward in her chair. "He come to see me."

"What did he say?"

Miz Barker looked at her a long time before she answered. "He thought somebody might be looking for him, to do him harm."

"He said that?"

Miz Barker nodded. "He said, 'He'll probably put his holy nigger on my tail. Don't worry. I've taken care of it.'"

Blanche frowned. What kind of conversation was that? Unless...

"He wasn't talking to you, was he? He was on the phone with somebody."

"That's right," Miz Barker said. "He called somebody."

"When was this?"

"Same day you come in the store asking for him."

"Before or after I came?"

"Before."

Blanche's heart did a hop. "Why didn't you tell me before?"

Miz Barker looked at Blanche from beneath her heavy eyelids. "I think maybe it had to do with Ray-Ray having something that didn't belong to him."

So that was what all that "protecting Ray-Ray" business had been about the other day, cagey old fox. "Did you tell the police?"

"I ain't 'bout to tell the police nothing like that! They already think we all thieves. Anyways, police don't care about no young black man's dying. All you got to do is read the paper to see that."

Blanche couldn't disagree. She just wasn't sure this ought to be the end of it. And neither was Miz Barker:

"That don't mean I don't want to know what happened to my boy. If somebody did hurt him, I want to know who it was, even if I can't do nothing about it."

And someone did hurt him, Blanche said to herself, as certain as if she'd been a witness. The memory of Allister Brindle calling Ray-Ray out by his name and raving about his stolen tape flashed quickly across her mind, followed by Allister's telling Sadowski to call Samuelson. She felt as though she were being drawn out of her body through the top of her head.

Miz Barker pinned Blanche with her eyes. "We got to do something," she said.

That was the second "we" Blanche had heard today, and she didn't like this one any better than the Malik-Aminata one. But she'd guessed there was a reason Miz Barker was telling her and not Pam or the police about this.

Miz Barker leaned back in her chair and rocked a little. A thin smile warmed her face. "I know I can depend on you, Blanche. Taifa told me about how you helped that lady up there in Maine and that white boy down home. I know you'll do as much for your old friend."

Blanche laughed. Did they put something in these old girls' food? How else could they sound so innocent and lay on so much responsibility, if not guilt? Then they made you feel good about bearing up under their orders even though you really didn't have any more choice than a stone had about being moved. How do they do it? And when do I get old and slick enough to participate? She wanted to know.

"Miz Barker, I don't think there's anything I can do."

"Yes, there is. Ask them ancestors I hear you talk to; then you git a good night's rest. You'll know what to do by morning."

This would make the third time Blanche had been mixed up in somebody dying too soon or in a wrong way. She felt both the weight of what Miz Barker wanted her to do and a kind of sizzle at the base of her spine, a kind of crackle of excitement over the prospect of trying to find out what had really happened to Ray-Ray.

She couldn't fool herself that she was agreeing to help for Miz Barker's, or even Ray-Ray's, sake. She was doing it because she liked doing it. She liked sticking her nose in where it wasn't supposed to be and finding out things other people didn't want her to know. She liked doing this the way some people liked jogging or dancing or going to the mall. It made her feel like she was putting all of herself to good purpose. She still got hits of feeling seriously useful when on the job and with the kids, but it wasn't like it had been when she was still learning her trade or when the kids were small. She hadn't realized how much she missed that feeling. She probably ought to be thanking Miz Barker instead of the other way around.

Blanche hurried home to make the call she didn't want to make.

"Cousin Charlotte, I hate to be the one to tell you this, but..."

"Somethin' happen to my baby?! What is it, Blanche, tell me what—"

"No, no. Shaquita's fine, Cousin Charlotte." Blanche paused and gathered herself. "It's Ray-Ray."

"Ray-Ray? What's wrong? What happened?"

"He's dead, Cousin Charlotte."

"Dead? Dead? Oh sweet Jesus! Sweet, sweet Jesus!" Cousin Charlotte's voice was a hoarse whisper as though shock had sucked up all the volume. "Tell me what happened."

Blanche told her about Ray-Ray's drowning, but not what Miz Barker had to say.

"Oh Lord! How'm I gonna tell poor Inez! He was her only child. The only one." Cousin Charlotte's sobs brought tears to Blanche's eyes.

"He was my godson, too, Blanche," Cousin Charlotte said.

"Oh, Cousin Charlotte, I'm so sorry." As a child, Blanche had always envied the kids with these backup parents.

"I can't talk right now, Blanche. I'll call you back." Cousin Charlotte's voice was choked with tears.

Blanche tried to just sit, to clear her mind for a couple of minutes, to just breathe and be there. She couldn't manage it long. Thoughts of Cousin Charlotte trying to tell Miz Inez about her only son's death quickened Blanche's breath and made her want to run from herself. Her skin felt raw, as though Ray-Ray's death had mauled her like some ugly beast.

She roused herself and took a large plastic container of red beans and one of black from the fridge, gathered onion, garlic, cumin, tomato paste, and chili powder, and got out the big pot. Ray-Ray watched her, not saying a word, only grinning his grin and moving his arms so that his muscles rippled. She didn't try to pretend that it was all her imagination. Ray-Ray, or at least a part of him, was walking around her kitchen like he owned it. But since he wasn't talking, she held her tongue, too.

She opened a pack of chicken franks and washed them. She'd throw them in the chili when it was done for chili dogs. She checked the fridge for salad greens, took out the ears of corn she'd bought the day before, and put them back again. Too much trouble. The kids could clean and cook the corn themselves. More and more she was trying not to be responsible for every bite that went into their faces. Twice a month Taifa was responsible for dinner, and so was Malik. They were rarely the greatest dinners she'd ever eaten, but that wasn't the point.

She wondered when Cousin Charlotte was going to call her back, and willed herself not to look in Ray-Ray's direction. Finally, she couldn't hold out any longer. He was leaning against the refrigerator door. He crossed his arms and gave her a "Well?" kind of look.

Blanche sank into a chair. "May the Ancestors welcome you," she told him. "But if you're here, I figure you want a report. I don't really know nothing," she told him. "I mean, I know you stole that tape of Brindle's. And you were right, weren't you? Brindle did put his preacher on you." She looked at Ray-Ray, hoping he would add something to the conversation. He didn't. "Damn! You're as bad as that old lady! Both of y'all expect me to do it all by myself." She sighed and closed her eyes for a second, trying to relax the tension in her back. "You could at least tell me who you were talking to on the phone. Was it Marc?"

No answer.

She opened her eyes: Ray-Ray was gone.

"Smart-ass," she mumbled. "Death don't change everything."

She wished Ardell were home. Why'd she have to be playing Miss Nanny of the Sea just now?

Blanche grabbed the phone on the first ring.

"Well, at least everything's under control," Cousin Charlotte said. "Lionel, Ray-Ray's daddy, is going to bring Ray-Ray's body down here for burial. That's what Inez wants, poor woman. Her heart's broken, just broken." Cousin Charlotte snuffled a few times. "Well, the Lord's will be done," Cousin Charlotte sighed.

If it gives you comfort, Blanche thought, but she didn't say it. Everybody ought to have something that helped life work for them, especially at a time like this—even if it was something that didn't work for Blanche personally.

"We'll have to stay on another week, Blanche. You can hold Inez's job a little longer, can't you?"

"No problem, Cousin Charlotte," Blanche said, and stifled a sigh. It was the least she could do.

The kids came home separately.

"Moms! You hear about Ray-Ray?" Taifa bellowed from the kitchen doorway.

Blanche stirred the chili and told her about the conversation with Cousin Charlotte.

"Yeah, that kinda stuff is really tough on old folks, I guess. I feel sorry for Miz Inez. You makin' chili? Great!" She sauntered off to the living room and turned on the radio.

"Yo, Mom, Ray-Ray drowned!" Malik told Blanche when he came in ten minutes later. "Dude was just trying to take a swim and bam!" Malik sniffed the air. "I hope there's dogs in that chili. We got hot dog buns?" He went to the bread box to make sure, then thundered up the stairs.

Blanche wondered what it meant that both Taifa and Malik moved quickly from Ray-Ray's death to chili. She could see the connection, one being necessary to ward off the other. Was that why there was always food after funerals? Maybe Malik and Taifa just reacted to something inside that was stronger than the polite sadness they'd learned to show when someone they knew died, something that automatically turned them away from death toward food, the thing that meant life. Or was it simply that they were young, and death, even when it brushed the edges of their own family, was still a myth in their minds?

"I hate it when people die!" Shaquita announced when it was her turn to come in and tell Blanche about Ray-Ray. "Poor Grandma! She was pretty close to him. And poor Miz Inez!"

Shaquita leaned over the stove to look down into the big pot. "That's a lot of chili!"

Blanche laughed. Three for death and three for the chili. Life was still in balance. "Some for leftovers," she told Shaquita. "It'll be even better after it sits a day or two." Blanche waited, suddenly positive Shaquita had something else on her mind.

Shaquita shifted from foot to foot and looked everywhere but at Blanche for half a minute more before she spoke again: "I know tomorrow's a school day and everything. But I already did my homework, and I know what I'm going to wear tomorrow, so that's all ready, so . . . I know how you feel about company on Sunday nights, Aunt Blanche, but could I . . ."

"Pookie?" Blanche interrupted. She couldn't stand but so much stammering and futzing around.

Shaquita nodded. "I talked to him. We straightened everything out. I . . ."

"What does 'straightened everything out' mean?" Blanche stirred the chili so hard, some slopped onto the stove.

"About Saturday, why he didn't show up. I haven't told him I'm . . . I wanted to, but I didn't want to do it on the phone, and he was tied up all day, so . . ."

"So you plan to tell him tonight."

Shaquita nodded again. "And I want you to meet him."

Blanche told herself to relax. Just because she wanted to twist that boy's testicles tight enough to keep him from ever knocking up somebody else's child didn't mean she'd actually try. After I meet him, I'll have a nice long, hot soak with lots of bubble bath and read the Sunday papers, she promised herself as a reward for being decent to Pookie.

"Okay, he can come over. But you gotta tell him tonight, Quita."

Blanche shooed Taifa and Malik upstairs to do the last of their homework when Pookie came. His slouchy posture and side-swinging arms were so common among young men these days, he seemed familiar. He had two gold chains around his neck and a diamond stud in his left ear. So this is our Pookie, she thought, every gangly, bullet-headed, low-talking bit of him. His wide, deep eyes added warmth to his lean face. He smiled and his prominent lips looked even more kissable. Poor Shaquita—she hadn't had a chance. Pookie had that irresistible-loving thing that some black men oozed like sweat. He might as well have had "Bad News" stamped on his baseball cap. Blanche looked at him as though he were a cat hair in her soup.

Pookie stuck out his hand. "I'm pleased to meet you, Miz Blanche. Quita says you're really special."

And charm, too. She gave him a toothy smile before he and Shaquita drifted off to the living room. Blanche fixed herself some tea and carried it upstairs. She decided to read the paper in her room instead of the tub. She'd get her bath once the kids were down for the night. She didn't want to be naked and soaking wet when Shaquita broke the news to Pookie.

She settled down with the Sunday *Boston Globe.* She started with the funnies, then went through the magazine and entertainment sections, working her way into the hard stuff. She didn't know why she bothered. Neither paper was worth all that much, unless you liked to read about criminals in the *Herald* and what to do about them in the *Globe.* Of course, she always read the black paper, the *Bay State Banner,* but was still partial to the *Amsterdam News,* warts and all.

She thought she heard the front door close, and she definitely heard Shaquita coming up the stairs. Blanche opened her door. "You okay?"

Shaquita looked like she'd been hit over the head with something heavy and was trying to decide whether or not to fall down.

Blanche took her wrist and pulled her inside.

"Did you tell him?"

Shaquita nodded.

"What did he say?"

Shaquita shrugged. "Nothing, really. I mean he... he didn't say anything. It was like I never said it or something. Like he didn't hear me or something."

"What do you mean?"

"He... He just sat there! I said, 'Pookie, did you hear me?' and he just looked at his watch. 'I gotta make a run, schoolgirl,' he said, like he was making fun of me or something. 'Gotta go.' And he was out of here, just gone." She looked up at Blanche as though she might be able to explain Pookie's behavior.

"Maybe he was just shocked and couldn't..." Blanche stopped talking. It wasn't her job to dredge up an excuse that made Pookie's walking out on Shaquita make sense. Maybe twisting his little nuts is an idea whose time has come, she thought. On the other hand, his acting like a first-class dickbrain could only help her convince Shaquita to make the right decision. Shaquita slumped where she stood.

"You need to get some rest, Shaquita. The important thing is that you told him and now you can turn your mind to deciding what to do."

"How can I decide anything if he..." Shaquita shook her head.

Lord! Had she ever been this blind?

"People say things in more ways than just with words, honey. He told you something by not saying anything."

"But what? What did he tell me? I still don't know if he..."

"If he what? Wants you to have a baby?"

Shaquita just looked at her.

"It's not his decision to make, Shaquita. It's yours. He's not pregnant. You are." Blanche knew she was preaching at the girl, but she couldn't seem to stop. "It's your body. You might have shared it with him, but you're the sole owner, honey, and you're the one that's got to decide what's going to happen to that body now."

Shaquita looked so alone, so tender, sympathy finally stilled Blanche's tongue. She put her arm around Shaquita's shoulder and felt the girl lean into her.

"I want to talk to you and Pookie before you make a decision—okay?" Shaquita nodded. Blanche walked her to the door.

Blanche had just settled on the toilet when Taifa knocked on the door, then slipped into the bathroom.

"So, when you gonna tell me?" Taifa demanded to know.

"Tell you what, Taifa?"

"About Shaquita."

Blanche's first impulse was to say it was none of Taifa's business, then to complain about not even being able to poop in peace. Both thoughts dissolved under the don't-bullshit-me look on Taifa's face and the memory of how insulted Blanche used to feel when Mama pulled that mess on her.

"I didn't tell you 'cause I'm hoping it won't last long." They'd had enough conversations about abortion so that Blanche knew she didn't have to explain.

"But she wants to have it, don't she?" Taifa sat on the side of the tub and crossed her long legs.

"Why you so sure she wants to have it?" she said.

"Well, you remember the other night she was talking about wanting to be an archy-whatever?"

"Archaeologist."

"Right. Well, remember, she said she wished she didn't have to go to college to learn how to dig up dead people? See, she don't really want to go to college. Every time I hear her talking to her girlfriends all they talk about is their boyfriends and babies. It's stupid."

"I'm glad you think so."

"Does Cousin Charlotte know?" Taifa asked.

Blanche shook her head and added, "Shaquita's got some hard decisions to make."

"Cousin Charlotte's going to make her butt!" Taifa rose and stretched. She patted Blanche on the shoulder. "Don't worry, Moms, I'm not gonna want to have a baby when I'm in high school, and I ain't afraid to go to college, either."

"Excuse me? What makes you think she's scared of going to college?"

Taifa wandered over to the medicine cabinet. She pumped some hand lotion into her palm, sniffed it, and stirred it around with one finger. "Well, maybe not exactly scared, but like, well, you know." Taifa studied her face in the medicine-cabinet mirror as though she were considering it for a prize. "Like she won't be part of the 'hood anymore, but what will she be part of? And Pookie, man, lots of girls like him, so . . . I'm gonna make a sandwich, you want one?"

Blanche could only shake her head. She was still taking in all she'd just been told about Shaquita *and* Taifa. Taifa was full of noise: loud talk, louder music, arguing about every little thing. But inside that noise there was somebody taking in everything happening around and to her and doing something with it. So much for that old saying about empty barrels. Noise and empty didn't necessarily go together.

Blanche thought about the many conversations she'd had with Shaquita about college. Not once, *not once*, had she picked up what she could clearly see, now that Taifa had pointed it out. Blanche had thought Shaquita's nervousness was about getting *into* college. But why would that concern somebody who'd gotten good marks since first grade? Poor child. She had to be truly confused to think that having a baby and raising it was less scary than going off to college. But of course, that wasn't all that was happening. The boyfriend had plenty to do with it, too. Was getting her pregnant his way of keeping Shaquita out of college and with him? No. He probably hadn't thought about anything past the head of his dick.

In the middle of the night, Blanche woke and tiptoed first to Malik's and then Taifa's room. The urge to bundle them into her arms and guard them against the worst of life made her rock on her feet. But she stood longest looking down at Shaquita, willing her not to let her life go reeling off a cliff because she'd done the natural thing, the thing that would be expected of a girl her age if she'd grown up in a real third world country instead of a neighborhood that was treated like one. It occurred to her that Shaquita's pregnancy meant she and Pookie had had unprotected sex, or at least had used a leaky condom. In either case, Shaquita needed to get tested for AIDS on top of everything else.

Sleep had gone elsewhere when Blanche returned to bed. She had a hard time calling it back. It arrived with a dream of Shaquita with six kids, homeless, living in a broken-down cab, but laughingly happy. Taifa and Malik lived two cars over.

SIX

DAY FIVE—MONDAY

Dreams chased Blanche from one side of the bed to the other until nearly dawn. In between dreams, she'd played the night sweats game: sweat and fling the blankets off, shiver and pull them back up again. She'd had her first night sweat six months ago. It had taken her a week or two to understand that they were the beginning of the end of her monthly investment in the tampon industry. Now she woke feeling as though she'd been jogging half the night. She leapt to her feet when she realized she'd slept through her alarm. She rushed in and out of the shower, covered her hair with a scarf instead of rebraiding it, praised and thanked the Ancestors while she dressed, but was still late for work.

Yet the closer she got to the Brindle house, the slower she walked. The sooner she got there, the sooner she would have to try to prove that she and Miz Barker were right—that Ray-Ray's death was no accident, and that her employer and his chief negro were responsible. But how? That was part of what slowed her steps: She didn't have a plan. She should have been more honest with Miz Barker, should have told her there was no way to do anything more than guess about what happened to Ray-Ray. But no, she had to act like she was some kind of detective or psychic or something. She could already see the look of disappointment on Miz Barker's face. Guilt prickled her like porcupine quills. She was walking so slowly now, she was hardly moving.

There was one other thing that slowed her steps: She needed to be careful. Very careful. She most certainly didn't want Brindle to realize she was on to him—not if the Ray-Ray solution was how he settled his differences with people. She pushed her double-minded self into the Brindles' kitchen.

"Well, if we ain't that glad to see you, darling!" Wanda was sitting at the kitchen table changing her shoes for carpet slippers. "I was afraid our Carrie was goin' to have to take over the cooking." Wanda punctuated her statement with a wink.

"Humph!" was all Carrie chose to say, but she whacked a grapefruit in half as though she meant to do it harm.

Blanche wasn't about to join Wanda in teasing a sister, especially one as sensitive as Carrie. "Thanks for doing the grapefruits and juice," she told Carrie instead. She hung her sweater and bag in the closet, put on her apron, and went to the stove.

"So, Miz Wanda, I thought I only had the pleasure on Tuesdays and Thursdays. Today's Monday." Blanche washed her hands and took over laying out breakfast.

Wanda pulled the vacuum from the utility closet. "Didn't I mention last time I was here? Tomorrow's me grandniece's graduation. Wouldn't miss that, would I? I'm not so much on the sittin' and listenin' to speeches part, but there'll be lovely cream buns and other bits afterward. Wouldn't miss that, would I, darlin'?" She pushed the vacuum into the front of the house.

Blanche set about making sure that even though she'd been late to work, breakfast was on time. She hummed to herself as she moved around the kitchen, bopping to the rhythm of cooking—a dance she knew well enough to improvise on with ease. She moved lightly from stove to fridge, buttering pans, slicing and dicing tomatoes, crumbling feta. Her mind was free of everything but the moment—the sure movements of her hands, the slight, circular motion of her body as she beat the eggs, the certain knowledge of just the right mix and amount of artichoke hearts, feta, and tomatoes to fill but not overpower the frittata.

She felt the deep and satisfying pleasure of knowing that she not only knew what she was doing, but was doing it to death.

When she finished her breakfast number, Blanche went to the bathroom and undid her cornrows. She combed and brushed her soft, thick, graying hair, parted it down the middle, and gathered strands, sweet with coconut oil, for rebraiding. She hummed softly and rocked a little as her body remembered sitting between her mother's legs having her hair plaited: the smell of her mother's newly washed and starched dress, like fresh-baked pie crust; the weight of the can of Dixie Peach Pomade she held within her mother's reach; the sound and vibration of her mother's humming that traveled down her mother's arms into young Blanche's scalp, connecting them as totally as they'd been joined before Blanche was born. Gonna call Mama tonight, Blanche said to her mirror self.

Carrie was waiting for her in the kitchen. "Need more coffee, Blanche. They sucking it up today."

Blanche sniffed the air. Each time Carrie or Wanda opened that door a wave of sour air rushed into the kitchen—not sour-smelling, but air that had been hanging around people in an evil mood: damp and mean and edgy. It surprised her. She'd expected Allister and Sadowski to be at least content, if not downright happy. By now Allister must know his Ray-Ray problem was permanently solved.

Carrie picked up the coffee tray. The front doorbell rang. Carrie stepped forward, then back, trying to decide whether to take the coffee first or answer the door. The bell rang again.

"You get the door; I'll take the coffee," Blanche said, removing the tray from Carrie's hands.

Brindle and Sadowski looked almost as bleak as they had the morning Brindle's run for governor had had to share the front page with Saxe's death. Felicia was doing all the talking:

"...hasn't been to work, and none of his friends have seen or heard from him." Her voice didn't get any louder, but it kept getting higher. Blanche imagined a spring in Felicia's chest winding her tighter and tighter as she spoke.

Allister shrugged. "Probably holed up in some hotel in Provincetown with..." He stopped talking when Blanche approached the table. He watched her without a word while she served the coffee. Blanche never looked directly at him, but she could feel his suspicion like a hungry hound sniffing at her ankles. No one spoke while she poured. So, of course, she did her door trick and listened from the hall.

"Mrs. Brindle, I'm sure your son—" Sadowski began.

Felicia turned on him. "Shut up, you weasel. I may allow you at my table, but I do not allow you to speak on family matters, at least not to me."

Blanche imagined Sadowski turning a vivid shade of red. Allister Brindle spoke up: "Felicia, I have far too much on my mind to worry about—"

"Oh, that's right!" Felicia said. "The missing photographs, or love letters, or autographed panties, or whatever. I thought you'd have taken care of that by now."

Do it, girl! Blanche mouthed. Worry about her son hadn't taken a bit of edge off Felicia's tongue.

Carrie turned from the front door with an armful of flowers. She headed for the breakfast room door, where Blanche stood listening. Carrie rolled her eyes in disapproval.

There was a thump and the clatter of dishes from the breakfast room, as if someone had slammed his fist down on the table.

"The whereabouts of your son is of no interest to me," Allister said in a slightly louder voice than usual. "There, I've said it. Are you happy? I've saved you the trouble of accusing me of not caring. I hope he stays lost permanently. The last thing I need is—"

Blanche knocked on the door and quickly opened it, just in time to see the glass in Felicia's hand and then the orange juice on Allister's face. Shock loosened Allister's features so that his nose and lips seemed to flow down to his chin along with the juice. Felicia stared at him from narrowed eyes. Sadowski hurried to Brindle's side, fluttering around him like some mammy in a 1940s plantation movie. No one noticed Carrie standing in the doorway with Blanche peering gleefully over her shoulder. These rich white folks sure knew how to rumble!

Allister waved Sadowski off and dabbed at his face. He threw his napkin on the table, rose, and headed toward the door.

"Get Samuelson," he growled at Sadowski.

Allister almost knocked Carrie over when he came storming out of the room. Blanche was already scooting back to the kitchen, chuckling over the look on Allister's juice-spattered face and the way Sadowski had buzzed around him. But Felicia! She could get the Bitch on Wheels Award if she kept up the good work. Damn Ardell! Why couldn't she call from that stupid boat she was on? I'm likely to burst with all this stuff before she gets home, Blanche complained to herself. She was somewhat cheered when the back door opened and Mick stepped inside.

"Hey! I forgot you were coming today."

Mick hitched her glasses further up her nose. "But you're glad to see me, right?"

Today her black T-shirt said DYKES DO IT BETTER in big white letters inside a pink triangle.

"Honey, you don't know the half."

"You hear about Miz Inez's son?" Mick asked before Blanche could tell her about the Brindles' little run-in.

"Did you know him?" Blanche asked.

"Yeah. I can hardly believe it! I mean, we were the same age! Went to English High together!" She spoke as if these facts were supposed to prevent death. "It really takes me out!"

"I just saw him the other day," Blanche said. "I feel awful for Miz Inez, too. She goes on her vacation and..."

"Yeah. That's rough." Mick looked at her watch. "God! I'm late. Gotta get moving."

"You got your work cut out for you today, girl," Blanche told her.

Mick turned back from the stairs. "Something happen?"

Blanche filled her in on what she'd seen and heard at the breakfast table. "I swear Allister looked like somebody had goosed him with an icicle," she said.

"Be plenty knots in Felicia's muscles this morning." Mick chuckled. "Wonder what's up with Marc?"

"You know him, too?"

"Not know him, know him. Him and Ray-Ray were tight." She ran up the back stairs.

Blanche stared after her for a moment or two in which she wondered exactly what "tight" meant.

Carrie had brought the flowers to the kitchen and left them on the sink counter. Blanche hunted up a vase and filled it with weak bleach water and sugar and began snipping stems and arranging flowers. The doorbell rang again, and Carrie scurried to get it.

Blanche had assumed that Brindle's order to Sadowski to "get Samuelson" meant to get him on the phone, so she was surprised when Carrie came back to say she'd just shown Samuelson into the library.

And don't I need to take these flowers into the living room and do a quick house inspection, especially around that library door? Blanche asked herself.

Sadowski barged into the kitchen like the place was being raided. "The boss wants to see you. Now."

Blanche gave him her I-know-you-ain't-talking-to-me look and turned to the sink. Carrie managed to shrink to the size and substance of a dust bunny. Blanche picked up the cut flower stems and dropped them into the disposal one by one. She wiped the counter, rinsed the dishcloth, and began slowly folding it, carefully lining up the corners and smoothing each fold.

"I said ..."

Blanche looked over her shoulder at Sadowski: "Just 'cause you stop pissing in midstream when your lord and master calls don't mean I'm going to rupture my lungs running down the hall."

"Now look here . . ."

Blanche sucked her teeth and turned her head. She finished folding the dishcloth and hung it on its hanger. She straightened her dress, retied her apron, and smoothed her hair.

"Out, out!" She made shooing motions at Sadowski and grinned behind his back as he turned on his heel and huffed out of the kitchen. She followed him into the hall, mimicking his loopy white-boy walk.

Rivulets of hard rain striped the library windows, silver on darkest gray. Brindle's face seemed to float just outside the puddle of yellow light from the lamp on his desk. His folded, spotlighted hands made Blanche think of animal traps covered with snow. Samuelson was standing in the corner where the bookshelves met. His arms were crossed, his head tucked in just like the TV magician before he disappeared into a cloud of white smoke. She made sure Samuelson saw her seeing him. Sadowski was now behind her, guarding the closed door.

Allister stared at her as though he had some hope of reading her mind.

"Do you have it?" Allister's words leaped across the desk at her like well-aimed knives.

"Excuse me?"

"Don't play games with me! I want it back, goddammit, and I'm willing to pay! Do you have it?"

He needs a tic, a hand-washing routine or something, Blanche thought, something like a valve on a pressure cooker, to ease some of the strain making him look like the top of his head's about to blow off.

"Have what, sir?"

"Don't lie to me! You let him in and you . . ."

Blanche put her hand on her hip and opened her mouth to tell Allister what he could do with his accusations and his job.

"I asked you a question!" he shouted at her before she could say anything.

She gave Allister's heaving chest and panicky eyes the kind of once-over that said she wasn't looking at much while she decided whether to do her Hurt Faithful Retainer routine or to go for Outraged Dignity. She pulled herself up an extra inch and took a deep breath. She considered folding her hands in front of her belly and decided that was going too far. She lifted her chin.

"There ain't a man living that I got to lie to, including you," she said—without pointing out the difference between having to lie and choosing to. "And I'm through being called a liar."

She reached behind her and began untying her apron as she turned and walked toward the door, contemplating punching Sadowski in his gut if he didn't get out of her way. He hurried around her toward the desk. She heard him whisper something to Allister.

"Don't go off in a huff," Allister said as she reached for the doorknob. "No one's accusing you of anything."

Blanche looked over her shoulder at him, but she didn't turn around, didn't walk back to the desk.

"Will that be all, sir?" She didn't wait for Brindle to answer. She was tempted to let the door slam or at least close with a definite thud, but she couldn't afford that. She stood with her ear pressed to the almost-closed door.

No one spoke for a couple of seconds. Then: "Insolent bitch! She's lying. He might have used the key to get in, but she's in on it. She put his note with the mail, and if she doesn't have the tape, she knows where it is. I'm sure of it," Brindle said.

Sadowski agreed. "But better to have her here, sir, so we can—"

Samuelson interrupted: "But why would Ray-Ray give her the tape? She's not—"

"I don't care why, Maurice." Brindle said Samuelson's first name as though it tasted bad on his tongue. "I just want that tape found, Maurice, and I want it found now. If you hadn't fucked up and ki—"

"Boss..." Sadowski sounded like a parent warning a child against saying a bad word. Brindle didn't finish his sentence.

"How many times do I have to tell you I—" Samuelson began.

"I don't give a shit about how you fucked up or why! Just get me that goddamned tape!" Allister shouted.

Blanche went to the kitchen wishing, once again, that she'd torn that damn note up and flushed it down the toilet. Ray-Ray should have just put Brindle's business in the street without selling wolf tickets. It was amazing how simpleminded some black men could be about white folks. What happened to all that mother wit that had helped them survive more than three hundred years in a cold, cruel country? What had Ray-Ray expected Brindle to do? Beg him to please not tell anybody? Offer him the guest room? Apologize for whatever it was she was sure Brindle had done to make Ray-Ray hate him enough to want to ruin Brindle's run for governor?

And what had Brindle done about it? The question made her stomach rumble. Maurice Samuelson is what he did about it. Why else would Brindle have him in the room? Listening, watching. A scorpion waiting to strike. Like Ray-Ray was struck. But why kill Ray-Ray without getting the tape? Brindle's got to be hot over that. That's what he meant when he said Samuelson had fucked it up—he didn't get the tape. Maybe Samuelson made Ray-Ray tell him where it was, but it wasn't there. Maybe he gave Samuelson a phony tape. And what was on the damned thing anyway? Now Ray-Ray was dead, the videotape was out there somewhere, and Brindle thought she had it. She wished Samuelson had let Sadowski finish his sentence about why it was a good idea to have her in the house. Shit! She wanted to find out what happened to Ray-Ray, but she didn't want to have a so-called accident of her own in the process. She jumped when the intercom buzzed.

"Such a shame about Ray-Ray," Felicia said when Blanche went up to her room. "Inez called last night. She is *so* thoughtful, even at a time like this. Of course, I told her to take all the time she needed, that you were doing just fine."

"Did you know Ray-Ray, ma'am?" Blanche asked, even though she already knew the answer. She wanted Felicia's version of what Ray-Ray had been to the family.

"Oh yes! He and my son, Marc, were great good friends. Ray-Ray was probably in this house as much as he was in his own."

Blanche wondered how many times Marc had been to Ray-Ray's house.

"Things sure have changed between y'all, haven't they, ma'am? I mean Ray-Ray was your son's friend, but your husband doesn't seem to think much of Ray-Ray now." Blanche hoped this would prompt Felicia to tell what had soured Ray-Ray on Allister.

Felicia looked surprised. "Yes, well, that's life, isn't it? People we think are our friends, who we think we can trust . . ."

Felicia's voice was suddenly so thick with sadness, Blanche was sure it wasn't Ray-Ray she was thinking about.

"But that's another story," Felicia said without finishing her comment about friends and trust. Instead, she gave Blanche a speculative look. "Have you any idea what it is my husband is missing? I could ask that ass, Sadowski, but I'd rather not."

Blanche was surprised by the question. Clients were generally more roundabout when they pumped her about another family member's business. She was tempted to say "It ain't my place, ma'am," but she found that usually worked only on Southern women and women with dreams of grandeur, not the ones who could actually afford it. She liked the fact that Felicia had come right out and asked her, like a grown woman, instead of trying to trick or bribe her into telling.

"A videotape," she said.

"Do you know what's on it?" Felicia asked, and was obviously disappointed when Blanche said no.

"Well, if you hear anything or know someone who might know where this tape is, please come directly to me. I promise you, I'll be extremely generous."

Blanche decided not to respond to that. She never liked being in cahoots with a client. They rarely had your back when shit got stinky. Still, she was glad Felicia wasn't in on what had happened to Ray-Ray. Felicia was still avoiding major eye-to-eye; Blanche wondered what she thought her eyes might show.

Around noon, people poured out of the house like water: Neither Wanda nor Mick had time for a snack; the Brindles went out and took Sadowski with them; even Carrie had an errand to run. Blanche called home. The line was busy.

The person Blanche sensed approaching the back door banged on it in a way that really got her back up. She opened the door eager to give hell to whoever it was. The sight of the red-eyed young man the color of just-done toast made her pause long enough for him to speak.

"Would you ask Miz Inez to come to the door, please. I have to see her. I'm not leaving until she talks to me." He crossed his arms over his slim chest and stuck out his chin like somebody willing to start trouble but not likely to be able to handle it.

Despite his badass attitude, Blanche had to smile. Just as cute as he can be, she thought, taking in his pert nose and dreamy brown eyes, the way his lips lifted at the corners even while he was trying to be tough. She liked the way he dressed, too, in a kind of old-fashioned dark gray suit with wide loose pants and a long square jacket. He had a clean, crisp smell, like limes or juniper berries.

"Well, honey," she said. "If you're planning to hang here until Inez comes out, you gonna be standing here for a long time, 'cause she's not here."

The young man swayed like a hypnotized snake as he tried to see around her.

"I told you she's not here, and I don't appreciate you acting like you think I'm lying." She wasn't about to tell him anything more. Cute or not, for all she knew, he could be a bill collector. She made to close the door.

"Wait, wait, please. I'm sorry. I'm just so upset." He gave Blanche a sad, haunted look. "She's not home. I've been to her house. It's locked tight. I called her all day yesterday. I just want to know when the viewing and the funeral are going to be. I got a right. I loved him, too. Maybe more than she did. At least I loved him for what he was ... He'd want me there, want me to ..." The young man broke off in an attempt to stop the tears already flowing down his face.

"Who are you?"

"It's not fair. It's just not fair," he said. "We loved each other. We'd just found a place over in ... He was going to ..."

Oh shit. The boyfriend! And she hadn't even realized Ray-Ray was gay! That's what Miz Barker meant about Ray-Ray being different. Why hadn't Mick told her? Blanche stepped outside the back door and closed it behind her.

"Listen, honey. I'm sorry, but Ray-Ray's body is on the train headed for North Carolina, where his people are from."

The young man turned his face away, his pain too private to share. This was not a good neighborhood for a black man to be walking through looking half crazy. But she wasn't about to let him in the house. He might be Ray-Ray's lover, but that didn't necessarily stop him from being a hatchet murderer. A lot of serial killers looked and acted like the nice boy next door when they weren't gouging out people's livers.

He took a snowy handkerchief from his pants pocket, wiped his eyes and face, and blew his nose. "Thanks for telling me," he said. "You're the first person who ..." He struggled not to cry again.

"What's your name?"

"Donnie. Donnie McFadden."

"Donnie, I'm real sorry about your loss. I'm Blanche White. I'm taking over for Inez until she gets back. I can't invite you in, but if you want to sit out here for a few minutes until..."

"No, no. I'm okay." He put his handkerchief away and straightened his shoulders. He looked so tender, she thought he'd bleed if she touched him.

"Look, I gotta get back to work, but I really appreciate... you're the only one I know who... Could I, I mean, could we talk later, after you get off?"

And listen to you talk about Ray-Ray? Blanche said to herself. You betcha. Who was more likely to know the whereabouts of that tape than Ray-Ray's lover? She agreed to meet him at Connolly's bar at eight-thirty.

She called home again and was almost sorry she did.

"You let me do the interviews, why can't I go to City Hall with Aminata?" Malik wanted to know. "She can't go till around three-thirty on Thursday. I can skip the Mediation Committee, so why can't I go?"

Blanche would have told him if she'd had a good reason. But "No" had just popped out of her mouth when Malik mentioned Aminata's name. Got to get over this! She told herself.

"You're right, honey. Yes, you can go. I just don't want you to spend so much time on this project you get behind in other subjects." She cringed at the excuse-making whine in her own voice.

She talked to Taifa next, or rather listened to Taifa tell every detail of her not-very-interesting conversation with her friend Rasheeda. They'd had a big fight and were trying to make up. Shaquita came on last and said there was no mail, except bills, and Blanche hung up.

She figured out which of her regular clients Cousin Charlotte's niece was supposed to be working for right then and called her.

"Aunt Charlotte already called me," Larissa said.

"Well, I'll call all my clients and tell them. Is everything going all right?"

Blanche couldn't decide whether to be happy or nervous when Larissa, and later, all her clients, said everything was going just fine without her.

Felicia reached for her martini almost before she was in the door. Allister Brindle sprawled in his chair.

"Who is it tonight?" Felicia asked.

"The Garrisons. Oil money. He could be very helpful with—"

"A campaign contributor, of course," Felicia interrupted. "Why else would we go there for dinner? God forbid we should have dinner with someone you weren't planning to fleece."

"There was a time you enjoyed going out with me," Allister said. His eyes spoke of missing those times.

"We used to be on the same side, believe in the same things, like the same people." Felicia said. "Now . . ." She looked as though she had more to say, but didn't.

"Does everything have to be about politics?" he asked.

"You tell me. You're the politician," Felicia said. "I'm going to get dressed."

Blanche was always interested in the way couples conducted their fights. Walking out of the room before Allister could get his two cents in seemed to be one of Felicia's major battle techniques—that and pitching orange juice. Blanche chuckled.

Allister took a long swallow from his glass and set it down before he, too, left the room. Blanche caught a glimpse of him in the sunroom on her way to the kitchen, nursing his hurt feelings and his plants. Two hours later, they were both gone, with Carrie right behind them.

Blanche had planned to take a good look around Allister's rooms and office before she left, but that would have to wait. She wanted to spend some time at home before she went off to meet Donnie.

Taifa was at a low spot on her hormonal roller coaster. If she wasn't laughing like a ten-million-dollar lottery winner, she was evil as a drunk on a water diet or so fresh Blanche could see steam rising from her.

"I don't know why I gotta take some old Spanish noway. None of my friends have to take it."

"That's between your friends and whoever is in charge of their education."

"Gawd! It's just too stupid!" Taifa stomped up the stairs.

Blanche was sometimes tempted to tell Taifa and Malik that she understood it was their job to rebel against her, to twist and turn and chafe themselves to independence so they didn't have to work at it so hard—but that information could backfire. She had a flash fantasy of Malik bringing home his Aminata look-alike girlfriend and there was Taifa in a see-through blouse and beat-me-daddy stiletto heels. She shook those thoughts off. Reality was scary enough.

"Moms! Phone."

The voice on the phone was so much less oily than in person that Blanche didn't recognize it at first. When she did, she made a face and wished like hell she hadn't taken the call.

"How'd you get this number, Maurice?"

"I got my sources, I got my sources." He laughed in a way that made her think he was at least uncomfortable, if not nervous, about calling her.

"Your choice for governor tell you to call me?"

"Now, don't be like that. The man don't mean you no harm. He's just worried. A lot's riding on his finding that tape Ray-Ray stole."

"How do you know he stole it?"

"Like I said, I got my ways. The real question is, where's the tape now?" He paused as if he actually expected her to tell him.

"Well?" she said.

"I wouldn't fool around with Brindle if I were you, sister. He's serious as a heart attack. Whoever has that tape is going to end up in some deep stuff."

"Like Ray-Ray, in the deep end of the pool," she said without thinking.

There was a moment of silence before Samuelson said, "I don't know nothing about that, sister. Not a thing. I just hope ... I just wanted to make sure you were okay and not taking Brindle's attitude personally. Like I told you, the man's upset. Very upset." Another pause. "So, if you can help him out ..."

"You mean contribute to his campaign, or make sure his shorts don't get starched?"

Samuelson's laugh was as real as the tooth fairy. "I thought maybe you could talk to Ray-Ray's mama, see if she might know where he ..."

"If Ray-Ray stole something from his mama's employer, I doubt he'd call her long-distance to brag about it."

"Just trying to be helpful, sister, trying to save you some trouble."

"Yeah, right. And my name's not sister." She hung up the phone and slumped against the wall. When she'd been listening at the library door, Samuelson had sounded as if he didn't believe she had anything to do with the tape. Had he changed his mind, or was he hedging his bets? Bad news in either case. He hadn't actually threatened her, but it was definitely time to start looking for that tape. But first, it was time to meet Donnie and see what he knew.

Connolly's was Blanche's favorite bar and live jazz outlet. It was the only bar she knew in Roxbury where a mature, lone woman could go without carrying a baseball bat. She thought the jazz called in the old heads and chilled out the young.

Donnie was waiting for her at the last small table in the back, beyond the long oval bar. He rose and waved to make sure she saw him. Blanche ordered a gin-and-tonic from the bartender.

"Hey, girl." Blanche turned around. Lucinda, who worked at The Steak Shop near Dudley Square, sat a stool away.

"I didn't know you ran with the quick-change artists," she said, tipping her head in Donnie's direction.

"Cab!" a voice hollered from the door.

"That's me!" Lucinda jumped off the stool and hurried out the door before Blanche could ask her what she meant. Blanche had a feeling it was some kind of slur against gays. She left the money for her drink and a tip on the bar. She took a sip from her glass, then carried it to the table, where Donnie was making rings on the tabletop with the bottom of a full glass of beer. He looked calmer, but sorrow hung around him like heavy weather. He had on the same clothes but managed to seem just-showered and newly pressed.

"Look, I'm sorry about this afternoon," he began before Blanche could speak. "I know I was out of line, going on Miz Inez's job like that, but I didn't know what else to do." He took a swig from his beer. "I didn't think she'd be glad to see me. Another friend told me how she treated him when he went to her house to pick up Ray-Ray. She called him a freak! Can you believe it?" Donnie looked at Blanche as though it had just occurred to him that she might be on Inez's side. "You a close friend of hers?"

"Relax, honey. I'm holding Inez's job because she's a friend of a relative, not because I believe she knows sunshine from shoe polish."

Donnie relaxed against the back of his chair.

Blanche stirred and sipped her drink. She wondered why Donnie had bothered to go to the Brindles'. If Miz Inez didn't want gays at her own door, she certainly wouldn't put up with one at her white folks' house, especially one claiming to be Ray-Ray's lover.

"Listen, Donnie," she told him. "I don't want to beat around the bush. Ray-Ray's funeral will probably be the day after tomorrow. I'm sorry."

Donnie covered his eyes with his hands. Blanche patted his arm. He lowered his hands and held his head back as if his tears were a bloody nose. They sat quietly for a minute or two. Someone put money in the jukebox—something slow and sad. Donnie excused himself and went to the bathroom. His eyes were red-rimmed when he returned. He avoided meeting Blanche's gaze.

Men, she thought, gayness notwithstanding. "It's normal to cry when someone you love dies," she reminded him. "Old folks say the dead need our tears to get where they got to go."

Donnie sighed a shuddery after-tears sigh. "Ray-Ray would have liked that. He believed in the hereafter and stuff like that. God! I miss him." He rubbed his eyes. "We had a fight the last time I saw him."

"When was that?"

"Four days before he died. We'd been staying at my place most nights until our place was ready, but that night..." Donnie sighed and closed his eyes for a moment before he went on. "That night... It was a real fight. I said things... we both said things that... Ray-Ray walked out. And that was that." His eyes glistened. "I never saw him again." Donnie quickly wiped at his eyes.

Blessed Ancestors! Blanche thought, Could this story get much sadder? She hoped Donnie would say more about the fight, but he didn't. Asking him to go into detail seemed a little like poking a finger in his wound.

"How long were y'all together?" she asked instead.

"I've been in love with him for years." Donnie's eyes and expression went someplace else.

Blanche was aware of a kind of translation going on in her brain, changing Ray-Ray—the overmuscled, confident jock—into a gay man somebody had been in love with for years. She chided herself for assuming Ray-Ray was straight because he had muscles and didn't swish.

Donnie's voice drew itself up to its full weight: "I'm the first black lover Ray-Ray ever had." He sounded every bit like a grand-prize winner.

Blanche was surprised. But why? There was no reason gay men should escape the pink pussy jones, just because there was no pussy involved. Being gay didn't relieve you of your white-is-better slave heritage. But that wasn't what she wanted to talk about.

"Did Ray-Ray ever talk about the Brindles, those people his mama works for?" she asked.

Donnie took a couple of slow sips of beer. Blanche watched him. Thinking or playing for time? She wondered.

"No. He never did." He stared at her face but not in her eyes—just the way Taifa did when she was lying.

"I asked because I heard that he and Marc Brindle were old friends, and I wondered if Marc knew, or if..."

"I don't know him."

Blanche watched him closely. If he and Ray-Ray had been as tight as Donnie said, and Ray-Ray and Marc had been close from childhood, how likely was it that Donnie hadn't at least heard of Marc? Or the Brindle family?

"I don't know anything about who Ray-Ray knows... knew, or what he was into. I didn't want to know and I still don't. We'd both... We'd both been around. Ray-Ray said he wanted a fresh start, to have a new life with no... so did I."

Maybe, Blanche thought. He and Ray-Ray may have wanted to start fresh, but the way Donnie reacted when she asked him about Marc made her sure that Donnie knew enough about Ray-Ray's old life to know what Blanche herself now realized: that Ray-Ray and Marc had been lovers. She gave Donnie an examining look. His jealousy certainly didn't show. She hoped her feelings about Aminata were equally invisible. She finished her drink.

"Well, I'm real sorry about Ray-Ray. I hadn't known him long, but I liked him. The way he..."

Donnie ran his hands over his face. "Half the time I can't believe it's true." He leaned toward her. "There's something I want to ask you. A favor. Ray-Ray had a picture of us together, taken at a friend's party," he said. "Do you think you could get it for me? It would mean a lot to me. And some letters I wrote him when ..." He worked to keep his face from crumbling. "I looked through the things he left at my place and they weren't there. I guess they're at his mother's or wherever else he was storing stuff until we could ... I guess his mom would know. Maybe you could ask her?"

"I'll see what I can find out," Blanche said. "He didn't give you anything special to hold, did he?" she asked.

Donnie poured more beer into his glass. "All I have are his weights and some clothes."

Blanche took her gas bill from her handbag and pushed it and a pen toward Donnie. "Here, give me your number. I'll at least try to get you some remembrance from the funeral. Inez'll be back in a week. I'll call you."

Donnie wrote two digits, then crossed them out and began again. "It's easier to get me at work," he said. "I have voice mail there. Since Ray-Ray ... I can hardly stand to go near my place. Can I have your number, too?" he added.

Blanche tore off a bit of flap and wrote the Brindles' kitchen number and her home number on it.

Donnie reached across the table and touched Blanche's wrist. "Blanche, I really appreciate you taking the time to talk; I mean, you don't know me but you ..."

Blanche rose from her seat. She couldn't take any more stoved-up male emotion this evening.

Donnie offered her a lift. She accepted but told him to let her off near Dudley Square. She wanted to walk the rest of the way. It was a bright, clear evening. The streets were alive with people and the promise of summer soon to come. She let herself feel the cool air on her cheeks and was grateful to be alive, in this body, at this time, no matter what was going on around her.

She was looking forward to a nice cup of tea when she got home. But the minute she saw Shaquita and Pookie talking on the stoop, she knew that she was going to do something that was probably a waste of time—and that tea would likely be replaced by a large gin. She hurried toward them before she could think up a halfway decent reason not to do what she knew she was about to.

"Hey, you two. I'm glad you're here. I want to talk to you. Come on inside."

Shaquita blinked at Pookie; he shut his face down so completely, he might have been asleep. He threw himself on the sofa and tugged at his cap. Shaquita sat next to him, stiff and wide-eyed as somebody in shock.

"Look, Miz Blanche," Pookie said while Blanche was thinking how to begin. "I know what you want to talk to us about. I know I'm going to have to take care of the baby, help Quita get a place."

Blanche bit down on her irritation at the tone of his voice—like she was a bill collector in a bad mood and he'd just put the check in the mail.

"You don't have to worry. I been thinkin' about it; you know what I'm sayin'? I was kinda like shocked when she tole me, but I'ma take care of my woman and my child."

Woman! Blanche nearly screamed. "With what?" she asked instead.

"Whatchu mean?"

"I mean, how are you going to take care of Shaquita and a baby?"

"It ain't none of your business how I make my money."

"Shaquita's my business."

Shaquita took his hand. "It's not Pookie's fault that the only way he can make decent money is selling drugs."

"*Decent? Decent?* It may be the only way he can make money, but there ain't a thing decent about it, and you both know it!"

Blanche turned to Pookie. "And when's the last time you thought of getting enough education to maybe get a job that don't get you thrown in jail or murdered?"

Pookie stared at her, his whole body straining toward her as though he was having a hard time holding himself back. "What? You want me to be like one of them downtown suits with they briefcases and tasseled loafers, actin' like where they be goin' is the onliest place in the world to get to? You think they ain't doin' worse shit than me? Do they boys meet 'em and greet 'em, make 'em feel like somebody? No. Do they got each other's back? No. They do that dog-eat-dog shit. I ain't into that. You can ask anybody. Yeah, I carry a gun for protection sometimes, but I ain't never pulled it on nobody who didn't mean me serious harm. I'm down with bein' black, doin' the right thing for the folks. I help out my moms, my sister, and her kids. I look out for my people. Ask anybody."

"Yeah? Then how come you knocked up somebody's sixteen-year-old child? You call that 'bein' black, doin' the right thing for the folks'?"

Pookie jumped up from the sofa. "You don't know nothin' 'bout what I been tryin' to do. Nothin'!" He jabbed his finger at Blanche. "I ain't just out there on the corner. I went to get my GED, see? I went to almost every class for weeks."

"Then what happened?" Blanche asked him.

"I flunked the test," he said in a near whisper.

Shaquita tugged him down beside her. "I tried to convince him to take it again, but..."

Blanche could feel a throbbing in her right temple. In any sane world, it wouldn't even be legal for these two to lip-synch the word "baby."

Shaquita covered her face with both hands. Pookie touched the back of her hand with his. Shaquita uncovered her face and looked at him as though he were a life raft and she were drowning.

Poor child, Blanche thought. Poor children. Pookie looked like a little kid afraid somebody was going to take his lollipop. He probably knew less about the world outside of his neighborhood than Shaquita.

Blanche leaned forward in her chair. She spread her hands as if to show she was unarmed, on their side. "Look, you two are so young, with so much to do to get your own lives together, it just doesn't make sense for you to have a baby right now. I mean, what's the hurry?"

Shaquita crossed her arms over her chest. "My grandmother didn't raise me to have no abortion."

Blanche almost laughed. The girl sounded as righteous as a jackleg preacher.

"Did your grandmother raise you to have sex without using birth control? Did your grandmother raise you to have sex at all?"

Shaquita lowered her eyes.

"Okay, you two. Let me ask you a couple questions. What kinds of things should a baby be able to do by six months?" She looked from one to the other. They looked at each other. "Well, Shaquita? Pookie?"

No answer.

"Okay, then, about how old should a baby be before you start giving it solid food?"

Pookie and Shaquita looked at their shoes. Blanche was sure most people about to have kids wouldn't be able to answer her questions either, but she sure as hell thought they *should* be able to answer them.

"Both of ya'll know more about how to drive a car than you know about how to take care of a child."

"We can learn!" Shaquita insisted.

"Yeah, but will you? If you don't know how to take care of the child before it's born, when are you going to learn, what with school and . . ."

Shaquita shot forward in her seat. "School?!"

"Girl, if you think for a minute that Cousin Charlotte is going to let you quit high school and give up college 'cause you're pregnant, you need to think again."

Shaquita was holding Pookie's hand with both of hers.

"How'm I going to take care of the baby and go to college? That doesn't even make sense."

"Why you so worried about Pookie's education when you're ducking out on your own?" Blanche silently thanked Taifa for telling her how afraid of college Shaquita really was.

"What?"

"You know it's true, Shaquita. Having this baby is as much about not going to college as it is anything else."

"It is not!"

Pookie gave Shaquita a questioning look.

"It's not. It's not. I swear it."

"Then why don't you want to go to college?"

Pookie was watching Shaquita closely. Blanche wondered if Shaquita noticed that Pookie didn't jump to her defense as she'd done to his.

Blanche turned to Pookie. "So what you planning to be doing while she's going to college?"

Pookie shrugged. "I'ma take care of my baby and my baby's mother; that's all I know."

The two of them seemed to melt together like overheated chocolate bars. You couldn't slip a knife blade between 'em, Blanche thought, and that dampness on my face is from spitting in the wind. But that didn't stop her from pressing on.

"How many couples you know who had babies together are still together?" she asked.

Pookie and Shaquita looked at each other and then away.

"Some of them is," Pookie said. "Lotta my homies ... they kids is all that's left. If something happens to me ..."

Of course. She should have thought of that. Shaquita might be trying to avoid college, but Pookie was trying to avoid death—trying to make sure some part of him remained after the next gang bang or drug war.

"Babies can't stop bullets, Pookie," Blanche said. "I don't know if you had a daddy growing up. I didn't. And I still sometimes think how unfair it was that he left my mother alone to take care of us. I'll always wonder how my life mighta been different with him around. And I resent him for it, wherever he is."

For the first time, she saw real attention in Pookie's eyes.

"It's not gonna be like that for us!" Shaquita interrupted with tears in her eyes. "Pookie's gonna get a job, and we'll stay together. I know we will!"

And dogs will sprout wings and take up the tango, Blanche thought. But the memory of being sixteen kept her from saying it. At Shaquita's age, hadn't she, too, believed bad things happened to other people, that even if she did the wrong thing, it would turn out right? That's what it meant to be sixteen.

She looked at Pookie and saw him—not as some swaggering teeny thug who was a threat to everything she was trying to teach Malik, but as somebody's child. Yes, he had an attitude; yes, he was involved in dangerous shit; but all he was doing was what was expected of him in a country that loved young men like him on the basketball court and in concert and spit hate in their faces everywhere else. Pookie was just trying to be exactly who America told him he was: everybody's worst nightmare. What she hadn't thought about before was that Pookie and boys like him might be even more afraid of what they were becoming than the people who labeled them.

Shaquita shifted in her seat. Was there any way to make her see her future in the nervous, screaming, blank-eyed motherettes who regularly wheeled, screamed at, and even smacked their babies on the buses and through the streets? Blanche was suddenly weak with how little she could say that would actually make sense to these two at their age, in their world. She felt suddenly old and stupid.

"Well, at least promise me you'll think about what I said." She rose from her chair; all her joints felt stiff. "I'm going to bed."

Of course, she immediately wished she'd handled the whole thing differently. She should have been nicer to Pookie. But she couldn't. She couldn't get past wanting to shake the shit out of both of them.

She closed the door of her room and headed straight for her Ancestor altar. She lit a candle and a stick of incense. Like the old folks she grew up around, she believed that dead ancestors returned through the children born to the family. Mama said Taifa walked, talked, and looked enough like long-dead great-great-aunt Freda to be her twin. Blanche herself had always been told how much she was like her grandmother's dead sister, Nell. Now she stared at the crouched ebony figure meant to represent her earliest ancestors back to the first mother, including all those lost to slavery. She spoke directly to them, explaining that she didn't like trying to convince Shaquita to abort, but whatever ancestor was planning to return through this girl's belly needed to pick a better time in Shaquita's life. She owned the fact that it was the Ancestors' and Shaquita's decision, and it was all out of her hands. She could only do what she thought was right.

By the time she put out the candle, her bed was beckoning to her like a horny lover.

SEVEN

DAY SIX—TUESDAY

Fortunately, she hadn't expected to be able to loll in bed until she felt like getting up, even if it was her day off. Taifa and Malik must have been saving up their morning nuttiness until a day she was home. They both slept through their alarms, got up at the same time, and fought about who got the bathroom first, since the rule was that the first one up got the bathroom. Taifa swore the only blouse she could possibly wear needed ironing, and pouted when Blanche told her there was time for her to iron it herself. Malik couldn't find any socks even though his sock drawer had been full of them two days ago, and told Blanche she was unnatural when she suggested he go sockless. Then he screamed at Taifa and Taifa screamed back. Shaquita vomited in the hallway, they were out of milk, and the handle fell off the tea kettle.

It was mornings like this that made Blanche know there was no way she was going to put in the years of hand-holding she saw other women doing with their grown children. She loved Taifa and Malik. But she was determined to figure out when she could step back from being a mule—on days like these, that's what she thought mothers should be called. That way, women choosing to have kids would have a better idea of what they were getting into. She didn't deny the pleasures of the profession. Even mules felt good sometimes. But no matter how much she loved and enjoyed them, no matter how proud they might make her, there was no way to get back the years and days and months of her life that she'd given to them as surely as if they were wrapped gifts with the children's names on them.

Thinking about motherhood reminded her that she hadn't called her own mother yesterday. When the house cleared out, she picked up the phone.

"I figured you was gonna call today," her mother said before Blanche even spoke. "How's my grandbabies? I dreamt about 'em last night. We was having a picnic out there by . . ."

Blanche flopped onto a kitchen chair and slumped against the table, weakened by the difference between the idea of a thing and the real thing. Yesterday, when she'd decided to call, she'd been thinking about talking to the warm, loving, wise, advise-giving woman who was the Mama that lived in her head. The Mama who lived in the world, who was on the phone right now, was the Mama who asked questions but didn't give you time to answer, who asked about the children but not about you, who talked on as though her voice were the only one needed to make this a conversation.

". . . rubbed the mayonnaise all over her face, and we just laughed like it was the funniest thing. Course that's the way things is in dreams, ain't it? Why, I remem . . ."

I'm too old to keep forgetting what I know, Blanche told herself, and sat up a little straighter.

"I just called to say hello, Mama. You okay? We're all fine. I know you were glad to see Cousin Charlotte, weren't you? I'll tell Taifa and Malik you asked about them. You need anything, you let me know. 'Bye now." Two could play at motormouth as well as one. Before she hung up, she could hear Mama sputtering. The sound turned Blanche's half-evil grin into a real smile. More important than that, the whole conversation, if you could call it that, reminded her that it wasn't just the mothers who paid. Being a child, of any age, was a mixed blessing. If you were lucky enough to be fed and clothed and all of that, you were expected to pay by behaving yourself and obeying whatever other rules and routines those in charge of you demanded; and if you were lucky enough to be loved, you weren't always lucky enough to be loved in the way you needed.

She gathered the children's clothes and the sheets and towels from their various hampers and sorted and soaked. She filled the washer from the mound of jeans to be washed, emptying pockets before stuffing them into the machine.

She found the foil-wrapped packet in the back pocket of Malik's favorite jeans. She didn't get it at first, maybe because it wasn't the square packet with the round imprint she was accustomed to. This silvery rectangle with the impression of something oblong in it could have been a snack pack from the space shuttle. She had to laugh when she finally understood what it was, but her laughter collapsed in her throat and her knees went weak with the realization of what a condom in Malik's pocket likely meant. She eased herself down on a pile of sheets and towels. The smell of Taifa's hair cream, the liniment Malik used on his basketball-battered knee, and her own Jean Naté wafted around her.

Oh Jesus! He's only twelve! She immediately thought of newspaper stories about fourteen-year-old fathers. She saw Malik's face in her mind and realized he could probably pass for eighteen, at least for seventeen. If he looked that old to her, he looked that old to girls who were sixteen, eighteen, twenty. She slammed the door on visions of Malik being wooed by a thirty-year-old woman in an outfit that advertised "Free Pussy." Dear Ancestors! She wasn't ready for this. She was just coming to terms with Taifa's teenhood. She wasn't supposed to have to deal with Malik's stuff for at least another year—or that's what she'd wanted to believe. Which is how I landed here in Surprise City, she thought. She'd been so busy worrying about Taifa and the possibility of her getting pregnant that she'd ignored the fact that Malik was just as capable of bringing home a baby as his sister. Maybe parenthood got on her nerves because she wasn't very good at it. She pulled her knees closer to her body and suddenly saw her dead sister Rosalie's face. She was smiling. Blanche frowned at her. "It may be all right with you," she said, "but what about me? You ever think of that?" Rosalie chose to disappear instead of replying.

Blanche rose and continued filling the washing machine. She would talk to Malik tonight. Maybe by then she'd know what to say. Right now, she needed a little time out, a little pampering. She took her old gym bag from the closet and grabbed a couple of towels.

As usual, she stopped to look at the mural on the front of the Roxbury YMCA building. It affected her heartbeat each time she saw the mystery of it: planets and moons set in a field of blue above what looked like ocean on the right and a black sky on the left. The pyramid in the middle threw a shadow onto an orange platform. The whole thing seemed to float on the top of the wall. Underneath, in a field of light blue, the words AFRICA IS THE BEGINNING seemed to leap out at and embrace her.

The sound of children shrieking and feet pounding on hardwood floors rolled out the front door, followed by that familiar Y smell: sneakers, chlorine, floor polish, roach killer, basketballs, and humans. Six little girls in snowy martial arts jackets ran by her while she waited for the receptionist to get off the phone. When she did, she took Blanche's card and told her the combination to the lock on the door of what was called the Women's Health Club—a title much too big for the two rooms full of lockers with adjacent sauna and a steam room the size of a large closet. The adjoining showers were hung with multicolored curtains. The place was small and modest but looked like people cared about it. Today, every face she saw was a black or brown mirror of her own deep-black, full-featured self. This was what made the place special.

"Hey," Blanche said to the woman already in the locker room—a short, muscular, dark-brown-skinned woman with closely cropped natural hair. She had a wide, inquiring face. She gave Blanche an easy smile and a hello with the West Indies in it. Blanche chose a locker in a corner. She dropped her bag on a metal bench and undressed. She was joined in the showers by the West Indian woman and her friend, who'd just come out of the steam room. They talked to each other in loud, laughter-laden voices.

"Elmira, he ain't no mon, dat one, he a worm!"

"For true, he is dat. For true!" Elmira agreed, and both women laughed.

"I tell him, buster, what you tink? I'ma put pus-pus in a drawer till you come bock? No way, buster. No way!"

Blanche had no idea who they were talking about, but the ritual of their talk was one by which she lived. She thought of Ardell and friends in Harlem. The phone, a drink at the corner bar, dinner, a walk in the park, whatever occasion they could arrange to ease each other over the humps in the road with a nudge or a laugh, or a loan. She followed the two women into the sauna and watched the grace and strength of their movements as they slathered their bodies with coconut oil. They all grinned when Blanche took out her jar of the very same oil. But Elmira and her friend continued to talk in that girlfriends way that excluded Blanche and made her aware of how much she missed Ardell. Blanche oiled her feet and waited for the quiet to come.

The hush thickened while they oiled their arms and legs and bottoms, sighed from deep in their bellies, then lay back into the waiting arms of the heat. Sweat rolled down Blanche's back, silken as the silence surrounding her. What little light there was seemed to gather on her thighs and breasts, like the first few stars in a blue-black sky. Now, she thought, now. The silence deepened and turned purple. She closed her eyes and was free of her body, air-light, sheer as the finest hose, floating in a coconut-scented sea of heat and black women breathing one breath. She lolled there, completely relaxed.

Someone's cough finally called her back to her body. She opened her eyes. Elmira was gathering her towel around her. Her friend followed her. Blanche stretched and rolled to a sitting position, rested and strengthened.

Elmira and her friend had already taken up their conversation when Blanche joined them in the showers.

"... I gotta pick up my grandson at the pool down the street. I wanted him to come here, but his mama got her own ideas."

"Somebody drown in dat pool just the other week, ya know."

"Leastways, wasn't no little one this time."

Blanche's ears perked right up.

"I know his mama," Elmira's friend said. "She a good woman. Decent woman."

"It's hard for a mother," Elmira added. "Especially if the son is, you know."

"I heard he was holding hands with some mon dat very night, you know."

"You mean somebody was wid him when he drown?"

"Leastways somebody snuck in the pool wid he, and somebody leave widout he, and that somebody waren't no stranger, you know."

"Speakin' of strangers," Elvira said, launching into a story about her sister's new man while Blanche was still taking in their news about Ray-Ray. The two women were dressed and gone before Blanche thought to ask them who they'd heard this story about Ray-Ray from. She was sure they hadn't heard who the man with Ray-Ray was or they would have said so, or at least hinted about it.

She sat on the bench fiddling with her hair and trying to fit what she'd just heard into what she knew.

Donnie said he hadn't seen Ray-Ray again after their fight, so unless he was lying, he wasn't the man with Ray-Ray at the pool. And from what she'd seen of Donnie, he was more likely to poison somebody than knock their brains out. But if Ray-Ray and Donnie were as much in love as Donnie claimed, why would Ray-Ray be holding hands with someone else? Of course, there was nothing like a fight to make you do something unfaithful.

A little bell rang in her brain. What about Marc Brindle? She remembered how Donnie had reacted when she'd mentioned Marc's name. Maybe Donnie and Ray-Ray's fight had been about Marc? But no, if the man with Ray-Ray had been white, one of the women would have mentioned it. Then who? Somebody hired to bash Ray-Ray on the head and make his death look like an accident on the diving board, of course. But holding hands? She saw Ray-Ray preening himself, loving himself, and assuming everyone else felt the same. It probably wouldn't take much to pick him up, to convince him you couldn't wait to hold his hand, especially if he was on the outs with his lover. She finished dressing and tied a scarf around her damp hair.

She stopped by the supermarket and picked up some chicken parts, potatoes, and broccoli for one of Malik's favorite dinners. Did she think filling him full of what he liked to eat would make it easier to talk to him about the condom she'd found in his pocket? There wasn't that much oven-fried chicken, garlic potato spears, and broccoli in black bean sauce in the world.

She walked up M. L. K. Boulevard to Humboldt to Miz Barker's store. She meant to ask Miz B why she hadn't come right out and said that Ray-Ray was gay instead of going through all that he's-special-and-different business, like gay people didn't shit between two shoes and cry when they got the blues just like everybody else. She hoped by the time she got as old as Miz Barker, there wouldn't be a damned thing she wasn't prepared to say out loud.

From a block away, she saw people standing outside Miz Barker's store. Something about them made her want to turn around and quick-walk in the opposite direction. The skin on her upper arms and neck prickled the way it did when she saw a child run into traffic after a ball. She slowed her steps, but Karen, her borrowing neighbor, came to meet her. The voice inside told her to push Karen away, to cover her ears and run.

"It's a damned shame, killing that poor old lady like that." Karen's voice was loud and bugle bright.

Something in Blanche's chest closed like a fist and began to ache. "Miz Barker?"

"Yep. Somebody hit her in the face. Hard." Karen took a drag from her cigarette. "Knocked her down. They think she had a heart attack. You could see the nasty sucker's handprint on the side of that poor old soul's face." She blew more smoke in Blanche's direction. "These damned kids is goin' to kill us all if we don't figure out how to—"

"Why you say kids?"

" 'Cause just this morning she had a big fight with some of them boys been hanging round her store. I didn't see it, but I heard one of them was all up in that old lady's face. Don't none of them have no respect for nobody. Somebody said one of them come back by hisself. The next time anybody saw poor Miz Barker, she was dead on the floor."

They were both silent for a moment before Karen spoke again.

"Funny thing is, I was just heading for her store to get some toilet paper. You got any I could borrow? I don't want to have to go all the way down to ..."

Blanche was already walking past Karen toward Miz Barker's store. She stopped in front of the padlocked door with an X of police tape over it and stared at the store as if it could tell her why her old friend, who had helped so many hereabouts, should be so completely without help this one time she herself had needed it so badly. Blanche remembered how many times she'd been irritated with Miz Barker lately, and the fist in her chest closed tighter, until tears stung her eyes and she had to turn away.

"... same boys who broke into her store a couple weeks ago," a man behind her said.

"It's a damned shame, old lady like that!" a young woman responded.

Other people were shaking their heads and talking the same kind of bad-kids talk. Blanche could smell their anger and sorrow—hot and moist like a storm brewing.

She went around to Miz Barker's house and knocked. Pam opened the door and grabbed Blanche's arm and held on to it. Blanche could feel the chill of Pam's hand through her sweater. A few older neighbors were in the living room. Pam pulled Blanche along to her bedroom and started talking, still clutching Blanche's arm.

"I wanted her to stay home and wait for me to come back from the market. I knew something was up. You know how you can feel it sometimes?" Pam laughed without humor. "You know she didn't listen. When did Gran ever lis—"

"There's nothing to blame yourself for, Pam. Nothing."

"But I'd have been there if I had a car! I missed the bus and I couldn't find a gypsy or a regular cab and ..." Pam increased the pressure on Blanche's arm.

Blanche pried Pam's hand loose and held it in both of her own. "No. If you'd found a cab, you could both be dead," she said as gently as she could. "Leave it alone, Pam. You're not responsible, and feeling guilty won't bring her back."

"But I came here to protect her, Blanche, to help her!" Pam fell into Blanche's arms. Blanche held her until her sobs were finally stilled and the ache in Blanche's own chest eased a bit. Pam pulled away to answer the ringing phone.

"Oh, Mama!" she said into the receiver. Need and relief made her voice waver. Blanche could almost see Pam reaching out to her parent for solace. From the way Pam's shoulders relaxed, Blanche knew Pam had made the connection she needed. Blanche patted Pam's shoulder and left her quietly talking to her mother.

As she'd hoped, the house was empty. She needed some time alone. Sadness lay heavy and hot on her chest. She didn't cringe from it or wish it away. She knew that avoiding pain didn't pay off. Tears came with memories: the times she'd watched Miz Barker slyly signify at folks, the way her voice took on a soothing tone when she talked to little children, the stubborn independence that made her her very own person. Blanche wiped her eyes. "May the Ancestors welcome you, dear friend," she said.

All three children had heard the news by the time they got home, and Miz Barker was the main topic at dinner.

"I hope I don't know him," Shaquita said, looking worried.

"Why it got to be somebody from around here?" Malik challenged Shaquita.

"Boy! You got to be kidding!" Taifa said. "Of course he's from round here. You heard what they said. He had on a Bulls jacket, dark green jeans, Air Jordans, and a black cap. You think somebody come in here from out in Randolph or someplace, dressed like the Germantown Street gang to give Miz Barker a heart attack?" Taifa laughed.

Malik's lower lip jutted out. He leaned across the table toward his sister. "You think guys from the suburbs don't kill people? You sound just like those white people on TV, always calling us names, accusing us of every... It's stupid. Stupid!" Malik's palm slapped the table so hard, his juice jumped over the side of his glass.

Blanche suddenly understood why Malik was so hot for Aminata's lead poisoning–teen violence idea. He wants a reason for kids killing kids, she thought, a reason that says it's not something in all black teenage boys' blood, that violence *isn't* natural to them. How could she not have realized that what kids were doing in the streets was even scarier for Malik than it was for her?

"No matter what they say on TV we all know there are a lot fewer kids who get in trouble than there are decent teens out here," she said.

Malik looked at her as though he wanted to believe her but couldn't. Blanche wished some of those so-called experts on black teen males who say it's up to parents to keep kids out of trouble could feel the pain in Malik's voice and on his face. They needed to know firsthand how it felt to be treated like the white world's worst enemy. How was she supposed to overcome that?

Blanche waited until Taifa was doing homework with Shaquita at the kitchen table before going upstairs and knocking on Malik's door. He didn't answer. She rattled the doorknob. Finally he opened the door and stood in the doorway like a housewife barring a salesman. Blanche held out her fist and slowly relaxed her fingers. She had to stifle a laugh at the look on Malik's face—and the way he jumped back when he saw the silver packet on her palm. She looked in his room, smelled it, and beckoned him to follow her to her room. She'd lost the advantage of catching him off guard and getting him to talk before he had a chance to think, but there was no way *she* could think in all that boy funk.

"Look, Moms," he said the minute her bedroom door was closed behind them. "It's no big deal."

"Oh? You mean this isn't a condom and I didn't find it in your pocket?"

He flinched at the word, but either they were going to talk or they weren't.

"How old is the person you're having sex with?" she demanded, and knew instantly that was the wrong question asked the wrong way. She watched him withdraw ten feet deeper into himself. An opaque window shade lowered over his eyes. She'd screwed that up. She had to remember she needed him to talk to her more than he wanted her in his business.

"Sorry, honey," she said. "I guess I'm kind of in a state of shock. I mean, you're only twelve!" Shit! That wasn't right either. "I guess I'm just not ready for you to be having sex yet."

Malik shifted from one foot to the other. "Why are you searching my pockets?"

Blanche had to laugh. Did males learn how to play that defensive game when their penises first developed?

"Boy, don't try that guilt-trip crap on me! I was washing your funky jeans as a favor to you. Now let's get back to your sex life."

Malik sighed and swayed, scratched his arm, put his hands in and out of his pockets. "Just because a person might have something doesn't mean he's doing what you think he's doing."

"Excuse me? Does that mean you are not having sex yet?" Too direct, she realized, but too late. "Look, honey, I'm not handling this too well, I know. But if you are having sex, then we need to talk about it. If you're not . . ."

"I'm not." He spoke so swiftly and softly she almost didn't hear him.

She moved closer. She held his chin and lifted his head. "You sayin' that 'cause you don't want to talk about it," she half asked, half told him.

Malik shook his head. "Nah. Some girl was handin' 'em out at school. I had to take one."

He didn't have to explain. Not taking a condom would mean he wasn't getting any.

"Girls don't even . . ."

Blanche waited for him to complete the sentence; when he didn't, she prompted him with an "I'm listening" kind of sound, but he shrugged—the teenager salute. Blanche was torn between relief and suspicion. She hoped what he was saying was true, but it sounded just like the type of lie she used to tell *her* mother.

"Let's talk anyway," she said.

Malik squirmed and said "I know, Moms" a hundred and fifty times while Blanche told him everything about his own and girls' bodies that she thought he needed to know, as well as giving him a good strong talk about AIDS and other STDs. It wasn't the first time he'd heard it all, but that didn't stop her.

"You know, Joycelyn Elders got fired as the surgeon general because she said she thought everybody, especially young people, should masturbate more and..."

Malik leapt off the bed where he'd been sitting beside her. "Ah, Moms! Come on!"

"It's not like this is the first time we've ever talked about masturbation, Malik." She waited for him to settle down. "Like I told you before, masturbation is nothing to be embarrassed about. It's healthy. When you feel all sexy, it's another way to satisfy the feeling. It's the only real safe sex, you know. And at your age, masturbating can prevent POTB."

"POTB? What's that?" He sounded like he thought it might kill him.

"The last three letters stand for 'on the brain.' You figure it out."

"Mom!" he roared with shock, then bounded out of her room.

Blanche fell back across her bed. She deserved a reward for this. At least a paycheck. She ran her hand down the front of her body and chuckled. She could have told Malik she was a masturbation champion, it had been so long since she'd had any other kind of sex. She pressed her hand against her crotch and sighed and dropped her hand to the bed. It wasn't a do-it-yourself orgasm she wanted, but sex with all the trimmings. A shower would have to do.

She was wrapping a towel around herself when Shaquita knocked on the bathroom door and told her Ardell was on the phone. Blanche grabbed her robe and ran to her room.

"At last!" Blanche nearly shouted at her old friend. "Girl, how are you? How was it? I sure missed your ass. Did you have a good time?"

"Humm. Now, Blanche, if I was to tell you that with all those questions you ain't giving me a chance to answer, you sound just like your mama, I guess you'd wanna cuss me out, so I ain't sayin' nothin' like that, but..."

"Oh yes, your smart ass is back!"

"But no, I ain't back yet. I'm down here in Bermuda with these fools for two nights, and then it's back on the boat. We won't get home until late next week. And will I be glad! A cruise to Bermuda ain't exactly a cruise to Bermuda when you're with the world's two wildest children and their simpleminded parents. I'd probably make out better if the parents had stayed home. Every time I get these two ignorant little maggots actin' like they might be third cousins to human beings, along comes mummy and poppy to let the kids kick and cuss and generally act like they need to be locked up and drugged."

Blanche had told Ardell the trip would be more than a notion, but neither one of them needed for her to say it again. Blanche wanted to talk about Ray-Ray and Miz Barker, but she could tell Ardell needed to be listened to, spoken to in words that hugged, then given an order to go directly to bed—which was exactly what Blanche gave her.

She hung up wishing she could put her own self to rest, but there was someone else she needed to talk to tonight. She didn't want to do it, but she couldn't figure out how else to get into Inez's house without breaking in. She sat in the middle of the bed with the phone in her lap. She stared at it for a few moments. Did she really need to do this? She'd told Miz Barker she'd try to find out what had really happened to Ray-Ray, but now Miz Barker was dead. Better just to let the whole thing drop. But then she remembered the way Allister Brindle had spoken to her about Ray-Ray's note and the tape and the way he had looked at her—as if she were something ugly and suspicious that had just crawled into his house. She thought about Samuelson's phone call and understood what neither of those pig suckers had said: They were prepared to do whatever was necessary to get that tape back. And at least one of them thought she had it or knew where to find it. She punched in the number Cousin Charlotte had left for her and reminded herself not to mention Miz Barker's death. That news could wait until Cousin Charlotte came home.

She let Cousin Charlotte talk about the plans for Ray-Ray's funeral, how Inez was holding up, and how good it was to be back in her girlhood home.

"Everything all right up there?" Cousin Charlotte asked when she'd wound down.

Blanche went right to one of her reasons for calling. "Why didn't you tell me Ray-Ray was gay? Did you know he had a lover who might like to know about the funeral arrangements?"

"Now calm down, Blanche. You know how excited you get. You sound just like your mother when you—"

"Don't even try it, Cousin Charlotte. You can't wiggle out of this. I got a right to get just as excited as I want. You loved Ray-Ray, and so did Donnie. And Ray-Ray probably loved him back. I'm sure Ray-Ray would want all his loved ones to at least know about his funeral. What about that?"

"I can't force nothing on Inez. She's got her own ideas."

"I bet she does! Does she make a sign to ward off the evil eye when she talks about Ray-Ray's gay friends? I hear she called one of his friends unnatural when he came to her house looking for Ray-Ray."

"It *was* kinda ugly," Cousin Charlotte admitted.

"You were there? What happened?"

Blanche could feel Cousin Charlotte settling into her chair like a hen on a couple of eggs.

"Well, I was in the front room when the, er, young man came to the door. In fact, I'm the one who opened the door. He said he was a friend of Ray-Ray's and asked me if I was Ray-Ray's mama. Well, I said, 'No, honey, I'm his . . .' "

Blanche tuned out on the filler. But she didn't want to interrupt. When Cousin Charlotte was interrupted while telling a story, she often started all over again from the beginning.

"... wished I hadn't opened the door, but it was too late by then. Inez was a mess, girl. Just a mess. Crying and screaming and trying to push Ray-Ray's er, um, friend off the stoop. 'My boy ain't no freak like you! Don't come round here tryin' to act like my boy's unnatural.' Inez was screaming at the top of her lungs. She said she knew that young man was trying to turn her Ray-Ray."

"Trying to what?"

"You know! Turn him into some kind of homo. But Inez said she knew her prayers had protected Ray-Ray. She's sure he wasn't really gay. Maybe a mother knows these things."

Blanche had always suspected Miz Inez didn't have enough sense to breathe when it came to Ray-Ray. Maybe Cousin Charlotte needed breathing lessons where he was concerned, too.

"Course I tried to calm her down, her blood pressure being what it is and all, but she was right out of control. So, I had to tell that young man he was doing her harm and had no right to come to her house looking for Ray-Ray being, you know, like that."

Cousin Charlotte had hardly finished talking when Blanche launched into a lecture on the stupidity of black people being prejudiced against anybody for any reason and moved on to homosexuals in particular.

"Far as I'm concerned, love is love." Even so, the memory of how she'd recently had to change her own views of Ray-Ray caused her to cut Cousin Charlotte some slack. "It ain't how you was raised, but that don't make it wrong."

Cousin Charlotte responded with one of her silences—the kind that gave new meaning to the saying "If you can't say anything good, don't say anything at all."

Blanche ignored the silence. She reminded herself that she was the one doing the favors and it was time to move on. It would take more time than she could spare to change Cousin Charlotte's mind, but that didn't mean she was off the hook.

"Well, you can make up for not telling me about Ray-Ray by bringing Donnie a pressed flower and a burial announcement from Ray-Ray's funeral."

More silence.

"And you better tell me where you keep the key to Inez's house so I can go through Ray-Ray's things and get them love letters Donnie told me he wrote to Ray-Ray before Inez finds them and has a heart attack."

Cousin Charlotte cleared her throat. "I'll see what I can do 'bout a flower and so forth," she mumbled. "Inez's key is in my kitchen drawer, the one in the cabinet under the window."

Blanche thought her next question might smooth Cousin Charlotte's feathers, or at least distract her.

"How come Ray-Ray stopped working for the Brindles?" Blanche could feel Cousin Charlotte struggling with her indignation at being criticized on the one hand and her natural inclination to talk on the other. Nature won.

"Now, you know, I wondered that very same thing myself. All Inez would tell me was that Ray-Ray and Mr. Brindle had some kinda shouting match. When I asked her about what, she shut them skinny lips of hers tighter than a clam. Course, Inez always was tight-lipped. Why, I didn't find out she'd bought a new washer until she ..."

Yeah, yeah, yeah. Time to try to get Cousin Charlotte off the phone. About as easy as getting honey out of your hair.

"... tell her how you're holding down poor Inez's job, gettin' them letters and all," Cousin Charlotte said.

That's what she got for half listening. Cousin Charlotte had switched subjects on her.

"Tell who what?"

"Your mama! When I talk to her tomorrow. Ain't you been listenin' to me, Blanche? How's my Shaquita?" she added. "Tell her her grandma misses her."

"One last thing, Cousin Charlotte. You know anybody who knows Maurice Samuelson at that Temple?"

"What you want to know 'bout that no-'count negro for?"

Blanche sat up a little straighter. "Why you say that?"

"Well, I don't want to talk out of turn about a man of the cloth, but... well, you know how some of them ministers are. Keep their brains in their pants and do a lot of thinking, anywhere they can find a spot, if you get my meaning."

Blanche remembered what Lacey had said about Samuelson's appetite for young white prostitutes. It sounded like that wasn't the only Juicy Miss Lucy he hankered for.

"So he likes his poontang, does he?"

"Don't be nasty-mouthed, Blanche. You know I don't hold with that, but yes, he surely do. I know a woman used to belong to that Temple of his. Knows something about him before he come here. She got a story to tell, honey."

"What kinda story?"

"I don't remember it exactly, except I remember he had a wife and didn't do right by her."

Blanche carted out the best lie she could come up with on such short notice. "Well, I got a friend who's thinking about joining his Temple. I keep telling her there's something not quite right about the man, but she don't want to hear it. If she could talk to the woman you know, maybe..."

"Call her up! I know for a fact she been warning people to stay away from there. Bea Richards. She's in the phone book. Over on Handel Street."

Blanche thanked her, ended the call, and lay back against the pillows, panting and feeling like she'd just finished a wrestling match. Cousin Charlotte was so much like Blanche's mother, Blanche could feel herself slipping back into childhood, even while she talked her most adult talk. Maybe having to deal with both of them in one day, especially a day when she'd talked back to Mama, was more than she was ready for. She had to look down to make sure she wasn't wearing a pinafore and Mary Jane shoes.

When she finally did come to rest, she saw Miz Barker sitting in her rocking chair, worrying about who might have hurt Ray-Ray. Poor old dear. Poor old dear. Tears gathered in Blanche's eyes, but she was grabbed by another thought before they could fall: Why did Miz Barker think Ray-Ray's death was related to something he had that didn't belong to him? Of course, Ray-Ray wouldn't necessarily have had to say anything. Miz Barker had loved Ray-Ray most of his life. She could have known something was up with Ray-Ray the same way Blanche knew when someone she loved was about to arrive or was calling on the phone. Still . . . She drifted off to sleep before the thought could fully form.

That night, for the first time in a long time, she dreamed of having been raped.

EIGHT

DAY SEVEN—WEDNESDAY

Dawn was just pulling the stars down to sleep when Blanche got Inez's key from Cousin Charlotte's kitchen drawer. It was nearly full light when she let herself into Inez's place.

She never liked being alone in the homes of people she knew. The minute the house sensed she understood it to be a living, breathing, watching creature with a personality and intentions of its own, the house confided in her, directed her attention toward things that told her more about the occupants than she wanted to know. Right now, her eye was being pulled toward a big green armchair with a floral slipcover, a mashed-down seat cushion, and a slightly greasy headrest. An old brass floor lamp stood behind it. Copies of *Ebony* were stacked on the floor on one side, and a Bible lay open on the table on the other side. Nothing much to see, just Inez's favorite chair.

She turned her eyes away, but it was too late. From the corner of her left eye she saw a tin can peeking from beneath the chair's slipcover skirt. Throughout her growing up in North Carolina, Blanche had seen these cans with the labels removed tucked beneath the chairs of older black women—men were bolder with theirs, leaving them in plain sight. She was surprised to find one here. Inez was someone who needed her religion to be hard on her, to forbid her everything but breathing and bathing—no movies, dancing, smoking, drinking, fornicating, idol-worshiping, or ego-tripping allowed. But despite her dedication, it seemed she still took a pinch of snuff and got rid of its juice in the usual down-home way. Blanche put on a pair of rubber gloves and hurried down the hall to the bedrooms before she saw anything else.

There was no question which room had been Ray-Ray's. Inez's room was overrun with crucifixes. Ray-Ray's was just overrun: two large plastic bags like plump slick green pillows in the middle of the floor, boxes of clothes lined up against the walls. All of his clothes seemed to be in boxes—a sign of his packing up to move in with Donnie? The bedside table drawer was jammed with old lottery tickets. Huge barbells guarded the window. Black high-topped sneakers and backless brown leather slippers looked like they had been thrown across the room.

The plastic bags seemed to be filled with throw-away stuff—old newspapers, socks without mates, raggedy, stained jockstraps. She turned to the boxes. The first one was fall of bulky sweaters. Jockey shorts, T-shirts, and socks were in the second box. Folded jeans and a couple pairs of corduroys were in the third one. There was a box of shirts, too. She looked from box to box. Some of the jockeys and tees were tightly rolled; others were half rolled and half folded. Most of the socks were organized in matched pairs; other pairs were separated. The sleeve of a sweater hung over the side of a box. She could almost see someone feeling around in the boxes, lifting the top layers and poking around underneath, making sure nothing was hidden among the clothes.

She went to the window that looked out into Inez's backyard. It wasn't quite closed. Outside, there was a cemented yard the size of a hot minute, enclosed by cinder-block walls. Two large blue plastic trash barrels stood against the far wall. There was an outline of a square etched in dirt beside the trash barrels. Blanche stood on her toes. A dark green plastic milk crate stood under the window—just the right size to have made the dirt square. There was also dirt on the windowsill. Somebody had beat her to it. No wonder Ray-Ray's things looked thrown around. But had they found the tape? She stood very still for a moment. How long ago had someone been here? Could they still be here? She turned to the room, held her breath, and listened. She didn't hear anything but street noises and didn't feel anyone else in the house. But she picked up a piece of lead pipe from beside Ray-Ray's bed and tiptoed from room to room, opening closets, looking under Miz Inez's bed and behind the sofa, ready to scream, swing, and run, all at the same time. But whoever had broken in was gone, and if the tape had been there, it was probably gone now, too. She wrestled disappointment to the ground and checked her watch. She had over an hour before she was due at the Brindles'. She went back to Ray-Ray's room to see what else she could see.

One of the big plastic bags brushed against her ankle. Something hard jabbed at her foot. She opened the bag wide enough to see the cardboard box inside. It was larger than a shoe box, but smaller than four shoe boxes. She took it out and set it on the floor. She didn't expect to find the tape inside, but what about Donnie's letters and picture? They weren't in the box either. But she was interested in what she did find: miniature racing cars; birthday cards; four new ties still in their boxes; a pair of child-sized mittens of thick, probably imported, yellow-and-blue wool; ten Christmas cards and one graduation card of the kind you put money in; three get-well cards; six U.S. Savings Bonds; four pairs of new argyle socks; a tightly folded silk robe; an envelope with an invitation to Marc Brindle's sixteenth birthday party with no name on the envelope. The gift cards had fallen into the bottom of the box, each with "To: Ray-Ray" and "From: the Brindles" written on them.

Ray-Ray's Brindle stash.

She looked at the other things in the plastic bag: bunches of torn-up bills, old shoelaces, more old lottery tickets, and other junk. So, he'd put his Brindle stuff in the trash. He'd kept some of it for a long time. Why throw it out now?

Was this how Ray-Ray's big fight with Allister had ended, with Ray-Ray throwing out everything the family had ever given him? But the fight was at least a year ago; would Ray-Ray stay mad that long? And why keep all these gifts this way in the first place? The toy cars didn't look as though they'd ever touched the floor. The gloves, ties, and socks had never been worn. The money gifts were missing; probably couldn't afford to horde them. Ray-Ray had just kept it all, like prizes or souvenirs, things too special to be used because of who had given them to him. Ray-Ray had told Blanche that he'd always used the front door, just like one of the family. Is that how he'd thought of himself before the fight that made him want to hurt Allister Brindle? Certainly, growing up listening to Inez talk about the Brindles in a holy tone of voice had made some impression on him. And how powerful it must have felt to a poor little black boy to be able to come and go pretty much as he pleased in a place like that, to be taken to ball games by Allister, as though he were the other son. And then it was over. She closed the box and put it back in the bag. She rose and began opening bureau drawers, looking for the letters and picture Donnie wanted. The drawers were empty except for a smaller one. It was half full of little boxes and packs of matches from clubs and restaurants, mostly from a place called Le Club, but there were no letters or pictures. She hesitated in the doorway.

Ray-Ray's room was the only one that looked like it had been searched. The tape could be somewhere else in the house. With Miz Inez out of town, Ray-Ray didn't have to worry about her finding the tape he'd tucked under her mattress—but it wasn't there, or in the bureau drawers with their cotton snuggies and undershirts, bras and slips bleached nearly blue and neatly folded dark brown panty hose. Blanche went down the hall to the bathroom. The cabinet under the sink smelled of Listerine, Bengay, and Lubriderm lotion and held little else. Miz Inez's kitchen cabinets were as organized as the ones at the Brindles'. If there was anything in them that shouldn't have been, Blanche couldn't find it. She even checked under the lining bag in the trash can. The built-in china closet and the old dark sideboard were full of dishes and cutlery, tablecloths and old magazines. The living room was equally tapeless. Disappointed but not surprised, she locked the front door and hurried to the bus stop. It was time to go to work.

As soon as she got to the Brindle house, Blanche looked up Bea Richards's phone number and called her. If she was a working woman, which she likely was, she'd be up by now. Blanche only planned to talk long enough to convince Bea to meet her and tell what she knew about Samuelson. But there was no answer.

"This my half day, you know," Carrie reminded Blanche.

The doorbell rang before Blanche could ask Carrie how she intended to spend it. Carrie and Blanche gave each other who-could-that-be-at-this-hour looks. The Brindles had only just finished breakfast.

"So?" Blanche asked when Carrie came back from answering the door. "And don't start that Massa's business ain't none a my business bull hockey."

"Weren't gonna say that noway," Carrie whispered. "Things is gettin' wilder and wilder around here. I just showed a private investigator into the library to see the mister and missus—least that's what his card said."

"Yeah, he was here the other day."

"Ain't nobody told me nothin' about it."

Carrie was right. If Blanche wanted Carrie to tell all, she needed to give up some information herself. So she told Carrie about Cleason's first visit with Felicia. "Maybe he's got something to report," she added, and went to find out.

First, she fussed with the flowers on the sideboard in the dining room, then slipped down the hall to stand just to the side of the open library door.

"Allister, be reasonable. He's our son!" Felicia said.

Allister didn't bother to respond.

"Mr. Brindle," Cleason said in his big voice, "Mrs. Brindle told me your son had a friend who recently died. Some people become very disoriented, some even become self-destructive when—"

"My son is none of your goddamned business! You're not going to create havoc in my campaign to serve whatever twisted animosity she... Marc is not missing, and my wife damned well knows it! And if a word of this gets out, I'll sue you until you bleed! Ted! Get him the hell out of here!"

Blanche hurried back to the kitchen. Full-scale war broke out once Sadowski showed Cleason to the door. Blanche had only to open the kitchen door to hear Allister shouting at Felicia.

"This is all your fault, all your fault! You and that limp-wristed son of yours, dragging his perverted habits into my home!"

"Your home? Your home? That's a laugh. If I didn't—"

"Stop right there, Felicia. I'm not going to listen to your—"

"Fuck you, Allister."

A door slammed. Felicia laughed.

Sadowski cleared his throat. "Mrs. Brindle, it's important to the campaign that I know anything that might—"

"Get out of my sight, you toady. And stay away from my breakfast table. I'm tired of seeing your ass-kissing face before I've had my morning coffee."

Damn! Felicia was taking no prisoners today. Things could be different around here when Inez got back.

"Missus sittin' in her room looking evil as sin," Carrie said when she came down from making the beds. "I know that woman needs extra prayers."

And it was only ten-thirty. Blanche looked at the house schedule. Allister would be gone for the rest of the day. Felicia was having friends in for lunch. She and Allister were out for dinner again. Blanche hoped their fight wouldn't change their dinner plans.

"You're gonna need lots of strength in them hands today, honey," Blanche said when Mick arrived. "They just had a fight."

"Another wasted massage," Mick said when she came downstairs. "Felicia's so pissed, her back and neck muscles were tighter than a virgin's snatch."

Blanche wondered aloud if Felicia would be calm by the time her guests arrived for lunch.

"Don't worry," Mick told her. "These girls are champions at fronting. They all pretend to be happy, fulfilled wives with wonderful husbands who don't ignore them, sleep around, kick their asses, or pat the paper boy's butt. I know more about all of them than they'd ever tell each other."

Blanche was curious as to what Mick knew about her employers, but not as curious as she was about Ray-Ray. "Forget them," she said. "What I want to know is why you didn't tell me Ray-Ray was gay."

Without moving, Mick seemed to pull back, putting more space between Blanche and herself. "If Ray-Ray was straight, would you expect me to say so?"

Blanche had one of those moments when she felt like she'd been walking around with a paper bag over her head and someone just yanked it off.

Mick flung herself into a chair and looked up at her. "It's like, the minute you say you're gay, or somebody's gay, it's like all the other parts of who we are don't count. So I decided to stop saying people were gay when I talk about them." Mick lowered her head, but not before Blanche saw the sadness in her eyes.

Blanche thought of herself as being not simply open-minded but a cheerleader for people who were different from what the rule-setters said was the way to live, behave, or feel. But looking down at Mick's bowed head, she realized that cheering from the sidelines didn't mean you knew how the game was played. She'd figured black lesbians had a sisterhood strong enough to carry them through all the nastiness the straight world dished out to them. But why should all black lesbians be able to do what so many straight black women couldn't do, no matter how hard they tried?

"I see your point, but I just don't know if not saying who's gay or straight helps or just confuses things. Maybe we ought to go the other way and always say what everybody's sex thing is instead of acting like everybody's straight until told otherwise."

"Yeah, maybe people'd get tired of hearing it after a while and figure out that it ain't all that important," Mick said.

"Maybe," Blanche told her. "All I do know is that it's a mess out here, girl, no matter who you love."

"Maybe the people who stay in the closet have got it right."

"You think that's why Ray-Ray wasn't out to his mom?" Blanche asked her.

"Well, he was and he wasn't," Mick told her. "He was more like behind the curtain than in the closet. I mean, I don't think he ever lied to Miz Inez, but he probably never said, 'Mom, I'm gay.' But the only way Miz Inez missed it was because she wanted to, like lots of our families."

"What about your family?

"My family?" Mick chuckled, and shook her head. "When I came out, my dad didn't talk to me for almost two years. Now he speaks. But that's all."

"What about your mom?"

"She's okay as long as I don't talk about it."

Mick didn't have to say how she felt about that. Her tone was bitter as week-old coffee.

"You got sisters and brothers?"

"One of each. My sister tries to be cool, but she hasn't asked me to baby-sit for her two girls since I came out. My brother completely wigged out about it. You should have heard some of the shit he said to me! Every time I think about it, I wish I'd decked him."

Men, Blanche thought, still trying to control that vagina, even when it was officially off-limits. Not that Mick's mother and sister seemed to have much more sense than their menfolk.

"You got anybody?" Blanche asked her.

Mick sat up straighter. The lines in her forehead disappeared. "Been together two years." She reached in her back pocket and pulled out a worn brown leather wallet. She took out a picture and handed it to Blanche.

Blanche looked at the short plump woman standing next to Mick. She had long straight hair nearly to her waist, cheekbones as sharp as Blanche's own, and a slight slant to her eyes.

"Pilar," Mick said in a whispery voice full of pride and something that sounded to Blanche like pure lust, although she admitted that might be due to her own giant-sized case of horniness.

"She's beautiful," Blanche said. Years ago, she'd have had an attitude because Mick's lover wasn't black, but the older she got, the more certain she became that someone you loved who loved you back was what was important.

"She teaches in the Women's Studies Department at Brandeis," Mick said.

"You're lucky." Blanche's growing sense of aloneness roughened her voice.

Mick nodded. "Yeah, I know. Before Pilar I used to get so lonely sometimes... not for sex so much, but for somebody to talk to. Somebody who cared about me. But you know what? It doesn't make up for the other parts. I mean, having Pilar is great. She's just so amazing! And we... but sometimes, I just miss my mom and dad so much. You know, the way it used to be when they were in my corner, no matter what. Or at least I thought they were."

'Cause that's what they told you, Blanche thought. That's how people set their children up: telling you they'll always love you no matter what, but forgetting to add that they might decide to love you from a distance and without speaking to you if you grew up to love someone just like you. She wondered what Mick's parents had done with all their growing-up memories of her once they'd decided she was no longer daughter quality. Mick ought to be able to take them back—every tender moment, every single kiss good night.

"They'd do better by you if they could," Blanche said.

Mick stared at Blanche for a few seconds. "You're right. I never thought of it that way. I keep thinking, like, they're my parents, they have to know what's right, do what's right. But they're also just people, people who just can't... Thanks, Blanche. I'm glad we talked."

Blanche grinned. "Now tell me about Ray-Ray,"

Carrie came down the back stairs and gathered her hat and coat. "I'll be going now. See ya." She didn't look at either of them. Well, at least she didn't just say good-bye to me by name and act like Mick's invisible, Blanche thought. But there was still a lot of work to be done on our Carrie. She turned back to Mick.

"So, do you know Donnie?" Blanche asked.

"Donnie? I don't think so. What's his last name?"

Blanche told her. "He said he'd been after Ray-Ray for years. He's in a bad way about Ray-Ray's death."

"What's his name again?"

Blanche told her.

Mick shook her head. "He's not from the old neighborhood. Anyway, the only real lover I ever knew Ray-Ray to have was Marc. All the rest were strictly for fun and games."

"You mean Marc Brindle, right?"

"Yeah. Remember? I told you Marc and Ray-Ray used to be tight."

"Yeah, I finally figured him and Ray-Ray were lovers, even though you never said they were a couple or even that Ray-Ray was..." Blanche scolded, then remembered Mick's thing about not saying people were gay and veered off. "When did they break up?" she asked.

"Well, they had this puppy thing going when they were kids. Then Marc went away to college, and I think he went to Europe, too. Anyway, like a lot of guys back then, Ray-Ray was screwing everything that moved. He was lucky he didn't get AIDS," Mick said.

"So that was it?" Blanche prompted her.

Mick pushed up her glasses. "I don't remember exactly when they hooked up the second time. Over a year ago, at least. But it didn't work. It was like they were trying to get back what they had when they were kids."

Blanche was too impatient for Mick to get to the parts she was interested in. "Is that what Ray-Ray and Allister fought about? Is that why Ray-Ray don't work here anymore?"

Mick nodded. "Ray-Ray never would say exactly what happened, except that it was about Marc. Ray-Ray really changed after that. A bunch of us hang out together, go to clubs, and you know, hang out. Ray-Ray was a regular, but he stopped showing up. At first I thought it was because of breaking up with Marc. But I really think the fight with Allister hurt him more."

Blanche thought about Ray-Ray's box of Brindle gifts in the trash in his room and knew Mick was right. And she was right, too: Ray-Ray's fight with Allister was the reason why he stole the tape, the reason why Ray-Ray wanted to ruin Allister.

"It's a shame Ray-Ray's funeral's gonna be out of town, with none of his friends there," Blanche said, wondering if there was someone beside Donnie close enough to Ray-Ray to keep Allister's tape for him.

Mick pushed up her glasses. "I don't think he had what you'd call really close friends except for Marc."

Blanche wasn't surprised. She knew how tiring and irritating Ray-Ray's overconfidence could be. She *was* surprised that he hadn't shown Donnie off to his old crowd—especially since cutie-pie Donnie had wooed *him*.

"No, that's not true," Mick amended. "He did have one other close friend, but she just died, too. Miz Barker, who had the store over on Humboldt. You know her?"

Blanche nodded.

"They were tight. Her and Ray-Ray. Since we were little kids. He used to tell her all his business—and ours, too, I bet. I think she used to let him stay with her sometimes when him and Miz Inez were buggin'. Now they're both dead."

And both of them murdered. Both of them—the one who'd stolen the tape and the one to whom Mick said he told all of his business. Something heavy hit the bottom of Blanche's stomach. "You going to Miz Barker's funeral?" she asked to distract herself.

"You want to go together?" Mick said. "I'll pick you up." She looked at her watch. "Damn! Late again!" she said, and was out the door.

Blanche called Gourmanderie Groceries for the pears, greens, and salmon steaks Felicia had requested for lunch. The delivery boy was at the door by the time she'd gotten her pans and condiments together. She trimmed and washed the watercress and endive. She spun the greens dry, wrapped them in a dish towel, and let herself fall into a kind of trance from which her body did the cooking while her mind was busy elsewhere.

She returned to the path of thoughts that had begun last night as she was falling off to sleep and had lengthened during her conversation with Mick: If Ray-Ray was in the habit of telling Miz Barker all his business, then Miz Barker had had good reason to think Ray-Ray's death was related to something he'd stolen: He'd told her what he'd done. Blanche peeled and began mincing a small clove of garlic. She stopped, knife raised two inches from the cutting board, instantly and completely sure not only that Ray-Ray had told Miz Barker about the tape but that he'd given it to her to keep for him. Miz Barker must have made up that business about overhearing Ray-Ray on the phone so she didn't have to admit what she knew. Blanche finished mincing the garlic. She lay the knife down and looked out the window into the backyard, giving herself a few more moments free from the knowledge that lay at the end of this trail of thought. She tried to concentrate on the squawk of a nearby blue jay, but her thoughts were like crying children refusing to be ignored. She swept the garlic into a bowl, added low-fat yogurt curd, and blended in some sour cream. Her legs felt like twigs too weak to hold her. She leaned against the counter as the thought that Miz Barker had most likely died because of Brindle's tape seeped through her like poison.

She closed her eyes and opened them only when she was sure the questions bouncing off the inside of her brain wouldn't make her scream out loud: How would things be different if she'd told Miz Barker about Ray-Ray sneaking into the Brindle house? Or how crazed Allister Brindle had been over his missing tape? Or the tone of his voice when he'd ordered Samuelson to find the tape? Would Miz Barker still be alive? Would Ray-Ray?

"So sorry, so, so sorry," she whispered as regret permanently etched those awful questions on her heart.

She drained the capers and folded them and a bit of their juice into the sauce. The least she could do now was to find the tape they'd died for and try to make somebody pay. She wanted to at least know who had killed them. She doubted Samuelson had dirtied his own hands, but didn't he have a couple of goons with him at the lead poisoning meeting? "I need to talk to Pam," she muttered, relieved to have something to do. She wiped her hands on her apron and reached for the phone. But she didn't use it. Miz Barker had just died yesterday. She'd call tomorrow. She washed and dried the pears for poaching. She also needed to decide what exactly to say to Pam.

Felicia's four friends were as interesting as three-day-old meat loaf. Blanche immediately nicknamed them The Nices: They had nice—not too long, not too short—haircuts; nice navy, green, or gray, or quiet plaid skirts; light-colored blouses or sweater sets;

sensible-looking pumps or high-end walking shoes. They had nice voices, too. None of them laughed loudly or leaned too far back in her chair. Of course, no one raised her voice, brought up sex, money, or their husbands' prostate problem. And Blanche was sure if she squinted just so, she could see right through them. They talked about some benefit auction they were working on. It all sounded so very nice, Blanche didn't bother to listen. She figured that by the time she served coffee, they'd need it to keep from boring each other to sleep.

Felicia came to the kitchen after lunch. "Lovely meal, Blanche. The pears were heavenly." She added that she and the girls were off to do some impulse buying.

Blanche made quick work of the after-lunch cleanup, put the last of the dishes away, and went upstairs to see what she could see.

It was Allister's rooms that interested her. She didn't expect to find a note on his bedside table explaining what was on the tape or what he had on Samuelson. Still, there might be something she could use.

She put on her rubber gloves and opened Allister's door. Of course, the vibe in there didn't suit her. She decided to work up to it by checking out Felicia's rooms first. She didn't expect to find anything useful. Felicia didn't know as much about Ray-Ray and the tape as Blanche did. But she'd figured a quick look around Felicia's rooms would put her in a searching frame of mind.

She'd already seen the bedroom, so she opened the door to the dressing room: a chest of drawers, a vanity table, and at least ten feet of clothing and shoe racks behind mirrored sliding doors. She went in the bathroom and opened the door to the sauna. A part of her longed to get undressed and climb in, but the rest of her knew this was not a house to get naked in. She opened the door on the far side of the bathroom expecting a closet, but found an exercise room—Nautilus equipment, an exercise bike, two workout benches, and a massage table. A stereo and small refrigerator sat in one corner, a chair in another. She closed the door and turned back to covet Felicia's bathroom for another minute. She lingered in the dressing room, a favorite hiding place of women she'd worked for. It was as if they thought this room was a good hiding place because no one but them and those they thought they controlled entered it. She checked the walls for a safe: behind a round mirror with a frame made of ceramic tiles painted with miniature scenes of mountains and lakes, fields of flowers, and snowy countryside scenes; behind the clothes in the closet; and behind the dresser. Nothing.

Even though she was wearing her rubber gloves, she used a long nail file from the vanity to stir the contents of the wastebasket: puffs of cotton stained with beige makeup and a cream that smelled of vanilla; a half-finished copy of the schedule of household events and meals they'd talked about a couple days ago; a postcard telling Felicia when the suit she'd ordered from Chez Simone would be delivered; a postcard from someone called Bibi—"Having a grand time! Such gorgeous waiters!"—on Mustique. Were foreign waiters favorite boy-toys among Felicia's set? She'd like to be a fly on the wall when the waiters talked their side of things.

Carrie did a good job of keeping Felicia's clothes in order. Blanche looked at, but didn't disturb, the bureau drawers full of creamy satin and lace-edged underwear, nightgowns, and so forth. The bottom drawer held a black dildo with a strap and two vibrators of different sizes. Blanche chuckled at an image of Carrie opening this drawer and breaking out into instant prayers for Felicia.

On the desk in the alcove was the first picture of all the Brindles that Blanche had seen. Within the silver frame, younger versions of Allister and Felicia stood side by side. A young man who had to be Marc had his arm around Felicia's shoulders. Marc looked to be in his teens. He had his mother's eyes and his father's chin. They were all laughing. Blanche put it back. She needed to move on to Allister's room, but she was halted by the feeling that there was something here. But what? She took another walk through. The door to Felicia's exercise room seemed to glow in the corner of her left eye. This time she went inside.

One long wall was paneled floor to ceiling with mirrors. She walked to the end of the room, turned sideways, and looked at herself. Oughtta put all this butt on that bike. Probably can't touch my knees, let alone my toes. So, of course, she had to try. She leaned over and was at least able to reach her calves. On the way up, she noticed a small button beside the last wall mirror. She pushed it. A door popped open to reveal a closet. Sweats, sneakers, bath sheets, a big fluffy terry-cloth robe. Blanche pushed the hangers aside. Halfway down the back wall was a cubby door—the kind that housed plumbing and electrical stuff. Blanche pulled the handle, and the whole door fell away. There were large elbow pipes behind it. Wedged behind them was a Bloomingdale's shopping bag—a heavy bag that clanked and clinked as she lifted it out of the closet.

She'd never seen an Olympic medal up close before. There were three gold medals and three silver ones. There were also six trophies, all for swimming contests. All of them had SAXE WINTON engraved on them. The newspaper had said Saxe's medals and trophies were missing. Maybe Saxe gave them to Felicia before he died. But why? She tried to think of a way Felicia could have gotten Saxe's things without having anything to do with Saxe's death. She didn't have any success. Shit! She'd been really glad Felicia wasn't involved in Ray-Ray's death. Now this! Still, her having these things didn't necessarily mean Felicia had killed Saxe. And if she had, why take his trophies? The answer came to her almost before she'd finished the question: to make it look like a robbery. But why kill him in the first place?

She took the last item out of the shopping bag. A packet of photographs. Twelve of them. Pictures of Saxe leaning against a boat deck, about to dive off the side of a boat, lolling in a deck chair in oversize sunglasses and an undersized G-string. He was alone in all of the pictures, except the last one. Blanche looked at it closely. It sent her back to the picture on Felicia's desk. Yes. The young man standing with Saxe was definitely Marc Brindle.

Saxe was looking directly into the camera, smiling that same closed-lipped smile that promised to top your best sexual fantasy. Marc was beaming at Saxe and leaning toward him in a way that reminded Blanche of lips puckered for a kiss. She turned the picture over. Nothing on the back, not even a date. But it wasn't when it had been taken but what it showed that mattered.

If Felicia really looked at it, she had to know how Marc felt about Saxe. Unless, like Mick had said about Miz Inez, she didn't want to know. Blanche held the picture under the lamp shade and looked at it under direct light. Oh shit! Were they really...? She brought the picture closer to her eyes. There was a shadow between Marc and Saxe, which is why she hadn't noticed it at first. But there was no doubt about it: Saxe and Marc were holding hands. Damn! She could feel heat rising from the picture. She thought back to the afternoon Saxe had come back looking for his photographs. Had Felicia seen this picture the day Saxe lost it? She'd been plenty down in the mouth when she went out that afternoon. It wasn't every day you found out that your son and your lover had a thing going on. Blanche could certainly see herself taking a swing at some dog who was screwing her and her child. But self-defense was the only reason to kill anybody.

There was such a thing as knowing too much about your employer's business. But maybe she was wrong. Felicia wasn't the only one with reason to want to hurt Saxe. There was Marc, too. Maybe that was why Felicia was so anxious to talk to Marc. Maybe she knew that he... No. How would Felicia get the trophies and medals from Marc if she hadn't seen him in months? And if his mother was helping him cover up a murder, wouldn't Marc have at least asked to speak to her when he called the house? Blanche remembered how Felicia had stopped making eye contact after

Saxe was killed. And hadn't Allister said something about her disappearing from some reception the day Saxe was murdered? She really wished she hadn't found this stuff. She put it all back in the bag, put the bag back where she'd found it, and closed the closet door. She went downstairs and made a cup of tea. Her hand shook as she poured the water.

"I don't have to do jackshit about this now," she told herself. She was half sure this was a lie. But was the truth? She knew she wasn't going to call the police and tell them Felicia had Saxe's trophies and medals. She knew she wasn't going to get in Felicia's face about things she had in her closet. She thought about Felicia chastising her for having poked Samuelson. Woman had plenty of nerve. Blanche finished her tea. Miz Barker and Ray-Ray first, she told herself. She went back upstairs.

Allister's rooms were the same size and layout as Felicia's. His bedroom was full of dark mahogany furniture that probably belonged to his great-grandfather and looked to Blanche like big hunched creatures crouching around the room. Duck prints hung on the walls; silver-backed brushes caught the light from the window. Everything in the room—furniture, rug, picture frames—were done in either hunter green or dark brown, with a little baby-shit mustard thrown in. A room that said "I'm a missionary-position kind of guy." She wondered if it was true. Did he and Felicia still have sex, or was he screwing someone else, too? Cream silk pajamas and a much-used paisley silk smoking jacket hung from hooks on the back of his dressing room door. He seemed to own every man gadget that ever came down the pike: a wooden valet station with a pants holder and jacket hanger, an electric nose hair trimmer, a Bose Acoustic Wave radio, a lighted notepad with a pen attached. She pushed the button on his tie rack. A light came on and the ties marched around in a circle. She liked his silver-and-black bathroom better than Felicia's blue-and-green one. He, too, had his own Jacuzzi, shower, and sauna setup. There were weights in his exercise room, as well as a rowing machine and a big black punching bag on a stand with buttons in the base like it had a computer built into it. She looked around his dressing room but didn't touch anything. She felt the walls of this windowless room inching toward her, as walls did when she was in enemy territory. She left the dressing room without looking around. It was her experience that men and women hid things differently. In addition to safes, women seemed to look for places that weren't really hiding places—like coat pockets and shoes. Men seemed to like trick hiding places: a secret panel in a wall, a desk with a hidden drawer, suitcases with false bottoms. She'd once found a shallow compartment built into the seat of an employer's desk chair. He'd kept pictures of naked children in it. She'd poured ammonia on the pictures and never went back.

A bookcase, an easy chair, and an end table occupied the alcove that in Felicia's room held her desk. Blanche circled the furniture, fighting her way through Allister's vibe as she walked among his things. It was a large armchair—big enough for two. Its dark wooden arms and feet shone from Wanda's labor. It was a chair Allister liked. The back cushion showed a slight darkness where Allister's head rested and just the barest indentation from his butt in the seat. The arms were wide enough to set a glass or cup on or to lean on and write. Blanche gathered herself to herself, took a deep breath, and sat down. Experience also told her that men liked having their hiding places in sight. If it was behind a picture, it was a picture in front of rather than behind their favorite chair so that they could keep their eye on it. She scanned the room from where she sat, then rose to inspect the pictures on the wall, all of which were just that. She went back to the chair and looked closer in: From the corner of her left eye, she saw the bookcase; in front of her, the footstool; on the other side, a table. She sat up and pulled the footstool to her. It was heavier than it looked. She ran her hand around the edge of the cushion until she felt a small hinge. She pulled at the cushion. It rose to reveal a small safe that was of no use to her without the combination. Or to anyone else.

She looked down at the gray combination lock. If this was where Allister kept his film, how had Ray-Ray gotten into it? She shut the cushioned lid. As she got up, her hand slipped from the arm of the chair, down into the space beside the seat cushion. Her fingers automatically snagged the item she felt there: a matchbook. A familiar-looking matchbook: LE CLUB was stamped on it in raised silver letters on a slick black background.

She'd found one just like it in Ray-Ray's bureau drawer. She went downstairs and called Joanie at the hospital where she worked. She played with the shiny black matchbook while she waited for Joanie to pick up the phone in the dieticians' office.

"Hey, girl. I know you're busy. I just want to know if you've heard of a place called Le Club."

"Never heard of it. Is it a nightclub?"

"Maybe. I don't really know."

"I just wish I had some nightclubs in my life! I can't remember the last time I was in a club. But I bet Lacey would know."

Blanche hesitated, wondering if Lacey would even remember her.

"Give me your number. I'll tell her to call you," Joanie said.

Blanche didn't hang around the library while the Brindles had their drinks. She could hardly look at Felicia. The minute she saw the woman, she could feel the weight of that bag of trophies and medals. And she couldn't stop herself from feeling bad about what that bag likely meant. As for Allister, just being in the room with him soured her stomach. She could tell from the way he watched her without seeming to that she wasn't brightening up the world for him either.

"Blanche, you sly fox, I had no idea," Lacey said when she called. "Of course, I'd love to sponsor you, honey. My, my, you are a one."

Blanche gave Lacey a couple seconds to clear her throat of that I-know-your-business chuckle before declaring that she didn't know what kind of a place Le Club was.

"If you don't know anything about it, why do you want to go there?"

"I'm superstitious," Blanche told her. "I've found two matchbooks from there—one in a place that surprised me."

"Superstitious and curious. Just where did you find these matchbooks?" Lacey wanted to know.

Blanche didn't answer.

"Fine, if you won't talk, I won't tell you about Le Club. You'll have to see the place for yourself."

Which was fine with Blanche. She agreed to meet Lacey the next afternoon while the Brindles went out. Lacey suggested she pick Blanche up to save time.

Tongues came running up to Blanche as she got off the bus.

"You'll wanna be my girlfriend, now, un-hunh, you'll give me a little kiss, too, Blanche, I know it. I know it."

She gave him a level look and waited for him to go on. It didn't make sense to encourage him with a question until it was absolutely necessary.

"I saved all your stuff, all of it. If it wasn't for me, they'd a taken everything you got, so…"

Blanche stopped walking. "What are you talking about, Tongues? What stuff of mine did you save?"

"Everything! Blanche, everything you got. You gon' be my woman now, I bet, un-hunh, un-hunh."

Blanche stopped herself from screaming at him to tell her everything right away. She didn't want him to go off just now.

"You mean stuff in my house, Tongues?"

"That's right, girl, now you talkin', girl. I saved it all. Me, Tongues. You got to at least give me a hug, Blanche, 'cause…"

Blanche willed herself to stay calm, to believe everything was fine. She gave his arm a gentle shake. “Maybe I will, Tongues, maybe I will. But first you gotta tell me what happened.” She was walking fast now, dragging him along with her.

Tongues’s grin was wide enough for two. “Oh boy! I got me a girlfriend now, un-hunh, un-hunh.”

Blanche felt her patience draining away quick as money from a gambler’s pocket. “Tongues, you gotta tell me what happened. Did somebody try to break into my house?”

“Un-hunh, that’s right, un-hunh, un-hunh. Two of ’em. Big niggers!” He lifted his hands way above his head.

Blanche’s breath caught in her chest. They were nearing her door. She was anxious to get inside, to check on the children and her territory, but she wasn’t about to let Tongues into her house.

“Did they try to break in the door?” she asked him.

He shook his head from side to side. When they reached her house, he walked around to the back and pointed at the kitchen window, which was open about an inch. The aluminum frame was bent.

“There, right there. Un-hunh, un-hunh.” Tongues made prying motions with his hands and arms.

Blanche left him there and hurried back around front. She unlocked the door and opened it. “Hey, y’all, I’m here. Everybody in?” she called, and was relieved when Shaquita said they were. “I’ll be back in a few minutes.” She closed the door, making sure it was locked.

“What did you do, Tongues?”

He covered his mouth with a nail-bitten hand and giggled. “I tricked ’em, tricked ’em.” His two-person grin was back.

“How, Tongues? How did you trick them?”

He spun around in a way that made Blanche fear she’d lost him.

"Here she come! Here she come!" He shouted toward the window, as though talking to the men who'd tried to pry it open. "Smart, hunh, Blanche, hunh?"

"What did they look like, Tongues?"

"I told you, Blanche. Big niggers, real big. I—"

"Did you know them, Tongues? Ever see them before?"

He gave her a blank look. "I tricked 'em, didn't I, Blanche, didn't I? Now I know you gonna give me some, I know it, un-hunh, un-hunh."

Blanche gave up. "Yeah, right, Tongues, I owe you. Maybe I'll bake you a cake, honey, but forget about getting any." She kissed him on his forehead. "Thanks for stopping those thieves. Now I got something to do." She gently pushed him off her stoop and headed back down the hill.

"Wait, Blanche, wait!" Tongues ran after her a few paces, then gave up.

Her mind raced along with her feet. What if one of the children had been home? What if those thugs had gotten in? What if they weren't your everyday thieves but were looking for something specific? How could she be so stupid, so smart-assed as to tell Miz Barker she was going to find out who killed Ray-Ray? If her life was so dull she needed to stick her nose in other people's business, maybe she should get a second job or volunteer somewhere.

Blanche looked around the McDonald's parking lot until she spotted the security guard's car. She yanked open the door before he had a chance to pretend he was awake.

"Where the hell were you when those creeps were trying to break into my place!" She grabbed him by his shirt and dragged him out of the car. "The children could have been home!"

The guard pulled his shirt out of her hands and stepped back. "Hold on there, hold on!"

He was a short portly man who looked old enough to have retired from some other job before he took this one, and probably had.

"You don't have no call to be pull—"

"Can that shit and listen to me! Somebody tried to break into my place this afternoon. I live in number forty-seven. They were right out in plain sight trying to get in my kitchen window. You tell me where you were when that was going on, and then we'll talk about me grabbing your shirt. Or should I call your boss and ask him?" She folded her arms across her chest to keep from grabbing him again, from slapping him and kicking him until he was silly.

"Now, missus, don't go making no calls. We can work this out. Number forty-seven, you say? I was up there all day, I swear. Musta been when I went in the market to get a..."

"We ain't paying your ass to go to no market!"

"I know, I know. It won't happen again, missus. I'll keep a special eye out on your place and make a report about what happened if you'll tell me wh—"

"Fuck a report! Keep your eye on my place, or I'm going to report you right out of a job. I got kids, you understand that! Anything coulda..." Shit! He was looking at her as though she was crazy, and she was. She took a couple of deep breaths.

"Look, I'm sorry about going off, but like I said, the kids coulda been home, coulda come home when somebody..." She shook her head to discourage the tears, hot with rage.

"Don't worry none, missus. I swear, I'll be on the watch. I need this job, I..."

Blanche raised her hand to stop him. "Okay, okay." She turned and headed back up the hill. Tongues was waiting in front of her house.

"Blanche! Blanche!" He ran toward her.

Blanche gave him The Look, the one she saved for Taifa and Malik when they were closest to making themselves the kind of pain in the behind that she was about to make them regret.

Tongues saw her face, spun around, and: "Oohgalta majinica sambalala dicoty..."

Blanche had never heard of anyone scaring Tongues into talking his talk with just a look. He was still doing his number when she let herself in the house.

Taifa was coming down the stairs. Blanche had hoped to be able to run up to her room and pull herself together before she saw the kids. If she tried to talk to them now, she wouldn't be able to keep fear out of her voice.

"Hey, Moms, whatsup? You okay?" Taifa lay her hand on Blanche's forehead. Blanche pulled Taifa close and hugged her hard. To her surprise, Taifa leaned into her and returned her hug with equal force. We don't do this enough, Blanche thought.

"I needed that," Taifa said as she pulled away. "My gym teacher made me feel so bad today!"

With half her mind, Blanche listened to the story of how Taifa had tried to weasel out of gym class, got caught, was loud-talked by her teacher in front of the class, and made to do extra exercises to boot. With the other half, she wondered if she might be wrong about the break-in being related to Brindle's tape. The neighborhood *was* a pretty high crime area, after all.

"That's what you get for trying to get outta class," Blanche told her. "You didn't—"

Taifa sighed with relief when the phone rang, and leapt for it.

"Hi, Grandma. How you doin'? Yes, I'm fine. Yeah, I mean yes, school's fine. We were just talking about it." She looked at Blanche and rolled her eyes. "Yes, Grandma. She's right here." She held the phone out to Blanche and escaped upstairs.

"Hey, Mama."

"Blanche? Is you all right? You acted kinda funny last time I talked to you. I wasn't even done talkin' and you—"

"And I will again, Mama, if you don't let me get a word in edgewise every once in a while. Now, how you doin'?" Blanche waited for her mother to get over her shock enough to answer.

"Well, I'm fine, I guess. How're you?"

Blanche smiled. So much for old dogs and new tricks. She gave her mother a short, clean version of how she was, how the kids were doing in school, and what a handful they both were.

"Ship them wild things down here. I'll straighten 'em out. Course, the Lord's just paying you back for all the grief you caused me when you was coming along."

Grief! What grief? She'd had too many chores to be a handful, but she didn't get a chance to disagree. Her mother was still talking, new tricks notwithstanding.

"... a shame about Inez's boy, poor woman. I know how hard it is to lose a child. Charlotte says that granddaughter of hers is a right smart young lady."

You couldn't tell it from the way she's acting now, Blanche thought, but told Mama what good grades Shaquita got and about her plans to become an archaeologist, as if saying it might help make it happen.

"Well, I don't want to run my phone bill up too high. I just wanted to holler at y'all."

"Thanks, Mama. I'll call you soon," Blanche said, as pleased with this conversation with her mother as she ever expected to be.

Blanche waited until they were nearly done with dinner to tell the children about the near break-in. They were full of silent attention when she showed them the bent window frame.

"That's why I want you to let the security guard go through the house before you come inside from school."

"That weird old man! Why we got to let him go in the house first, Moms?"

Blanche heard the little squeak of worry in Taifa's voice.

"I just want him to make sure everything's okay. If the thieves come back, I don't want you to meet 'em. Tongues scared them off this time, but..."

"Tongues? That fool? He probably made the whole thing up." Taifa said.

Blanche almost chastised her for talking about Tongues as though he weren't still her elder, despite the state of his mind, but thinking Tongues was too foolish to be telling the truth had lessened that squeak in Taifa's voice.

"I don't need that old dude to protect me!" Malik wolfed. "I can take care of myself. If some . . ."

Blanche waited him out. There was nothing she could do with that testosterone thing.

Shaquita was the only one who didn't seem to have a problem. She promised to be waiting on the stoop when Blanche's two got home.

That's done, Blanche thought, and went in the living room to listen to the news on the radio and to give the kids a chance to mumble and grit in private. She caught the end of *All Things Considered* on National Public Radio. Her friend Carmen in Harlem had introduced her to NPR. Being able to listen to it in Boston made her feel connected to folks in the other places she'd lived, all listening to the same thing.

She waited until the children settled down for the night before she took over the bathroom: candles, incense, her jambox and earphones, and Ida Cox reminding her that "Wild Women Don't Get No Blues." She tried to slip into the space between sleep and wakefulness where her body was practically weightless and her mind was free, but she'd had too much of a day for that. She could depend on the security guard for a couple days because she'd just gotten on his butt, but the effect of that wouldn't last. She needed to find that tape—or whatever Brindle had on Samuelson—something to stop the heat she felt rising around her. But protecting the children couldn't wait for that. She remembered that at the lead poisoning meeting Othello Flood had said the Ex-Cons provided security. Maybe he could help her. She stretched out in the tub and closed her eyes.

Ray-Ray's ghost walked through the bathroom door and sat on the lid of the toilet seat. She'd noticed that the older she got, the more time the dead spent with her. Ray-Ray crossed his legs and arms and gave her another "well, girlfriend" look.

"Don't look at me like I'm supposed to do something unless you came in here to tell me where you hid that damned tape. You gave it to Miz Barker, didn't you? At least tell me what's on it and whether I'm right about what made this Brindle-bashing year?"

Although she left plenty of space between questions, Ray-Ray only grinned at her through the rising steam. And when she rose from the tub, he left.

Before she went to bed, she thanked her ancestors for protecting her house. After all, the thieves didn't get in.

In her dreams, the detective Felicia Brindle had hired was peeping through Donnie's keyhole, which was also in the doorway to the YMCA, except inside, instead of the Y, there was Allister Brindle's bedroom, where Ray-Ray and Pookie were having a pillow fight, and Wanda was playing the mouth organ in the city pool.

NINE

DAY EIGHT—THURSDAY

The corn on her left baby toe drummed out a rhythmic pain before Blanche was fully awake. A bad sign. She reminded herself she didn't have to have an attitude all day just because her foot hurt, even though her evilness and her throbbing corn always seemed to hang together.

This is a new day, she told herself. I can do anything I want. If that were really true, she'd call the Brindles and tell them to cook their own damn meals, then take herself to a podiatrist and have this corn removed. She'd shop for comfortable shoes, have a nice lunch: soup, a mesclun salad, a nice plump piece of cornmeal-battered catfish, and the richest dessert on the menu. She'd read and nap the rest of the day away. If she could really do anything she wanted.

Instead, she looked back along the path of her life for a point where she had been free of work. She couldn't find one. Her earliest memories were of baking bread with her mother, her own child nose just clearing their old pine table while her little sister played in the corner under the window. She remembered pulling herself up as tall as she could, imitating her mother's proud stance. She could still smell that dry, chalky raw wood tabletop and feel the tickle of flour dust coating the inside of her nostrils. Her mother's loaves had glistened on the table, looking light enough to float to the oven. Little Blanche's bit of dough, stamped with pudgy fingerprints and heavy and limp with handling, went into the oven right alongside Mama's loaves. "This is how you learn," Mama would always say when little Blanche complained about the difference between Mama's loaves and her own. "Keep trying. Yours'll look like mine, someday."

Child Blanche also loved to climb beneath that hand-me-down table and pretend it was the roof of her snug and pretty little house. She'd mimic her mother's cleaning behavior—washing and drying her make-believe dishes, polishing her pretend windows until they shone, washing her imaginary clothes, and filling her playhouse with the smell of heated starch as she pressed them. By the time she was ten, her play-baking and -cleaning had become the real thing. Her father was gone before Blanche could form a lasting memory of him.

With two children to feed, Mama left for work early and came home late. Blanche could still taste anger—bitter and salty—at always having to drag baby Rosalie everywhere she went, of having to end her game of jacks because she had to peel the potatoes or stop jumping double Dutch to scrub the kitchen floor. She knew better than to sass, and she didn't really want her mother to have to do all the work, but in her mind, she'd often railed against her mother for making her work so hard so much of the time. By high school she'd stopped thinking of herself as an overworked child and understood that she was simply paying for what she got in the way of food and clothes and a home. A fair trade.

But no longer. She had done more work than she'd been paid for in her life. She was tired: tired of other people's houses, other people's meals; tired of keeping other people's worlds beautiful and peaceful while risking her own children growing wild as a stand of bamboo. She stomped into the bathroom and slammed the door in a way that told everyone else in the house to back off. For once, the children showed their good judgment by staying out of her way.

⚜ ⚜ ⚜

The sight of Jamaica Pond and the sound of a mockingbird running through her repertoire lightened Blanche's mood enough for her to step back and look at what was bothering her.

Part of her attitude was worry. She'd given up the dream that she could protect Malik and Taifa from the worst of life, but today, she wished she could follow them around all day to make sure nothing and no one touched them that shouldn't.

The rest of her attitude was about the Brindle house: She didn't want to go anywhere near it. She knew Allister was behind Ray-Ray's death, but she was positive he hadn't done his own dirty work. She couldn't say the same for Felicia. She didn't feel the kind of disgust toward Felicia that she felt toward Allister because Saxe's death didn't touch her the way Miz Barker's and Ray-Ray's did. Still, how was she supposed to go to work and act as though she didn't know that Felicia was a woman who'd killed a man with her own hands? The answer came in a parade of faces of past employers whom she'd seen coked up, giving the chauffeur some head, neglecting to bathe for a week, exchanging tongue with their schnauzer, pilfering money from a guest's handbag, and engaging in various other acts she'd pretended not to see or know about. Just keep your mouth shut and your eyes straight ahead, she warned herself.

The first thing Blanche did when she got to the Brindles' was call home.

"You over being evil already?" Taifa asked her.

"It's okay," Taifa told her when Blanche apologized. "Like you always say, Mama Blanche, everybody's got a right to have a bad day. Did you want something special?"

"Just to remind y'all to let the security guard go through the house when you come home from school."

"Ah, Moms!"

"I mean it, Taifa. None of you can go in the house until he looks around. You understand?"

"Whatever."

"Excuse me?"

"Yeah, I understand."

"That's better, and don't forget to tell Malik and Shaquita what I said. I'm depending on you. Don't disappoint me," she added before she hung up, knowing that Taifa understood the consequences of being an undependable disappointment.

Blanche's next call was to Bea Richards. Again, no answer. Was there someone else who might have the dope on Samuelson? Maybe she'd ask Joanie.

Blanche gathered ingredients for eggs Benedict. Cooking something that needed attention always settled her nerves. After breakfast, she checked the household schedule to see how it meshed with her plans for the day: Felicia would be off to the hairdresser's shortly. Allister was probably already gone, and neither one of them was in for lunch or dinner. Perfect. They would be home for drinks, but she'd be finished by then. She called Miz Barker's house.

"Hey, Pam. It's Blanche. You okay?"

"As I can be. You know how it is."

"It's gonna take a while, honey, but the pain will ease. It will."

Pam sighed. "I know. But that doesn't seem to help much right now. I've been trying to keep busy."

"Well, I may be able to help with that," Blanche said. "I talked to Miz Inez last night. She reminded me how close Ray-Ray and Miz Barker were."

"Yeah. I used to be jealous of him when I was a kid."

Blanche crossed her fingers. "Miz Inez thought maybe Ray-Ray might have given Miz Barker a box to hold for him. A kind of souvenir box. His first pair of baby shoes are in there, and his high school diploma. Now he's gone, Miz Inez'd really like to have them."

"But why would he give it to Gran?"

"Well, Miz Inez didn't exactly say. But she did seem to know a lot about what was in Ray-Ray's private box. Maybe that's why he wanted it out of the house."

"Could be," Pam said, "but I never saw it."

"Well, is there someplace special Miz Barker might have put it, if he did give it to her?"

"I already started going through her things," Pam said. "And I haven't seen any box like that." She paused for a minute. "There's the attic. Gran probably hadn't been up there in years. I sure haven't."

"Could we look?"

When Pam agreed, Blanche made a date to come by later that morning. She hung up and tried to convince herself her lies were justified. When this mess was all straightened out, she'd tell Pam the truth.

She took the piece of envelope with Donnie's number on it from her bag and called him. This time she wouldn't have to lie; she just didn't intend to tell the whole truth. There was no sense adding to Donnie's grief by telling him somebody had killed Ray-Ray—and that she thought she knew who'd done it.

"International Autos, Sales Department," a crisp-voiced woman told her. Blanche asked for Donnie and waited.

"Donald McFadden, how can I help you today?" His voice was louder, deeper, and more pushy than she'd heard it before.

"Donnie? It's Blanche White. You got a minute? It's about Ray-Ray."

"Hi, Blanche. Did you find my letters and the picture?"

"They're not at his mom's place," she told him.

"Maybe he has some stuff in storage, or a friend I don't know might have them. You could ask his mother, maybe she—"

"Listen, Donnie," Blanche interrupted. "You remember I asked if he ever mentioned the Brindles, the people Miz Inez works for? Well, he may not have mentioned them, but they, at least one of them, have been doing a whole lotta talking about Ray-Ray. Allister Brindle—"

"Don't tell me! I don't know anything about Ray-Ray and those people, and I don't want to know, especially anything that... I told you! We wanted to start fresh. We didn't talk about old..." Donnie's voice quivered.

"Donnie, I'm sorry. I know you're having a hard time right now, but somebody tried to break into my house yesterday. I think they were looking for—"

"Don't. I told you, I don't... Look, I gotta go."

The phone was dead before Blanche could open her mouth. "Chickenshit!" she said to the dead line. He'd have likely pooped in his drawers if she'd told him the whole story.

"Hello, darlin'. " Wanda eyed the teapot.

"I'll make a fresh pot of tea if you've got a minute. There's some biscuits and ham."

Wanda unwound her layers and sat down. She looked around the room, then turned to Blanche.

"Somethin'different about this place. Feels like sad times coming."

"You feel it, too." Blanche poured tea.

"What's been goin' on?"

What hasn't? Blanche thought.

"Course, it's what's comin' that's the thing. I had an old auntie who could tell you at what o' clock death would be knocking at a neighbor's door. I can't tell the comin' of death from the comin' of a broken arm. All I know's when something bad's headin' this way." She stopped to bite into her ham biscuit. "Christ! You can cook, darlin'! I never quite got the knack of it meself."

Blanche was glad Wanda had drifted away from talk of the Brindle house. She liked what she'd seen of Wanda. Blanche smiled to herself when the phrase "even though she's a white woman" tried to work its way into her thinking. Wanda was definitely not who she meant by "a white woman." But liking Wanda was not the same as confiding in her. That kind of trust took longer than the two weeks they'd have together. They sipped their tea and ate their biscuits in companionable silence.

Wanda went off to her work. Blanche checked the time and gathered her bag and jacket so she'd be ready.

As soon as Felicia left for the hairdresser's, Blanche assured Carrie that she'd be back long before Felicia was finished trying to turn back time. She called a cab and went upstairs to tell Wanda she had to leave for a while.

"Mind how you go, darlin'. I'll be rootin' for ya," Wanda said, as if she knew something Blanche hadn't told her.

Blanche climbed the slim, fold-down ladder to Miz Barker's crawl space and gritted her teeth against the mental exertion of forcing herself to thrust her head into the small opening above her. She took a deep breath, closed her eyes, and stepped up another two rungs so that her head and shoulders were in the crawl space. It smelled of dust and mildew and looked like a rest home for cardboard boxes and dilapidated valises, their leather peeling away like shedding skin. Pam was already on the other side of the space. A layer of fine undisturbed grit covered the floor, except where Pam had walked. The dust that covered everything else in the room like an afghan was also undisturbed. Pam was right. No one had been up here for years. Blanche was delighted to back down the ladder and out of the tiny place before it got too hard for her to breathe. She checked her watch—still fine on time.

They left Miz Barker's house and went to the store, where Blanche was almost bowled over by the spirit of the old woman. She stood in the middle of the floor, feeling Miz Barker moving slowly round her. The echo of the old woman's voice mingled with her sharp liniment smell. If she tried, Blanche was sure she could reach out and touch Miz Barker's arm. The look on Pam's face as she stared at Miz Barker's stool made Blanche think Pam knew the old lady was still there, too. Pam drew a ragged breath.

"This is the first time I been in here since..." Pam's voice was thin and sad.

Blanche looked up at the dusty shelves and at the ancient cash register and wondered again about the woman whose life was in this store. Had the store given Miz Barker pleasure? Or had she run it for so long she couldn't do without it? Had she reached a point where, like Blanche, she felt she had worked too hard and too long for too little? And would she do it all the same if she could live again? Or would she, too, want to take a flying leap out of here to parts unknown?

Blanche leaned over and pulled out the drawer under the cash register: receipts, paper clips, small pads of paper, pencil stubs. She lifted a lid from a box on a shelf behind the cash register, and it crumbled in her hand. Most of the other boxes they opened were empty. What little stock there was had mostly been nibbled by mice.

"I don't think what you're looking for's in here," Pam said, wiping dust from her hands onto her jeans. She looked around her. "It's like the store died, too," she said.

Blanche didn't think the tape was there either, and it was time to get back to the Brindle house.

"We could look down in the bomb shelter," Pam said.

"In the what?"

"Underneath Gran's house. It runs the length of the whole block. These houses were built back in the fifties when everybody was paranoid about the Russians, but now it's just storage space. I doubt most people leave anything much down there."

Blanche was interested. "I gotta get back to work," she told Pam reluctantly. "Maybe we can do it later this evening?" She remembered the date she'd made with Lacey yesterday. "No, I can't this evening, what about..."

"I'll just give you the keys and you can go when you get a chance," Pam said. She took Blanche to Miz Barker's house and showed her the outside door to the shelter.

"Don't forget to bring a flashlight when you come back," Pam said as they stood looking down a short flight of cracked, litter-strewn steps at the shelter door. "It's got electricity, but I don't know if the bulbs are any good."

Blanche began crushing ice for the Brindles' cocktails when she felt the car coming up the drive. She knew it was them the same way she always knew when an employer was approaching.

Both of 'em look like they need mouth-to-mouth resuscitation, Blanche thought. Allister reminded her of one of those never-quite-finished sweaters Taifa used to knit: limp and lumpy and coming loose around the edges.

"Ah, drinks! Just what I need," Allister spoke like a man being rescued. Felicia looked as though a volcano were about to explode from her belly.

Blanche held the drinks tray out to her.

"Leave it, please," Felicia, said, instead of taking her martini from the tray. And quickly, her tone seemed to add.

Blanche did as she was bid, but of course this didn't stop her from lingering outside the door.

"Allister, there's something I need to talk to you about."

"Not Marc again, I hope."

"No, it's not Marc. At least not in the way you—"

"I don't suppose it could wait? I've had—"

"Until when? After the campaign? Felicia's volcano was beginning to rumble. "Never mind. I don't know what could have gotten into me." Felicia took a sip from her glass.

"Felicia, I'm tired. I only meant—"

"You only meant, 'Shut up, Felicia, and stop expecting to be treated like anything other than a large purse.' I bet you'd have enough energy for a conversation about your missing tape! Oh yes," she added. "I know about it. And I hope whatever is on it is enough to destroy you!"

Felicia's volcano had erupted, but it didn't wilt Allister.

"I doubt you'd really enjoy seeing me destroyed, my dear." Allister's voice was full of what Blanche could only identify as privilege: the sound of ownership—not just money but ownership of government, museums, and colleges, of the right to run the world. "You see, I remember how eager you were to join my penniless little world, how delighted your vulgar, wig-manufacturing, nouveau riche, social-climbing parents were when ..."

"You bastard!"

Something shattered in the room. There was rustling, movement. Blanche tiptoed down the hall toward the kitchen.

She didn't know when they went upstairs to dress. Felicia clicked into the kitchen on high, high heels to tell Blanche they were leaving. Blanche had been too interested in their conversation during drinks to focus on Felicia. Now she looked at this woman, the second woman she'd met, she realized, who had killed someone. The first one had been mad as a monkey on LSD. Was this one? If anything, Felicia looked more like herself, as though killing her lover had simmered her like stock, until there was only the thickest, richest part of her left.

"Is everything all right?" she said under Blanche's long gaze.

"Yes, ma'am, *I'm* fine." Blanche put more emphasis on the "I'm" than she'd intended. Felicia didn't miss it.

"So am I," she said, her voice just a tad too high. "How do I look?" She posed in her form-fitting ankle-length off-the-shoulder number in deep red and hard orange.

"Like fire," Blanche said. "Just like fire." She wondered whether Felicia was about to burn something up or go up in flames herself.

They were hardly out of the house before Blanche called Lacey to come pick her up. The phone rang as she put it down.

"Blanche? It's Donnie."

"Yeah?"

"Look, I'm sorry about the way I, about hanging up earlier. I was just so ... And then somebody came in and I couldn't really talk."

"Well, I appreciate your calling back, Donnie. When I called you, I was hoping maybe Ray-Ray had told you..."

"Listen, Blanche, I loved Ray-Ray but I can't get mixed up in anything he might have..."

"Anything like what?"

Donnie hesitated, then: "Look, I shoulda told you when you called. But I was so... Two guys came by my place asking questions about Ray-Ray, who he used to hang with and where, stuff like that."

Blanche immediately saw Samuelson's goons towering over Donnie. "Did they say what it was about?"

"No. But they got a real attitude when I told them I didn't know anything about Ray-Ray's business. I'm not sure they believed me."

"They didn't hurt you, did they?"

"No, but..." Donnie took a deep breath.

"What is it?"

"They scared the hell out of me, Blanche."

Blanche could feel his fear seeping like cold air through the phone.

"So, what are you going to do about it? You—"

"No! Nothing! I'm not doing a damned thing about it! I don't know what Ray-Ray did, but if it got him... if he was in trouble with those guys who came by my place, they could have... what if they're still watching me? Maybe the way he died wasn't..."

"We could work together," Blanche said, "try to find out..."

"Ray-Ray's dead," Donnie said. "Nothing can change that."

"I know that," Blanche said. "But it ain't that simple. I got kids, I can't have..." She let the sentence trail off. Not only did Donnie not want to know anything about Ray-Ray's business, she realized she didn't really want to tell him what she'd learned, either. As scared as he sounded, if Samuelson's Muscle Brothers paid Donnie another visit, he'd likely tell them every word she said faster than a lizard could catch a fly.

"Well, I'm sure you'll be fine," she told him, although she had no idea if it was true. "If those men thought you were lying, they wouldn't have left without trying to make you tell what you know."

"You think so?" He sounded like a child wanting to believe the bogeyman was out of town.

"Sure, I'm sure."

"Look, Blanche, I'm sorry to sound so..."

Weak and wussy? Blanche thought. "Take care of yourself, Donnie." "Gutless wonder!" she muttered when she hung up. She was on her own, as usual. What a joke that Ray-Ray should fall for such a little weakling.

She was locking the back door when Lacey arrived.

They drove down Tremont Street, passed Connolly's, turned right on Massachusetts Avenue and then onto Washington Street. Lacey made a couple turns down narrow streets whose street signs Blanche didn't see.

"Where are we?"

"In the South End," Lacey parked on a side street, near a row of apartments with torn window blinds and dirty stoops—not an Allister Brindle kind of neighborhood. A BAR AND GRILL sign glowed neon red in a small front window across the street. The place was just as dreary on the inside; they didn't stay long. Lacey motioned Blanche to follow her down a dim corridor. Hair rose on the back of Blanche's neck when a man stepped out of a doorway near the far end of the corridor.

"Hey, Lacey," he said. He gave Blanche a brief once-over, and handed Lacey two black half masks. When Blanche and Lacey put them on, the man turned and knocked on the door behind him.

The room they entered was huge. The walls were painted a dark, vivid blue lit by track lights. Black leather banquettes surrounded onyx tables that also glowed blue, lit from inside. The banquettes rose in three tiers above a dance space with mirrored floors. Two large, empty cages hung from the ceiling on either side of the room.

"My favorite seat," Lacey said as she slid onto one of the banquettes in the third tier.

Blanche could see why. From here you could see most of the club—and there was plenty to see. Had that man worn those bottomless leather pants and short jacket on the bus? She folded her arms across her own breasts as if the large gold ring in a passing woman's nipple might attack her. A man in handcuffs and a T-shirt that said I'M YOURS threw himself on the floor in front of a woman carrying a whip. She lifted her foot, and he began passionately licking the bottom of her shoe. Blanche turned to find Lacey watching her with amused eyes.

"What can I bring you, ladies?"

Blanche couldn't stop herself from staring at the waiter's see-through plastic shorts and his pink penis with its cock ring clearly visible. Lacey could hardly order for laughing. Blanche didn't mind. She had no doubt that if her mask wasn't covering it, the expression on her face would warrant a chuckle or two.

She looked around the quickly filling room as rolling ladders were moved beneath the two cages. There was light applause. A couple climbed into each cage. All four people were dressed in form-fitting black leather. The woman in the cage on the right also wore a half mask. The man with her wore a tight leather hood with openings only for his mouth and nose. The woman carried a whip. In the other cage, the head and face gear were reversed and the man carried the whip. The room grew quiet. The background music died down, and something with a more driving beat began at a higher volume.

Blanche felt her mouth hanging open; she didn't even notice the waiter when he brought their drinks. She flinched as the whip cracked against the back of the woman on her knees in the cage to her left. She turned to her right. The man in that cage was on all fours, his head buried in his arms and his behind in the air. The woman had one stiletto heel planted on the small of his back. She was leaning over, teasing his bare butt with the whip handle—more than teasing, Blanche realized when she saw the tip disappear between his buttocks.

She turned from the cages and looked around. There was a woman on all fours being used as a footstool by two men in suits; two other men with leashes attached to collars around their necks were being led around the room by a woman in a skin-tight pink jumpsuit. Was this supposed to have something to do with sex? She thought about the kind of pain and shame black folks suffer in America, and wondered how many were into pain for pleasure. She didn't have a problem with people who needed handcuffs and a good spanking to get their rocks off, but for her, being bound and hit and shamed were too much like slavery to be a good time. Still, people sat at the bar the same way they sat at any bar, couples cuddled in corners, and a few folks were grinding their hips on the dance floor. As the room filled, there were more worsted pin-striped suits than black leather.

It was just after six in the evening. Blanche wondered what this place was like about midnight, when folks were really loosened up. She felt Lacey watching her, and turned toward her.

"I don't meet a lot of women in your line of work," Lacey said.

"Likewise," Blanche said. "But I meet a lot of women who *were* in my line of work, at one time or another, or one way or another. I imagine the same is true for you."

Lacey laughed and clapped her hands. "Brava, Blanche! Most women like to pretend that being in the life is something only sluts and junkies do. I'm glad you know better."

Blanche decided not to mention the big difference between women who traded sex for a new house, a better car, and so on from the men in their lives and pulling down your panties for men you didn't know, and who would never acknowledge you if you met them in church. Instead, she took off in a direction she hoped would lead to where she wanted to go.

"And what about men? The backbone of the industry?"

"Ah, yes, God love 'em; what *would* we do without their appetites! You'd be amazed at what some of the big-money boys want from a woman. Course, they have to pay big for the pleasure." She rolled her eyes in emphasis. "But you don't want to talk about my business. It's Allister Brindle you want to know about, isn't it?"

Blanche couldn't hide her surprise. "Why do you say that?"

Lacey gave her a sly smile. "You told me. That's another thing we working girls do well: listen."

"When did I tell you?"

"You told me that you'd found two packs of matches from Le Club, and you found one of them in a place that surprised you. You didn't say where you found the matches, but I called you at the Brindles' place. So it stands to reason that you found at least one of the packs there. Am I right?"

Blanche grinned at her. "You sound like a detective."

"I'd be good at that, too."

"So," Blanche said. "What about Allister Brindle?"

Lacey picked up her drink and jiggled it. "He's not a Family Values client."

It took Blanche a couple seconds to remember that Family Values was the name of Lacey's call-girl business. "Shit!" she said, not bothering to hide her disappointment.

Lacey smiled at her. "You don't get it. If Brindle were one of ours, I couldn't tell you anything. Client confidentiality, you know. But since Brindle isn't one of ours..." Lacey shrugged and grinned.

Blanche leaned across the table, almost knocking over her drink. "Tell me!"

Lacey laughed her hearty laugh. "I wish Marcella were here. She's the one to tell the story about your employer! But she's left town. It must have been right here, at her going-away party, when she told us about him." She tilted her head in a remembering way. "It was me, Ray-Ray Brown, God rest his soul, and one of his dates—I don't remember his name—and Marcella and her sister, Joyce. Girl, Marcella had us dying! Drunk and maudlin as she could be. Sniveling about how moved she'd been that afternoon when Brindle insisted on making a tape of—"

"Did you say a tape? Like a videotape?"

"That's right—Allister Brindle dressed up like a little girl, and Marcella giving him a good spanking with the hairbrush. Marcella told us: 'Movies always make me look fat, but he looked so cute in that frilly little dress, how could I say no?'" Lacey howled with laughter. "He told her he wanted it to remember her by, since he was bankrolling her move to LA."

Blanche had to turn her head to hide the tears of disappointment that sprang to her eyes. She'd been hoping Allister's tape would at least have some kind of illegal payoff on it, or a deal with the mob—something important—not some silly shit, like Allister skipping around in a pinafore. While she could understand why Allister wasn't eager to have the voters see him in girl-wear, she'd been expecting something more important than bottomless britches. Like something that would land him in jail. She'd also been hoping whatever was on the tape would jam Samuelson up, too. Shoulda known life wasn't about to get that simple, she thought.

"Did you say Ray-Ray was with somebody? Was it a guy called Donnie?" Blanche couldn't remember Donnie's last name no matter how she tried. "He's kinda slim, light brown-skinned, well-dressed, dreamy brown eyes, with real short hair?"

Lacey shook her head. "Unh-unh. This was a white guy. Dark hair, nice-looking. Kinda quiet, or shy."

Blanche sat up straighter in her seat. "Marc? Was his name Marc?"

Lacey thought for a second or two. "Could have been. Yes, maybe so. You know him?"

If only, Blanche thought, and shook her head.

Lacey went on: "I don't care what people do, as..."

But Blanche's attention was elsewhere. If Marc and Ray-Ray were together when they found out about the tape, Marc was also probably the answer to the question of how Ray-Ray had gotten into Brindle's personal safe. She'd bet serious money that Marc supplied the combination.

"... hate a hypocrite," Lacey said. She put some money on the table and stood to leave.

Blanche added to the tip and nodded, although she didn't know exactly which hypocrite Lacey was referring to. She followed Lacey toward the door and looked around Le Club one last time.

She didn't remember what she'd expected when she'd found the two matchbooks, but it had turned out to be a surprise in more ways than one. Now she knew what was on Allister Brindle's tape and had a good idea who'd helped Ray-Ray steal it. But she had more questions than information: Had Ray-Ray and Marc talked to each other before Ray-Ray died? Did Ray-Ray give Marc the tape? Did Marc know where it was now? Did he know what had happened to Ray-Ray and why? And now that Ray-Ray was dead, did Marc intend to take up Ray-Ray's plan to use the tape to bring Allister down? Where the hell was Marc, anyway?

Maybe it was thinking about Marc Brindle and his dad and the many ways that parents and children got separated that made Blanche want to snuggle right in with the kids when she got home—like when they'd first come to live with her, after she'd finally settled down to being their parent. They'd been so lost without their real parents, so afraid that nothing was permanent. On Sunday mornings, she'd bundled them into her bed and snuggled with them under a mound of blankets. She'd read the funnies to them, tell them knock-knock jokes and make up silly stories. She remembered how sure she'd been that she could, in time, provide what they needed to grow and prosper; that she could and would do whatever was necessary to keep them safe. Fool!

They were finishing up homework at the kitchen table when she came in. She took a chair at the table and asked them about their day. Taifa started a story about volleyball practice, but Malik was too full of his trip to City Hall with Aminata to wait his turn.

"We got the name of the corporation that owns the abandoned building, but not the names of the officers. Aminata says we should wait till Sunday, then go see her friend Teddy. He's a computer geek. Aminata says he can probably nd out the head find out the head of the corporation." Malik sounded like a proud father whose one-year-old just sang "Lift Every Voice and Sing."

"I never would have thought of that. Would you, Moms?" he added, just in case she didn't get it.

She smiled, lifted her eyebrows, slowly shook her head, and hoped it all added up to looking impressed. She didn't know how much more Aminata the Goddess crap she could handle.

Nestling in with the kids wasn't working. She was tighter than a new girdle. She felt like an icy finger was poking her in the back, reminding her of what had happened to Ray-Ray, of the near break-in and Donnie's visitors pushing her to hurry up, as though she had only a little bit of time to find the tape before the whole thing blew up in her face.

She left Shaquita in charge and said she'd be back in an hour. She put a flashlight in her handbag. A big dark car almost ran her down on Dale Street. She shook her fist at it, then hurried to the bomb shelter under Miz Barker's house.

Someone had recently thrown a beer bottle against the door. Glass lay shattered at the foot of a long, spidery stain. She looked around to make sure she was alone, then lifted the padlock on the heavy steel door. Both the lock and the edge of the door were scratched, as though someone else had tried to get in. Without a key. The harsh howl of a cat in heat almost made her drop the keys. She was relieved when the lock slipped open. She made sure her flashlight was on before she opened the door. The couple of dim bulbs that came on when she flipped the inside light switch didn't help much. The place was big enough so that her scalp didn't immediately begin to prickle with sweat the way it sometimes did when she was in a small, closed space, but tiny windows near the ceiling made her want to get out of there before she was all the way in. She took a deep breath and locked the door behind her.

The shelter was broken up into large cubicles made of wire fencing, like numbered jail cells, one for each house. Despite what Pam had said, most of the spaces were locked and held furniture, boxes, bikes, stacks of old newspapers, and bulging plastic bags. The rest hung open, dusty and creepy. Inside each cubicle there was a set of stairs that led up to the house above. The old, fetid air was chilly.

She found Miz Barker's cubicle and unlocked the padlock with one of the keys Pam had given her. She'd already seen Miz Barker's crawl space, so she didn't expect to find any clutter and she didn't. On the left side of the space, metal shelves held items draped with pillowcases. An armchair, two floor lamps with fringed shades, and an occasional table with a pedestal shaped like an elephant's foot sat together on the other side of the space beside a folding bed covered with a bedspread. Five taped boxes were lined up at the back. Blanche laid her flashlight on one of the boxes and rifled through a box filled with women's clothes. Nothing. She turned to the next box: odds and ends of dishes. The third box held thirties-style felt hats, but no tape. There was no tape in the final two boxes either. Tiredness suddenly dropped over her like a large, heavy net. She struggled with it for a few moments. She hadn't finished looking around in here. She yawned. It was no use. She'd come back tomorrow. On the way out, she peered into corners, half expecting something or someone to jump out at her. She sighed and relaxed her shoulders when she'd clicked the lock in place. As she crossed the street, she chided herself for letting the place spook her, and looked forward to her bed.

Car headlights suddenly threw her shadow down beside her like a black velvet cloak. She raised her hand to shield her eyes from the glare. The urge to run rumbled through her like a dose of salts. She turned back toward Miz Barker's house, but it was too late. The car was in front of her, vomiting out shoulders and biceps in dark suits. She opened her mouth to yell. A cologned hand covered her lower face. Someone snatched her handbag.

"Just a little talk," the one holding her whispered. He and his friend hustled her into the backseat of the car.

Samuelson was waiting for her. One of the biceps boys climbed in front, while the other squeezed in the back seat after her. She was close enough to Samuelson to smell roast beef on his breath.

The hoodlum beside her dumped the contents of her handbag into her lap and stirred them around. "Nothin' here, Rev."

Samuelson turned toward her. "Where is it?" His eyes were so cold, his face looked frozen.

"What?" Blanche locked eyes with him and vowed that she would eat cow shit before she let him see the fear that was curdling her stomach and causing her heart to bang against the wall of her chest like it was trying to escape.

"No games. No games," Samuelson told her. "I ain't got time. I tried to treat you nice, called you up, tried to help you, but you disrespected me. Now I just want that fucking tape." All his oily minister-speak was gone. His voice was rough and sharp as cheap sandpaper.

"I don't have it." She snatched her handbag from Mr. Muscles and started stuffing her things back inside. He began patting her down and feeling her up at the same time. He chuckled at her attempts to ward off his hands. She made a grab for his nuts, but he twisted his body away from her and quickly crossed his legs. Samuelson grabbed her arm but snatched his hand out of reach before she could sink her teeth into it. He dug his hand in her hair and yanked. She elbowed him in the chest and took strength from the way the air whooshed out of him. He released her hair. His goon managed to grab both her wrists. She kicked at his shins.

"Damn, old lady!" he said. "She strong, ain't she, Rev? You want me to fuck her up?"

Fear jumped through her like jolts of electricity. She could tell from Mr. Muscles' tone that fucking people up was his favorite flavor of ice cream. She tried to stop fighting him, but she was trembling so violently, she seemed to be resisting when she wasn't. She felt her throat tensing for a scream, her tongue pushing her to beg this shit to please not punch her, hurt her, please. She took a couple of deep breaths and clenched her sphincter muscles to keep her bowels from letting loose.

"Okay, okay." She fell back in her seat. Mr. Muscles let go of her wrists. She wound her arms around her body to hide her shaking hands. She needed to be calm and reasonable to convince Samuelson she was telling the truth.

"Look, I don't have no tape," she told him in a voice so firm and sure it surprised her. "I never even saw the tape. Ray-Ray wasn't no friend of mine. Why would he tell me where it was?"

"Then what was you doing down in that cellar?" Samuelson asked. "Sneaking over here at night. Almost walked right into my car, you was in such a hurry to get here. Gotta be a reason for that."

"Well, I wasn't gettin' no tape, or I'd have it on me, wouldn't I?" She took a long, deep, ragged breath. "Excuse me, but I ain't used to being dragged off the street, searched and—"

"Listen, you..." Samuelson began with enough menace in his voice to make Blanche's stomach cramp again.

"Okay, okay," she said. "I was looking for the tape. I admit that. I mean, shit, you and Brindle been all over me about it. I figured if I could find it, you'd get off my case."

"So you was planning to give it to Brindle if you found it? Right."

She knew he didn't believe her, but she pressed on. "Well, not exactly. I was planning to give it to you so *you* could take it to him and not let on I was the one who found it. I don't want to fuck up Miz Inez's job. But now, after what you and your boy here just did to me, maybe I'll—"

Samuelson twisted toward her and grabbed her chin. His boy threw his arms around her to keep her from raising her hands.

"Bitch, stop yanking my chain." Samuelson pressed his fingers into her jaw and pulled her face closer to his. "At first, I thought Brindle had his head up his ass about you being in on this shit. But he was right. You got two days to bring me that tape. Two days. You got a nice family. Nice kids. It sure would be a shame if one of them was to get hit by a car or ..."

Blanche yanked her face out of his hands and tried to butt him with her head. His boy opened the car door and dragged her out. Blanche kicked him in the knee and put her head back in the car.

"You got a mama, Maurice? A wife or a girlfriend? Anybody in this world you love?" The thug was pulling at her, but she wouldn't let go of the car. "Anything happens to those kids, I swear, I'll find your people and break your fucking heart. You hear me? That's a promise!"

Samuelson just laughed. The thug shoved her into the street. She fell on her side, skinning her knee and ripping her skirt.

"Rotten fuckers!" she yelled as the car roared off.

Her knee hurt like hell, her back was screaming and her teeth ached from where Samuelson's fingers had dug into her jawbone, but she ran home faster than she'd ever thought she could move. She had to hunt for her keys and was afraid for a second that they were still in Samuelson's car. When she finally got the door open, she half ran, half crawled up the stairs to Taifa's and Malik's rooms. Only when she saw them asleep and safe did her mind begin to work again. She went back downstairs and made sure all the windows and doors were locked. Then she got out the phone book, but her hands were shaking too badly to separate the pages. She called information for Othello Flood's number.

He answered after two rings.

"Yeah, you're the mother of the young brother Aminata's working with," he said when she told him who she was.

"Look, I need some help, some protection. Someone is... Someone tried to..." She fought back tears. She leaned against the wall and held the phone with both hands to control the tremors of rage and fear that made her knees knock.

"Where you live? I'll be right there."

She'd had two slugs of gin by the time he arrived, and had cleaned the snot and tears from her face. She opened the door before he could ring the bell.

He took her hand. "Everything's gonna be fine, sister."

Blanche didn't tell him it was already too late for everything to be fine, that she was already scared half out of her mind, bruised and ashamed of not being able to protect Taifa and Malik. It would take a while before fine had anything to do with anything. Instead, she thanked him for coming and offered him something to eat or drink before she told him what had happened.

"You ain't the first," he said. "The Reverend's building up quite a rep for hassling people he don't like. We've had to deal with his boys more than once. Why's he after you, if you don't mind my asking?"

Blanche explained about Brindle, Ray-Ray, and the tape.

"You really think they killed that brother?"

"I'm more sure of it than I was before. I just don't have any proof. If I could find somebody who saw the man who went to the pool with Ray-Ray, somebody who knew who he was..."

"Let me check it out," Othello said, then sat forward in his chair. "Look, there's something you got to understand. We don't half step. When you get help from the Ex-Cons for Community

Safety, you get a hundred and ten percent. You know what I'm sayin'?"

It was exactly what Blanche wanted to hear. She only wished she'd called him sooner.

He took a small notebook and a pen from his shirt pocket. "Okay, then. What school your kids go to?"

Blanche told him.

"We already got somebody working around that school, keeping an eye out for dealers and other punks. The brother who does the school can pick 'em up and bring 'em home. We'll come by early tomorrow morning so I can introduce him. Somebody'll be taking you to work and picking you up. Name of Roger. I'll bring him around tomorrow, too."

They agreed on six-thirty the next morning. She could easily get to work by seven-thirty with a ride.

"A brother'll be stationed outside your house. Round the clock. It'll always be the same car, so you'll know he's your man."

"Oh! My cousin's granddaughter is staying with me until her grandmother gets back to town. She's in METCO, the suburban school program." Blanche talked really fast, embarrassed at having been so focused on Taifa and Malik that she'd forgotten about Shaquita. "She gets the school bus."

"What time does she leave and get home?"

Blanche told him.

"No problem. The brother who's taking your two to school can take her to the school bus. The brother outside your place can take a break and meet the school bus and bring her home."

He reached in his jacket pocket. "Here, take these whistles and leave 'em around the house. Anything goes down, use 'em. Otherwise, just leave the brother to his job."

Tears of relief sprung to Blanche's eyes. "I really appreciate this, Othello. Can I make a donation to the Ex-Cons?"

"Thanks. We got our expenses like everybody else, so anything you can give will help, but we know about tight money, too, so don't stretch yourself out of shape. Anyway, who knows? We may need a favor from you someday."

He wrote down the license plate number of the car that would be stationed outside and also jotted down her work and home phone numbers. She was tempted to ask him to stay a little longer when he rose to leave. He looked down at her for a few seconds then excused himself to make a phone call.

"Brother Warren will be outside your house in about half an hour," he said. "Dark blue Accord. You got the license number and your whistle. Now try to get some sleep."

Blanche thanked him again and dragged herself upstairs to the bathroom. She fell asleep in the tub and woke up only when the water turned cool. She looked out her front window before getting into bed, and was comforted by the sight of the blue Accord in the parking space closest to her house.

TEN

DAY NINE—FRIDAY

She woke before first light from a dream in which whoever she was running from kept getting in front of her, forcing her to run backward. When she tried to stand up, her scraped knee buckled, which triggered a series of aches and lightning-sharp pains along her back and thighs. She sat on the side of the bed, gently massaging her legs and fighting the strong desire to roll back into bed and pull the covers over her head. She didn't try to stop the tears that made hot channels down her cheeks and chin to her nightgown. She also didn't try to stop the flash of Samuelson's grinning face as his car sped off, or the feel of his pig-boy's hands squeezing her breasts and ass. She let herself imagine that car careening into a telephone pole and exploding while she watched and listened to their screams. But this only made her cry harder. She was never going to be able to make them feel the fear that had socked her in the gut so hard she'd nearly soiled her pants when they'd thrown her in that car and threatened Malik and Taifa. Tendrils of fear inched across her chest at the thought of what Samuelson and his shitheads might have done to her, might still be planning to do to the children. She eased herself off the bed and went to the window to check on the blue Accord. There it was. At least that, she thought, at least that. She turned to her Ancestor altar and lit a stick of incense.

"Ancestors of the blood, the spirit, and the heart, ancient to infant, known and unknown, I salute you this morning, thanking you for the goodness you have brought to my life, for the goodness you . . ."

She couldn't go on with her usual salutation. Yet she believed asking the Ancestors for something directly was risky—as though, "Be careful what you ask for, you just might get it" was the Ancestors' motto. So she clamped her lips on asking them for her children's safety. There was nothing safer than death. But she also couldn't talk to them as though everything were fine. She took another direction:

"Ancestors, you saw what happened to me. You heard what those lice said about hurting Taifa and Malik. I know they're your young, too, so I know you look out for them, just like you protected me from getting hurt worse than I did. I light this candle in thanks for your protection of all of us."

She lit the candle and watched the flame grow steady before she went to the bathroom.

A hot shower eased her aches and loosened her joints. She dressed, started the French toast and bacon, then woke the children early. They tumbled into the kitchen, so drawn by the scent of a Sunday breakfast on Friday, they didn't complain about being roused extra early. Blanche waited until they were sopping up their last drops of syrup to begin talking.

"Something happened last night," she said, and wondered what there was in her tone that brought all three of the children to silent attention.

"Some men tried to . . . it has to do with this job I'm working for Miz Inez. Something's missing and they think Ray-Ray took it and gave it to me. He didn't give it to me, but they don't believe me. Last night, some men tried to . . ."

"What, Moms?! What?" Taifa was out of her chair. She threw an arm around Blanche. "Are you all right? Did they hurt you? What . . ."

"Hurt! Who said anything about hurt? You always jump to conclusions!" Malik shouted, but he sounded like he might cry.

Shaquita stared at Blanche with fear in her eyes.

"No. I'm okay, honey." Blanche put her arm around Taifa's waist and kept it there.

"And everything's gonna be fine. Some people are going to be looking out for all of us for a while, until this is all over. Othello Flood with the Ex-Cons for Community Safety. He..."

"Aminata's boyfriend," Malik said.

Blanche nodded. "That's right. Somebody from the Ex-Cons will be taking you to school in the morning and bringing you home."

"Aw, Mom! No way! I can look out for myself, and I got things to do after school that..."

Blanche sighed. That guy thing again. She let Malik talk on about soccer practice, his class mediation committee meeting, and basketball practice with his Y team—all things she was supposed to believe were more important than his safety.

"I'm sorry, Malik. You're going to have to come home with your ride. And stay home. Both of you. It's only for a few days, I promise," she said, and hoped it was true.

"But, Moms! They're criminals!" Taifa shrieked.

"They *committed* crimes. Just like you *were* a baby with shitty diapers. They've changed, too," Blanche said.

The doorbell saved her from further argument.

The sight of Othello called to mind a snug house and a full cupboard—things she associated with security. She also conjured up a big, firm bed lit only by a candle or two in a room filled with music—things she associated with good sex. Even last night, in the middle of her fear, she remembered that melting feeling in her crotch when he'd held her hand. She wondered how much her attraction to Othello had to do with her Aminata thing. Maybe it wasn't just Malik's relationship with her that rankled. And how horny was she that she'd think of sex at a time like this? But when did a person need to be held and stroked as much as when things were going to hell in a hurry?

She wasn't the only one with an open nose: Taifa's objections to being guarded by a convict seemed to dissolve at the sight of the muscular, almost pretty-faced young man assigned to drive her and Malik back and forth to school. Roger, Dennis, and Louis, the three men with Othello, were all polite, quiet, and formal. After they were introduced, they went back to their respective cars to wait for their charges. Blanche liked that, too.

Before she left the house, she decided to call Bea Richards one last time. She was almost tongue-tied when Bea answered the phone.

"Yes, this is Bea Richards. Who is this?"

Blanche untwisted her tongue enough to explain that she'd gotten Bea's name from Cousin Charlotte. "She thought maybe you could give me some information that might help a friend of mine."

"What kinda information?"

"About Maurice Samuelson."

"What about him?" The curiosity in her tone was replaced with something that sounded more like suspicion.

"Well, my friend's thinking about joining his Temple and..."

"Who you say give you my name?"

Blanche told her again.

"She shoulda told you I ain't much for talking business on the telephone. Certain people round here might be trying to find out what I'm sayin' and who I'm sayin' it to."

Blanche kept quiet. The woman sounded a little bit like a lady she'd known in Harlem who thought the FBI was trying to take nude pictures of her to sell to *Playboy.* On the other hand, she sounded a lot like Blanche was beginning to feel, as though her life and world were on the verge of being seriously invaded.

"Let's meet somewhere," Blanche said.

They made a date to meet in the Tropical Foods market off Dudley Square on Saturday.

"I'll be wearing a red sweater," Bea told her.

Blanche's ride to work with Roger was something she could easily get used to—complete with a cup of tea to sip on the way. She thanked him and said she'd see him at seven-thirty.

The air inside the Brindle house felt moist and wild. Blanche moved slowly and quietly around the kitchen, careful to stay relaxed and in the center of herself, as though her calm and quiet could be a model for the house.

Carrie almost leapt into Blanche's arms when the front doorbell rang. She burst back into the kitchen and pointed toward the front of the house. "It's Mr. Marc."

Blanche grabbed a pair of flower shears from the utility drawer. She went out to the front hall to the table between the breakfast room and the library, where she began grooming the fresh flower arrangement. All the while she eyed Marc Brindle. He looked like a person who'd given up sleep a long time ago. The heavy shadow of his beard was long past five o' clock. His pants and jacket hung from his body in folds and creases. Even from this distance she saw the dirt on his shirt. He looked in her direction, but she wasn't sure he saw her. She gave him a good-morning nod but didn't speak. She was right behind him when he opened the breakfast room door, and she caught the door just before it clicked shut. Then she peered into the room with her left eye.

The forces Blanche had felt in the house gathered in the breakfast room. She could feel the electricity in the air and something else—something like a fast train coming that couldn't be stopped.

Felicia rose from the table. Allister didn't move. Felicia flung her arms wide. She had a look on her face that Blanche sometimes sensed on her own—that combination of relief and irritation when Taifa and Malik came home after being gone long enough for the worst possibilities to begin whispering in her ear.

Marc held out his arm to ward his mother off.

Felicia stopped halfway between him and the table, her arms still partially outstretched.

"Marc, darling. I'm so glad to see you!" Felicia took a slow step toward him. "I was so worried. I—"

"Don't, Mother, please don't!"

"But, darling, I just want to …"

Marc grasped his hair with both hands. "Why, Mother? Just tell me why him? Why?"

"I didn't mean to, Marc. It was an accident. He—"

"An accident?! An accident?! How do you seduce someone by accident, Mother?"

Felicia looked confused for a few seconds. "Oh, I thought you … but you mean you think I … No, Marc. Darling, no! You can't think I'd do such a thing! I didn't know! I swear I …"

"He loved me! I know he loved me! Until you …"

Something crumbled in Felicia's face. "No, no, it wasn't like that. It wasn't just me! He had other … He was just a … I swear I never knew about you. Never knew he even liked …"

"Liar! We were happy until you—"

"Marc! I would never have … never do anything to hurt you, darling, you know that. You must know that."

Blanche had forgotten about Allister until he rose from his chair. "What the? Both of you? Both of you were fucking that trainer? Jesus Christ! If this gets out, I'll …"

Marc and Felicia ignored him. Felicia took another step toward her son. "Marc, please, I'm telling you the truth."

"Oh, God, Mother!" Marc reached for Felicia with one hand and cradled his face with the other.

Felicia rushed to him and threw her arms around him, murmuring motherese and hugging him hard.

Marc put his hands on Felicia's upper arms and gently put her aside. He murmured something to her that Blanche couldn't hear. Felicia smiled even though there were tears in her eyes. Marc turned to Allister.

"Dear old Dad." Marc made the title sound like the worst possible curse. "You and your fucking political career and your fucking family name! I might have had a norm—"

"Get a grip on yourself, boy! No son of mine…"

"Son of yours! Son of yours! When did I graduate to being your son? I thought I was *her* son. That's what you always—"

"Don't speak to me in that tone of voice, boy! I can't stand hysteria in a man, especially a Brindle."

"What do you like in a Brindle, Dad? Handcuffs? Leather underwear? Blonds with big tits and whips? What makes you better than me?"

Allister's eyes bucked. "You! You have it!" He banged his fist on the table. The dishes rattled like chattering teeth. "Where is it? Where's the tape?" He leaned across the table toward his son. "Your black fag boyfriend stole it for you, didn't he? You told him about the safe, didn't you? Didn't you?"

"I told him where to find the combination, you filthy, lying hypocrite!" Marc screamed at him. "'Don't be such a sissy, boy! Get yourself in the missionary position with a fast tart and forget this homo business,'" he said, imitating his father's clipped voice. "And all the time you've been…" Marc shook his head, as if he couldn't go on.

"Where is it? Where's the tape?" Allister sounded as though he were being strangled. "That rotten nigger stole it for you, didn't he? After all this family did for him! He wrote me. Did you know that? Threatening to—"

Marc interrupted him. "Fuck you! What about me? Standing there listening to a drunken prostitute talk about how you liked your spanking was bad enough, but that tape! God, it made me vomit."

Felicia looked from her son to her husband.

Marc's shoulders were heaving. Blanche couldn't see his face, so she didn't know if he was gulping for air or crying. But she was all too sure of the gun Marc pulled from his jacket pocket. The house quivered when the gun appeared.

Felicia squeaked like a mouse under a cat's paw. Allister looked at his son with widened eyes.

"It's you I should have killed instead of Saxe," Marc said to his father. The gun was dead steady in his hand.

Felicia's body jerked. Her mouth worked, but no sounds came out.

Allister sat back down. "You don't have the balls to kill a rabbit." Allister spoke as though Marc hadn't said anything about killing Saxe. He leaned back in his chair. "Remember the time Uncle Randolph and I took you hunting?" he went on. "You couldn't even …"

Felicia turned on him. "Shut up, you fool! Didn't you hear …?" She turned back to Marc. She held out her open right hand as if she expected him to lay his troubles in her palm.

"Listen to me, Marc, please." Felicia sounded calm, but Blanche didn't believe it. "Don't do this. Don't ruin your life for him. Allister's not worth killing! And I know you didn't kill Saxe. I killed him."

Allister's mouth fell open. Marc lurched forward. Allister recovered first.

"What are you saying?" he shouted at Felicia. "What are you talking about?"

Neither Felicia nor Marc seemed to hear him. Marc touched Felicia's cheek with the back of his free hand.

"I almost wish you had killed him," Marc said. The sadness in his voice filled the room and oozed out into the hall. "Then I wouldn't know how it feels to … Then I could sleep, think, I wouldn't have this … this …"

Allister looked from his son to his wife. Marc let his gun hand fall to his side. He was looking at Felicia.

"He was rubbing ice on the lump you'd raised on his head when I got there. He told me you'd hit him. He said everybody in my family was crazy. I asked why you had hit him. 'A lover's quarrel,' he said. And laughed. He asked me if it turned me on, knowing he was screwing my mother."

Felicia flinched and reached out to touch Marc's sleeve.

Marc kept talking. "He said he didn't give a damn about me, that he'd rather fuck a sheep than ... I laughed. I *knew* he loved me. He told me! He showed me! I thought he was making it all up because he was angry about something else. He was so moody, and he didn't always tell the truth. I figured he'd be all right if ...

"I asked him why he kept seeing me if I was so ... He said for fun and profit. He said in a way he was fucking the whole family because dear old Dad was going to be really fucked when he threatened to go to the papers with pictures of both of us with him. He said he'd make a bundle. I knew he was telling the truth that time. It was almost funny. He didn't know about the tape, you see. That I told Ray-Ray where to find the combination. Saxe always said I was too spineless to really do anything against ... So I wanted to show him ... to make him proud of me. But when he said ... I was glad I hadn't told him. I laughed in his face. Nobody was going to care about his little photographs once I took the tape to the press."

A momentary spasm twisted Allister's face. He opened his mouth as if to speak but didn't. Marc went on talking. "Then he told me to get out and to stay away from him. He started pushing me." Marc's voice went thin. "Just little shoves." He jabbed his stiff-fingered hand into an imaginary chest. "He kept talking about me and you, both nympho pushovers who let him do anything he wanted. He kept laughing and talking and pushing me. I saw the trophy where he'd put it on the table ... I picked it up. I just wanted to make him stop talking and pushing me and pushing me—"

"Oh God, oh God, oh God." Felicia covered her mouth with a hand and crumpled to her knees as though the weight of Marc's words were too heavy for her to bear. When she looked up, her face was skim-milk white.

"I went back," she said. "I ... I thought I'd done it. I thought—"

"You took his things!" Marc interrupted, looking down at her. "I should have realized it was you." He jerked his head in Allister's direction. "I thought maybe he'd sent some of his henchmen to make it look like a robbery, or got some police official who owed him a favor to fix it up."

Blanche wished she could see Marc's face, but it wasn't really necessary. Sorrow and grief flowed between him and Felicia like a fast-moving river.

Allister leaned forward over their abandoned breakfast. "The tape," he said. "Where ...

No one else even looked at him. Felicia was still on her knees crying quietly. Marc moved closer to her. He reached down and gently put his hand on her head. She threw her arms around his legs and laid her forehead against them.

"Oh, Marc, I'm so sorry, so sorry," she moaned. "We'll get you out of this. We can—"

Allister stood up. "Marc, son, listen." He spoke softly and slowly, as though Marc were a frightened child. "It's not just me who'll be hurt by the tape. Your mother, you. Just give me the tape, son. I know I've been—"

"You did this!" Marc shouted at Allister, and pointed the gun straight at him again.

Allister looked like he thought Marc might have less trouble shooting him than he'd had with that rabbit. "Now, son." Allister raised his hands in a surrendering way.

"Don't call me that, you bastard! Don't call me that!"

"But you are my son, you ..."

Marc looked down at Felicia, her face buried against his legs, her arms wrapped around them as though they could save her.

"I'm sorry, Mother," Marc said, touching her head once again. "I can't. I just can't."

Allister paled and shut his eyes, so Blanche was the only one actually looking at Marc Brindle when he turned his face from both parents and put the barrel of the gun in his mouth. She was the only one who actually saw his head explode, flinging chunks of dripping red flesh and bone on the walls and on Felicia's bowed head, depositing freckles of blood and brains on the floor. All done before Blanche could wrench open the door and scream out the "No!" that was a deafening roar inside her head.

ELEVEN

DAY TEN—SATURDAY

Blanche woke with the smell of blood still fresh in her nose. Her mouth felt slimy and tasted like rancid butter. She licked her lips—hot and chapped, as though she had a fever. Her mind replayed the scene she'd been seeing all night. Would the sight of Marc Brindle's exploding head ever fade? How long would she have crouched outside the breakfast room door if Carrie hadn't come running out of the kitchen at the sound of the shot?

"OhJesusOhJesusOhJesusOhJesus!" was all Blanche could remember her saying. But Carrie must have called the police and ambulance. She remembered that Carrie had also helped her to a kitchen chair where she'd sat staring, trying not to be present, not to have seen. The house rang with Felicia's screams.

Blanche was still sitting, staring at the floor, when the ambulance and police arrived. When the policeman asked Blanche where she'd been at the time of death, she told him she was about to make tea when they heard the shot. She pointed to the kettle sitting in the sink waiting for water as proof. When he asked what else she'd heard, she had the presence of mind to tell him the house was too well built to hear anything but the loudest noise from the front rooms when the kitchen door was closed. He'd turned to Carrie.

If he'd asked Carrie where Blanche had been during the shooting, Blanche was afraid Carrie might have told him rather than blemish her soul with a lie. Blanche had had a she's-a-jealous-hearted-underling-trying-to-get-me-in-trouble story ready for the police in case Carrie did talk. But he asked only had she let Marc in, what time, and how did he seem—to which Carrie had said, "Like hisself." Carrie, like any sensible poor person whose knowledge of the police came mostly from their storm-trooping through her neighborhood, had answered his questions and volunteered nothing. Blanche was damned grateful and planned to tell Carrie so, just as soon as she could get her nerves together enough to call her.

Joanie, Aminata, and Lacey had all heard about Marc on the noon news and were at Blanche's house when she got home. Aminata and Joanie took the kids. They'd spent the night next door. Lacey had made Blanche a pot of ginger tea with more rum and honey in it than ginger. She'd let Blanche tell the story of what she'd seen over and over again until Blanche's shoulders began to droop. Then she'd given Blanche the best back rub she'd ever had, and put her to bed.

Should have had a couple more cups of Lacey's tea, she thought. The clock by her bed said 2:30 a.m. Middle-of-the-night stillness lay over the house and neighborhood. She was alone in the quiet night—a situation that usually soothed her. But right now, the desire to be held, to be hugged in strong arms until she no longer felt bruised by what she'd seen was a full-body ache. Don't go there, girlfriend, she told herself. Like Mama says, you didn't come into this world holding hands with nobody. Still. She rolled over on her side, drew her knees toward her chest, wrapped her arms around her body, and rocked herself back into sleep.

The phone woke her at 7:00 a.m. She recognized Sadowski's voice but pretended not to remember immediately who he was. "Oh yeah, Allister Brindle's boy," she said.

Sadowski took a deep breath but held whatever he'd wanted to say in favor of telling her why he'd called. "The Brindles are closing the house for a while. They're really..."

She listened to his stiff little speech about the Brindles' pain and grief and need for complete rest and solitude.

"Your check will be in the mail this morning, and Mrs. Brindle will be in touch with Inez."

When he was finished talking, Blanche hung up without another word. Talking to Sadowski was one less nasty thing she had to do in this life. But that didn't mean the Brindles were gone from her mind.

She now knew who had killed Saxe and what part Felicia had played in his death. She knew that Marc, not Ray-Ray, had Allister's tape; she wondered if Allister had found the tape among his son's things. She hoped he'd remember to tell Samuelson the tape hunt was off, or at least off her, before he and Felicia left town. The thought of Felicia triggered the sound of her scream echoing through the Brindle house and the smell of blood and the noise and the way Marc's body had fallen so slowly to the floor. She knew she needed a good cry; her eyes stung, but no tears fell. She considered getting up, saw herself in the bathroom brushing her teeth, taking a shower. The thought of so much effort made her drowsy. She snuggled back into bed.

It was ten-thirty when the phone called her out of sleep once again.

"Is that you, Blanche?" It was Mick.

"I guess so."

"You were there when Marc did it, weren't you?"

Blanche said she'd been there, but didn't say that she'd seen it.

"You okay? It's a terrible shock to have something like that happen, Blanche. If you don't feel up to the funeral, Pam'll understand."

Miz Barker's funeral! She'd forgotten! She threw back the covers. She'd have to get Taifa and Malik organized to at least go to the viewing. Shaquita was baby-sitting for the Mortons, so she was out. Blanche remembered buying apples the other day—too many for the kids to have eaten them all already. The funeral wasn't until three. She had time to put together a couple of pies.

"I'm going," she told Mick.

"Moms?" Taifa tapped on the door. Malik was right behind her.

"You okay, Mama Blanche?" Taifa put her arms around Blanche and held her. Malik stretched his arms across both their shoulders. She leaned into the hug and let them warm and soothe her.

"Tell us what happened, exactly," Taifa said. "Was there a whole lotta blood and stuff?" Taifa's eyes were all curiosity.

"Oh, Ife, I can't even tell you how awful it was. One second he was standing there screaming at his parents and the next second he was..."

Once again, she saw Marc Brindle's head blow apart.

"Wasn't nothin' you could do, Moms. Don't feel bad," Taifa said.

Blanche stared at Taifa and wondered how she knew. Even though it was in her mind, Blanche was only this moment letting herself look at the question of whether she could have flung open the door, lunged for Marc, screamed, done anything that would have made a difference.

"Yeah," Malik added. "You know how you are, Mama Blanche. If there was anything you could have done, you would have."

The tears nearly leapt from Blanche's eyes. She sank to the side of her bed and buried her face in her hands. She cried for all that had happened: Miz Barker's and Ray-Ray's deaths, Pam's and Inez's grief, Shaquita's pregnancy and the pain it was going to cause Cousin Charlotte, the shock of Marc's suicide, Samuelson's attack on her, the fear that the need for guards had put in the children's eyes.

Taifa and Malik sat on either side of her and held her, patted and murmured to her in just the way Blanche had done to them over the years.

"Oh Lord! I feel so much better." She blew her nose on the tissues Malik handed her.

"Thanks," she said, looking from one to the other.

Taifa shrugged. "It's a family thing."

Blanche didn't think she could take any more. She sent them to wash and change, which meant a fight about who got to shower first until Blanche made them flip for it.

The sun drew her to the bedroom window. The Accord was in the parking lot. She went to the phone to call Othello, but realized she'd better make another call first.

"Temple of Divine Enlightenment."

Blanche asked for Samuelson—remembering to put the "Reverend" in front of his name. She was tempted to lie about her own name when asked; Samuelson might not be willing to talk to her. But he was.

"My sister." The oil was back in his voice.

"If the way you treated me the other night is how you treat your sister, I'm glad we don't have the same mama."

Samuelson went so silent, she began to think the line was dead.

"All right, all right. A misunderstanding." He didn't sound like he meant it.

"So Brindle told you his son had the tape."

"He told me."

"Well?"

"Well what?"

"Apologize," she demanded.

The line really went dead this time. Bastard! But at least she'd found out what she needed to know. She called Othello.

"It's funny you should call," he said. "I was planning to call you."

Blanche told him about Marc and the tape and her call to Samuelson.

"So I'm off Samuelson's list," she told him.

"Yeah, well, the good reverend still needs to be dealt with. He can't be goin' around jacking people up like he's the king of the community."

"I just wish there was some way to find out what Brindle has on him. I swear I'd spread it all over town!" Blanche said.

"Yeah, you mentioned that."

Blanche liked his thinking-about-what-to-do-about-it tone.

"I'll be hanging out with your son tomorrow, you know. Him and Aminata."

He said Aminata's name as though it were sugar on his tongue. Lucky Aminata, Blanche thought. I will not hate her!

"Doing what?" she asked without a hint that she was trying to put out an invisible green fire.

"Driving them to a friend's house out in Framingham. He thinks he can help them find out who's behind the company that owns that abandoned building."

"Oh yeah, the Internet thing." Blanche half remembered Malik talking about it.

"Aminata says your boy is really hyped. Good to see a kid his age interested in the environment. You gotta be proud."

"I keep my fingers crossed," she told him, and knew he understood.

"That's all you can do after you've done the rest," he said.

They were about to hang up when Blanche said, "Why were you going to call me, Othello?"

"Remember what you told me about somebody being with the brother who drowned at the pool? I had one of the our members ask around. You were right. There was somebody with him, an older guy, is what we were told."

"What do you mean, 'older'?"

"There's a woman lives on Washington Street, near the pool. She says she knew Ray-Ray from when she used to go to the same church his mom goes to. She said she saw him and another man heading for the pool the night he died."

"Somebody she knew?"

"She couldn't see the other dude's face, but she said she knew he was old by the way he was dressed. 'Old-timey,' she said."

Blanche's stomach rolled over twice. "What did you say?" she asked as a picture of Donnie in his old-fashioned, long, square-cut jacket and baggy pants formed in her mind.

"An older dude," Othello told her.

"No, about his clothes."

"An old dude in old dude's clothes," he said.

Blanche opened her mouth to tell him what she was thinking, but what if she was wrong? This was something she wanted to be very sure about. Donnie wasn't the only one who wore vintage clothes. The picture of Donnie in her mind began to fade, like a photo left too long in the sun—but its shadow remained.

"We'll keep checking around," Othello said. "Maybe somebody else saw him, too. Somebody who recognized him."

"I really appreciate all your help, Othello. I won't forget it." She made a mental note to give the Ex-Cons a goodly chunk of her income tax refund—the next piece of money she expected to have.

She told herself she had too much to do to get hung up on her conversation with Othello. She tuned the radio to WBUR and listened to *Car Talk*. She didn't have a car or want one, but the show was always good for a laugh. She rushed together a couple apple-raisin pies, showered and dressed in her gray, brown, and tan funeral-going dress and the gray-and-brown low-heeled shoes she'd found on sale in Filene's Basement. She wrote Shaquita a note saying where they'd all gone, and was ready when Mick rang her doorbell.

The kids rushed outside to admire Mick's Jeep Cherokee—an insult to Native Americans and to people whose legs weren't long enough to take a giant step up into the damned thing.

Blanche couldn't take her eyes off Mick. The combat-booted, very butch lesbian she'd been talking to for the last week or so was now decked out in a navy blue pin-striped suit with a straight skirt, a white blouse with a ruffle down the front, and navy blue pumps with matching handbag. Blue-and-white earrings dotted her ears.

"Who you pretendin' to be?" Blanche joked without thinking, then checked Mick's face to see if she'd offended her.

Mick laughed. "That's just what my girlfriend said." She kicked off her shoes.

"How do women walk all day in these damned things!" She plopped on the sofa, legs as sprawled as her skirt would allow.

"Why wear 'em? Or any of it?" Blanche gestured at Mick's shoes and outfit.

"It's easier this way," Mick told her. "You know what black folks are."

"I ain't black folk?"

Mick pushed up her glasses. "You know what I mean, Blanche. It's hard being an out lesbian in the 'hood. That's why I moved. I grew up around here, remember? And I caught hell."

Blanche knew about catching community hell from the many, many times she'd been wounded by blacks for being too black. She remembered when she would have done anything to make the teasing stop, to turn herself into a mid-range brown girl instead of being out on the extreme edge of blackness. As a girl, she'd even tried rubbing her body with lemon juice because she'd heard somebody say it would lighten your skin. How old had she been when she'd learned to treasure her blackness in a way that made other people's negative comments about it sound just plain crazy? How many times would Mick have to put on this getup before she realized it wasn't worth it?

"You got a lot of faith in clothes makin' the woman, honey," she told Mick.

Mick lowered her head and smoothed her skirt. "It's a kind of respect thing, too. For Miz Barker, I mean. She never said she approved of me, but she acted like she did, even though she used to tease me about looking like a lumberjack. So, I figured this one time . . ." Mick trailed off.

Blanche remained silent, waiting for Mick to acknowledge that her last reason was not as important as her first.

"It's stupid. You're right. But God! It just rips my guts out when black people look at me like I'm evil or dirty. Like I don't belong here. Or anywhere."

Blanche wished she could tell Mick she was wrong, that no black person had anything against lesbians or gay men, but she knew Mick was right. She'd once heard a black historian say that hatred of homosexuals was taught to African slaves because slave babies could only be made by female-male couples. Somebody ought to tell gay-hating blacks that slavery was over and loving was about more than baby-making.

They stopped by Miz Barker's house to drop off Blanche's pies and the ham Mick had baked. The kitchen was under the control of a quartet of women Blanche thought of as part of The Regulars—the women in the community who always helped the sick, made sure all the food a grieving family could use was prepared and presented, made sure their street was kept clean. They were the women she always thought of when she heard some right-wing jackass—black or white—going on about how black people needed to do for themselves instead of blah, blah, blah. If we didn't do for ourselves, she thought, we'd all be dead by now.

The viewing and funeral were at Roland's Funeral Parlor on Columbus Avenue. People were going in and coming out as Mick cruised the block for a parking space.

Pam and other members of the family sat to the left of the coffin. Blanche went straight to the front and hugged Pam.

"We're very sorry about your grandmother," Malik told her as he shook her hand.

Taifa nodded her head. "She was a good person," she added.

Blanche looked from Malik to Taifa, pleased with them.

Mick added her condolences, and they all shook hands with Miz Barker's son and his wife, Miz Barker's sister, who sat in a wheelchair looking confused, and Pam's mother, who presided over cousins, grandkids, and great-grandkids swelling the ranks of family mourners.

What was left of Miz Barker looked like no one Blanche had ever known. In death she seemed to have shrunk to the size of a wizened child in adult clothing, her skin stretched across her face like a rubber mask. She was laid out in a gunmetal-gray coffin filled with a foamy white lining like frozen shaving cream.

After a minute or so, Blanche walked Malik and Taifa to the door. She'd told them before they left home that there was no more need for the Ex-Cons, so they were eager to be on their own. But first Blanche made sure they'd done their homework.

They'd be out all day tomorrow, Malik with Aminata and Othello, and Taifa and Shaquita on a mall trip with Joanie to New Hampshire sponsored by Rudigere Homes, during which Taifa expected to sell a lot of candy.

"There's ground turkey for burgers in the fridge and leftover chili," Blanche told them. "Taifa, do you have exact change for the bus? You remember the last time you—"

"Chill, Moms, chill. I got it covered."

Blanche looked from one to the other. "Don't get into no foolishness on the bus. Like I told you, act like—"

"Mom, we ride the bus all the time. We're not babies." Malik laid his hand on her arm as though he were trying to calm a fretful child. They both kissed her on the cheek. She had the distinct feeling they felt sorry for her.

She took a seat in the last row of folding chairs. She believed a funeral was the place to leave your sorrow and pain piled around the coffin like so many baskets of flowers and walk away ready to be healed, if you could. But she'd already shed most of her misery when she'd cried into the children's arms. Even so, she felt the gathering tide of grief—as though all the people in the room had pooled their heartache over Miz Barker's death and whatever else they needed to cry and moan about. She felt it in herself, too, a kind of opening up on the inside, like moving closer to the people around her without moving at all.

A young man rose and went to the podium in the corner of the room opposite the coffin.

"My name is Calvin Barker. I want to thank you..."

Blanche judged him to be a great-grandson.

It seemed everybody—including Blanche—and every business in the neighborhood had sent a card or telegram to the family, all of which Calvin was reading. Particularly touching messages got a loud "Umm-humm" from the mourners. Each time it happened, Blanche felt the grief tide rise a little higher.

When the cards were read, Calvin asked people to come to the podium if they had anything they wanted to say about Miz Barker. Most people stood and spoke from their seats about what a good neighbor and friend Miz Barker had been. Finally, a young woman rose from her seat and went to the podium.

"My own mother put me out after her boyfriend raped me. This woman"—she pointed at Miz Barker's coffin—"took me in."

"Praise Jesus! She was a good soul," someone called out.

The young woman went on: "She helped me to understand that what had happened was not my fault. She helped me get my life back together and encouraged me to keep on moving on."

"Amen, child, amen," a mourner replied.

"I am here to praise her and to thank her. To tell the world that there was no more decent human being in the world, God rest her soul."

"Tell it, child!"

The current swelled as the young woman stopped talking and began to sing "Nearer My God to Thee," punctuated by sobs from members of the family. The room was swamped by a wave of grief. Tears flowed, family members hugged, and other mourners clasped hands as they were all washed in one another's sorrows and released from them in a way that was easy and sweet and hard as birthing. Just as Blanche thought she would drown in so much feeling, a small child asked, "Momma, is that lady gonna sing *another* song?" and dried their eyes with laughter.

Mick didn't want to go to the cemetery and neither did Blanche. When they arrived at the Barker house for the after-funeral gathering, it was already nearly full of people juggling paper plates and plastic cups. The house smelled of ham and turkey, greens, pig feet, chitterlings, corn bread, garlic, and lesser spices that made Blanche's stomach growl. She worked her way toward the sideboard spread, with Mick right behind her.

Blanche filled a paper plate and found a not-too-crowded corner where she could stand and eat. She exchanged greetings with folk she knew and didn't know. All around her people were talking about everything from buying a house to how to get rid of bill collectors. Whatever sadness there was for Miz Barker had been left at the funeral home in favor of celebrating her life with a plateful of good food. Chili and death, she thought.

Pam was moving through the room thanking people for coming. She looked worn to the bone. Blanche drew her away, made her sit down and sip some tea. But Pam couldn't stop talking. It was as though words were a fence she'd built between herself and her grief, one that needed constant repair.

"She wouldn't have liked all these people in her house. She'd talk to people all day in the store. But only family came here."

"What about Ray-Ray? Didn't he come here, too?"

"Yeah. But he was family as far as she was concerned. He came by the store to see Gran right before he died, you know. Him and his friend."

"His friend?" Blanche felt the blood draining from her face. "What friend?"

Pam shook her head. "I didn't know him. Ray-Ray said he needed to talk to Gran, so I didn't hang around. Lots of people did that, you know, came by the store like they needed to buy something, but really they came to talk to Gran. I think that's why she was so irritable about me being in the store with her, afraid I'd stop people from talking. Once I figured that out, I knew when to leave for a while."

"So was Ray-Ray's friend just a friend, or..." Blanche tried not to seem too eager to hear Pam's answer.

"Boyfriend. Cute little dude. Kinda clean cut. Had on a sharp old suit. I think Ray-Ray called him Donnie. I could tell they had a thing going from the way Ray-Ray looked at him. Didn't faze Gran. She was just glad to see Ray-Ray. And now they're both dead." Pam sighed, a long, fluttery sigh.

Blanche hardly heard what Pam was saying. She was suddenly so cold, she was sure she'd see her breath if she spoke. The picture of Donnie that had formed and faded in her mind when she'd talked with Othello earlier was returning in full color. She saw him in Miz Barker's store with Ray-Ray, then again days later, alone with Miz Barker. Did his slap cause her heart attack, or was it the shock of being slapped by her Ray-Ray's lover that had killed her?

"... first time I ever saw Gran go around the house and check the doors and windows before she went to bed. It was like she knew death was coming and was trying to lock it out. But it didn't work, did it?" Tears sprang to Pam's eyes. She excused herself and ran quickly up the stairs.

Blanche wanted to reach out to Pam, but she was afraid of blurting out what she was seeing in her mind's eye about who had killed her old friend and why. It would hurt Pam too much right now. And besides, Blanche wanted to be sure. Really sure.

"Blanche!" Aminata tapped Blanche's shoulder and made her jump. Blanche locked thoughts of Donnie in the back of her mind and nervously turned to Aminata.

"How you doin'?" they asked simultaneously, and laughed about it.

"You first," Aminata said. "Musta been terrible seeing that boy kill himself like that. You still look kinda strained around the eyes."

Blanche nodded. "Thanks for looking out for the kids. I really appreciate it."

"I was glad to do it. I'm half in love with that son of yours anyway, you know. I only wish my own son..."

Blanche was tempted to change the subject, but figured that's what most people likely did to Aminata, as though her son were a birth defect too ugly to talk about.

"How is your boy holding up, Aminata?"

Aminata crossed her arms. "Sometimes I think he's doing better than me. Sometimes... I don't know. Every time I see him, I see a change. Not growing-up kinda change. More like he's learning things in there that... I still can't believe it, you know. I still wake up thinking I dreamed the whole thing, expecting to hear him in the... I raised that boy to respect life, to love life. He was so gentle and sweet when he was little that he could have been..." Aminata bit her lip and lowered her eyes.

Blanche grasped her hand hard. "It's not your fault, honey," she said.

"That's what Othello always says. But God! I wish..." The pain on Aminata's face was as fresh as if her son had just been arrested. "If I'd just known what lead can do, I'd..."

"That's just it," Blanche said, remembering what her children had said to her about Marc Brindle. "If you had known, you'd have done something. You couldn't do something about what you didn't know, honey."

Aminata squeezed Blanche's hand, then released it. "Most people don't ask me about him." She gave Blanche a sidelong look. "Afraid I'll go off on my son thing," she said with a smile that made Blanche aware of how foolish it was to assume you knew more about a person than the person knew about herself.

"Except for Othello," Aminata added. "He always asks. Always listens."

They both looked across the room at him. Othello was searching Aminata's face with his eyes. Did he feel her wave of unhappiness from that far away?

"You may be half in love with Malik, but I'm half in love with Othello, so that makes us even," Blanche said, to her own surprise.

Aminata nodded. "He is special."

He grinned when he saw Aminata smile, as though his smile were as dependent on hers as moonlight on sunlight.

"I really got lucky."

"It ain't just luck," Blanche said, and suddenly understood how her jealousy of Aminata was related to Malik becoming very much his own person, with his own ideas, and secrets that didn't include or revolve around her. This woman was his friend. Lead poisoning was his issue, both chosen without the least bit of concern for her two cents worth of opinion.

"But how are you feeling, Blanche? Musta been awful being in that house."

"I'm okay. I had a good cry, so I'm all right, for now." She told Aminata about the children's arms around her as she sobbed. "It felt strange to be the one getting the comfort."

Aminata nodded. "They're growing up. I can already see what kind of man Malik is going to be. Working with him really gives me a lift! You know we found the name of the company that owns those abandoned buildings, right? If we can get the names of the officers tomorrow . . . I can't wait to bust these suckers! It'll be good for the organization, too. Make folks see we can really do something about this mess. 'And a little child shall lead them,' isn't that what they say?"

Aminata left with Othello, and Blanche looked around for Mick. She was talking to Lacey. Blanche wondered what folks in the 'hood thought about Lacey being a very up-front sex worker.

She noticed a clutch of women cutting their eyes at Lacey. The set of their shoulders and their expressions made it clear they weren't admiring her outfit, sharp as it was. Had Lacey noticed? Did it matter to her?

"Hey." Blanche put her arm around Lacey's waist. "You make a mean cup of tea, honey!"

Lacey laughed. "And you can suck it up, too, girl!"

"We were just talking about Ray-Ray and Miz Barker, their being friends and dying so close to each other," Lacey told Blanche.

"He came to see her right before she died," Blanche said. The Donnie door in Blanche's mind threatened to swing open. She leaned firmly against it.

"Weird," Mick said. "Like they were saying good-bye to each other."

Blanche and Lacey exchanged amused looks in memory of when they'd believed life lined up that neatly. But Blanche was aware of the true connection between Ray-Ray's and Miz Barker's deaths: The same hand raised against both of them. One hand belonging to one man. One man. Cold once again crept up Blanche's spine and encircled her midriff as though she'd stepped into a walk-in freezer. Beneath the ice, a whole sea of emotions swirled through her—anger at her own stupidity, a sadness for what had happened to Miz Barker and how it might have been prevented a fury against Donnie and everyone else involved in the search for that foul tape, a longing to just sit down alone somewhere and cry.

Lacey and Mick switched to talking about how sad it was when all the old folks started to die off, and naming all the recently dead elders from the old neighborhood. Blanche was hardly present. She hoped that what was happening inside of her wasn't written on her face. Apparently it was.

Lacey lay her hand on Blanche's arms. "Sweetie, you're looking a little peaked. You had a real shock yesterday. You need to take it easy for a couple of days."

Blanche left, but she didn't head for home and rest. She had to meet Bea Richards.

Blanche was early. She slowed her steps and watched the gypsy cab drivers who worked the Tropical Foods market. She didn't think she'd ever seen a regular cab outside of this store. The gypsy drivers looked for fares in both directions—making reservations for after-shopping rides with folks going in the store, and asking people leaving the market loaded down with bags if they needed a ride. In the few years she'd lived here, the gypsy drivers had changed from older American-born black men to younger men from Africa and the Caribbean, especially from Haiti. Had the older men moved on to a spot where they made more money? She hoped so but doubted it. Retired? On what? Mr. Raymond, a black Santa Claus look-alike who was her usual gypsy driver, was just pulling off.

"Hey, Miz North Carolina!" he called as he rolled by with two women in the backseat and the front passenger seat full of grocery bags.

"Hey, how you doin', Mr. Raymond?"

"Tryin' to make a dollar, tryin' to make a dollar." He waved and kept on going.

Mr. Raymond's words repeated in her head as she watched two people—one on either side of the street. One was trying to sell homemade baked goods; the other was offering to carry people's groceries to their car, their house, or even the bus stop for a quarter a bag. Where were all these lazy, shiftless, don't-want-to-work black folks politicians and newspapers were always going on about? All around, there were street vendors selling everything from incense to little black dolls in hand-crocheted outfits. Making work, she thought: doing what poor black people did to get money enough to get by. She'd read there'd been a lot of jobs created in Boston. What they didn't say was who had gotten those jobs. She rarely saw black people working construction in this town, and there weren't even that many blacks in the post office. She could easily count on one hand the number of black salesclerks she dealt with downtown or at the malls. The last time black people had full employment in America was during slavery. She joined the stream of mostly women and children entering the market and was immediately in another world.

The smell of fruit in various stages of decay, the peppery aroma of spices both known and unknown, the earthy odor of roots not native to these parts reminded her of barefoot women cooking over old fires. Languages swirled around her: Spanish, Jamaican patois, Portuguese, African languages she ached to recognize. She felt herself an ingredient in a rich gumbo, simmering down to a nourishing thickness in a broth made of all their juices.

A slim, honey-brown woman in a red sweater rolled a shopping cart up to Blanche.

"Bea Richards?"

Bea nodded and wheeled her cart down the aisle. Blanche wished she had a bit more information about Bea. For all she knew, Bea could be one of what Ardell called the Sanctified Suckers: women silly enough to fall for the kind of minister who considered screwing as many women in the congregation as possible a fringe benefit of his job as God's go-between. Bea didn't look like a fool—but what did a fool look like? Blanche vowed not to say anything sharp, no matter how tired Bea's story.

Bea gave Blanche a sidelong glance. "You're maybe thinking I'm some kinda kook, meeting you here like this." They stood at the end of the meat counter in the back of the store. From there they could see who was seeing them.

"No, I don't think it's kooky. I know what Samuelson's like."

Bea carefully examined a woman checking out the nearby pork roasts.

"He come to see me. Told me not to talk to anybody about his business. Told me too much talking could be bad for my health. Course, he didn't stop me talking. I just try to be more careful." She gave Blanche a slightly panicky look. "You did say you weren't a member?"

"No, no. I'm not a member. I just wanna know..."

"Who told you to talk to me? Oh yes, Charlotte." Bea's eyes followed a woman who'd looked in their direction when she passed by.

"Why did you leave the church?" Blanche asked her.

"Temple," Bea corrected her. "I dreamed about him, you see. Saw him plain as I see you. Didn't know who he was until I saw his picture in the paper a week later. I knew right off I was meant to join him, to help him in his mission."

"His mission?"

"To bring all religions and races together. At least that's what he said he wanted to do. Now I know better." Bea's eyes narrowed. "Now I know..."

Blanche waited for Bea to go on for as long as she could. "Know what?" Blanche asked her.

Bea clutched the handle of her shopping cart until her knuckles stood out like huge marbles. "I gave that man five years of my life. Five years... I did everything for that man."

Blanche stifled a yawn. He-did-me-wrong stories were never her favorites.

"I didn't have no family here, no children. All my spare time went to working for the Temple. I brought in new members, did the typing, and even swept up sometimes."

"What happened?" Blanche was eager to have it all told and over with so that she could go home.

"I tried to tell people when I left the Temple, but nobody listened to me. I even wrote a letter to the newspaper. But they didn't print it."

Blanche was two seconds short of tearing at her hair and running from the store. "I really want to know what—"

"In time," Bea interrupted, "my relationship with Maurice Samuelson became what you might call close."

Blanche grimaced.

"Nothing improper!" Bea said. "I'm not that kinda woman." She drew herself up. "Besides, I wasn't born yesterday. I know how some of these ministers like to take advantage. But Maurice was devil enough to seem sincere. In fact, he asked me to marry him. This was before he married the wife he got now."

"Oh!" Blanche said, beginning at last to sense a little more than just the usual ministerial sex story. "What happened?"

"The Lord saved me from the devil's clutches, that's what happened! Well, like I said, I don't have no family, but I got friends. Good friends. Right here in Boston and down in Delaware. That's where I'm from.

"Course, when I decided to marry Maurice, I called my dearest friend, Rachel, to tell her the news. She still lives in Delaware. That's when she told me about Laconia Waterford and poor Murleen."

"Who are they?" Blanche was having a harder and harder time concentrating as it began to sound like the same old story with a few extra twists.

"Didn't matter that she wasn't alive. She was dead because of what he did to her."

"Excuse me?"

"She was already dead when he asked me to marry him, you see, but it was what killed the woman that made me know he was just a devil pretending to be a man of God."

Blanche didn't think it was Bea's friend who was dead, but who the hell was? She'd have to bluff it.

"What did he do to her?"

"Poor woman come home and find that low-down negro in their marriage bed with her own daughter."

"What woman? Laconia or Murleen?"

Bea gave her a sharp look. "I don't like to keep repeating myself," she said.

"I'm sorry. I'm kinda tired today, and I got lost when you were telling me about…"

"What I'm telling you is that Maurice Samuelson married a woman down in Delaware. Her name was Laconia Waterford. She was a widow with a grown daughter, name of Murleen. You understand me this time?"

Blanche nodded.

"Well, Laconia had a heart attack and died when she come home and found Maurice in bed with poor Murleen, who was born slow as a white-faced mule. After Laconia died, Maurice put poor Murleen in an institution for the retarded! She's still there, for all I know. Folks down Delaware was quite upset about it. That's why that Samuelson negro left Delaware and come here to do the devil's work, after he got all Laconia Waterford's savings and insurance money and deserted her only child by a previous marriage.

"Course I gave him a piece of my mind, trying to marry me after what he did to that woman and her child! I wasn't having none of that, and I told him so, you can be sure!"

Blanche stared at Bea for a moment, partly hypnotized by her story and half hoping to hear something more, something she could use—like Samuelson's stealing the money instead of having it left to him, something that made him ask "How high?" when Brindle said "Jump."

"How old a child was Murleen?" she asked Bea.

"Wasn't no child by then, except in her mind."

So that's that, Blanche thought. But it was kinda funny. Samuelson must have got the shock of his life when Bea got in his face with his skanky business. Blanche could see why he didn't want it talked around town. But it couldn't hurt him in the way she needed to.

"Well, I sure thank you for telling me about him," Blanche said. "If this doesn't convince my friend to stay out of that Temple, nothing will."

"You send her to see me! I don't care what that sinful man says, I'm gonna tell the truth and shame that devil!"

"You be careful," Blanche said as they parted.

Disappointment dogged Blanche's steps. It wasn't right that Samuelson was going to get away with all he'd done to so many people—murder, rape, thuggery, lies, the boy had been at all that, although she was no longer so sure about the first and worst of his crimes. But even without that, Samuelson was guilty of plenty. It wasn't fair that he should be the religious star in the community when he was really a mangy dog showing signs of rabies. She'd stopped expecting life to be fair when she was about eight years old and had yet to be proven wrong. Still, that didn't mean she couldn't try to even things out a little bit.

She stopped at the hardware store and picked up two spray cans of red-orange paint. She also bought herself a pocket-sized container of pepper spray. From now on, she intended to be better prepared for pigs like Mr. Muscles.

By the time she got home, her head felt swollen with the need to think about all that she'd learned, to figure out what she needed to do. She went up to her room and undressed. She lay on her bed and relaxed her body. As her breathing slowed, she let the picture of Donnie float once again to the center of her mind's eye. She sighed and willed herself to accept the meaning of what Othello and Pam had told her: Donnie had lied about not having seen Ray-Ray for four days before Ray-Ray died. He'd lied about being afraid Ray-Ray's killer might come after him. What else had he lied about?

She shifted back to the evening she'd met Donnie at the bar. What was the remark Lucinda had made about him that night? Something about artists. Maybe it wasn't a slur against gays, as she'd thought. Maybe it was about Donnie himself.

She got out the Yellow Pages again.

The woman who answered the phone at The Steak Shop said Lucinda wasn't working today. Blanche knew better than to ask for Lucinda's home phone number, but she tried to get the woman to pass her number on to Lucinda.

"Can't," the woman said. "She outta town. Be in Monday." She hung up.

Blanche made herself a cup of tea. Nothing she could do now but wait. She turned on the radio and switched the station from the children's preferred WILD to WGBH. *Blues After Hours* was on tonight. She'd ride the music away from here for a little while.

TWELVE

DAY ELEVEN—SUNDAY

Joanie came to fetch Taifa and Shaquita at 8:30 Sunday morning. Othello picked Malik up at nine. None of them would be back before evening. Blanche had planned to go back to bed and sleep another hour or two, but the prospect of a whole day on her own was too exciting to waste on sleep.

She turned on the radio before she turned on the kitchen light. For once, her station hadn't been changed. Maybe the children finally accepted that this was her radio, not to be mistaken for family property—just like Grandma tried to teach me. She chuckled to herself, then stared at the radio:

> . . . His father, Allister Brindle, recently declared his candidacy for governor. The Brindle family is one of the . . .

The reporter droned on in his best we're-so-sorry-to-have-tell-you-this voice saved for the tragedies of the well-to-do and famous. If sympathy for the family was how the press was playing it, there'd be no ambitious junior reporter poking around for the story under the story, and the cops had no reason to ask any more questions. For once, rich folks' privilege was paying off for her, too.

The doorbell rang as she was pouring some of the bubbling bath salts Malik had given her for her birthday into the tub. She jerked upright and caught her breath. She knew who it was, just as she always knew when somebody close to her was calling on the phone or ringing her doorbell. But it can't be! she thought. They hadn't done any more than exchange birthday cards since he got married. Her mind argued with the hard, pimply flesh at the tips of her breasts and the first hint of a throb between her legs. It couldn't be, but it was.

She turned off the water and looked in the mirror on the medicine cabinet. She smoothed her hair, then ran down the hall to her room. Where had she put that condom she took from Malik? She found it in her night table drawer and put it under her pillow. The bell rang a third time. She straightened and retied her robe before she went down to the door. She laid her palm flat against it for a moment, then flung it open.

"Y-Y-You surprised?" Leo held his hat between those knowing hands. A grin squinted his deep, dark eyes and creased his broad forehead. His stutter, which showed up only when he was really nervous, told her he wasn't sure of his welcome. She stomped on the urge to run her tongue over his full, red-black lips.

She stepped back to let him in, then quickly locked and chained the door. She turned to face him. Damn, he looked good! She tried to wipe the lust off her face, although she was sure he'd felt it already. The heat that sprang between them when he passed her in the doorway had nearly singed her hair.

"What brings you to Boston?"

"My brother Roscoe's wife's mother died. They live over in New York. I was the only one of the brothers who could get up here to the funeral. So... I took the bus here from New York. Nice ride."

Blanche felt him searching for something more to say. She didn't help him out. He was the one who got married.

"Nice funeral, too. Real nice."

Blanche wanted to laugh. She'd never seen him squirm so, like he had to pee or something. She folded her arms across her chest and waited.

"I thought I'd surprise you. Maybe buy you a drink, or ..."

"You want some coffee? Hot tea? Iced tea? Orange juice? Gin? Water?"

"Uh, yeah, coffee. Coffee would be good." He followed her into the kitchen.

"Nice place you got here."

Blanche measured coffee into the coffeemaker and let the silence between them settle into something a little less nervous.

"Saw your mama last week. Spry as ever."

Blanche put cups, cream, and sugar on a tray.

"Haven't seen Ardell for a while. Somebody said she's away. Course you'd know more about that than me." He gave Blanche a help-me-out kind of look.

"How about something to eat?" she asked him.

"Uh, I'm fine, I'm fine."

There was no argument about that. She carried the tray into the living room and put it on the coffee table. She invited him to sit. He took the sofa. She took the armchair to his left. She poured coffee and handed him a cup. They stared at each other over it until she sat back in her chair.

"So how's everything down home?"

"Fine, just fine. Everybody's healthy. Weather's good." He sipped his coffee. "How's Taifa and Malik?"

"Growing fast. What's up with Luella? How she doing?" Blanche asked, knowing he knew she didn't give a damn about the answer. She wondered if he also knew she was going to have him even if he said Luella was standing just outside the door. But that didn't mean she was going to make it easy for him.

Leo looked everywhere in the room except at Blanche. "She's okay."

"Just okay? That don't sound like newlywed talk to me. Why didn't she come with you?"

Leo squirmed like the sofa was heating up beneath him.

"Well?"

Leo's usually slow, clear voice became a quick mumble: "Seem like she don't want to be a wife no more than you. Spends all her time in that new church."

Blanche threw her head back and laughed.

Leo leaned forward and set his coffee cup on the table and looked at her as though her name were Cake.

"Goddammit, Blanche! What you want me to say? Okay, okay, maybe I made a mistake, maybe…" His words were like groans from deep in his gut.

Blanche unfolded like brand-new butterfly's wings.

"Serves you right for quittin' me." She crossed her legs and let her robe fall open.

Leo stood and reached for her. Blanche let him pull her from the chair. "Aw, shit, woman. Don't nobody ever quit your fine ass." He cradled the cheeks of her behind with his hands and slid his tongue between her lips, slowly, deliberately exploring her mouth. She felt light as laughter. And greedy. She wrapped her arms around his neck. His hand slid between her legs. She yanked his shirt from his pants, lifted it, and moaned at the touch of his velvet chest, the muscles in his back. She pulled away to take off her robe. Leo helped her with one hand while the other stayed between her legs, touching everything she owned and turning it to a hot stickiness. Those magic fingers. Dear Ancestors! This was the sweetest man. She traced a circle around his left nipple with her tongue. They almost didn't make it to her bedroom.

He stayed all day, most of it in Blanche's bed. In the middle of the afternoon they showered and played in the tub until they were both hot enough to sizzle. Blanche didn't tell him anything about what had been happening, but she leaned into him and let him pet her in ways she could see surprised him and made him happy. She fed him lightly, not wanting to waste his energy on digestion. She rode him like he was the last train away from certain disaster, and lay panting and sweaty next to him, more relaxed and present in her body than she'd been in months, her floor littered with Leo's condom supply. Laughter rolled up from her belly and rocked the room.

"Damn! I missed you, woman! Just hearing you laugh, I..." Leo rolled toward her. "Listen, Blanche, I..."

She put her tongue in his mouth. What was there to say? He was the one who'd gotten married.

Leo pulled away from her. "So, this is it?"

"You always was greedy, Leo. That's what got you Luella."

He frowned down at her. "What you mean?" He made small circles around her navel with his index finger.

"You wanted somebody to own. That's why you got married. This wasn't enough, just being happy as two pigs in slop." She slid her hand along the shaft of his penis. "You had to own a wife. Well," she laughed, "you got one. And God, too, it sounds like."

Leo wanted to talk. "Can't we work something out?"

"Something like what?"

"Something regular, something sweet and..."

Blanche laid her hand on his cheek. "Leo, honey, you know better."

"Blanche, baby, I miss you so much. You don't know what it's like. Every time I look at Luella, I know I made a mistake."

"Then fix it," she told him, but softly.

"That could take awhile. In the meantime..."

"I haven't changed, Leo," She almost wished it weren't true. "It would be just like before. You don't know how to do open-handed loving, and I can't do it any other way."

"Aw, Blanche, we..."

She leaned over and kissed him. "Don't waste what time we've got talking about what we can't have." She rolled toward him. There was one last condom on the night table.

An hour later, she shooed him into a cab, which gave him exactly forty-five minutes to make his bus.

Blanche was still in her bathrobe when Malik flew into the house.

"Moms! Guess what?" He threw his backpack on the sofa. "We found the names of two officers in the company that owns the abandoned building. They're related. Two ladies named Laconia and Murleen Waterford. We don't know who they are yet, but..."

"That's great, honey," Blanche said from the one corner of her attention not engaged in savoring her day.

"Man, that computer was awesome! And guess what else? These Waterford people own some other buildings, too, where people are living, and we... Why're you smiling like that?" Malik asked her.

"Like what?" Blanche swung her crossed leg.

"Like *that!*" He looked at her as though she might have stolen something.

When Shaquita and Taifa came in, Taifa stood in front of Blanche, where she sat in her favorite chair.

"Whatsup, Moms!" She leaned over and looked deep into Blanche's eyes, then stood back with a frown on her face. "Anybody been here?" she asked with a hint of Malik's suspicion in her voice.

Blanche laughed, told them there was food in the fridge if they were hungry, and went upstairs to slip her sweetly aching body into yet another tub of warm water.

She drifted off to sleep with the ease of an otter slipping through water. She dreamed of water, too, of floating on a calm blue sea, bobbing to the rhythm of it breathing beneath her. Then she was standing beside a road. Two women stood nearby. They smiled and spoke to her as if she knew them. The plaid headdresses and old-fashioned long skirts they wore were like those she'd seen on Caribbean women in ads for vacations to Jamaica. Dream Blanche was tired and sweaty and knew that she was waiting for some kind of ride. The two women began applauding as a Model T Ford chugged toward them. Bea Richards was driving. She waved to the two women, then opened the door and beckoned to Blanche, but the car turned into a crumbling building just before Blanche stepped in. Bea barely escaped. The two women threw buckets of water at the dust rising from the falling building. Bea. Water. Ford. Building.

Blanche's eyes flew open. Her feet were on the floor before her legs were fully awake. She staggered down the hall to Malik's room, reached out to shake him, and changed her mind. He needed his rest. She moved his backpack and the Jockey shorts and shirt he'd worn Sunday. The notebook for his environmental paper was on his desk. She stepped out into the hall, where she could see better, and flipped the book open to the last used pages. Excitement made her fingers clumsy. Did she have the right name? The state she'd been in when Malik told her about the owners, who knew what he'd said. But there they were, Laconia and Murleen Waterford, the dead wife and the locked-away, retarded stepdaughter of Maurice Samuelson. They were the named officers of the corporation that owned the abandoned building where lead poisoning may have killed a child.

THIRTEEN
DAY TWELVE—MONDAY

Blanche couldn't wait for Malik's alarm to go off. She shook him awake. "I know who owns the abandoned building!"

Malik rubbed his eyes and blinked at her as though trying to make sure he wasn't dreaming.

"The officers of the corporation that own the abandoned building are Maurice Samuelson's dead wife and stepdaughter."

"Who?"

"Maurice Samuelson. Reverend Samuelson."

"You mean that creepy minister who was at the meeting?"

"The very same lowlife."

"Moms! Moms!" He grabbed her by the shoulders and bounced on the bed. "You did it, Moms! You did it!" He gave her that you're-Wonder-Woman look he usually saved for Aminata. Blanche was embarrassed to be so pleased by it.

"I gotta call Aminata!" He leapt out of bed and rushed to the phone.

Blanche sat on the side of his bed grinning from Malik's praise and the deep, gut-warming possibility of having finally gotten something on that so-called minister of God.

"She wants to talk to you, Mama Blanche!" Malik said after he'd told Aminata the news.

"Girl, you are something! How'd you find out who they were?"

Blanche told her about Bea Richards. "But who knows if I'd have remembered hearing their names before if I hadn't dreamt about them."

"Well, I'm gonna try to get up with Computer Teddy, as Othello calls him," Aminata told her. "We need a marriage certificate or something to tie the Waterford women to Samuelson."

"I guess Laconia could have started the corporation and bought the buildings without Samuelson knowing anything about it." Blanche thought this as likely as a flying footstool, but they had to be sure.

"Un-huh. And maybe I'm really the queen of the Nile," Aminata said. "I never did trust that man! I'm betting it's the other way around. I'm betting Samuelson didn't even start the corporation until after Laconia was dead. I'd like to know what else his corporation owns besides buildings that probably have phony deleading certificates. I'm checking that out. I got a feeling it ain't just buildings he's hiding behind that woman's name. And what about the stepdaughter? Where's she, I wonder."

Blanche told her what Bea had said about Samuelson putting Murleen in an institution.

"I bet she don't know she's an officer in some corporation. That man really oughtta be ashamed of hisself!"

If only, Blanche thought. "You really think your computer friend can find a marriage certificate for them?" Blanche's doubt was as clear as her words. "They probably got married down in Delaware. Did I tell you that?"

"It don't matter. Teddy's one of them information junkies. Hooked into everything. That's all he does, all he talks about. And they got everything on that Internet, girl," Aminata said. "Keep your fingers crossed. If we find what we need, we'll call a community meeting for Thursday night. Turn this sucker over to the 'hood first, to the people whose kids he poisoned. Then we go to the authorities. The rotten bastard."

Almost as soon as Blanche had waved the children off to school, Malik ran back to tell her Cousin Charlotte had called while she was in the tub last night. "She'll be back on Wednesday." He dashed back out the door.

Blanche moaned and wished she didn't have to deal with Cousin Charlotte's reaction to Shaquita's pregnancy. And what about Miz Inez? Blanche didn't want to be the one to tell her the truth about how Ray-Ray had died. There was only so much bad news she was prepared to deliver.

She waited until nearly noon before she walked down to Dudley Square and around the corner to The Steak Shop.

The shop was small and narrow: a counter running along one wall, three tables with cracked Formica tops and four wooden chairs each. The grill was behind the counter. The place smelled of cigarettes and burnt grease smoke mixed with the scent of cooking meat. The large front window was so cloudy, the outside world seemed lost in fog. Lucinda was wiping the counter, her head cocked hard to the side to avoid the smoke curling up from the cigarette in the side of her mouth. There was no one else in the place.

"Hey, Lucinda, how you doin'?" Blanche took a seat in front of her.

"Nothin' to it, Blanche. What can I get you? We just got some fresh cold cuts; I could make you a real decent hoagie."

Blanche looked down at Lucinda's three-inch bright-red-with-rhinestones nails and remembered an article she'd read about the germs under fingernails. Of course, it would be interesting to see Lucinda work in those things, but not worth the risk, she decided.

"I'll just have one of those orange drinks, thanks."

Lucinda brought Blanche the bottled drink and a straw. She put out her cigarette and leaned against the counter.

Blanche jumped in before Lucinda could start a conversation about something else.

"Lucinda, remember when I saw you in Connolly's the other day? When I was with Donnie and you said something about him being an artist, or something like..."

Lucinda grimaced. "Quick-change artist," she said. "But I didn't mean nothing by it, Blanche. It's none of my business who you..."

"Lucinda! Just tell me what you meant. He ain't a friend."

A woman and a little girl came in and took a table. Lucinda went off to wait on them. Like Blanche, they only wanted drinks.

"Tell me what you meant," Blanche said when Lucinda came back. "Do you know him?"

Lucinda chuckled. "I useta work at Plug's before it closed. You know what I'm talkin' about?"

Blanche didn't.

"It was a bar. It wasn't a gay bar. Lotta neighborhood people hung there, especially in the daytime. But a lot of gays hung out there at night. Not the kind who shake they ass and say 'I'm gay, get over it,' and not the kind who was pretendin' to be straight. I mean the ones that act like regular people, you know what I'm sayin'?"

Blanche didn't want to get into a thing about "regular people," but she wasn't going to agree with her either. "Go on," she said.

"Well, you know what it's like tendin' bar; people talk to you like listenin's what you get paid to do. When they ain't talkin' to you, they talk in front of you like you can't hear."

"So, you know anything about him?"

Lucinda gave her a stop-interrupting look.

"Anyway, Donnie useta hang in there and meet dates there."

"So? What was so quick-change about that?"

Lucinda widened her eyes and crossed her arms. "A big change. From his wife and kiddies out in Taunton to Miss Thang in the bar. Is that quick-change enough for you?"

Blanche frowned, trying to make sense of what Lucinda was saying. Lucinda gave her an exasperated look.

"Donnie useta come in and meet gay guys and go out with them, but his wife probably ain't hip to it."

"Donnie's wife?! You mean Donnie has a wife?"

"Sure. My girlfriend lives right around the corner from him. She went to school with Donnie's wife. Their kids go to the same school. She came to meet me at Plug's one night and almost shit when she saw Donnie there."

"A wife," Blanche said, trying to get used to the idea that the man she'd thought was gay, who'd told her he was gay and in love with another gay man had a wife and…

"Did you say kids?!" She sounded as shocked as she was.

"Yep. Three or four, I think." Lucinda looked amused. "Donnie ain't the only one, you know. A lotta the so-called 'straight' men who hung out at Plug's were married or had girlfriends." She laughed and shook her head. "They all acted like people were stupid. Donnie and those other married dudes would come in, buy a drink for one of the fags, sit with him, and chitchat. Then the straight guy would leave by the front door. Five minutes later, the gay guy would leave by the back door. In fifteen minutes to a half an hour, one or both of them would be back. And I ain't talking turning tricks, here. I'm talking boys just like to have fun," she chortled. She went off to collect from the woman and child.

Blanche was stunned. Only a few days ago she'd had to rearrange her thinking to include Ray-Ray and Donnie as lovers. Now Lucinda was adding another branch to that family.

"Well, maybe his wife does know," Blanche said when Lucinda came back. "I mean, if he's bisexual, maybe she is, too, or…"

"Girl! Get real! How many black women you know agreeing to that share-and-share-alike shit? Anyway, if that was the deal, my girlfriend wouldn't have been so shocked to see Donnie in Plug's doing his guy thing."

Blanche thought of Leo's brother George, who'd done time for armed robbery. She remembered him talking about guys who were straight on the street but had male lovers in jail. Blanche had always thought George was one of those men, although he'd never admitted it. Did men like that consider themselves bi? Or gay? Not from the way George talked. Or Lucinda.

Lucinda checked her nails. "Yeah, girl, the bartenders used to talk about it all the time. We used to joke about somebody needing to call Donnie's and those other dudes' wives to make sure those suckers were using condoms at home."

"Did Ray-Ray Brown hang out at Plug's?"

"You sure know your Donnie. Ray-Ray was all up in that boy's face. I useta wonder if there was something more than a quickie goin' on between those two. I think if Ray-Ray had had his way, there woulda been. He died, you know." Lucinda leaned on the counter. "Donnie ain't bad-lookin'," she said, "but I never could see what Ray-Ray saw in him. I always got a real weird vibe from Donnie."

Blanche leaned toward her. "Weird how, exactly?"

Lucinda hunched her shoulders. "The nigga's just strange!"

"You don't mean because of the gay sex thing, do you?"

"No, no. This didn't have nothin' to do with sex. This is about… I don't know, but I never heard him talk about anything but money: how much he needed, what he'd do with it if he had it, why he didn't have it, what he was gonna do to get some. If he came in while people were talking about the rain, he'd turn the conversation to the cost of umbrellas and raincoats. Always money. It ain't natural.

"Why you so interested in him, anyway?" Lucinda asked.

"It's kinda complicated," Blanche said, and scolded herself for not having a ready answer to a question she should have expected. "Donnie's messing around with a friend of a friend, and I was just curious about what he might… it's kinda, you know, personal."

Lucinda gave her a skeptical look. "Whatever," she said in a way that told Blanche she'd gotten her last bit of information from this source.

Blanche paid Lucinda for her drink and hurried home. She was stepping fast but hardly quick enough to keep up with the thoughts tumbling around in her mind like laundry in the dryer. She felt her ideas about what had happened to Ray-Ray and Miz Barker shuffling like cards in a hustler's hands. She unlocked the door and went right to the phone. She called Information for Taunton. There was one Roberta MacFadden and one McFadden, initials D. A. Blanche punched in D. A.'s number.

"Mrs. McFadden?" she said to the woman who answered the phone.

"Yeah?"

Blanche could hear children very nearby. One of them was crying.

"Mrs. Donnie McFadden?"

"Yeah? Who's this? Leave your brother alone, Donnella!"

"This is Mary Green for Boston City Hall, Mrs. McFadden. I just need to verify your husband's address. He does still live with you at . . ."

"Darnell! Get down from there. Now! Of course he lives—who did you say this was?"

"Can I reach Mr. McFadden at his place of employment at . . ." Blanche scrambled around in her purse for the piece of paper Donnie had given her, and read the number.

"Well, yes, but . . . Awright now, I'm warning both of you!"

"Thank you." Blanche hung up.

So there it was. Donnie was still living with his wife. He'd made Blanche think he had a place of his own. Of course, that could still be true. Yeah, if he owned the company where he worked. He'd lied to her about having his own place and about getting a place with Ray-Ray. He'd lied to her about being gay. She was both pissed and embarrassed about that. Like any good scam artist, he couldn't have done it without her help, without her believing that he had to be gay because he moved his hands and body and used his voice in ways the movies and other bullshit artists said were signs of being gay. She couldn't blame a damn bit of that on Donnie. From what Lucinda had said, he was probably lying to himself, too.

He'd lied to her about everything and she'd believed him. Why? Looking back, she couldn't find any good reasons. When he'd told her he didn't know Miz Barker or Marc, why hadn't she known then that she was being suckered? She was like a person who got hit by a truck because she looked the wrong way on a one-way street. Although Samuelson and Brindle had given her plenty of reasons to look their way, Donnie had given her a couple, too. Still, that business about being afraid of Ray-Ray's killer was a stroke of evil genius—one for which she fully intended to find some way to pay him back.

But if money-hungry Donnie had the tape, he'd have been in touch with Brindle, trying to turn that tape into cash. At least as late as yesterday, that hadn't happened—which probably meant Donnie didn't have it. Did he know where it was? Or was he waiting for her to find it for him? Of course, she could be wrong about Miz Barker having the tape. Marc could have had it, but all she'd heard him say was that he knew what was on the tape. He never actually said he had it. Donnie must have thought he knew where it was, or he wouldn't have killed Ray-Ray and Miz Barker before he laid hands on it. Ray-Ray had probably given Miz Barker the tape in the store while Donnie was watching. But then, crafty as usual, she'd moved the tape and started watching her back.

Blanche put on her old Keds and changed into her housecleaning pants and sweatshirt. She threw on a jacket, grabbed her handbag and flashlight, and made sure her pepper spray was in her jacket pocket. Minutes later, she was back in Miz Barker's bomb shelter.

She ignored the boxes she'd already searched, and lifted the covers off the items on the shelves: an old electric toaster, the kind with fold-down doors on either side; an upright black manual typewriter with a cutout front; a curling iron and straightening comb in their own little heater.

Like a retirement home, she thought. Nothing broken, everything past its time. She imagined the items talking together, reminding one another of the lives they'd lived when they'd been the star of the kitchen or the latest gadget on the market, of how people had gathered round, eager for what they had to offer.

Time. Everything and everybody had only a thin slice and that was all. When your time was up, you got put on the shelf in the basement. She didn't want to go there, to wind up in a nursing home with a bunch of discarded souls trying to outdo one another with stories from the past.

There was a cathedral radio like the one her grandmother had owned. She fiddled with its knob. Granny had never liked for Blanche to touch that precious box. She looked more closely at the little window where the tuning dial once glowed, all dingy now, like the window in an old lady's apartment. She also didn't want to live alone in some Blanche-smelling room talking to herself and a couple of cats. She didn't want to live with Taifa or Malik and feel herself becoming somebody's child. But she didn't want to die before she was eligible for any of that either.

What she did want was to get used right up. Not simply to use up her years and days, but all of herself—her laughter and loving, her dance steps and good times. All of her juice. Juice she felt beginning to dry up, just a little, like the first skim on cooling milk.

She turned her mind back to trying to picture Miz Barker coming down here with something Ray-Ray has asked her to keep for him, to hide for him. Did she know what it was? Was she excited? Blanche walked to the back of the space. Excited. That was a funny word to use about hiding something, but it stayed with her. She imagined Miz Barker in here looking for someplace to hide a videotape. Not big, not small. Where would it fit? Blanche walked slowly among the bits of furniture. She closed her eyes and saw Ray-Ray down here without Miz Barker, looking around for a good hiding place like she'd just done. She opened her eyes, but nothing leapt out at her.

She checked underneath the cushions in the armchair and examined the elephant-foot table. She flopped into the chair and tried to relax. She knew the tape was here. She knew it. She also knew that finding something was often a matter of thinking like the person who hid it.

"All right," she said to both Miz Barker and Ray-Ray. "You two been buggin' me and buggin' me about this business, now give me a hand here." She sat still and called up her memory of Ray-Ray when he'd came to the Brindle house. He'd been full of himself, no doubt about it. Sure of himself, but righteous, too. He was going to get his revenge on Allister for kicking him out of the family. He also knew that diming on Allister was a good thing to do. Was he scared? Did it occur to him that Skanks One and Two might send somebody to shut him up? If he wasn't scared, he must have expected trouble. Why else hide the tape? Was he really planning to put Brindle's business out on the airwaves? She stared at the radio on the shelf.

She found an old table knife, used it as a screwdriver, and removed the back of the radio. And there, where all the tubes and wires should have been, was a black plastic videocassette.

On the way home she peeped around corners and peered over her shoulder so often, she looked like she had a tic. She clutched her bag tightly to her chest and held her pepper spray in her right hand.

Once she got home, she locked the door behind her and even closed the curtains. She was so excited, she dropped the cassette twice before she could get it in the machine. She sat on the floor in front of the machine and took a deep breath. Half a minute into the film she whooped out loud at the sight of a bored-looking blond smearing chocolate syrup on Allister Brindle's crotch and licking it off in slow motion. Damn! So much for the Mr. Family Values candidate!

The next segment was the one Lacey had told her about—Brindle in a pinafore and knee socks being given a good spanking with a black lacquer-backed hairbrush. Blanche wasn't amused anymore. There was something tired and desperate about the whole thing. Kinky, maybe, but no more so than men who went out on football and rugby fields to get kicked and gouged for so-called fun. Still, she'd never thought much of Allister Brindle, and she thought even less of him now—not because of the way he liked his sex, but because he was such a lying phony.

The next piece was even less funny: A large German shepherd's penis was just visible as the dog humped over Brindle's butt. No wonder Ray-Ray was so pleased with himself. This was definitely a career-busting tape. The dog had more dignity than Brindle. And Donnie! He could have retired with the money he'd have gotten from Brindle for the tape. But it wasn't until the final segment that she realized just how much Donnie could have gotten.

Allister was naked on a huge bed, his body looking almost rosy next to shiny black sheets. But it wasn't Allister that made her groan. She moved closer to the screen for a better look. She stopped the tape and replayed the picture of three little faces, their eyes looking off to the left, as though someone there was giving them instructions. The child pinching and twisting Allister's nipples couldn't be more than eight years old. None of the little girls had developed breasts yet. Blanche stared at the screen while Allister's eyes rolled and he squirmed beneath a child's mouth while his hand . . . She couldn't make it upstairs and barely made it to the kitchen sink before vomit flooded her mouth. Children. She couldn't pull her mind away from them.

Whose little girls were they? Where were the people who were supposed to protect them?

She hung over the sink, tears streaming down her face, bile boiling up and out of her as she gagged and groaned. She knew this kind of shit went on in the world. She knew that child molesters looked like salesmen, cops, the man across the street, the candidate for governor. She knew that children were stolen and sold into nightmares. She knew, but she had never seen. And now she could never not see, never not remember the look on those three small faces, each with her own way of looking like she wished she was anyone but who she was, that she was anyplace but where she was, that what would happen next wouldn't hurt too much, that whoever was standing on the sidelines telling her what to do wouldn't get mad and make her do these bad things over and over and over again.

Blanche cleaned her mouth and face and then the sink. She remembered the first time she'd seen Allister Brindle. What had he told Sadowski about black people? "They're not like us. You can never trust them. Different values." At the time, she'd been insulted that he would make such They statements. Now she was glad he felt he was so different from her. She wanted to be as different from the Allister Brindles of the world as possible. But he wasn't the only sleaze in this shit pile.

In the living room, the TV screen showed the gray-and-white end-of-tape pattern that looked liked static sounded. She turned off the TV, then rewound the tape. Her hand shook when she took the tape from the machine. Her fingers felt grimy from handling it. She carried the tape up to her room. She held it in her left hand and held that hand behind her—there was nowhere in her room where she dared to lay it down. She lit a candle on her Ancestor altar and thanked them for helping her find the tape. She also thanked them in advance for helping her understand what she needed to do with it, and she wished the awful thing were not in her house.

She went back downstairs. She wouldn't be able to sleep with it in her room. Would a night in the refrigerator hurt a videotape? No, not near their food! Finally, she put the tape in a plastic bag and took it to the laundry alcove between kitchen and living room. She shoved the tape deep in the clothes hamper. The perfect place for it. And guaranteed no one else in her family was likely to find it in there.

She stood in the shower with too-hot water pouring over her, the little girls' faces as present as the drops splashing in the tub. She stood there until the water ran cold. When she finally got out, her skin and everything else about her seemed tender. Even her eyes felt raw. But she knew what she needed to do. When she'd dressed, she called Othello and got his answering machine.

"It's Blanche White. Call me as soon as you can. I got news."

He called her back in twenty minutes and was at her door an hour after that.

"I know who killed Ray-Ray Brown and Miz Barker. His name is Donnie McFadden. He ain't old, but he wears kind of old-fashioned clothes," she told him. "The woman who saw Ray-Ray near the pool said the man with him was an old person 'cause that's how he was dressed. It was Donnie. I'm sure of it. All that bullshit he gave me about wanting his letters back from Ray-Ray was really to find out if Ray-Ray had things stashed somewhere else besides Miz Inez's house and Miz Barker's." Then she told him about all the other lies Donnie had told.

"Donnie probably tried to talk Ray-Ray into the money-for-tape idea, but Ray-Ray wouldn't go for it, so Donnie killed him. Donnie thought he knew where Miz Barker had put the tape, only she'd moved it and wouldn't tell Donnie where it was. That's why he killed her."

"It all adds up," Othello said, "but we don't want to make no mistake."

"I thought of that," Blanche said, and told him how she planned to get Donnie to tell on himself.

"If you're right, it could be dangerous."

"That's why I called you," she said, and saw her whole income-tax-return check going to the Ex-Cons. Cheap at the price.

"I'm game if you're game," he told her. "What about tomorrow night?"

"Hi," Taifa mumbled, and stomped upstairs when she came in from school. Blanche decided to wait a while before she tried to find out whether this snit was about something that ought to concern her.

Malik came in and went right to the phone to call Aminata.

"Nothing yet," he told Blanche when he'd hung up. "But she said Teddy's sure he can find what we need on his computer. Aminata's gonna call me."

Blanche smiled not so much at what Malik said as at the fact that the sound of Aminata's name no longer made her hackles rise. Progress.

"You really like working on this, don't you?" Blanche instantly saw his name over a column in the *New York Times.*

"It's okay," he said, adopting the hideout attitude of a teen who senses a career talk coming, but he couldn't keep the pleasure out of his eyes.

Blanche turned on the radio. "There's some sliced chicken if you're hungry." She enjoyed the surprise on his face when she didn't do her career talk. She could wait.

Shaquita's little butt was dragging low when she came home. Blanche called the girl to the kitchen after Malik went off to his room. Blanche knew Shaquita didn't want to hear the best advice Blanche had to give, so she decided to play it another way.

"You can't be moping around with a baby in your belly." Blanche handed her a glass of orange juice. "Baby needs a mother thinking positive thoughts, planning the future, and sending love."

Tears big as peas rolled down Shaquita's face. She leaned over in her chair and hugged her body, rocking back and forth.

Blanche knelt in front of Shaquita, put her arms around the girl, and held her until she was ready to talk.

"He doesn't want it. He..."

"You mean Pookie? What did he say?" Blanche held her breath.

"He... He... I asked him if he would come with me to talk to Gran. He said"—she took a deep breath—"he said he wasn't into being a father. He said I should..."

Sobs cut off Shaquita's words. Blanche put her arms around her again, in part to hide the smile that was blooming on her face. Thank you, Pookie, Blanche mouthed.

"I thought... I thought this was what he wanted. He kept saying..."

"But you're the one who has to—"

"But I wanted it, too! I was the one who said it was okay not to use a condom. He didn't make me."

"But you wouldn't have done it if he hadn't wanted you to," Blanche insisted. "And now he's changed his mind." Ancestors bless him, she added to herself.

"What am I going to do, Aunt Blanche? I'm so scared! I just..."

"So was I, Quita. And I was older than you."

Shaquita stopped crying and raised her head.

"I was eighteen when I got pregnant," Blanche told her. "Just outta high school. He wasn't even a boy I particularly liked. I mean, I liked him well enough. He was nice and all, but I didn't have a real thing for him. I just went out with him 'cause I was mad at Leo, my regular boyfriend." Blanche stroked Shaquita's head. "I wanted to be grown. Grown women had sex. So... the next thing I knew, I'd missed my period." Blanche shook her head and laughed a little. "I don't think I've ever been so scared since. I knew Mama would kill me, or at least make me wish I was dead. I sure didn't want to have to marry Sonny Jones. And I was already wondering if I ever wanted to have children at all."

Shaquita was dry-eyed now and totally caught up in Blanche's story. "What did you do?" she asked.

Shoulda told her this before, Blanche thought. "Well, I thought about just having it. Just not saying anything to Mama and letting the size of my belly give her the news. Then I stopped thinking about me as Mama's child and started seeing me as somebody's mama, having to do everything: go out to work, cook, clean, and take care of my own child at home, just like my own mother did. When was I gonna have fun? Be young? How was I gonna be able to stay home to take care of a baby? What was I gonna use to pay somebody else to watch the baby while I went to work? How was I gonna get to Harlem, USA, like I'd been dreaming about?" All the confused feelings of that time welled up in Blanche. She felt the weight of that never-born baby and the deep sorrow that had lingered for weeks afterward. She wiped the tears from her eyes.

"My cousin Murphy helped me. She was a lot older than me. Mama always called her 'worldly.' So I figured she might know what to do. She took me to a friend of hers, a nurse or a midwife. But first Cousin Murphy made me pray for what would not have a chance to become a full baby born to me, made me thank it for giving me my life back. Made me promise to give of myself to some child already in the world. Atonement, she called it. I thought that was really crazy stuff, but I didn't argue with her; I'da done anything, *anything.* Now I see she was right. Now..." She thought about the role Taifa and Malik had played in her atonement, and thanked her sister for the opportunity she'd given her. Now, using her experience to try to help Shaquita, she was aware of having found yet another way in which all of her life was connected.

Shaquita squeezed Blanche's hand. "Did it hurt?"

"A little pinch. I was about as far gone as you. I had cramps and bled some afterward. It wasn't no picnic. And I felt sad for a while. But at the same time, I was glad I did it. Glad to know that..."

"It was all over." Shaquita finished the sentence for her.

Blanche stood up. "Now you got to decide, Quita. Whatever you decide, you know I'm in your corner. And so is Cousin Charlotte. But think about it, honey, that's all I ask. Think about who you are, and what you've always said you wanted. Don't stand in your own way."

Shaquita rose and kissed Blanche on the cheek. "Thanks, Aunt Blanche," she said. The phone rang. "I'll get that!" Shaquita said, and was gone.

"Is that for me?" Malik called out, and thundered down the stairs when Shaquita said it was.

Blanche slumped against the table. Honesty was hard work.

"We got it, Moms!" Malik yelled, and ran into the kitchen. "When Laconia Waterford died, when they got married, and when the corporation was started! Aminata was right, the company wasn't started until after Laconia Waterford died. He musta forged her signature or something. There's gonna be a Community Reawakening Project meeting about it on Thursday."

"Congratulations, honey!" She hugged him and relished the knowledge that Samuelson was finished as the minister of truth and virtue. By the time Aminata and company got done trashing him for poisoning black kids and the state jacked him up for his bogus corporation and lead violations, the Reverend and his Temple might have to do what he'd done in Delaware: get out of Dodge. She let herself feel the full pleasure of that and wished she could add a kick in the balls to go with it. But she did have her own little surprise for him.

Her house and the neighborhood were enjoying middle-of-the-night quiet when Blanche left home carrying a pillowcase with paint, a funnel, a pair of rubber gloves, a small flashlight, and a box of sugar inside. She took her pepper spray from her jacket pocket and carried it in her right hand.

She stood across the street from Samuelson's house for almost ten minutes in which she wondered what the hell she was doing there. Samuelson's goons were as ready to push her face in as look at her, and here she was, sneaking around his house. She remembered that old thing about falling off a horse: The best thing to do was to get right back on before the fear of riding set in. Was that what she was trying to do? Keep her courage up by acting like she had some?

The house and the Temple next door were both dark. If Samuelson's boys were working security, she didn't see them. She walked down the driveway. The car was parked in back under a carport. It seemed to crouch there like a monster sleeping beneath a huge umbrella. She half expected the doors to spring open and Samuelson's boys to jump out and grab her again. She realized she was panting loud enough to be heard downtown. She took a deep breath and told herself to be cool as she moved closer to the car.

She set her pillowcase on the ground and put on her rubber gloves. She figured a car like this probably had an alarm as sensitive as a cat's whiskers, so she moved with the delicacy of that same cat on the prowl. She opened the lid to the gas tank, unscrewed the cap, and laid it on the ground. She opened the pillowcase, took out the sugar, the ice pick, and the funnel. She took off the protective cork that covered the tip of the ice pick and inserted the tip it into the opening around the gas tank cover. She moved the tip slowly around the gas cover until it popped open—a trick she'd learned from an old Harlem neighbor who'd kept his gas tank full of other people's gas. When the gas cover popped, she wedged the funnel into the gas tank. The sugar slid into the tank with a low hiss. Blanche smiled.

"And now for today's sermon," she whispered. She jumped at the sound of the ball bearings pinging against the sides of the paint can as she shook it up. Still mindful of the car alarm, she held the can high and leaned over the car without touching it. The result was worth the ache in her upper arm. The letters stood out like flames against the car's dark body. She used the other can of paint to draw arrows leading from the sidewalk down the driveway to the car. She chuckled all the way home at the thought of Samuelson and his Temple members following the arrow trail to the minister's car, which now proclaimed that GOD DON'T LIKE UGLY—a car that even with a new paint job wasn't going to be worth a teaspoonful of cat piss once that sugar made its way into the engine. He wouldn't be roughing up any other women in this baby.

Life might not be fair, but it sure as hell could be satisfying.

FOURTEEN

DAY THIRTEEN—TUESDAY

Taifa was moaning and whining about the state of her fried hair; Shaquita remembered a book report due today and was busy scribbling when she wasn't throwing up. Malik mumbled something about women and slammed out the door with a piece of toast in one hand and two slices of bacon in the other. And there were women who actually wanted to stay home with their kids. Amazing!

Blanche waited until ten-thirty to call Donnie at work. She wanted to make sure he'd be there. Her mouth went dry at the sound of his voice. She was careful to keep rage out of her voice.

"Donnie? This is Blanche White. I got something I want you to see. Can you come by this evening, say about seven-thirty? I won't have it before then." She didn't want him to surprise her by coming earlier.

"What is it? Something of Ray-Ray's?"

Blanche didn't answer him. "I'll have it ready when you get here. My kids will be out." She didn't expect him to refuse—and he didn't.

She walked around the room to calm herself, then called Othello and told him everything was set.

Blanche checked the Yellow Pages and made a couple of calls until she found what she was looking for. It was going to cost more than she expected, but her Brindle check came that morning. She'd been paid for an extra week. It seemed just right to use

Brindle's money to pay for his downfall. She fished the tape out from among the dirty clothes and put it in her bag.

The little girls' faces rose up from it like mist from a lake. Blanche hoped it wasn't too late for them. She was relieved to have the doorbell interrupt her thoughts—until she saw who was leaning on her bell.

"Hiya doin', Blanche?" Karen the borrower blew a mouthful of cigarette smoke past Blanche into the house.

If I was inclined to lend her whatever it is she wants to borrow, she won't get it now. Blanche waved the smoke back toward the door.

"I was wondering if you got any cornmeal I could…"

Something in Blanche snapped. She grinned at Karen.

"Now ain't this a coincidence. I was just heading for your house to ask you if *you* had some cornmeal *I* could borrow. And what about mustard? You got any of that?"

Karen's mouth fell open.

"And I could sure use a couple cups of rice and some flour."

Karen backed off the stoop.

"What about a roll of toilet paper? I guess I could use paper towels if that's all you got."

Karen began walking backward toward her own house. She kept her eyes on Blanche.

"What size shoe do you wear, honey?" Blanche called after her. "I could use a sweater, too! Blue would be nice," Blanche shouted.

She could hardly close the door for laughing. She was still chuckling when the phone rang.

"Hello. May I speak with Blanche White, please?"

Blanche sank into a chair. All laughter was gone now.

"I'm so sorry about your son, Felicia."

"Yes, my son." Felicia paused a few seconds.

In the long silence that followed, Blanche could feel Felicia's pain leaping through the phone lines like static.

"I wanted to ... you were here, you see, and I ..."

"Yes, I understand."

"Allister doesn't talk about it, except to remind me that I'm responsible. Of course, he's right. If I hadn't been ... Life is so, so ... I don't know."

Blanche could hear the tightness in Felicia's throat. She suddenly saw Felicia with Marc's blood in her hair, screaming as though her voice had the power to turn back time. Now she sounded like a person hit too often to expect anything but pain. Felicia's sorrow touched Blanche in that place all loving mothers shared, where death or danger to your child lived. It was not the kind of connection it was healthy for her to have with an employer. Even so, she couldn't help but feel for the woman—and Felicia wasn't her employer anymore.

"The funny thing is, I didn't even care for Saxe," Felicia said. "It was just a physical thing. Allister and I don't ... It was just sex. That's all I wanted. If I'd had any idea, any idea that Saxe and Marc ... that Marc would ..."

Here it is again, Blanche thought: Felicia blamed herself for not knowing her lover was screwing her son and for Marc's death. Aminata kicked herself for not having known the effects of lead paint. Pam blamed herself for not having been there to save Miz Barker. And she herself wondered whether Miz Barker and Ray-Ray might still be alive if she'd acted differently. She wondered if men thought they were responsible for things they couldn't control, or was this a woman thing?

"It wasn't your fault any more than it was mine, no matter what your husband says," Blanche told her, and clamped her teeth shut on the desire to tell Felicia she'd soon be getting a package that would show how little right Allister had to point a finger at anyone for anything.

"I hear you're going away," she said.

"We're leaving. But not together. I should have left him years ago. And if I know Allister, he's going to make me wish I had.

He'll use Saxe and whatever else he can against me in the divorce." Felicia paused, then went on. "It would help if I had... Did you ever hear any more about Allister's tape?" Felicia paused again, but not long enough for Blanche to answer. "As I said, I'm prepared to be very generous."

Blanche considered how to answer. She'd be happy to take Felicia's money any day. Of course, she didn't intend to admit to knowing anything about the tape, but she did want to make sure Felicia knew where to send the check.

"Lost things are found all the time," she said. "Maybe the tape will be one of them."

"I'll keep my fingers crossed," Felicia said.

"And your checkbook handy," Blanche added. "And, of course, you have my address..."

After she hung up, Blanche sat by the phone for a couple seconds, thinking about the harm Allister and Donnie had done to so many people. The children in the video, Miz Barker, Ray-Ray, Marc Brindle, Saxe Winton, Felicia bent almost to broken, Donnie's wife about to get one of the nastier surprises of her life, Pam, Miz Inez, and all the other mourners left to try to wade through their pain without drowning. Oh yes, she wanted to really fuck with both these boys!

She took the bus to Centre Street in Jamaica Plain. The two-story buildings on this main street made it look like a small town. Blanche gave the chubby young woman behind the counter of Rick's TV & Stereo Shop a can-I-trust-you? look before reluctantly handing her the videotape to be copied. When Blanche had called the place earlier, she'd made sure the tape wouldn't have to be viewed in order to be copied, so that was okay, but she still didn't like letting the tape out of her hands. The copy setup was right behind the counter, surrounded by rebuilt TVs and car stereos, jam boxes, and clock radios, so at least she could keep her eye on it. She watched the young woman's blue-and-red fingernails as she put the tape in the machine and pushed some buttons. Blanche waited with as much patience as she could muster for the copies to be made.

She immediately took the tapes up the street to the post office she'd passed on the bus. Unlike the Roxbury post office, this one didn't have a thick Plexiglas partition between the workers and the patrons that let folks know they were so dangerous a barrier was needed to keep them from what? Touching? She took a couple of deep breaths and told herself to just fill out the postal forms: one for Felicia, one for the Massachusetts Society for the Prevention of Cruelty to Children, and one for the Massachusetts Society for the Prevention of Cruelty to Animals. She figured that pretty much did it for Allister. She'd mail the original tape to herself at Ardell's address when she was done with it. She handed the lot of them to the woman behind the post office counter and waved bye-bye to Allister Brindle.

"I need you folks to do your homework at the library this evening," she told the kids after dinner. "And stay there till I come get you," she added.

"Is this about whatever was making you smile like that on Sunday?" Malik wanted to know.

Taifa came right to the point: "You got a boyfriend, Mama Blanche?"

"I wish!" Blanche told her. "This is about my needing this house for a couple of hours."

Taifa and Malik exchanged one of those brother-sister looks Blanche could never read.

"I ain't got much," Taifa said.

"You what?"

"I don't have much homework."

"Then read a book. Library's got plenty of them."

She didn't often refuse to give them a reason why they had to do something, so she'd expected a lot of questions and attitude.

But something in her voice must have told them that resisting would be a waste of time.

Blanche was more nervous than she'd expected. Even Othello's arrival didn't calm her. He had another man with him: Elroy Banks—light skin and eyes, short, polite, and quick. Blanche was glad he was on her side. He and Othello looked around for a place to put their tape recorder, which for some reason made Blanche even more nervous. Othello explained that the tape was voice activated and would pick up everything they said, as long as she didn't turn up the sound on the TV.

But what if Donnie had a gun and just walked in the door and shot her without saying a word? He'd already killed Ray-Ray and Miz Barker to get this tape. He could do the same to her. What if he grabbed her by the throat but went on talking to her as though they were having a normal conversation so Othello and Elroy wouldn't know anything was wrong? She was, she admitted to herself, afraid. She hoped she wasn't too scared to play her part.

At seven-twenty, Othello stepped into the downstairs coat closet. Elroy went to stand in the shadows at the top of the stairs. Blanche put the Brindle tape in the VCR, lowered the blinds, and turned out the lights, except for a small lamp near the TV. The revolver Othello had given her laid in her lap. Her pepper spray was in her pocket.

The sound of glass breaking in the back announced Donnie's arrival. The fact that he didn't simply knock on the door was all the proof she needed that he meant to kill her and make her death look like part of a break-in, the nasty little shit. She started the tape, although she couldn't look at it. She held the gun behind her and stood facing the doorway. Donnie soft-walked into the room. He wore a clear plastic raincoat and the kind of rubber gloves that doctors use. He looked from her to the VCR and back again.

"You planning to kill me for the tape the way you did Ray-Ray and Miz Barker?" She gripped the gun tighter. She hadn't expected the sight of him to make her want to hit him.

"If Ray-Ray had been more cooperative, he'd be alive today. I hope you got more sense." Donnie moved closer to the TV, watching Allister do his thing.

Blanche thought of all those crocodile tears Donnie had poured out over Ray-Ray, all the sympathy she'd wasted on his evil ass, and felt her dander rising like yeast rolls. Keep cool, girl, she cautioned herself. You can handle this. There's things I need to know before the boys take over.

"What I don't get is why you killed Ray-Ray and Miz Barker before you got the tape," she said.

Donnie reluctantly pulled his eyes away from the TV. "My one big mistake. I was sure I knew where the fucking thing was! I saw the old lady lock it in the drawer under the cash register. Who'd have thought that old bitch would move it and then have the nerve not to tell me where it was?"

Blanche held her breath to keep from screaming. It was one thing to think Donnie had killed Ray-Ray and her old friend, but hearing him admit it as if he were talking about the weather made her want to give him back some of his own. She clenched the handgrip of the gun and willed her finger away from the trigger.

"Is that why you hit her?" she asked him. "Because she wouldn't tell you where she'd put the tape?"

Donnie looked at her. Blanche shivered but didn't drop her eyes.

"Who knew the old bitch had a bad heart? She had so much mouth, I thought she was made of steel."

Something about his eyes made Blanche sure he'd have killed Miz Barker even if she *had* given him the tape.

"I hope *you're* not planning to put up a fight." He turned from the TV and stood directly in front of her.

"How'd you find out about the tape?" she asked him as if she hadn't heard his last remark.

Donnie turned his head toward the TV, where Allister's upturned ass glistened like Siamese moons.

"Ray-Ray was fucked up the night he heard about the tape. He came in the bar screeching at the top of his bitch lungs about Brindle being a hypocrite. The second he saw me, he headed for me like he always did. Only this time, he had more to say than how much he wanted to suck my dick." He looked at her now with a grin, clearly hoping she'd be shocked. "And for once, I was glad to see his switchy ass. I could smell money before he finished telling me the whole story."

"So you made it all up, about the two of you loving each other and getting a place together, all those tears, and being scared the goons who killed him were after you."

Donnie grinned. "Good, huh? I was in the drama club in high school. Always could get right into a part."

"Yeah, well you may have been lying about loving Ray-Ray, but you sure did appreciate fucking him, and don't even bother to say you didn't, you rotten hypocrite! You ain't even man enough to walk with your shit."

He moved closer to Blanche. She stood up.

He made a noise that was supposed to be a chuckle. "Yeah, I knew you was mouth from the minute I met you. But I got something that'll fix that." He slipped out a knife from somewhere in his clothes. The blade was wide and curved. "I wish there was another way," he said with what sounded like sincere regret—another bit of acting on his part. But she had some reality for his ass.

She gave him a big smile. "Oh, there is another way." She pointed the gun at his chest.

Donnie shook his head. "You're not the type, Mama."

Blanche used her left hand to release the safety. Donnie blinked. His smile did an instant fade.

"You're right," Blanche told him. "I'm not the type, but why don't you jump at me with that knife and see what happens?" She really wanted him to do it, wanted him to give her a reason to shoot him, one that wouldn't keep her awake at night, a way that would avenge Miz Barker and Ray-Ray and rid her of the rage at having been fooled by him.

"Take it easy, Blanche, take it easy," Othello said.

Donnie spun in his direction. Othello and Elroy landed on either side of Donnie and twisted the knife away from him before Blanche could see how it was done.

"Black bitch!" Donnie twisted and turned until Othello got an arm around his neck. Elroy stuffed a gag in Donnie's mouth and handcuffed his hands behind him. Blanche kept the gun trained on Donnie—not out of fear but because she wanted to see his face collapse in pain, his blood create a new pattern on his clothes. Despite the horror of having watched Marc Brindle blow his brains out, the desire to shoot Donnie was like hunger gnawing at her belly. And that shocked her.

Donnie continued to struggle as the two men hustled him toward the door. He gave Blanche a final look so hateful it might have made her step back if she hadn't fortified herself with the possibility of killing him. She raised the gun as if to strike him and thoroughly enjoyed the way he flinched. She lowered the gun and spit directly into his face. "A little present from Miz Barker," she said. It was an act so out of character, it made her feel peculiar.

Othello left Elroy and Donnie in the car and came back into the house. He fished the tape recorder out from under Blanche's chair, rewound a little, and listened. "Sounds like we got it all," he said.

Blanche was sitting on the sofa staring down at the gun.

"You okay?"

"I will be." She held the gun out to him.

Othello took it and her hand. "You did good, sister." He held up the small tape recorder. "And we got proof." He gave her hand a squeeze. "You want me to take that video off your hands?"

Blanche told him she'd take care of it. When he left, she went to the kitchen and fixed herself a drink. Lord, she needed Ardell! She drank the gin-and-tonic slowly, trying to see around the memory of her desire to commit murder and what it meant, then went to fetch her kids before the library closed.

FIFTEEN

DAY FOURTEEN—WEDNESDAY

Blanche woke feeling too heavy to move. The events of last night weighed her down like ten extra blankets. She could still feel the trigger of that gun against her finger, feel the surge of power, like a shot of pure caffeine, knowing she could end Donnie's life as easily as not. She had been in a rage before, wanted to hurt somebody bad before, but always with heat, with anger pouring off her like sweat, with the need to defend herself. It hadn't been that way last night. Last night, when she'd held that gun on Donnie, a part of her had been as cool and calm as if all she'd been thinking about doing was putting out the trash.

She spent the morning tearing her kitchen apart and cleaning—not because it was dirty, but because she needed to keep busy. It didn't help much. It didn't get rid of or answer the question of how she was different from some kid with a gun and a grudge. Violence was the national measles, and she'd been infected. Now she had to find a cure.

She took a large plastic container of her version of her friend Vanessa's special International Negro Spaghetti Sauce from the freezer. She had no energy to be creative about food. The sauce was a deep, deep red and so thick and rich with ground turkey and kielbasa, it completely coated the noodles and the garlic lit up the house.

After school, Blanche and Shaquita went to Cousin Charlotte's. She and Miz Inez were due back in a couple of hours.

They dusted and vacuumed and aired out the downstairs and Charlotte's and Shaquita's bedrooms. Blanche even bought a bunch of flowers for the dining room table. Anything to soften the blow. When they heard a car stop out front, they gave each other a nervous look. They hadn't talked about how to tell Cousin Charlotte about Shaquita's pregnancy, and now it was too late. They went to the door together.

Cousin Charlotte levered herself out of the cab, adjusted her hat, paid her fare, and harangued the driver into carrying her bags up the short stoop to the front door. Then she reminded him that Inez had already tipped him when they'd dropped her off. Cousin Charlotte smelled of trains and down home. She hugged Blanche and squeezed Shaquita half to death.

Cousin Charlotte gave them both a long look. "What's wrong?"

Neither Shaquita nor Blanche spoke.

"All right." Cousin Charlotte sank heavily into an armchair. She took off her hat and fanned herself with it. "Just tell me and stop actin' like you killed somebody." She stared straight at Blanche.

"It ain't my story to tell," Blanche said.

Shaquita raised her head defiantly, but when she looked at her grandmother, her eyes and her head both lowered.

Cousin Charlotte rose and walked slowly around Shaquita. She stopped in front of Shaquita and held the girl's chin in her right hand. "Whose is it?" she asked.

Shaquita began to cry.

Blanche stayed until Cousin Charlotte was through screaming "Oh my sweet Jesus!" before she hurried out the door and down the stoop. She knew she wasn't out of the discussion and the sweet Jesuses yet. Cousin Charlotte would likely call before Blanche got home, and would certainly be in her face tomorrow, but for the next three blocks she was free—until she got to Miz Inez's house.

Miz Inez looked as though she'd lost twenty pounds. There were new lines in her face, and she moved like a woman who wasn't sure where she was going.

"I'm real sorry about Ray-Ray, Miz Inez."

Inez was quiet for a long time, then heaved a huge, slow sigh that filled the room with shreds of the pain eating at her insides. "Everybody keep tellin' me I'll get over it in time. But I ain't got much time left." She tried to smile and almost managed. "Well, I ain't the only one. Poor Miss Felicia. We got something in common now, something awful. I called her the other day. She told me." Miz Inez cleared her throat and sat up a little straighter. "Course, that boy of hers always was unstable. Funny, you know."

Blanche watched Miz Inez building herself a dead son who wasn't gay. It was like killing Ray-Ray a second time.

They were both silent for a minute or two. Blanche had gone there wishing she could tell Miz Inez the truth about Ray-Ray's and Miz Barker's deaths. It would be so much better for Inez to hear it from her instead of the police. But if Miz Inez couldn't accept that Ray-Ray was gay, there was no way Blanche could figure out to tell her about Donnie without telling her how Marc, her son's other lover, had given Ray-Ray the combination to Allister's safe so that Ray-Ray could steal the tape. Blanche really didn't want any more people to know she'd even heard of the tape, let alone that she'd had it or had seen it. Allister Brindle was sure to catch hell over this, but that didn't mean he wasn't powerful enough to make her life a misery. Or end it. Her tongue felt thick and hot, swollen with what couldn't be said.

"They goin' away, you know. Miss Felicia and Mr. Allister."

"Long enough for you to have to get another job?" Blanche asked her.

"Wasn't goin' back there noway," Inez said. "Nothin' to keep me in this cold, prejudiced town. Goin' back to Farleigh soon's I can."

Blanche almost told her to go now, tonight, before the police showed up to break her heart beyond repair. She told Miz Inez good-bye and wondered whether her own life would now return to normal. She looked forward to her own day jobs. Most of the houses where she usually worked were empty when she cleaned them. In those that weren't, she'd already established that she was not the shrink or the girlfriend and wasn't interested in listening to secrets or giving advice.

Blanche and both kids went to the community meeting that evening. Blanche wondered how many people filing into the room had any idea of what was coming. Most folks looked grim, as if they at least had a feeling that the news wasn't good. Taifa wanted to go sit with some friends, but Blanche kept her by her side. She made sure their seats at the end of a row of folding chairs had a clear path to the door. She didn't really expect trouble, but Samuelson wasn't above playing rough, as she well knew. The same thing had obviously occurred to Aminata and the Community Reawakening Project. Ten men with orange armbands that said SECURITY stood around the room in clumps of two and three.

Aminata knew what she was doing. It was dinnertime. She didn't expect folks to pay attention on an empty stomach, so as usual, the back table was heaped with cold cuts and rolls, coffee and sodas, and milk.

The room nearly vibrated from the premeeting hum. An older woman with serious hips fanned herself with a folded newspaper. A belly laugh from the back of the room rippled the air like heat. Taifa twisted and rubbernecked, waving to friends who'd already seen her and shouting to those who hadn't until Blanche gave her The Eye. Malik was already up front with Aminata and Othello. They were joined by someone who appeared from the back to be a short, blue-suited white man with a briefcase, who turned out to be a very light-skinned black woman.

Aminata raised her hands for silence.

"First of all, I want to thank y'all for coming. I know this is a week night and folks have plenty to do at home, so I'm gonna try to make this meeting as short as possible." She looked around the room again. "We're going to get started in a couple minutes, but first, did everybody get something to eat? Coffee? You kids get yourselves a glass of milk," she told two little boys sitting in front. "Don't want anything to go to waste."

A few people got up and tiptoed to the food table. Aminata shuffled the papers she had in her hand, had a short conversation with the light-skinned sister, then gave the room another one of those silencing looks.

"There's only one thing on the agenda this evening. Community leadership." Aminata paused and looked around the room as if to make sure everyone was paying attention. "Now, I want to introduce you to the young man who made all of this possible with his determination, hard work, and concern for his community. He's going to tell you how this project got started."

Taifa was nearly bouncing in her seat, and Blanche had to keep her own grin under control. Malik, on the other hand, looked and sounded as though standing in front of a roomful of adults explaining why he wanted to do a paper on Roxbury and the environment was an everyday thing.

"... and I learned how to do a lot of things working on this paper," Malik went on. "Like getting information from the state and how to interview people to find out what happened to them or what they know. The biggest thing I learned was how good it feels knowing what I did is going to help Roxbury and maybe make some little kids safer. I know there are a lot of teens like me who would feel good about helping the community, too, if people would treat them like Aminata and the other people around this organization treated me. Thank you." He looked startled by the loud applause.

"Before I get to the point, for those of you who don't know her, this sister"—Aminata held her arm out toward the suited woman standing near her—"is Marilyn Wharton, the lawyer for the Community Reawakening Project." She paused, moved a step closer to the audience, and began speaking again. "You know," she said, "it's always hard criticizing our own. White America gives our leaders so much flack, we feel like we always got to be out in front with praise for them, and come to their defense, no matter what they do. Now, that would be just fine if our leaders weren't human beings like the rest of us. Being human, they do what humans do: They sometimes make mistakes. But what about when they *choose* to do wrong? What are we supposed to do then?" Once again, she stopped talking and looked around the room, this time waiting for a response. "Well?" she demanded.

"Fry their asses!" someone shouted. Not-quite-easy laughter washed across the room. "Give 'em hell!" someone else called out. "Chastise their butts!" a woman said in a commanding voice.

"That's right!" Aminata said. "That's right, chastise them. And that's why we're here this evening." She held up the papers she had in her hand. "These documents make it clear that the Reverend Maurice Samuelson, of the Temple of Divine Enlightenment, has made a mistake. Not by accident, but on purpose. One child may have died because of it. Other children were certainly poisoned by lead because of the mistake Reverend Samuelson chose to make."

A rumble rose up from the room.

"These papers prove that Reverend Samuelson is the owner of a boarded-up building on Register Street where there were once four apartments, apartments in which children were poisoned by lead. These papers show that Reverend Samuelson knew there was lead in this building. We talked to people who used to live there. They told us that someone who worked for the owner showed them certificates that proved the buildings had been deleaded. Those certificates were phony. And the good reverend hid his ownership of this building behind a corporation. His dead first wife is supposed to be the president, even though the corporation wasn't established till after she died. We also believe he bribed a..."

The door to the room crashed open. Samuelson and four of his boys stomped in. Security guards quickly formed a human fence around them, but allowed Samuelson to pass.

"I'm glad you decided to come, Reverend Samuelson," Aminata called out. "I was just planning to tell folks you'd been invited here tonight but had decided not to face the community. I'm glad you changed your mind. Please have a seat."

Samuelson hesitated. He'd obviously expected his entrance to stop Aminata in her tracks. He stood in the aisle, seeming uncertain about his next move. Aminata went on.

"As I was saying, Reverend Samuelson, here, has made some bad mistakes. Y'all know what lead poisoning does to our children. And you know what it does to our kids when they get older, making them violent, making them hurt their friends, like my sweet son did. My boy... but I ain't going to talk about that now." She turned and gave Othello a big smile before she went on.

Blanche thought she felt a shift in people's attention. She looked around the room. Was everyone as uncomfortable as she was with Aminata's wishful thinking about a connection between lead poisoning and violence? It was almost embarrassing to hear her talk about it.

"... four youths from Roxbury waiting to go to trial for killing somebody," Aminata said. "Three of those four boys had lead-paint poisoning when they were kids. The effects of mistakes like Reverend Samuelson's don't just make us sick. They can kill us and make us kill."

"Hold up, young lady. I'm a man of the cloth. I'm an upstanding member of this community. You better be careful about what you say. I could sue you and your ragtag organization for every nickel you got."

Aminata waved the papers in the air and spoke with even more vigor. "And furthermore, the Reverend's phony corporation owns other buildings in this neighborhood, too. We need to be talking to people who live in them to see if—"

"Woman! You don't know who you messin' with," Samuelson huffed. "I got friends downtown. Friends who won't take kindly to some crazy woman trying to make me look bad." Samuelson looked at the people around him. He spread his hands, palms up. "You all know me. You know what I done for this community. You gonna sit here and listen to this—"

"Man, just tell us what you gonna do 'bout this lead-poison mess you done made for our kids," a man called out.

"That's right!" a number of people agreed.

"I ain't got to explain nothing to y'all bunch of..." Samuelson changed direction and eased toward the back of the room, where his boys were still surrounded by security men.

"You need to pay attention to the message on your car, Rev," a deep voice down front suggested.

"His car? What's his car got to do with it?" someone else wanted to know.

"Somebody sent him a message," a deep voice replied. "It said 'God don't like ugly' in big orange letters, right on his hood."

The room rocked with laughter.

"That's what I call a serious monogram," a woman called out to more hoots of laughter.

Samuelson's eyes darted from side to side. He looked like a bully losing his first fight.

"You ain't heard the last of this," he shouted. "I got lawyers, too. And if any of you niggers is responsible for fucking up my car, I'll..."

Hoots and jeers cut him off.

"And God bless you, too, Reverend," someone called after him, which caused even more hilarity.

"Traitor! Slumlord!" people hollered after Samuelson. He tried to bluff as he turned and strutted toward the door, but everyone had seen the shock on his face. He slammed out the door, his boys close behind him. The room broke out in applause.

After the meeting, people milled around talking in excited voices and signing up for Aminata's reparations committee that would work with the authorities to break Samuelson's back. Blanche made her way over to Othello.

"What happened?" she asked him.

He looked puzzled.

"I thought you were going to tell folks who killed Miz Barker and Ray-Ray."

He looked at her for a long time. "Sorry, sister, but I don't know what you're talking about."

For a moment, Blanche was too shocked to protest. He was walking away when she found her voice. "Wait a minute, I want to know why—"

He held up his hand to silence her. He gave her a look so intense, Blanche could feel it trying to touch her brain.

"Remember what I told you when you first called me? A hundred and ten percent, remember? That's how Ex-Cons for Community Safety deals with problems. One hundred and ten percent. Forget him. I already have."

Blanche would have liked to pretend she didn't know what Othello meant, but she couldn't. "But he's got a wife and kids!"

"He should have thought of that," Othello told her. "So long, Blanche."

Blanche was as chilled as if she were outside in a snowstorm without a coat. She'd called on Othello because she never liked getting involved with the police, never trusted them to do the decent thing. She stared at Othello's back moving away from her. Why had she expected him to have more faith in the system than she did—he, who'd already been through it? Yet she really thought he'd turn Donnie and the recording of his confession over to the police. She'd thought there would be a trial where she'd get the answers to her questions—like how exactly had Donnie killed Ray-Ray, who was so much stronger? Had Donnie and Ray-Ray had a real relationship besides the one Lucinda saw in the bar? Had Donnie tried to talk Ray-Ray into whitemailing Brindle, or had Donnie decided from jump to kill Ray-Ray for the tape? Now she would never have her questions answered, because Othello hadn't turned Donnie over to the police. And never would. Never could now. But why did she care what Othello had done to Donnie when just last night she'd been ready to kill Donnie herself?

But I didn't, she thought, I didn't kill him. She'd known without thinking that pulling that trigger would have changed her into a different person—a woman who had taken somebody's life. Now she felt as responsible for and changed by Donnie's death as if she'd gone and killed him herself. She could feel the weight of his death like a fifty-pound hump on her back.

Taifa tugged at her sweater. "Let's go, Moms."

Blanche turned and headed toward the door, but Malik was still talking to Aminata. Blanche ducked her head. She didn't think she could talk to Aminata right now, not so soon after what she'd learned about Othello. She knew that men like General Schwarzkopf could send people's children into war and still be nice to their wives, that the men who dropped the atomic bombs on Japan were all supposed to be decent, sane people, but she didn't believe it for a minute. All she wanted to say to Aminata was "Run!"

As soon as she could, Blanche beckoned to Taifa and Malik, and the three of them left.

"We really nailed him, didn't we, Moms!" Malik was as excited as Blanche had ever seen him.

She threw an arm around his shoulders. "I'm really proud of you, Malik. I'm glad you dug your heels in about doing this project with Aminata."

Malik grinned at her.

"And to think," Taifa chimed in, "he couldn't have done any of this if he hadn't been lucky enough to be born my baby brother."

"Oh yeah?" Malik made a grab for her hair. Taifa shrieked and took off down the block with Malik right behind her. Blanche was surprised at how pleased she was to see them still doing their kid thing. Not yet, she thought, not yet.

The phone was ringing as Blanche put her key in the front door. She ran to it, a grin on her face.

"Hey, girl! How'd you know I needed to talk to you?"

Ardell laughed. "It ain't always about you, Blanche. I got some talking I need to do, too. Serious talk."

"What's wrong?"

"Ain't nothin' wrong. Ain't nobody sick and I ain't bringin' no bad news."

"Well, what's up?" Blanche settled into her favorite armchair, ready for a long listen. Then she sat up straight. "Wait a minute. Did you say 'bringing'?"

"Train gets into Boston at seven-twenty-five Saturday evening."

"Get off at Back Bay Station," Blanche told her. "I'll be waiting for you, you know that." She had fifty questions, but she recognized Ardell's I-ain't-talking tone of voice. Blanche decided to wait to tell Ardell her news, too. It was the kind of story that could wait.

SIXTEEN

DAY SIXTEEN—FRIDAY

Blanche spent Friday morning calling her clients to let them know she'd be back to work on Monday. They all seemed pleased, and none of them had any complaints against Cousin Charlotte's niece, who'd replaced her.

It was a real spring day, and she was eager to get out of doors, maybe find her way over to Jamaica Pond and walk along the other side—the side opposite the Brindle house. She stood in her doorway for a few minutes appreciating the coming green, watching the way the sun etched gold on the houses across the way. But she couldn't get herself out the door. She didn't know why until the phone rang.

"Well, darlin', what do you think of it all?"

"Wanda?"

"The very same. I got your number from our Inez."

"How you doin'?"

"All well on my end. You're the one, darlin', bein' there when the boy died, I mean."

"Yeah, it was rough, but I'm okay now."

"I should think so, darlin'. We don't get paroled from hell every day."

Blanche laughed. "Working for them wasn't no picnic, it's true."

"It's not workin' for 'em I'm talkin' about, darlin'. I take it you haven't seen the papers yet?"

"Tell me," she said.

"Well, darlin', it seems our Allister's been caught with his pants down in front of the underaged. It's all over the front page. Something about a video with children and animals. Quite a nasty business. Even I'm a bit shocked, and I never put anythin' past that lot!"

So it was out. "Have they arrested him?"

"Not yet, but there's talk of, how do they put it? Ah yes, serious criminal charges."

The memory of Brindle talking to her as though she wasn't fit to breathe faded beneath the picture of him being dragged away in handcuffs. "No more than he deserves."

"My very thought, darlin'. And what a blessin' for the people of this state! People can forgive a hand in the till or a pack of lies, but not fornicatin' with wee kiddies."

Blanche remembered Ray-Ray telling her that what he was doing would be good for her and everybody in the Commonwealth. Too bad there wasn't some way he could get credit for it.

"It was good working with you, Wanda. I truly enjoyed it."

"As did I, darlin', especially the lovely tea. Come to my place and I'll fix you a cup of my special blend."

"One of these days," Blanche said, and wondered if it was true as she wrote down Wanda's phone number and address.

She reminded herself to get Carrie's number from Inez. She owed her a call.

SEVENTEEN

DAY SEVENTEEN—SATURDAY

The next morning, Blanche spent nearly an hour in front of her Ancestor altar, trying to find a way to make peace with the knowledge that Donnie's family didn't and would likely never know what had happened to him. She knew she couldn't tell his wife, could never do anything that would endanger Othello and the Ex-Cons for Community. She also knew this wasn't justice, and apologized to her forebears for it. When she'd first gotten Othello's group to help her, she'd been glad to know there were black men in the community prepared to protect people, make the bad actors pay for what they did, and keep the neighborhood safe. She still thought this was a good idea—just as soon as folks figured out how to solve the same problem they had with the downtown system: Who polices the police? Who decides who should be punished and how?

She spent the rest of the day getting ready for the evening. She cleaned the living room, bathroom, and her own room—changing the curtains as well as the sheets, washing the windows and sprucing the place up for her friend's visit.

Cousin Charlotte stopped by around noon.

"So, what's Shaquita gonna do?" Blanche asked her.

Cousin Charlotte adjusted today's hat—a porkpie with a bright green band and a huge pink rose in the front. "We still talkin' about it," she said. Her voice told the disappointment her words didn't express.

Blanche took a deep breath. "Make sure the doctor tests her for AIDS, Cousin Charlotte."

Cousin Charlotte seemed to collapse like a deflated balloon, but only for a few seconds before her shoulders rose to their usual height. "Well, she's finishin' high school and goin' outta here to college, baby or no baby. I made sure she knows that."

"If she has it, are you gonna take care of the baby while she's in school?"

Cousin Charlotte set her lips in a firm line. "No, I ain't havin' that mess. I don't want no baby, and I ain't havin' no baby. If she want a baby, she gon have to take care of it. If she decides to have it, she *and* that baby goin' to college."

"What about Pookie?"

"She probably all up in his face right now, stupid child."

Tears filmed Cousin Charlotte's eyes. Blanche gave her a long hug before she left.

Blanche was too excited about Ardell's coming to pay much attention to Taifa and Malik's bickering. She fed them early and set them free to visit friends. She turned on the radio for the evening news and heard something that stopped her cold:

> A new study suggests that childhood exposure to lead increases the chances of juvenile delinquency. Low-level lead has previously been found to lower IQs in children. The latest study suggests that lead's effect on behavior could be even more significant. NPR's Richard Harris has the story.

Blanche ran to the phone and called Aminata. Her line was busy. Blanche grabbed a pencil and a piece of paper and wrote down as much information as she could, being extra careful to get the name of the doctor who had done the research, Herbert

Nedelman at the University of Pittsburgh, who certainly sounded like a brother to her on the radio.

She tried Aminata's number again. Still busy. The woman might be half crazy, but she'd been right about lead poisoning and violence in teenagers.

"I knew it. I always knew it," Aminata said when Blanche finally reached her.

There was no bus in sight when Blanche left the house to go meet Ardell's train, so she decided to walk a block or two and was almost instantly sorry she had: Just as she turned the corner, Pookie came out of a house farther along the block and began walking ahead of her. He hadn't seen her. Blanche felt her face tighten and her back do a ramrod thing. She was tempted to slip back around the corner until he got farther away. Why? Because he was one of those young men some people called an endangered species? Was that a reason to turn up her nose at him? After all, people didn't stop speaking to FDR's granddad when he was dealing drugs. His little enterprise got him into the president's family. Maybe Pookie would get lucky. He'd tried in his own way to get Shaquita to change her mind about the baby, and it still might work. Anyway, treating him like he was dog poop on the pavement wasn't likely to help him come to a good end. If nobody even wanted to speak to these kids, how could anyone then turn around and criticize them for their choices?

"Hey, Pookie! Wait up," she called.

True to her word, Blanche was waiting on the platform at Back Bay Station when Ardell's train arrived. They hugged for a long time. When they moved apart, Blanche could see tears about to fall behind Ardell's glasses, just as they were misting Blanche's own eyes.

Ardell reached down to pick up her bag. Blanche stopped her. "I've waited as long as I can, Ardell. Tell me what's up."

Ardell let a clot of people break around them before she spoke. "I've come to tell you that the old police headquarters burnt down last week, so any information they mighta had about why you left town in such a hurry is gone up in smoke. Your mama's gettin' old. And you and me both need less work and more money. I got an idea about how we can get both."

"Good!" Blanche grinned. She picked up Ardell's bag and they headed, arm in arm, toward the escalator.

ABOUT THE AUTHOR

Barbara Neely's short fiction has appeared in various anthologies, including *Breaking Ice*, *Things That Divide Us*, *Angels of Power*, *Speaking for Ourselves*, and *Test Tube Women*. She lives in Jamaica Plain, Massachusetts, where she is working on the next Blanche White mystery.

CPSIA information can be obtained
at www.ICGtesting.com
Printed in the USA
LVHW032249030322
712442LV00005B/733